일범의 평범한
사람 이야기

일범 손영징 지음

미다스북스

책 머리에

2000년 미국으로 가서 20년 동안 직장생활을 하다가 은퇴해서 2022년에 한국으로 돌아왔을 때, 아내는 '지난 20년이 마치 꿈만 같다'고 얘기했지만, 나는 모든 것을 새로 시작하는 기분이었다.

각 지방자치단체를 중심으로 20년 전과는 너무도 달라진 풍경들, COVID 19의 영향도 있겠지만, 회사 다니는 직원들의 근무 환경, 복잡해진 교통, 비싼 집값…. 어느 것 하나 낯설지 않은 것이 없었다. 어차피 퇴직 후에는 전국의 맛집과 풍광을 찾아 여행도 다니고, 좀 여유가 되는 대로 해외여행도 생각하고 있었다. 그러나 코로나 19로 인해 하고 싶었던 것을 생각만큼 할 수가 없었다. '여행가기 힘들면, 지난 인생을 정리나 해 볼까'하는 심정으로 2021년에 책을 두 권 출판했다. 이른 바, 일범 시리즈로서, 첫번째는 『일범의 비범한 인생 이야기』, 두번째는 『일범의 특별한 영어 이야기』였다. 어차피 판매용은 아니었고, 집안에 보관할 목적과 지인들에게 선물할 목적이었다. 훗날 나를 기억해 주는 사람들이 내 책을 언급해 준다면 그것도 보람 있는 일이라 생각했기 때문이었다.

이번에는 『일범의 평범한 사람 이야기』라는 제목으로 제3권을 출판하려고 한다. 영향력 있는 작가라면 조심해야 할 주제이겠지만, 나 같은 평범한 사람은 술자리에서 농담으로 할 수 있는 정치 이야기, 종교 이야기를 글로 쓴다고 해서 문제가 되지는 않을 것으로 생각한다. 그냥 평범한 사람들의 생각일 뿐이니까.

이 책은 총 4부로 구성되어 있는데, 1부는 평범한 한 사람의 가족애를, 2부에서는 평범한 사람이 바라보는 우리 사회전반에 대한 생각을, 3부는 한 평범한 사람이 겪은 고유한 경험을 그리고 마지막 4부에서는 미국생활을 할 때 틈틈이 써 놓은 영문 Journal 또는 Essay 모음으로 구성되어 있다. 특히 영어 부분은 영어가 유창하지 않은 한국인의 입장에서 쓴 글들이라 큰 부담 없이 함께 이해해 주리라 믿는다. 다만 GGU에서 MBA 과정을 할 때 쓴 Project Paper들은 전문적인 분야여서 일반인이 이해하기는 좀 어려울 것 같다. 그러나 이 책은 어차피 판매용이 아니므로 내 작품을 활자화해 둔다는 데 의미를 두고 싶다. '일범이라는 사람이 이렇게 살아왔구나'하는 것을 누가 이해해 준다면 나는 먼 길을 떠난 후에도 고마워할 것이다.

2023년 3월
일범 손영징

목차

제3부 나의 경험

제4부 미국생활

1장 미국Chicago에서 어학 연수할 때(1997) 쓴 글들

2장 LMC에서 영어공부를 할 때(2001) 쓴 글들

3장 LMC에서 영어공부를 할 때(2004) 쓴 글들

4장 LMC에서 영어공부를 할 때(2006) 쓴 글들

5장 GGU에서 MBA 과정을 공부할 때(2002~2004) 쓴 글들

미국 생활 초기

아들 결혼식

딸 결혼식

◀ 손녀 이룸

손자 열음▶

가족에게

The Story of an Ordinary Man

• • •

아들 결혼식 때의 축사
(2014.4.25 서울)

안녕하십니까? 신랑측 혼주 손영징입니다.

4월 25일, 오늘은 저희 부부의 결혼 33주년 기념일이기도 합니다.

저희 부부는 아들 하나, 딸 하나를 두었는데, 아들은 '자랑스러운 아들인'이란 뜻인 자아린이고, 딸은 '세상에 빛나는'이란 뜻으로 세빈이라고 합니다. 저희 부부는 자아린이와 세빈이를 키울 때, '바른 몸, 바른 마음'이라는 가훈을 정하고, 항상 몸 튼튼하고 마음 착한 사람이 되도록 가르쳤습니다. 그러나, 공부나 일상생활에 있어서는 모든 걸 스스로 하도록 하고 전혀 간섭을 하지 않았습니다.

자아린이는 자랑스럽다는 이름에 걸맞게 스스로 잘 자라 주었습니다. 고2라는 늦은 나이에 간 미국에서도 언어의 장벽에도 불구하고, 고등학교, 대학교를 잘 마쳐주었습니다. 다른 가족들은 아직 미국에 있지만, 혼자 귀국하여, 병역의무를 마친 게 자랑스럽습니다. 그리고, 작지만 장래성 있는 직장에서 성실히 일하는 모습이 자랑스럽습니다. 매일매일을 바쁘게 생활하면서도 자주 저희에게 안부전화를 해 주는 것도 자랑스럽고, 정치인이 아닌 것도 자랑스러우며, 세금 꼬박꼬박 내는 봉급생활자인 것도 자랑스럽습니다.

이런 아들이 제게 '결혼을 하겠다'고 했을 때, 저는 먼저 '너 클 때 우리집 가훈이 뭐였냐?'고 물었더니, '바른 몸, 바른 마음'을 잘 기억하고 있더군요. '그래, 그렇다면 여자친구는 바른 몸과 바른 마음을 가졌느냐?'고 다시 물었고, 자아린이는 '그렇지 않다면 제가 어떻게 결혼하겠다고 하겠습니까?'라고 답했습니다. 저는 마음이 너무나 흡족했고, 실제로 만나본 아현이는 건강한 몸과 아름다운 마음씨를 가진 최고의 며느리감이었습니다.

이렇게 잘 키운 따님을 저희 아들 자아린에게 짝 지워 보내 주시는 사돈 남이장군의 후손 남기봉 씨와 신재옥 여사에게 감사드립니다. 또한 이렇게 오셔서 축복해 주시는 하객 여러분에게도 진심으로 감사드립니다. 아들, 며느리에게는 건강하고 행복하고 자랑스런 가정 꾸려나가기를 기대하지만 한 가지만 당부하고 싶습니다. 자아린, 그리고 며늘아가야, 부모가 자식에게 물려줄 수 있는 최고의 선물은 자녀에게 형제, 자매를 갖도록 해 주는 것이야. 3남3녀정도는 낳아라. 결혼 축하한다. 그리고, 너희들 결혼기념일 행사할 때 아빠엄마도 같이하자. 감사합니다.

· · ·

딸 결혼식 때의 축사
(2022.5.1 Anaheim, 미국)

안녕하십니까? 신부측 혼주 손영징입니다.

Good afternoon, ladies and gentlemen. I am Young Sohn, Bride's father.

오늘은 남양 홍씨 집안의 준수하고 기품있는 준기와, 밀성 손씨 집안의 세상에 빛나는 세빈이가 이곳 미국땅에서 부부가 되는 예를 올리는 날입니다.

JOONKI means handsome and graceful, SEBIN means brilliant in the world.

저희 부부는 1남1녀를 두었는데, 아들은 '자랑스러운 아들인'이란 뜻으로 자아린이라고 하고, 딸은 '세상에 빛나는'이란 뜻으로 세빈이라고 합니다. 저희 부부는 자아린과 세빈이를 키울 때, '바른 몸, 바른 마음'이라는 가훈을 정하고, 항상 몸 튼튼하고 마음 착한 사람이 되도록 가르쳤습니다. 그러나 공부나 일상생활에 있어서는 모든 걸 스스로 하도록 하고 전혀 간섭을 하지 않았지만, 세빈이는 그 이름에 걸맞게 반듯하게 잘 자라 주었습니다. 21년 전 제가 회사에서 미국으로 발령받아 왔을 때, 세빈이는 High School 1학년으로 편입을 하였는데, 언어의 장벽을 이겨내고, 고등학교에서는 우수학생으로 상도 많이 받았고, UCLA에 진학해서는 Media Art Design을 전공하여, 현재는 유능한 Web Designer로 활약하고 있습니다.

준기도 22년 전에 부모를 따라 미국으로 와서, 열심히 노력한 결과, 현재는 규모는 크지 않지만 알찬 무역회사를 하나 운영하고 있습니다. 둘 다 자랑스러운 Korean American으로 자리 잡았다고 할 수 있습니다.

JOONKI came to the states 22 years ago and SEBIN 21 years ago. At this time, JOONKI runs a small trading company and SEBIN is a profitable web designer.

알아서 잘 커 준 세빈이에게도 고맙고, 준기가 이렇게 멋지게 될 수 있도록 뒷바라지해 주신 준기의 부모님 홍재명 씨와 홍용순 여사님 및 두 여동생들에게도 정말 감사를 드립니다.

내가 알기로는 두 사람이 만난 지 약 14년쯤 된 것 같은데, 14년을 한결같이 서로 이해하고, 서로 위해주며 지내왔고, 그 사랑의 결실이 오늘 맺어지는 것입니다.

COVID-19 이라는 한번도 경험해 보지 못한 어려운 상황에서도, 이 자리에 축하해 주러 온 세빈이 친구 희정이, Amy, Alice, 민정이 & her husband Jordon, 또 함께 일하는 회사동료 여러분 정말 감사합니다. 이상준 씨 부부와 김동진 씨를 비롯한 준기의 선후배와 친구들, 그리고 회사 동료와 가족분들께도 깊은 감사를 드립니다.

오늘 내가 신부의 아버지로서, 준기와 세빈이에게 몇 가지 당부를 할 테니 잘 들어래이…

먼저, The first, 세상에는 아름답고 본받을 만한 부부들이 참 많이 있지. 잉꼬부부의 대명사 최수종/하희라 부부, 기부천사 션/정혜영 부부,

입양한 애를 자기애와 함께 사랑으로 키우고 있는 항상 신혼 같은 차인 표/신애라 부부 등등… 물론 이런 사람들처럼 똑같이 살기는 어렵겠지만, 지금부터 영원히, 적어도 사랑하고, 봉사하고, 서로 아껴주는 마음은 닮도록 노력해라.

Love and take care each other and serve others now and forever.

두번째는, The second, 부모가 자식에게 해 줄 수 있는 가장 큰 선물은, 자녀에게 형제자매를 갖게 해주는 거란다. 둘 다 나이가 있는 만큼, 많은 자녀를 두기는 어렵겠지만, 준기 닮은 아들 하나, 세빈이 닮은 딸 하나는 있어야겠지? 기대한데이.

I hope you have a boy and a girl. What a good combination!

마지막으로, The third, 내가 노래는 잘 못 하지만, 요즘 많이 불리고 있는 결혼식 축가 두 곡을 소개하마.

먼저 윤종신이 부른 〈오르막길〉에는, '힘들겠지만 가파른 길을 함께 손잡고 사랑으로 끝까지 오르자'라는 다짐이 있어 참 좋더라.

또, 한동근이 부른 〈그대라는 사치〉라는 축가에는

'그림 같은 집이 뭐 별 거겠어요?

어느 곳이든 그대가 있다면 그게 그림이죠

빛나는 하루가 뭐 별 거겠어요?

어떤 하루든 그대 함께라면 뭐가 필요하죠'라는 가사가 있더라. 이러한 축가 가사처럼, 준기와 세빈이는, 함께 손잡고, 서로 격려하고, 서로 이해해 주면서, 작은 일에도 행복을 느끼는 그런 부부가 되어라.

신부의 아빠로서, 신랑의 장인으로서 하는 당부란다.

Go uphill with hands in hands and be satisfied with a little.

아름다운 날입니다. 오늘 와 주신 하객 여러분에게 다시 한번 감사드리며, 식후에 마련된 칵테일과 저녁식사를 마음껏 즐기시기 바랍니다.

It's a beautiful day today.

Thank you for coming and please enjoy the cocktail hour and dinner after this ceremony.

감사합니다.

Thank you.

. . .
만약 내가 먼저 가면
(2022.9.28)

  박무영, 나의 아내. 결혼한 지 40년을 한결같이 나를 사랑하고, 나 때문에 스트레스를 받고, 나를 위해 희생을 감수해 온 사람. 저 세상에서도 당신을 사랑합니다.

  우리가 처음 만나던 날, 회사 작업화를 신고 나타난 내게 이상한 생각이 들었었겠지요. 새로 받은 안전화라 낡은 구두보다 더 좋았기 때문이라오.

  거의 매주 만나 술을 함께 마시면서 '이 사람 너무 술꾼 아닌가?' 생각했겠지요.

  부모님께 처음 인사시켰을 때 엄마가 '병색이 완연하다. 몸 약한 사람을 집에 들였을 때 얼마나 힘든 줄 아느냐?' 면서 우리의 결혼을 반대했을 때 당신은 얼마나 마음 아파했겠소.
  그날 이후 당신과 결혼해야겠다고 내 마음이 굳어진 것은 엄마에 대한 반발인가요? 당신에 대한 사랑의 확인인가요?

  짧은 연애 기간 동안 해프닝도 많았지요?
남포동 어느 술 파는 카페에서의 첫 키스를 기억하오?
에덴공원에서의 데이트를 기억하오?

포항북부해수욕장에서 일몰 이후 해변을 거닐다 해경에게 단속당한 것도 기억하오?

내가 부산으로 가는 대신 처삼촌이 계신 포항으로 나를 만나러 매주 올라와 준 당신이 고마웠소.
결혼식 날짜는 봉급날로 내 멋대로 잡아버린 내가 황당했지요?

결혼식날 엄마가 '이제 보니 달덩이 같구나, 키도 크고 예쁘고 건강해 보이는구나. 내 사람이 될려고 그랬나 보다'라고 하신 말씀에 눈시울이 붉어지는 당신을 보았소.

'신혼여행을 우리끼리만 간직해야지 다른 사람에게 보일 필요가 있냐?'면서 카메라를 가져오지 않은 내가 황당하지 않았소?

외동딸을 낭떠러지 위로 아슬아슬하게 달리는 첩첩 산골에 시집보내기 위해 데려다 주면서 장인어른의 맺히는 눈물을 나도 보았소.

10평짜리 임대 주택에서의 신혼생활은 뭐가 뭔지도 모르고 지나갔지요?
내가 '유학가겠다'고 준비하는 동안 각종 서류 떼러 다니느라 고생 많았소.
유학을 위해 당신에게 운전과 매듭공예를 배우게 한 것은 괜찮았으나, 낙태를 하게 한 것은 두고 두고 후회하는 일이 되었소. 지금도 죄책감을 느끼고 있소.
공부한다고 서울 올라왔을 때 면목동 셋방에서 당신은 얼마나 힘들었소. 베데스다 기독병원에서 자아린을 낳고, 지혈이 되지 않아 수혈을 받은 순간은 정말 위험했었소.

짧은 서울생활을 뒤로 하고 다시 포항으로 내려올 때 나의 변덕에도 당신은 묵묵히 따라 주었소.

포항에서 한동안 내가 고스톱에 빠져 퇴근이 늦을 때, 당신의 눈물을 많이 보았소. 미안하오.

포항성모병원에서 낳은 세빈이는 우리의 또 다른 보물이 되었소.

포항 지곡동과 동해상도타운에서 사귀었던 아줌마들이 그나마 당신과는 자주 어울리는 친구들이 되었으니 다행이오.

포스틴 건설과 조업의 주역이었고 다시 석도 공장장을 할 때가 내게는 가장 바쁜 시기였지만, 당신에게도 그리 나쁜 추억은 아니었을 거요. 묵묵히 나와 애들을 뒷바라지 해 준 당신이 고마웠소.

미국 어학연수를 마치고 귀국길에 당신과 함께한 미국 서부 및 하와이 관광은 그 중에 압권이었소.

수염을 기르고 카우보이 모자를 쓴 나와, 두 달 동안 몰라보게 살 찐 모습으로 나타난 당신은 천상 부부였소.

당신에게 미국생활은 새로운 도전이었겠지요? 의사소통이 자유롭지 못한 상황에서 눈치 하나로 누구보다 잘 생활해 준 당신에게 감복했소.

20년 동안 미국, 캐나다, 멕시코, 유럽 및 남미 여러 나라를 여행해 본 것도 소중한 추억이 되었소.

당신은 맹장 제거, 자궁적출, 쓸개 제거 등 우여곡절을 겪었지만, 특히 당신이 원인 모를 병으로 힘들어할 때가 우리 결혼의 가장 큰 위기였지요. 그러나 자아린 낳을 때 받은 수혈로 감염된 C형 간염을 완치한 것은 축복이랄 수 있지요.

20년 만에 다시 한국으로 돌아와 새 집을 마련하고 정착하는 동안 나는 거의 도움이 되지 못하고, 혼자 힘든 일, 어려운 일까지 해내는 당신이 고맙고 또 미안해요.

'85세, 많으면 90세까지 함께 건강하게 살아야 되는데, 앞으로는 도움되는 남편이 되도록 노력해 볼게요' 이런 약속은 이번 수술이 아무일 없이 무사히 끝났을 때 할 수 있는 약속인 것 같소.

생각해 보면 지난 40년간 우리에게 남은 것은 자랑스러운 아들과 며느리, 이쁜 이룸, 열음, 또 세상에 빛나는 딸과 사위 그게 전부인 것 같소.

개인연금(UPI Pension)은 전부 내 앞으로 되어 있고, 아내에게 나오는 국가연금(Social security)은 얼마 안 되는데, 만일 내가 먼저 가버리면 당신의 생활이 너무 걱정되오. 당신을 위해서 내가 먼저 가면 안 되겠다는 생각이 듭니다.

順天은 하늘에 순응한다는 뜻이니, 이름에 걸맞게 꿋꿋하게 잘 살아 갈 거라 믿소.

자아린, 세빈, 나의 자랑스러운 아들과 딸.

태어나서 지금까지 한 번도 말썽을 부려 본 적이 없는 너희가 고맙다. 어릴 때부터 동생을 유난히 챙겨준 자아린이기에 너희 둘의 우애는 영원하리라 믿는다.

심시티 2000을 처음 사 주었을 때 너무 좋아하던 자아린이 생각나고, 엄마가 아무리 머리카락을 세게 묶어도 '예쁘게 한다'고 하면 아픔을 참아내는 세빈이가 생각난다.

초 · 중학교 때 항상 공부 잘하고 모범생이었던 너희 모습들도 눈에 보인다. 남들 다 하는 과외 수업 한 번 받지 않았는데도 항상 다른 아이들보다 우수했던 너희가 자랑스럽다.

자전거 타고 교통사고가 나서 아직도 후유증이 있는 자아린에게 미안하고, 넘어져 허리를 다친 줄 모르고 방치해둔 세빈이에게 미안하다.

처음 미국 갔을 때는 말 한마디 제대로 못하던 너희들이 금방 아빠보다 영어구사 능력이 뛰어나게 된 것도 너무 자랑스럽다.

키우면서 '이래라, 저래라' 한 마디도 간섭하지 않았지만 가장, 착하고, 정직하고, 마음이 따뜻하고 바라게 자라줘서 정말 고맙다.

대학과 전공과목을 스스로 선택하고, 거기에 걸맞은 직업을 가진 것도 고맙다.

자아린에게는 대학 졸업 후 혼자 귀국해서, 혼자 군대가고, 혼자 직장을 찾고, 혼자 생활을 헤쳐 나가게 해서 미안하다.

세빈에게는 아빠가 훌쩍 귀국해 버려서 혼자 미국에 남게 해서 미안하다.

자아린이 예쁜 아현이 만나 이룸, 열음 낳아 키우면서 알콩달콩 살아가는 모습 보니 고맙다.

늘 싸우지 말고, 이견이 있으면 조용히 대화로 해결하도록 해라, 불쑥화내는 아빠는 닮지 말거라.

세빈이 듬직한 준기 만나 예쁘게 살아가고 있으니 고맙다. 지금처럼 엄마와 자주 통화도 하고 더 늦기 전에 애기를 가지는 것이 아빠의 바램이다.

내가 먼저 가거들랑 화장해서 유골을 밀양 가족묘에 묻어라. 그래야 홍배와도 가끔 만나겠지.

유골을 썩지 않는 유골함에 담아서는 안 된다.

제사를 지낼 필요는 없다.

내 재산은 엄마까지 다 가고 나거든 너희 둘 반분해라.

이룸, 열음, 또 세빈이 2세 반듯하게 잘 가르쳐라.

둘은 물론 사촌, 외사촌, 고종사촌들과도 잘 지내거라. 우리은행 계좌에서 매달 유니세프에 후원을 조금씩 하고 있는데 그것은 너가 알아서처리해라.

아빠 휴대폰에는 아빠와 연락하며 지내는 모든 사람의 정보가 담겨있다. 연락할 일 있으면 이 휴대폰을 사용해라. 부고는 시골친구, 중학

친구(산동회), 고교친구(배정, 강선대), 포스코 입사동기, 냉연부 동료,
UPI 동료 등에게 알려라.

영실 고모에게 각종 보험을 가입해 놓았으니, 빼먹지 말고 찾아라.

세빈이는 내가 UPI에 든 생명보험 찾는 것 잊지 마라.

먼 곳에서도 늘 너희들을 생각하면서 미소 지을 것 같다.

사랑해.

한국 생활 적응기

코로나19 K방역의 실상

20년간의 미국생활을 청산하고 한국행 비행기를 탄 것은 2020년 7월이었다. 코로나 19가 기승을 부릴 때였는데, 미국에서 접했던 한국의 방역시스템, 소위 K방역은 세계 최고였다. 귀국 후 일산에 있는 어느 오피스텔에서 2주간 격리를 하게 되었다. 그 사이에 보건소에 가서 PCR 검사도 받고 정부에서 주는 구호품도 푸짐하게 받았다. '정말 K방역이 잘 되어 있구나'라는 생각을 했다. 다만, 보건소를 왕복할 때 나를 태워 준 방역택시 기사의 말을 빌리면, 방역택시는 다른 영업을 해서는 안 된다고 했고, 나와 같은 사람만 태워서는 '수입이 턱없이 부족하기 때문에, 시에서 보상을 해 주는 게 마땅한데 그렇지 않다'고 하소연을 했다. K 방역 이면에는 이렇게 희생당하는 분도 있다는 점이 안타까웠다. 그래도 초기의 K 방역은 잘 된 시스템이었던 것이 틀림없었다. 문제는 이게 지속되지 못한 것이었다.

2021년 5월, 미국에 거주하는 딸의 결혼식에 참석한 후 한국으로 돌아올 때였다. 미국으로 출국할 때에 병원에서 인당 10만 원을 내고 PCR 검사를 받았지만, 한국으로 돌아올 때도 미국 현지에서 PCR 검사를 받고 음성확인서를 소지하고 있었다. 샌프란시스코 공항에서 인천공항까지 약 12시간이 소요되었는데, 인천공항에서 파주시에 있는 우리집까지 오는데 6시간 이상이 걸렸다. 인천공항에 내려 정해진 절차대로 입국 수속을 밟는 것도 너무 시간이 많이 걸렸지만, 그 곳에서 일하는 직원들은 전혀 도움이 되지 못했다. '외국에서 입국하는 사람들은 모두 어디 어디에 가서 지정된 버스를 타세요'라는 안내를 받고 그곳 가는 방법을 물어보니, 군인으로서 K방역에 동원된 것 같은 직원은 전혀 길을 몰랐다. 절차 절차마다 너무나 많은 사람들이 방역에 참여하고 있었지만 정작 필요한 일을 하는 사람은 보기 어려웠다. 그냥 인건비만 낭비하고 있었다.

　'외국입국자는 전부 모처에 있는 현대자동차연수원으로 가서 PCR 검사를 받고 1박 한 후, 다음날 음성확인이 되어야 집으로 갈 수 있다고 했다. 버스를 타기 까지는 두시간 정도 기다려야 했다. 버스로 일산으로 이동중에 파주시 보건소에 전화를 걸어 '집으로 바로 갈 수 없느냐'라 물어보니, '바로 갈 수 있어요, 지정된 방역택시를 타고 보건소로 가서 PCR검사를 받은 후 다시 방역택시를 타고 집으로 가면 된다'는 것이었다. 두 시간을 기다려 버스를 타고 일산으로 가고 있던 상태라 이미 늦었다. 약 한 시간을 달려 일산의 집합장소에 도착했다. 그 곳의 직원은 '현대연수원으로 가는 버스로 갈아타라'고 했다. 내가 '파주시 보건소에 문의해 보니, 1박하지 않고 집으로 갈 수 있다고 하던데 어찌된 거냐'고 물으니, '그렇지 않다. 외국입국자는 무조건 현대연수원으로 가야한다'고 했다. 두 사람의 의견이 너무 달라, 내가 다시 파주시 보건소에 전화를 걸어 그 직원을 바꿔 줬다. 두 사람은 한참동안 전화로 싸웠다. 결국 파주시 보건소 직원이 이겨서 나는 방역택시로 이동하기로 했다. 보건소 직원이 알려준 전화번호로 전화를 했더니, 방역택시 기사가 '지금 인천공항이기 때문에 시간이 좀 걸릴 것'이라고 했다. 이런 황당한 경우가 있나? 다시 1시간 정도 그 자리에서 기다려 드디어 방역택시를 탔다. 파주시 보건소에서 PCR 검사를 받고, 그 택시로 집에 도착하니 맥이 풀렸다. 택시 요금이 문제가 아니라. 인천공항에서 집까지 오는 게 태평양 건너 12시간 비행하는 것 보다 훨씬 피곤하였다. K방역은 인력과 시간과 돈만 낭비하고 있고, 정부는 현장이 어떻게 돌아가는 지 모른 채 K방역 잘 한다고 자랑만 하고 있다.

- - -

나이와 호칭

미국에도 경로 우대 제도가 많지만 한국에 와서 경로 우대를 받으니 여러가지 생각이 든다. 개인적으로는 경로 우대는 적어도 70세 이상이 되어야 한다고 생각하고, 그 대상도 가난한 노인네 중심으로 되어야지 재산이 어마어마한 노인들까지 경로라는 이유로, 할인 또는 면제를 해 주는 것은 찬성할 수가 없다.

전철을 공짜로 탔는데, 경로석 외에는 좌석이 없다. 나는 평소에 스스로 '젊다'고 자신해 왔기 때문에 경로석에 앉는 것은 왠지 좀 꺼림칙했으나, 결국 경로석에 앉았다. 누가 '젊은 사람이 왜 경로석에 앉아 있어요?'라 물으면 모자를 벗어 보이면 될 것이다. 나는 전두환 전 대통령처럼 완전 대머리라 가능한 모자를 쓰고 다닌다. 모자를 벗으면 80대로 보는 사람들이 많다.

전철이나 버스를 타면 70은 넘었을 것 같은 아주머니들이 나에게 자리를 양보해 주기 위해 의자에서 벌떡벌떡 일어나서 '어르신 여기 앉으세요'라는 하는 분들이 많다. 나는 68세이다.

미국에서는 사람을 사귀는 데 나이는 문제가 되지 않는다. 내가 다니던 미국 헬스클럽의 PT(Personal Trainer)는 나를 만나면 'Hey, my friend'라 인사하는 것이 보통이다. 나도 나이나 지위에 상관없이 모든 미국인 직원들과 친구처럼 스스럼없이 지냈다. 존대말이 명확치 않은 영어를 쓰기 때문이기도 할 것이다. 한국에서는 나이에 관해서 대단히 민감하다. 한 살이라도 더 많으면 형님 대우를 받고 싶은가 보다. 이런 부류의 사람들을 만나면 나도 뻥을 좀 친다. '호적에는 55년 을미 생 양띠지만, 실제로는 52년 임진 생 용띠이다. 휴전 될 때 태어났는데, 아버지가 전쟁 통에 출생신고를 좀 늦게 했다'라 하면, 대개 내 말을 믿는다.

한번은 파주시 국민연금 사무실에 들렸다가 80대 아주머니 한 분을 조리읍 사무소까지 태워 주게 되었다. 이 아주머니는 연신 고마워하면서, 나에게 '부인과 함께 사느냐'고 물었다. '그렇다'고 대답하니까 '참 좋으시겠습니다. 나는 아빠가 몇 달 전에 돌아가셔서 너무 슬프다'는 뜻으로 신세 한탄을 하셨다.

나는 '이 아주머니의 나이가 80은 넘어 보이는데, 이 사람의 아빠라면 100세는 넘었을 텐데, 그건 호상이지 뭐 그리 슬퍼할 일인지 의아했다. 한참 후에 '내가 아내와 같이 살고 있어 좋겠다'는 말과 연계해서 생각해 보니, 나를 자기 연배로 생각했고, 아빠는 아버지가 아니라 남편을 의미하는 것으로 이해가 되었다.

한국에서의 호칭은 여러가지로 마음에 들지 않는다. 위에서 말한 남편을 아빠로 호칭하는 것도 문제이고, 남편을 오빠라고 부르는 것도 문제이다. 남매간에 결혼했는가? 오해받기 십상이다. 특히 반려동물을 키우면서, 주인이 개, 고양이의 엄마, 아빠라고 하는 것은 도저히 이해가 안 된다. 자신을 스스로 '개'라 하다니, 해도 너무 한다. 나를 꼰대라 해도 좋지만 안되는 것은 안되는 것이다. 개. 고양이의 엄마, 아빠가 아니라 가 아니라 개, 고양이의 주인인 것이다.

동물은 암수를 지칭할 때 암컷, 수컷 또는 암놈, 수놈이라 하지 남자, 여자라고 하지 않는다. 그런데 요즘 사람들이 흔히 동물에게 '남자, 여자'라 하니 황당하다.

병원, 은행, 관공서 등에 가면 나를 '아버님'이라 부르는 직원들이 많다. 존경의 표시로 그런 호칭을 쓰는 것 같지만, 나는 이해가 되지 않는다. 내가 그들과 같은 아들, 딸을 둔 적이 없기 때문이다, 존경하고 싶다면, 환자분, 손님, 어르신 정도로 충분하다.

'사장님'이라는 호칭도 마음에 들지 않는다. 내가 직장생활을 40년 이상 했지만 항상 남 밑에 있었지 사장이 되어 본 적은 없는데, '사장님'이라 불러주니, 황당하다.

나와 대화 중에 나에게 '자네'라는 호칭을 쓰는 친구가 있다. 친구 사이에 '자네'라는 호칭을 쓰지 못할 것은 없지만, 흔히 '자네'라는 용어는 아랫사람에게 주로 쓰는 호칭이기 때문에, 이 말도 나는 마음에 들지 않는다. 이름을 불러주는 게 훨씬 더 정감 있다. 더구나 나는 '일범'이라는 멋진 자(字)가 있지 않은가?

도감골 사람들

    2020년 7월, 20년간의 미국 생활을 끝내고 한국으로 이주를 결심했을 때, 가장 먼저 생각해야 하는 것은 '어디에서 살 것인가' 였다. 고향이 밀양이고 부산서 고교와 대학을 다녔기 때문에, 형제 자매와 친구들이 대부분 부산, 창원, 양산, 밀양 등에 살고 있었다. 따라서 그 중간쯤되는 김해나 양산에 살고 싶었다. 인터넷을 통해 그 지역의 아파트와 주택 시세를 알아보니 생각보다 너무 비쌌다. 코로나로 인해 집 구하러 한국에 나오는 것도 여의치 않았다. 일산 사는 아들에게 '집 좀 알아 보라'고 했더니, 며느리가 '아버님, 우리집 근처로 오세요'라 했다. 아내와 의논 끝에 아들이 사는 일산 근처로 이사하기로 마음먹고 한국으로 들어와 집을 보러 다녔다. 일단 일산의 아파트는 너무 비쌌다.

    미국도 10여년 전에 Financial Crisis가 왔을 때 부동산 거품이 꺼지면서, 집값이 반값으로 떨어진 적이 있었다. 그때 계속 값이 올라가는 집을 담보로 은행대출을 계속 받아 흥청거리고 살던 많은 사람들이 쪽박을 차고 나가는 광경을 목격했기 때문에, 한국의 이 아파트 가격도 반드시 거품이 빠질 거라는 확신이 들었다. 그리고, 미국에서 20년간 Front yard와 Back yard가 있는 주택에서 살았기 때문에 아파트는 쳐다보기만 해도 답답하였다.

    아내와 나는 결국 전원 주택에서 살자는 데 합의했다. 내 예산에 맞는 전원주택을 찾기는 쉽지 않았다. 부동산 소개소를 통해 고양시의 많은 주택들을 봤으나 마음에 드는 집을 찾지 못했다. 범위를 넓혀 고양시와 인접해 있는 파주시에서 새로이 짓고 있는 전원주택 단지에 오게 되었다. 말은 전원주택이나, 실제로는 집들이 너무 다닥다닥 붙어 있어 '전원'은 아니고, 옆집과 담장을 공유하는 미국의 타운하우스와 비슷했다. 아들이 사는 일산과 멀지 않고, 가격도 예산 범위에 맞아서 이곳으로 이사오기로 했다. 이사를 온 후, 마을 사람들과 친해지면서 이 시골마을의 유래도 듣게 되고 사람들의 정(情)도 함께 느끼게 되었다. 원래 이 마을의 이름은 도감골이었다. 도감(都監)이란 고려와 조선시대 국장이나 국혼 등 큰 국사가 있을 때 임시로 설치하던 관청을 의미하는데, 그 유래는 다음과 같다.

옛날 이 마을에 아들을 홀로 키우는 어머니가 지극정성으로 아들의 공부를 뒷바라지했는데, 안타깝게도 아들의 출세를 보지 못하고 세상을 떠났다. 훗날 아들은 높은 벼슬에 올랐으나, 어머니 생각에 늘 우울하였다. 그 연유를 눈치채게 된 챈 조정에서 어머니의 혼을 다시 국장으로 성대하게 모셨다. 도감무덤이 생긴 후로부터 이 마을은 도감골이라 불렸다. 도감골 사람들은 정(情)이 많다. 통상 시골 마을에 외지인이 이사오면 텃세라는 게 있는데, 여기는 그렇지 않았다. 앞산을 다녀오다 마을 어른 한 분과 인사를 나누었는데, 그날 이후 나도 이 마을 노인회 회원이 되었다. 누가 내 나이를 물으면 나는 늘 '작년에 스물 아홉이었다'라 대답했던 내가 노인회 회원이 되어 경로당에 출입하다니 세월이 참 재미있다. 도감골 사람들은 대부분 농사를 짓는데, 내가 어릴 때의 내 고향과 달리 의외로 부자가 많았다. 마을 옆으로 수도권 제2 순환도로 건설공사가 진행 중인데, 토지 수용 보상액도 제법 되는 것 같았다. 한 분과 얘기해 보니 재산이 30억 원쯤 되는 것 같았다. 내가 그 분에게 '아니 그 많은 돈을 가지고 왜 아직도 힘든 농사일을 하세요? 지금 살아 봐야 15년 정도인데, 1년에 2억씩 쓰면서 남은 인생을 즐기세요. 딸이 세 명 있다 하니, 15억은 딸들에게 나눠 주고 1년에 1억씩 쓰면 되겠네요'라고 했지만, 평생 농사를 지은 사람은 농사를 낙으로 여기는 것 같았다. 아침 일찍 일어나 자전거를 타고 논에 가서 미꾸라지, 메기, 참게 같은 걸 잡기 위해 통발을 설치하고, 그 다음날에는 통발에 잡힌 고기들로 매운탕을 끓여 마을 사람들과 나눠 먹는 게 낙인가 보다. 그런데, 도감골 노인네들 주량이 장난이 아니다. 나도 술을 많이 마시는 편이지만 함께 술을 마셔보면 감당이 잘 안 된다. 농사를 천직으로 생각하고, 낯선 사람과도 술을 마시며, 따뜻하게 맞아주는 인정 많은 사람들이다. '개는 훌륭하다'라는 TV 프로그램 촬영차, 강형욱, 이경규, 장도연 씨가 우리집에 오신 것도 좋은 추억이 되었다. 한국 와서 어쩔 수 없이 듣게 되는 수많은 나쁜 뉴스들이 이 도감골 사람들 덕분에 희석되어 참 좋다.

. . .

전화기 고장과 스미싱

  미국에서는 Apple 전화기를 사용했는데 한국으로 와서 삼성 휴대폰으로 바꾸었다. 'Made in Korea가 세계 최고인데 내가 한국사람으로 Apple 전화기를 계속 쓰면 되겠나?'라는 애국심의 발로였다. Apple에 익숙해진 터라 처음에는 약간 불편했지만 곧 적응이 되어 만족스럽게 쓰고 있었다. 그런데, 어느 날 남산에 놀러 갔다가 배터리가 얼마나 남았는지 보려고 하니, 휴대폰이 켜지지 않았다. 집에 와서 배터리 충전을 해 보아도 마찬가지였다. 삼성전자 대리점으로 가서 물어보니, 고장이라 했다. '이런 경우는 극히 드물지만 간혹 Source가 완전히 나갈 경우가 있다'고 했다. 어떻게 수리할 수 있는지 물으니 포맷팅을 새로 해야 한다고 했다. 'After service로 되느냐고' 하니 '돈을 내라'고 했다. 어쩔 수 없이 수리비를 주고 고쳤으나, 문제는 휴대폰에 저장해 놓았던 모든 정보가 전부 지워져 버린 것이었다. Apple을 사용할 때는 매주 Backup을 했는데, 삼성으로 바꾼 후에는 Backup을 하지 않은 게 문제였다. 연락처, 사진, 카카오콜 History, 은행 등의 Id와 password 모두 날아가 버렸다. 컴퓨터에 저장된 정보와 중복되는 일부는 복구할 수 있었지만 대부분은 복구가 쉽지 않았다. 가까이 살고 있는 아들이 어떻게 해 보더니, 카카오톡에 친구로 등록된 명단을 복구해 내었다. 그 명단 모두에게 카톡을 보내 전화번호를 받아냈다. 덕분에 평소 연락을 잘 안 하던 친구와 연락할 수 있었던 점은 다행이라 할까? 삼성이 만든 휴대폰에 이런 일이 생기다니, 조금 실망했다.

한번은 휴대폰에 누군가가 내 이름으로 물건을 구매했다는 내용이 떴다. '전화번호를 하나 주면서 이 물건을 구매한 적이 없다면 이 번호로 전화해 주세요' 라 되어 있었다. 나는 즉시 그 번호로 전화해서 '그런 물건을 구매한 적이 없다'고 했다. 그랬더니 전화 받은 상담사가 상냥한 말투로 친절하게, 구매물건 확인방법과 구매취소방법을 알려 주었다. 시키는 대로 다 한 후 전화했더니 '경찰청과 금융감독원에 신고를 다 했으며 잠시 후에 금융감독원에서 확인 전화가 올 것인데, 이 번호가 아니면 절대로 전화를 받지 말라'고 했다. 좀 이상한 생각이 들어서 금융감독원 전화번호가 맞는지 찾아보니 틀림없었다. 잠시 후 그 번호로부터 전화가 왔고, 거기서 묻는 대로 상황을 설명해 주고, 보상받는 방법을 안내받았다. 내 나름대로는 잘 처리했다고 생각했는데, 아내는 '뭔가 이상하다'고 했다. 나는 도리어 아내에게 화를 내고는 덮어 버렸다. 다음날 아들에게 얘기했더니 '스미싱(SMS Phishing) 당했어요, 전화기에 어떤 내용들이 있나요?'라 물었다. 아는 사람들 전화번호 외에도 은행 정보 등 모든 정보가 전화기에 다 저장되어 있었다. 아들은 '큰일 났다'면서 열일 다 제쳐 두고 나에게 왔다. 그리고는 전화기를 즉시 포맷팅을 시작했다. '금융감독원에서 아빠에게 개인적으로 왜 전화를 하겠어요? 그 사람들이 다 한패로 움직이는 사기꾼들이에요' 나는 그 날 아들에게 엄청 혼났다. 보이스피싱(Voice Phishing) 말은 들었지만 내가 당할 줄은 상상도 못한 일이었다. 전화기 내의 정보를 복구하는 것은 아들에게 맡겼지만 제일 걱정되는 것은 얼마 안 되만 내 전 재산이 들어있는 우리은행 계좌였다. 은행 계좌번호뿐만 아니라 비밀번호까지 전화기에 다 저장되어 있었기 때문이었다. 다음날 아침 일찍 조마조마한 마음으로 우리은행에 갔더니 휴~ 천만 다행으로 돈은 그대로 있었다. 우리은행뿐만 아니라, 농협은행과 Bank of America, 또 모든 id와 password를 바꿔야 했다.

· · ·

주택건설업자

　파주 도감골에 정착하는 과정에서 나는 한국 주택건설업자들의 문제점들을 많이 보았다.

　우선 땅 주인부터 문제였다. 이곳은 청송 심씨의 집성촌이었는데, 오래 전에 이곳에 살던 심 모 여인의 땅이었다. 심씨의 남편은 고양 모 고등학교 교사인데, 두 사람 다 공무원으로서 이런 주택 건설 사업을 할 자격이 안 되었다. 공직을 그만 두면 몰라도 공직에 있으면서는 할 수 없는 상황이었다. 그들은 딸을 대표로 해서 유한회사를 하나 만들었다. 내가 집에 문제점이 너무 많이 생겨 부동산 매매계약서를 보고 거기 나와 있는 유한회사 대표의 전화번호로 전화를 했더니, 부동산 중개인이 받았다. 계약서에 있는 대표의 주소로 내용증명을 하나 보내려고 했는데, 그 주소는 우리 옆집 주소였다. 알고 보니, 이 주택단지의 임시 사무소가 우리집 옆집 주소로 되어 있는 것이었다. 남편이 근무하는 학교로 찾아가지 않는 한 실소유주는 만날 방법이 없었다. 딸은 사업에 전혀 관여하지 않고 부동산 소개업자 한 명에게 모든 것을 일임하고 있었던 것이었다.

전원주택이라는 대대적인 선전과는 어울리지 않는 일종의 타운 하우스였다. 미국의 타운 하우스를 보면 옆집과 벽을 공유하는 데, 여기도 옆집과 담벽을 공유하는 게 꼭 같았다. 조용히 살고 싶어 전원주택이랍시고 이곳으로 이사 온 입주민들은 옆집이 보이지 않도록 담벽을 차단하는 사람들이 많았다.

나는 이곳 단지의 모델하우스로 지어 놓은 집을 계약했는데도 하자가 많았는데, 다른 집들은 훨씬 문제가 많았다. 가장 심각한 문제는 모든 집이 비만 오면 곳곳에 물이 줄줄 새는 것이었다. 집집마다 입주 후에 방수공사를 하느라 난리였다. 또 하나의 심각한 공통 문제점은 모든 집에 똥 냄새가 나는 것이었다. 특히 기압이 낮은 날이면 주차장 뿐만아니라, 거실, 1층, 2층 모든 곳에 똥냄새가 진동했다. 서울의 내로라 하는 하수구냄새 제거 전문가가 우리집에 여러 번 와서 고쳐 봤지만 똥 냄새를 완벽하게는 잡지 못했다. 아직도 간혹 냄새나는 날이 있어 정말 기분 나쁘다. 시멘트 바닥은 평평해야 하는데 울퉁불퉁하게 마무리하는 것은 기본이고, 잔디밭은 경사가 맞지 않아 비가 오면 물이 빠지지 않았다. 전기선이 잘못 연결된 것은 모든 집의 공통적인 문제였다. 알고 보니 공사감독 한 사람만 한국인이고, 일반작업자는 베트남, 방글라데시 등에서 온 외국인 노동자가 많았다.

내가 입주도 하기 전에 이미 Deck의 나무들은 뒤틀리고 부서진 곳이 많았다. 나는 내 돈을 들여서 Deck의 나무를 합성목재로 바꿨다. 합성목재 시공은 역시 외국인 노동자가 했는데, 시공사의 감독이라는 사람이 합성목재 교체작업도 자신이 공사감독을 하므로 하루에 25만 원씩 일당을 달라고 했다. 물 빠짐이 제대로 안 되는 잔디밭의 잔디를 다 걷어내고, 땅을 평평하게 고른 다음 자갈을 깔았는데, 전부 내 돈으로 스스로 했다. 한번은 다른 문제가 있어 시공사에 연락을 했더니, 솔직히 그 시공사의 대표도 내용을 잘 몰랐다. 내가 '아니, 당신이 지은 집에 대해서 당신이 모르면 누가 아냐?'라 했더니, 그 사람은 자기가 세 번째 시공사라고 했다. 첫 시공업자와 두번째 시공 업자가 모두 부도를 내고 잠적했다고 했다.

미국에서는 집을 지을 때, 제일 먼저 하는 일이 도로이다, 도로가 다 되면 그 다음은 하수처리설비, 그 다음은 소방설비, 전기설비, 공용설비… 이런 것들이 다 끝나면 주택의 기초공사를 시작하는데, 도로보다 높은 곳에 주차장을 비롯한 1층이 들어선다. 그런데, 여기서는 완전히 반대다. 우선 집부터 지어 놓고 본다. 하수처리설비는 아예 없다. 주차장은 도로면보다 낮아서 비가 오면 도로의 빗물이 주차장 안으로 다 들어온다. 우리 앞집은 주차장 벽에서 물이 새 보수공사를 여러 번 했지만 완전히 수리가 되지 않아, 항상 습기가 차서 24시간 대형 선풍기를 틀어 놓고 지낸다.

　계약서에 하자보증기간은 2년으로 되어 있다. 1년이 좀 지나서부터는 하자가 발생해서 시공업자나 부동산 중계인에게 연락을 하면 전화도 잘 받지 않는다. 수차례 시도해서 겨우 연락이 되면, '곧 조치해 주겠다'고 대답하고는 감감 무소식이다. 2년이 다 되도록 기다리는 작전이었다. 1년 반쯤 되었을 때, 우리집 목욕탕 타일이 왕창 떨어져 내렸다. 그때 보수하러 온 업자는 '처음부터 시공이 잘못된 것'이라 했다. 2년이 지난 후에 같은 목욕탕의 반대쪽 벽면 타일이 또 떨어져 내렸다. 2년이 지나버렸으니 하자요구를 할 수도 없고, 시공사 대표에게 카톡을 보내 '그 당시 보수했던 업체 연락처를 좀 알려 달라'고 했더니, '전화기를 바꿔서 자기도 연락처를 모른다'라고 답이 왔다. 현대 산업개발에서 짓고 있던 광주의 고층 아파트가 무너져 내리는 사고가 발생한 것도 비슷한 시기다.
　이것이 한국주택건설업체의 현실이다.

주차 과태료 이의 신청

이의신청사유:

저는 한국에서 대학을 나온 후, 포스코에서 초창기부터 20여년간 일을 하다가 미국으로 건너가, 미국 기업에서 다시 20년을 더 근무한 미국 영주권자입니다. 1년 5개월 전에 퇴직하고는 한국으로 이주를 결심했습니다. 여러가지 사유가 있었지만 한국으로 돌아와서 가장 하고 싶었던 일은 각 지역을 찾아다니면서 유명한 음식을 먹어보는 것이었습니다. 그러나 코로나19 때문에 멀리 가 보지는 못하고, 제가 살고 있는 파주지역만 자주 다녔습니다. 그러다가 아내와 '의정부의 부대찌개가 유명한데 여기서 가까우니 한번 가서 먹자'고 하여 인터넷에 검색해 보니 의정부동오부대찌개 금오점이 별점이 가장 좋더군요. 그곳으로 갔으나, 주차공간이 없어 10여 분을 헤매다가 신곡동에 있는 의정부동오부대찌개 본점으로 오게 되었습니다. 이곳에도 역시 주차공간이 없어 난처했는데, 도로가에 몇 대의 차량이 주차되어 있고, 주차금지표지판도 없었습니다. 노란 줄을 피하여 노란 점선구역에 주차를 해 두고, 부대찌개를 맛있게 먹었습니다. '역시 부대찌개는 의정부다'라 생각하며 포장 2인분까지 사서 집으로 왔습니다. 합계 '4인분에 3만 천 원' 값도 싸서 더욱 만족했습니다만, 하루가 지난 후 '주차위반'이라면서 벌금 9만 6천 원이 부과되었네요. 법을 위반했으면 벌을 받는 건 당연하지만, 몇 가지 측면에서 이의를 제기할 수밖에 없습니다. 첫째, 거기에는 주차금지 표지가 없었습니다. 둘째, 거기가 '스쿨존'이라는 것은 '주차위반 통지'를 받은 후 알았지만, 그날은 일요일이었습니다. 미국에서도 스쿨

존에 주차금지, 속도제한 등의 법이 있지만, 주차금지표지는 모두가 잘 볼 수 있게 되어 있고, 속도제한도 학생이 없는 시간대에는 적용되지 않습니다. 셋째, 이렇게 생각지도 못한 과도한 과태료는 한국문화와 한국지리에 익숙하지 않은 외국인이나 저같이 국적이 한국이지만 외국에서 오래 살다 온 사람에게는 한국의 이미지를 나쁘게 심어줄 수 있습니다.

위와 같은 사유로 과태료 부과에 대해 이의를 제기하오니, 선처를 부탁드립니다.

첨부서류: 영주권 사본

전화를 걸어 '결과는 언제 나오느냐?' 물어보니 매주 화요일에 심의위원회가 열린다고 했다. '심의가 끝나면 주차위반 고지서를 보낸 것처럼 전화메시지로 알려 주나요?'라고 물어보니, '위반 고지서는 메시지로 보내지만 심의결과는 본인이 직접 전화해서 알아봐야 합니다.'라고 대답했다. '시스템 참 개판이구나'라 생각했는데, 그 다음 주 수요일에 띠링 메시지가 왔다. '기각되었습니다.'

고객 서비스 점수 빵점 한화생명

 2022년 6월, 일산병원에서 '뇌수막종 제거수술을 해야 한다'는 진단을 받은 후, 보험설계사에게 '보험을 하나 들고 싶다'고 했더니, 한화생명의 한큐보험을 추천해 주었다. '한큐보험은 한 가지 질병에 대해서만 보험금 지급이 되는 보험'이라 했다. 암이나 협심증 또는 뇌졸중 같은 타질병은 안 되고 오로지 하나의 질병에 한해서 보험금이 지급된다고 하였고, 나는 그 보험에 가입하고 매달 89,115원씩을 납부해 왔다.

 몇 달 후 세브란스병원에서 뇌수술을 받고 70페이지 분량의 병원진료서류를 팩스로 보험설계사에게 보냈고, 보험설계사는 나 대신 보험청구서를 작성하여 병원진료기록과 함께 한화생명으로 보냈다. 며칠후 한화생명에서 전화가 와서 '본 건은 보험금이 100만 원이 넘기 때문에 팩스로는 안 되고, 원본이 필요하다'고 했다. '한 부 밖에 없는 원본을 한화생명에 줘야하나'라는 생각도 들었지만 일단 주기로 결정했다. 그런데 문제는, '병원진료기록 원본은 내게 있지만 보험금 청구서 원본은 내가 갖고 있지 않았다. 한화생명 웹사이트에 들어가서 보험청구서 양식을 찾아보았지만, 보험상품에 대한 선전만 가득할 뿐 내 실력으로는 보험청구서 양식을 찾을 수가 없었다. 고민 끝에 한화생명 지점으로 직접 가보자는 생각이 들었다. 네이버 지도에서 찾으니 한화생명 파주지점이 가까운 곳에 있었다.

 직접 차를 몰고 '파주시 금릉역로 84'로 찾아갔다. 그런데, 그곳의 직원은 '여기는 한화생명이 아니고, 한화생명은 9월달에 운정으로 이사를 갔다'라 했다. '이사 간 곳의 주소를 좀 알려 달라'고 했더니, '한화생명 콜센터에 문의해 보라'고 했다. 네이버지도에 나와 있는 한화생명 파주지점 전화번호(031-941-3817)로 전화를 했더니, '지금 거신 번호는 없는 번호입니다'라는 메시지가 나왔다. 한화생명 콜센터(1588-6363)에 전화를 하니, '죄송합니다. 지금은 통화량이 많아 잠시 기다려 주십시오'라는 자동응답 메시지가 나왔다. 약 20분간 계속 기다려 달라는 메시지가 나오더니 갑자기 전화가 뚝 끊겨 버렸다. 어처구니가 없었다.

한화생명 웹사이트에서는 왜 보험청구서 양식을 쉽게 찾을 수 없는지, 이사 간 지 2개월이 지났는데 왜 네이버지도에 주소와 전화번호를 수정하지 않았는지, 원래 사무실에는 왜 이사 간 곳의 주소나 연락처의 안내문을 안 붙여 놓았는지, 콜센터에는 왜 통화가 안 되는지, 한화생명의 모든 시스템이 엉망인 것 같은 느낌이 들었다. 마지막 수단으로 전국에 있는 모든 한화생명 지점을 뒤져서 경기도 일산에 있는 '한화생명 일산고객센터(031-941-3817)'로 전화를 했다. '한화생명 파주지점이 운정으로 이사를 했다는데, 주소나 연락처를 좀 알려 달라'고 했더니, 주소나 연락처는 알려주지 않고 '거기는 한화생명 영업점이기 때문에 보험상품을 판매하는 곳이지 보험금 청구서를 접수하지는 않는다'라 했다. '한화생명에서 원본서류를 요구하는데 내가 서류를 어떻게 전해 줄 수 있는가' 라 물으니, '한화생명 직원이 우리집으로 와서 서류를 받아 가게 하겠다'고 했다.

나는 한화생명 직원이 오기 전에 보험금 청구서를 준비해야 했다. 보험설계사에 연락하여 보험금 청구서 양식과 동의서 양식을 전화기로 받았다. 전화기로 받은 양식을 컴퓨터로 보내고 컴퓨터에서 프린터로 인쇄하는 작업은 내가 할 수가 없어서 가까이 사는 아들을 불러 도움을 받았다. 뇌수술 후유증으로 오른손이 많이 떨리는데도 불구하고 어렵게 보험금 청구서와 동의서를 작성할 수 있었다. 우리집에 컴퓨터와 프린터가 있고, 도와줄 수 있는 아들이 가까이 있으니 가능했지만, 그런 여건이 안되는 사람들은 보험금 청구서 준비는 거의 불가능한 일이었다.

며칠 후 한화생명 직원이 우리집으로 와서 병원진료기록 원본과 내가 자필 사인한 보험금 청구서와 동의서 서류를 받아갔다. 또 며칠 후 '한화생명 보험 사정인'이라면서 우리집으로 찾아와서 '병원기록을 조사하기 위한 것이라면서 여러 장의 동의서 서류에 사인을 해 달라'고 했다. 사인을 다 해 주었더니 '암만 아니면 문제없다'는 식으로 말을 했다. 나는 '100만원은 넘는다고 했는데 얼마나 나올까' 기대를 하고 있었는데, 며칠 후 한화생명에서 전화가 와서 하는 말이 '보험가입 시 이미 질병진단이 있었으므로 보험금을 지급할 수가 없습니다'라 했다.

'뇌수술을 받은 후 계속 머리가 맑지 못했는데 뭐 잘못 들었나'라는 생각이 들었다. 며칠 후 담당자에게 전화해서 '한큐보험은 한가지 질병에 대해 보상해 주는 보험 아닌가? 원본까지 가져 가 놓고 보험금 지급이 안 된다고 하니 이해할 수가 없다'라고 항의를 하니까, 이미 질병진단을 받은 상태이기 때문에 보험가입은 되지만 보험금 지급은 안 된다'라 했다. 이게 무슨 말인가? 보험료는 받지만 보험금은 지급할 수가 없다는 뜻이다. 한마디로 도둑놈 심보다. 현재 심정은 원본 서류를 돌려받고 보험계약을 해약하고 싶다. 얼마나 많은 다른 고객들도 나와 같은 생각을 할 지, 한화생명의 미래가 걱정된다.

한국에서 운전하기

나는 미국으로 가기 전에 한국에서 약 20년간 운전을 했었다. 그런데 미국에 들어가서 운전면허를 따기 위한 첫 실기시험에서 떨어졌다. 운전하는 데 전혀 문제점이 없다고 생각했지만 옆에 앉은 시험관이 차선변경을 해 보라고 해서 아주 능숙하게 차선변경을 했더니, 다시 한번 해보라고 했다. 또 재빨리 차선변경을 했는데, 다른 건 별 관심 없는 태도였고, 계속 차선변경만 시켰다. 사무실로 돌아오니 나의 운전이 너무 안전하지 못하다고 불합격을 줬다. 운전은 안전이 우선이지 빨리, 능숙하게 하는 것이 좋은 것이 아니라는 걸 이때 깨달았다.

미국은 자동차의 나라다. 땅이 워낙 넓어 자동차 운전은 필수이다. 나이가 들어 더 이상 혼자 자동차 운전을 못하면 죽을 때가 됐다는 의미이다. 미국 전역을 자동차로 여행 다니면서 20년을 살았다. 그리고 한국으로 돌아왔다.

한국에서의 운전은 낯선 것이 너무 많아 당황할 때가 많다. 여기 몇 가지 사례를 보자.

고속도로를 주행하다 다음 번 출구에서 빠져나가려면 맨 우측 차선에 줄을 서는 것은 당연하다. 출구 쪽 차로는 심하게는 1킬로미터 가까이 정체되는 경우도 흔하다. 그런데 옆 차선으로 쌩쌩 달리던 차량이 출구 직전에 쏘옥 끼어든다. 그리고는 비상등을 잠깐 깜박인다. 비상등을 잠깐 깜박이는 것은 '미안하다'는 뜻인지, '감사하다'는 뜻인지 모르겠지만, 비상등을 깜박일 짓을 하지 말아야지 왜 상습적으로 얌체 짓을 하는지, 아무리 점잖은 사람이라도 이때는 욕이 나온다. '끼어들기 단속 중'이라는 표지판이 있으나, 실제 단속하는 경우는 한 번도 못 봤다.

시내도로에서 차를 운전하다 보면 '빨간색 화살표 신호 시 U턴 가능'이라는 표시가 있다. 그런데, 화살표 신호는 녹색뿐이지 빨간색은 절대 없다. 왜 빨간색 화살표로 해 놓았는지 도저히 이해가 안 된다.

서울에서 파주에 있는 우리집으로 가려면 GPS에서 서울—문산 고속도로와 56번 지방도로 안내하겠다는 메시지가 나온다. 그런데, 56번 지방도에 들어서면, 길가의 표지판에는 '국지도'라 되어 있다. 국도 아니면 지방도이지 국지도는 또 무엇인가?
찾아보니 '국가지원지방도'라는 뜻이다. 미국 촌놈에게는 생소한 용어임에는 틀림없다.

미국의 교통신호는 교통상황에 따라 켜지거나 꺼지게 되어 있다. 모든 건널목에는 도로 바닥에 센서를 설치해서 차가 있으면 신호가 들어오고 차다 없으면 신호가 들어오지 않는다. 또 사람의 왕래가 드문 곳에서는 건널목을 건너려면 사람이 수동으로 스위치를 눌러줘야 신호가 들어온다. 그렇지 않으면 항상 차가 다닐 수 있다. 한국의 교통신호는 차가 있건 없건, 사람이 있건 없건 관계없이 일정한 시간간격으로 자동적으로 신호가 들어오게 되어 있다. 건너는 사람이 아무도 없는데 또는 지나가는 차가 하나도 없는데, 기다리기 귀찮으니, 그냥 신호를 무시하고 가 버리는 차가 너무 많다. 급한 운전자도 문제지만 신호시스템에도 문제가 많다.

GPS는 참 잘 되어 있다. 안내가 너무 많아 귀찮을 정도이다. 심지어는 '전방에 녹색운전 단속 지역입니다'라는 안내가 나오는데, '녹색은 환경을 뜻하니까, 매연차량을 단속하는가 보다'라 이해하고 지나갔지만, 나중에 알아보니, '녹색운전'이란 단순히 매연차량단속이 아니라, 경제속도 준수, 과적금지, 상하차 시 시동 끔, 혼잡구간과 시간을 파악하여 운행효율 높이기, 물류터미널 공동이용으로 화물의 수송, 배송 거리 단축, 차량의 주기적 점검으로 대기오염 감소, 필요할 때만 에어컨 사용, 화물 운송 시 덮개를 씌워 비산먼지 방지 등 여러가지가 포함된 아주 의미 있는 새로운 용어였다. 그러나, 녹색운전 단속 구역이라면서 실제로 단속하는 경우는 한 번도 못 봤다.

운전을 하다 보면 '전방에 시속 몇 킬로 고정형 이동식 단속 구간입니다'라는 안내를 자주 듣는데, '고정형 이동식'이라는 말은 아무래도 이해를 못하겠다. 고정형 이동식과 이동형 고정식은 다른가? 이동한다는 얘긴가? 고정해 놓았다는 얘긴가?

샌프란시스코 시내에서 자동차로 1시간쯤 걸리는 피츠버그까지 가려면 Bay Bridge의 맨 오른쪽 차로를 타고 차선을 바꾸지 말고 계속 직진만 하면 도착한다. 그런데, 한국에서 도심을 운전하다 보면 직진으로 잘 가고 있는 차로가 갑자기 좌회전 전용으로 바뀌어 버려서 당황한 경험이 자주 있었다. 물론 '땅이 좁다'는 핑계를 대겠지만, 잘 생각해 보면 답이 없지는 않을 텐데, 사고의 위험을 그냥 방치해 두는 것은 분명 잘못된 것이다.

서울, 부산 같은 대도시에서 운전하는 것은 정말 피곤하다. 막무가내

끼어들기, 잦은 크락션, 좁은 주차공간, 신호등에서 꼬리물기 … 한국에만 있는 무질서한 현실이다. 내가 한적한 시골로 이사 온 것이 정말 다행이다.

• • •

한국에서의 영어교육

일본사람들이 영어에 약하다는 것은 그들의 글자가 소리를 표현하기에 너무 부족하기 때문입니다. 우리의 한글은 이 세상의 거의 모든 소리를 정확하게 쓸 수 있습니다. 한글이라는 인류최대의 발명품을 가진 우리가 자랑스럽고, 선조들에게 감사합니다. 그런데 한국 사람들은 왜 영어에 약할까요? 그 이유는 재미 저술가 조화유 씨가 수없이 지적하고, 정부에 건의하고, 모는 노력을 다 해도 고쳐지지 않는 '한글 로마자 표기법(외래어 표기법)' 때문입니다. 6.25 때 우리를 도운 맥아더 장군을 모르는 한국인은 없지요. 그러나 정작 미국에서는 맥아더 장군을 아는 사람은 재미교포들 외에는 없습니다. 왜냐하면 그는 맥아더 장군이 아니고, 머카써 장군이기 때문입니다. MacAthur [məká:rθər]를 미국사람들이 발음하는 대로 한글로 적으면 머카써에 가깝습니다. 우리가 학교에서 맥아더가 아닌 머카써로 배웠다면 영어발음이 훨씬 좋아졌겠지요.

러시아가 우크라이나를 침공한 뉴스가 연일 화제인데, 미국인에게 '우크라이나'라 하면 아무도 이해하지 못합니다. Ukraine[ju:kréin]은 '우크라이나'가 아니라 '유크레인'이라 발음합니다. 한글로 '유크레인'이라 표기할 수 있는데 왜 '우크라이나'라 표기하는지 이해가 되지 않습니다. 액센트도 매우 중요합니다. 미국에 Dennis, Janice라는 이름이 있습니다. 한국 사람들은 거의 대부분 '데니스', '제니스'라 발음합니다. 융통성 있는 한국 사람들은 눈치로 알아차리지만 순진한 미국인들은 누구를 부르는지 모릅니다. '**데**니스', '**제**니스'라고 반드시 액센트를 앞 음절에 두어야 합니다. 별도의 액센트 표기법을 강구해야 합니다.

This [ðɪs], That [ðæt] 에서의 th발음과 something [ˈsʌmθɪŋ]에서의 th발음은 분명히 다릅니다. 지금은 사용하지 않는 옛 한글 자음을 활용하면 이런 차도 쉽게 쓸 수 있습니다. This는 씨스로, something은 섬띵으로 표기하면 되는 것입니다. 그러면 우리는 어릴 때부터 영어 발음을 정확하게 할 수 있게 됩니다. 앞에 말한 머카써도 머카떠가 되는 것입니다.

미국인의 Dr와 Tr발음은 은 우리가 아는 발음과는 다릅니다. Drive는 '드라이브'가 아니고 '주롸이브'라 발음하고, Tree는 '트리'가 아니고 '추리'라 발음합니다. 즉, Dr은 '주'로, Tr은 '추'로 발음합니다. 몇 가지 예를 보면 Drama(주라마), Dream(주림), Dragon(주레곤), Drink(주링크), Track(추렉), Truck(추럭), Trailer(추레일러), Training(추레이닝) 이런 것들입니다. 우리가 어릴 때부터 Dr은 '주'로, Tr은 '추'로 표기했다면 커서 영어가 훨씬 쉬웠을 것입니다.

조화유 씨의 책 내용 중 일부를 여기 소개하면 이해하기가 훨씬 쉬울 것입니다'

- 외래어 표기법에 'oo'는 전부 '우'로 표기하도록 한 것은 잘못된 것

입니다.

우리가 알고 있는 영화배우 Demi Moore(데미무어)와 Roger Moor (로저무어)의 미국 발음은 데미모어, 로저모어에 가깝습니다.

Roosevelt(로오즈벨트)대통령을 루스벨트라 발음하는 것은 미국인은 Loose Belt(느슨한 혁대)로 들릴 것입니다.

- p와 ph와 f를 모두 'ㅍ'으로, s와 sh를 똑같이 'ㅅ'으로 표기하는 것도 잘못된 것입니다.

voice phishing을 '보이스 피싱'이라고 표기하는데 이것은 'boy's pissing'(소년이 오줌 싸는 것)으로 오해하기 쉽습니다. 보이스 휫슁이라 하면 오해가 없을 것입니다.

English를 '잉글리시'라 하지 않고 '잉글리쉬'라 써야 합니다.

Fast food를 '패스트 푸드'라 하면 Pest pooed(해충이 똥싼 것)로 들릴 것입니다. '홰스트 후우드'라 쓰면 영어 발음에 아주 가깝습니다.

wife를 '와입흐'라 쓰면 정확한 영어 발음이 되는데, 표기법대로 '와이프'라 쓰면 wipe처럼 들려서, 아내는 평생 걸레질(wipe)이나 하는 사람이 됩니다.

- r과 l도 구별하지 않고 둘 다 'ㄹ'로 표기하는 것도 잘못된 것입니다.

이 때문에 rice(쌀)와 lice(이)를 똑같이 '라이스'라 발음하고 쓰게 합니다.

-s를 무조건 'ㅅ'으로 표기하는 것도 문제입니다.

s가 모음 앞에 가면 'ㅆ' 소리, 자음 앞에 가면 'ㅅ' 소리가 납니다. 그런데 s를 무조건 시옷으로 표기하라니까 sale을 '쎄일'이라 발음하면서

도 '세일'이라 씁니다. 또 시옷을 받침으로 쓰지 못하게 하는데, 그래서 Bush를 '부시'라 씁니다. '붓시'라 하면 더 좋고 '붓쉬'라 쓰면 완벽한데 말입니다. s와 sh를 구별하지 않고 다 'ㅅ'으로 표기하는 것도 잘못입니다.

- 장모음과 된소리를 금지하고 있는 것도 잘못된 것입니다.
식당, 호텔, 항공편 등을 예약하고 약속 시각에 나타나지 않는 것을 not show up이라 하는데 이걸 줄여서 한국에서는 no-show(노쇼)라 한 것인데, '노오 쑈오'라 써야 정확한 발음이 됩니다.

- ㄲ, ㅆ, ㅉ, ㄸ 같은 된소리도 쓰지 말라고 하는 것도 잘못된 것입니다.
영화의 장면을 scene(씨인)을 '씬'이라 발음하면서도 '신'으로 쓰라고 강요합니다.
THAAD를 입으론 '싸드'라 하면서 쓰기는 '사드'라 쓰는데, 실제 발음과 동떨어진 외래어표기법을 바꿔야 한국인의 영어실력이 늡니다.

한국에서의 종교

교회와 교인 : 나는 할머니와 고모들이 성당에 다니는 카톨릭신자였
지만, 내가 직접 교회에 가 본 것은 대학 때였다. 무슨 축제 때 파트너
가 필요했는데 친구 윤탁이가 소개해 준 분이 부산 연산동 동신교회에
다니는 J였다. 그녀를 따라 일요일날 교회를 몇 번 갔었는데, 거기서 고
향친구 이정석을 만나게 되어 깜짝 놀랐다. '아니, 고향서 사과농사를
짓고 있는 줄 알았는데, 이 교회는 웬일이냐?'는 내 말에, 정석이는 '얼
마 전 부산으로 내려와 조그만 철공소에 다니는데, 철공소 사장이 이
교회 장로이고, 일요일날, 일은 안 하지만 교회에 나오지 않으면 하루
치 일당을 뗀다'고 했다. 그의 가정형편을 잘 아는 나는 '헌금할 돈은 있
나?'라고 물었더니, '헌금바구니에는 손만 슬쩍 넣었다가 뺀다'고 했다.
목사, 장로, 또 여러 교인들이 교회에 처음 나오는 대학생인 나에게는
대단히 친절하게 대해 주었다. 나는 예배가 끝나면 목사와 함께 점심을
먹으면서, 믿음과 성경에 대해 토론을 하곤 했다. 그런데 창세기는 신
화인가? 삼위일체란 무엇인가? 침례냐 세례냐? 안식일인가 일요일인
가, 초기 기독교가 로마시대에서 왜곡되지 않았는가? 사람이 죽은 후에
는 어떻게 되는가? 등의 주제에 대해 의문이 많았던 나는, 목사와 믿음
에 대해 얘기하는 수준을 넘어 신자와 비신자 간의 논쟁이 되어 갔다.
내가 몇 주 째 계속 이렇게 물고 늘어지자 처음에 반겨 하던 사람들도
'저 사람, 이제 우리 교회에 안 나왔으면…'하는 눈치가 보였다.

이렇게 시작된 나의 성경공부와 교회에의 들락거림은 수 년간 계속

되었다. 몇몇 교회에 가 봤으나, 매번 비슷한 일들이 벌어졌고, 목사들과의 논쟁에서 지지 않기 위해서라도 더욱 열심히 성경과 과학, 역사에 대해서 공부를 하게 되었다. 믿음은 '그냥 믿어버려야 하는 것'인데 나는 그렇지가 못했다. 같은 하나님을 믿으면서, 카톨릭(로마, 그리스정교, 러시아정교), 성공회, 개신교의 각 교파들은 왜 자신들이 정통이고, 옳다고 주장하는지? 루터(루터교), 캘빈(장로교), 재침례파(침례교), 쯔윙글리가 종교개혁을 부르짖었듯이, 요한 웨슬레는 장로교의 바탕에서 감리교로 분리해 나왔고, 성결교는 감리교에서, 순복음교는 성결교에서 '보다 더 성경중심으로 살아야겠다'고 갈라져 나온 교파가 아닌가? 기독교가 유대교와 로마교의 박해를 받고, 신교가 구교로부터 박해를 받았듯이, 역사적으로 보면 항상 새로운 교파는 기존 교파로부터 박해당해 왔다. 따라서 지금 기존 교단으로부터 이단시되는 문선명의 통일교, SDA(재림교), 몰몬교, 여호와의 증인, 박태선 장로의 신앙촌(천부교) 등도 언젠가는 오십보 백보가 될 것 아닌가? 이런 생각을 했다.

성경의 해석차이 또는 저마다의 교리에 대한 실망보다, 나를 더욱 교회로부터 멀어지게 한 것은 교인들에 대한 실망이었다. 기독교인 즉 Christian이란 무엇인가? 그것은 성품과 행위에 있어서 Christ(예수 그리스도)를 닮은 사람, 또는 닮으려고 노력하는 사람이다. 성경에 묘사된 예수의 성품과 행위를 보면, 가난하고 힘든 사람의 친구이며, 자기의 이익을 구하지 아니하고, 이웃을 심지어는 원수까지 사랑하고, 죄인들을 대신하여 목숨을 버리신 분이다. 예수를 생각하면 우리는 사랑, 온유, 희생, 봉사, 화목, 용서, 믿음과 같은 단어들이 떠오른다. 그런데 내가 만난 자칭 Christian이라는 사람들은 거의 대부분이 입술로는 '주여, 주여'라 외치면서, 그들의 성품과 행위를 보면, 자신과 자신

주위의 구복(求福)을 위해 기도하고, 금전적으로는 조금도 손해 안 보려고 교묘한 술책을 고안하고, 교회와 교인을 자신의 출세와 장사에 활용하고, 종교를 빙자하여 탈세와 불법을 저지르고, 자신과 생각이 다르면 배척하고 심지어는 증오하고, 비기독교인에 대해 다리를 놓기는커녕 장벽을 치고, 사람을 피곤하게 광신(狂信)적으로 선교하며, 교세를 키우고 헌금을 더 많이 거둬들이기 위해서 전도하고, 생색내기 또는 광고목적으로 헌금하고, 하나님 사업을 빙자하여 사기를 치고… 기독교인(Christian)이 아니라 그냥 교회 다니는 사람들을 보면 구복(求福), 집착, 편견, 분열, 구속(拘束), 독선, 이기(利己) 같은 단어들이 떠오른다. 모든 것이 예수의 성품과는 정반대다. Anti-Christ, 즉 사탄과 다를 바 없다. '교회에 다니면 나도 선(善)을 빙자한 악(惡)에 물들겠구나'라는 생각이 드는데 어떻게 교회에 나갈까? 문제는 종교 자체에 있는 것이 아니라 종교인에게 있다.

성경 : 내가 나름대로 성경을 공부해 보니, '구약성서는 유대민족의 고대역사서이고, 신약성서는 Jesus Christ라는 성현(聖賢)의 말씀과 행적을 그의 제자들이 기록한 것'이 나의 결론이다. 성경 창세기의 내용은 종교적, 철학적인 진리일 뿐이지 과학적 진리는 아닌 것이다. 창세기를 글자 그대로 믿고, 수억 년의 지구 역사와 수백만 년의 인류 역사를 부정하는 기독교인들을 보면 그들의 폐쇄성이 정말 답답하다. 구약의 얘기들은 지구상 많은 나라의 역사책에서 흔히 볼 수 있는 내용들이다. 나는 왜 목사들이 이스라엘 민족의 역사책은 그렇게 열심히 연구하면서, 우리민족의 자랑스러운 역사인 한인천제(桓因天帝) 7대 3301년, 한웅천왕(桓雄天王) 18대 1565년, 단군(檀君) 47대 2096년에 대해서는 관심조차 기울이지 않고, 일제에 의해 왜곡된 단군신화만이 전부인 양

알고 있는지? 나는 왜 기독교인들이 삼성기(三聖紀), 단군세기(檀君世紀), 북부여기(北夫餘紀), 태백일사(太白逸史)와 같은 역사책은 있는 줄도 모르고, 삼국사기, 삼국유사가 최초의 우리 역사책인 줄로만 알고 있는 지 정말 이해가 되지 않는다. 예수의 얘기는 토씨 하나에도 의미를 부여하면서 우리민족의 경전인 천부경(天符經), 삼일신고(三一神誥), 참전계경(參佺戒經)은 왜 공부하지 않는지? '하나님이 천지를 창조했고, 성경은 하나님의 말씀이기 때문이라고?'하는 분들에게 "천만의 무식한 말씀 그만 하시고 성경이 만들어진 역사부터 공부하시라."는 게 내 충고다.

신약성경에서 예수의 성품과 가르침은 완전한 사랑이지만, 아쉬운 부분은 '예수의 12세부터 30세까지의 성장 과정과 구도 과정이 기록되어 있지 않다'는 점이다. 보병궁 복음서(成約聖書)를 보면, 예수께서 12세에 인도로 유학하여, 베다성전, 페르시아의 아베스타 경전, 마니법전, 인도의 의술(醫術), 불교 경전과 석가 부처님의 지혜를 공부했으며, 인도의 승려, 학자들에게 '우주신(본체신)은 한 분이고, 신(인격신)은 '한 분 이상'이어서 모든 것은 신(개체화된 인격신), 모든 것은 하나이다'라 말했다고 한다. 인도에서의 예수의 이름은 이사(ISSA)였으며, 이미 인도 최고의 현자(賢者)중 한 명이 되었다. 예수는 한편 티벳에서 밀교계 고승으로부터는 심령 치료의 비법을 전수받았으며, 그리고 이집트에서는 애굽 밀교의 경전도 공부하고 그리스도(하느님의 사랑)라는 최고의 법명(法名)을 받았다고 한다. 29세에 유대로 귀국한 예수가 '유일신교인 유대교파들에게 모든 인간의 절대 신성을 부르짖으며 이적을 행하고, 군중을 모아 신의 사랑과 평등 사상을 전파하였음'은 당연해 보인다. 결국 예수는 유대교파의 질시와 저주를 받아 십자가에 매달려 처형되었는 데, 이 때 예수가 마지막 숨을 거두기 전 외친 "엘리엘리 라마 사박 다니(Eli Eli Lama Sabachthani: '하나님, 왜 저를 버리셨나이까'로 번역되어 왔음)"라는 말은 티벳트 라마불교의 진언(眞言)인 "엘리엘리 라마 삼약 삼보리(Eli Eli Lama Sammach Sam Bori)"라는 다라니(Dha－rani, 呪文)라고 하니, 예수의 인도에서의 구도생활이 그에게 얼마나 큰 영향을 미쳤는지를 알 수 있다.

다른 종교 : 나는 다른 종교에 대해 직접 경험해 보지 않았기 때문에 함부로 말할 수가 없다. 그러나 책을 읽고, 혹은 경전을 공부하기도 하여 '그 종교들이 무엇을 추구하고, 종교인은 어떻게 살아야 하는가'는 알고 있다. 모든 종교의 가르침은 사랑이다.

내가 아는 佛敎의 가르침은 가만히 듣기만 해도 저절로 경건해지지 않을 수 없는 사상이다. '모든 존재는 無常하다'는 〈공(空)〉의 사상, 욕망과 집착을 멀리하는 〈무아(無我)〉, 구제기원(救濟祈願)의 자비(慈悲), 평안이 있고 어지러움이 없는 깨달음, 적정(寂靜) 그 자체의 열반(涅槃 ; nirvāna)을 이상으로 하는 해탈 ….

스스로 깨달아 부처가 되는 것(成佛)은 불교 최고의 가치다. 불교에서 흔히 얘기하는 '일체유심조(一切唯心造)'라는 말은 '세상 모든 일이 마음먹기에 달렸다'라는 뜻으로 고통을 극복하는 것도, 깨달음을 얻는 것도 바로 자기자신의 '의지'에 달린 것이지 다른 어떤 것으로부터 얻을 수 있는 것이 아니라는 것이다. 그런데 현실은 어떤가? 불교신도들에겐 깨달음은 없어지고 求福만 남았다. 내 자신이 부처가 되려고 하는 종교가 불교인데, 이제는 부처에게 福을 달라고 빌기만 하는 종교가 되어버렸다. 그러다 보니 승려들도 타락하여 해탈을 구하는 노력은 없고 신도 위에 군림하려고 하고, 종파로 나뉘어 권력과 재산 다툼에만 몰두하고, 금전관계와 여자관계로 사회 지탄의 대상이 되고 있는 스님의 탈을 쓴 짐승들이 속출하는 것이 아니겠는가? 스님 생활을 오랫동안 했던 친구는 '스님들이 면벽수도에 들기 전에 곡주와 돼지나물을 실컷 먹고 들어가지 않으면 힘들다'고 말 했다.

내가 아는 이슬람은 평화의 종교다. 이슬람이란 말은 평화, 청결, 순종, 복종을 뜻하며, 종교적 의미에서의 이슬람은 오직 하나님의 뜻에 순종하고 그분의 법에 복종을 뜻한다고 한다. 그런데 왜 거기에는 시아파, 자이드파, 암살단파와 같은 과격한 파들이 활개를 치는가? 종파가 갈라져 나가 대립하는 것이 그들이 믿는 유일신 알라의 뜻인가? 아니면 내가 최고가 되겠다는 욕심인가?

모든 종교는 사랑을 가르치며, 거룩하고, 경외로우며, 자기를 희생하고, 정의롭다. 이것은 확실한 진리다. 그러나 인류역사상 또 하나 확실한 것이 있으니, 그것은 '전쟁의 90%는 종교 전쟁이었다'는 것이다.

나는 모든 종교의 가르침을 존경한다. 그러나 종교인이 되기는 싫다.

통행세 : 경북 포항에는 내연산이라는 명산이 있다. 보경사 입구에서 맑은 물이 흘러내리는 계곡을 따라 이어진 등산로는 절경의 연속이다. 관음폭포를 비롯한 12폭포를 지나, 향로봉까지 오르는 등산코스는 산을 좋아하는 사람이라면 누구나 꼭 다시 가고 싶은 곳이다. 그런데, 이곳에 갈 때마다 사람의 기분을 망치게 하는 것이 있으니, 바로 통행세

다. 등산로 입구 도로를 막아 놓고 보경사에서 '사찰 관람료'라는 명목으로 통행세를 걷는 것이다. 등산객은 보경사 사찰안으로 들어가지 않지만, 사찰 관람료는 내야한다. 2021년에는 정청래 의원이 해인사를 두고 '봉이 김선달처럼 돈을 빼앗아 가고 문화재 보호 목적으로 통행세를 내고 있다'고 하여 불교계와 큰 마찰을 빚은 적이 있다. 물론 조계종의 사유지이고, 오래전 정부에서 국립공원을 설치하면서 문화재보호법으로 강제로 공개의무를 지우자, 조계종에서 떠밀려서 공개하면서 문화재 관람료를 받기 시작한 것이 연유라고 하지만, 이것을 현시점에서 잘하고 있는 정책이라 보는 사람은 아무도 없을 것이다. 양심 있는 스님이라면 역시도 잘못된 것이라 생각할 것이다. 조계종에서 대승적 결단을 내리든지 정부가 무슨 대책을 세우든지 해서 등산객에게 통행세를 강제로 받아내는 일이 없도록 해야 할 것이다.

· · ·

한국의 정치와 사회

나는 국민의 한 사람으로서 항상 집권 여당 편이었다. 왜냐하면 나는 정치를 역사의 관점으로 보기 때문이다. 누구나 대통령을 뽑기 위한 선거운동 때는 이편 또는 저편을 지지할 수 있다. 그러나 누군가가 대통령으로 선출이 되는 순간 그것은 역사가 되는 것이다. 역사를 되돌릴 수가 있나? '선출된 대통령이 국민의 행복과 미래의 한국을 위해 일을 잘 할 수 있도록 최대한으로 지지하고 성원해 줘야한다'고 생각한다. 그렇게 하는 것이 국민 된 도리이다. 잘못하는 점이 있으면 다음 선거 때

투표로 심판하면 되는 것이고, 대통령이 일을 잘 할 수 있도록 지지해 줘야한다.

한국의 역대 대통령들은 다 공(功)과 과(過)가 있었다. 이승만 대통령은 3.15 부정선거 등 독재권력을 추구하다가 결국 하야를 했지만, 대한민국 정부를 수립한 초대대통령이지 않은가? 박정희 대통령은 긴급조치 등으로 장기집권을 꾀하다 결국 부하의 손에 의해 비참한 최후를 맞았지만, 경제발전을 이루고 대한민국을 가난에서 벗어나도록 하는 데 크게 기여한 것은 누구도 부정할 수가 없다. 전두환 대통령은 집권과정도 문제였고, 집권 후에도 인권탄압, 이순자 일가의 부정 축재 등 문제가 많았던 것은 분명하지만, 인재를 적재적소에 등용하여 물가를 안정시키고, 마이너스 성장이던 한국경제를 다시 일으킨 공로는 인정해야 하지 않은가? 인정 못한다고 달라지나? 이미 지나간 역사인데. 노태우 대통령도 김옥숙, 박철언 등의 부패에도 불구하고 북방정책으로 한국 외교의 폭을 넓힌 것은 인정해야 한다. 김영삼 대통령은 아들 김현철의 한보관련 비리에도 불구하고, 그가 추진한 금융실명제와, 하나회 척결 등은 잘한 일이었다. 김대중 대통령 또한 홍삼트리오(홍일, 홍업, 홍걸)의 부정축재가 발목을 잡았지만, 갈라진 영호남을 화합시킨 공은 누구나 인정하는 바 아닌가? 노무현 대통령은 국익을 위해서는 좌우를 가리지 않고, 최선의 선택을 했으며, 가장 서민의 심정을 알아주었다. 살아 계시는 이명박, 박근혜, 문재인 대통령에 대해서는 말을 아끼자. '미우나, 고우나, 마음에 들거나, 아니거나 모두가 한국의 역사다'라는 걸 잊지 말자.

한국에는 국회의원 수가 너무 많다. 국회의원이 아니라, 개 구(狗), 불쾌할 쾌(快)를 써서 구쾌의원이라 해야 맞겠다. 여의도에 개똥 냄새가 진동한다. 진정으로 국민을 위하고 나라의 미래를 위한 법을 만들 사람 100명 정도면 될 것이다. 정당 소속은 중요하지 않다. 오히려 정당 소속이 아니면 더 좋다. 우리나라 정당이란 게 자기 집단의 이익을 위한 싸움 외에 국민의 행복과 나라의 미래를 위해 해 온 일이 있나? '우리나라같이 좁은 땅에 지방자치가 과연 필요한가?'라는 의문부터 든다. 광역단체장은 그렇다 치고, 기초단체장은 왜 정당 소속인가? 대통령과 광역 단체장이 협의하여 임명하는 게 맞다. 선거비용 절감뿐만 아니라, 행정의 효율성 측면에서 그렇다. 광역단체의회는 그렇다 치고, 기초단체에 의회가 왜 필요하냐? 처음 도입될 때에는 무보수 명예직이었는데, 어느 순간에 자기들이 급여 받게 법 만들고, 무슨 대단한 권력을 쥔 것처럼 거들먹거리고 시민을 위한 봉사정신은 티끌만큼도 없는 지방조폭들이 모인 집단 같다.

미국의 경우, 경찰이나 공권력에 덤벼 드는 경우는 절대로 용서가 안 된다. 경찰이 총으로 쏴 죽인 경우에도 과잉진압 또는 과실 치사 혐의로 기소되어 재판에 회부되지만, 대부분 정당방위나 정당한 공무집행으로 무죄로 판결 난다. 한국의 실정은 어떤가? 한국에는 헌법 위에 떼법 있다는 말이 있다. 경찰관을 두드려 패는 사람도 있고, 공권력 자체를 아예 무시하는 불법 집단 행동이 판을 친다. 이광요 수상이 장기집권을 하면서 싱가포르 국민들의 정신개조를 시켰듯이 한국도 한 세대 (30년) 정도 모든 불법에 대해 가차없이 엄중 처벌해서 국민 의식 수준을 개조할 필요가 있다.

대한민국의 법이 너무 관대하다. 수백 명 또는 수천 명의 눈에 피눈물을 나게 한 경제 사범들에게 왜 솜방망이 처벌만 하는가? 아동 성범죄를 저지른 조두순은 고작 12년 감옥 살고 나와 버렸고, 수십명을 연쇄 살인한 유영철은 사형선고를 내렸는데 왜 사형집행을 하지 않고 비싼 교도소에서 밥 먹여주고, 관리하면서 국민 세금을 낭비하고 있는가? 마땅히 사형시켜야 할 중범죄자들은 가차없이 사형을 집행하고, 신문, 방송에서 매일 아침마다 톱뉴스로 '어제는 총 몇 명이 사형 집행되었는지, 어떤 범죄를 저질러 사형되었는지'를 상세하게 보도하길 바란다. 매일 이런 소식을 1년 정도만 계속하면 이 나라에 더 이상 범죄는 발생하지 않을 것이다. 잠재적 범죄자에게 '죄를 지으면 죽는다'라는 걸 인식시켜야 한다.

국민을 위한 법 만들 생각은 않고 매일 자신의 이익을 위해 거짓말만 하는 구쾌의원에 대해서는 주민 소환제를 만들어야 한다. 더 이상 거짓말 못하도록 사회에서 매장시켜야 한다. 방송에서 정치인들이 패널로 나와서, 자신이 속한 당을 위해 말도 안 되는 변명을 늘어놓는 것을 보고 있으면 구역질이 난다. 다음 선거에서는 반드시 심판해야 하는 것이 국민의 도리이자 유권자의 의무이다. 국민을 분열시키고, 사회를 파탄 시키고, 민족의 미래를 어지럽히는 모리배들이 정치를 해서는 안 된다.

국회의원을 지낸 코미디언 고(故) 이주일이 국회를 떠나면서 '4년동안 코미디공부 많이 하고 갑니다'라 한 말이 생각난다. 지난번 한동훈 법무장관 청문회 때, 이모(李某)교수를 이모(姨母)라고 우기는 K 의원과 '한oo(영리법인)'을 보고 한동훈의 딸이라고 주장하는 C 의원을 보고 있으니, 개콘이 다시 부활한 줄 착각할 정도로 웃겼다. 한국 구쾌의원의 현주소다.

20년 동안의 미국생활을 접고 한국으로 돌아왔을 때, 오랫동안 만나지 못했던 친, 인척들을 보고 싶었다. 사촌, 외숙모, 외사촌, 고종사촌, 이종사촌 등을 만나 옛 추억을 나누며 혈육의 정을 느꼈다. 그런데, 단한 분, 막내이모를 만날 수 없었다. 막내이모와 연락을 하고 지내는 친인척은 아무도 없었다. 내가 만난 이종사촌들은 큰 이모의 자녀들이었는데, 그들도 막내이모의 연락처는 몰랐다. 막내이모는 내가 미국으로 가기 전에는 광화문에 있는 동아일보 구내 식당에서 일을 한 적이 있었다. 나는 수소문 끝에 아현동에 있는 무료 배식센터에 이모가 자주 간다는 소문을 듣고 그곳으로 찾아갔다. 그곳에서는 '이름만 가지고는 알 수가 없다. 구청으로 가보라'고 했다. 구청으로 가서 이름을 대고 사정을 설명한 뒤, '연락처를 알고 싶다'고 했더니, '개인정보는 알려드릴 수 없다. 사람을 찾는 일이라면 경찰서로 가 보라'고 했다. 다시 해당 경찰서로 갔지만, 경찰서에서도 '개인정보는 알려줄 수 없다' 했다. 라떼에는 114로 전화를 걸어 '어디 사는 누구 전화번호 알려 주세요'하면 바로 알려 주었는데, 세상이 바뀌긴 바뀌었다. 범죄예방을 위해서는 좋은 지 모르겠지만, 좋은 일을 하자는데 법이 방해하고 있다. 이런 법은 당장 고쳐야 한다. 경찰의 임무에 사람 찾아주는 일을 추가해야 마땅하다.

한국의 현대자동차는 미국인들 사이에서 참 인기가 많았다. 현대자동차가 좀 잘 나간다 싶으면 반드시 우리를 실망시킨 것은 노조의 파업이었다. 현대자동차에 강성노조만 없었다면 진작에 현대자동차는 세계 최고의 자동차 회사가 되었을 것이라 확신한다. 귀족, 강성 노조의 불법 파업은 엄중히 처벌해서 다시는 국가 경쟁력을 약화시키는 일이 없도록 해야 하겠다.

북한의 김일성, 김정일, 김정은 왕조는 끊임없이 우리에게 위협을 가하고 있는 상황에서 전교조의 일부 교사들이 북한의 주장과 사상을 아직 어린 학생들에게 주입시키고 있다는 뉴스는 듣고도 이해할 수가 없다. 북한을 동경하고 주체사상을 신봉하는 사람들은 북으로 가면 될 것 아닌가? 자유민주주의 국가인 남한에서 누릴 것 다 누리면서 북한에 동조하는 것은 엄청난 모순이다. 하루 빨리 법을 만들어, 북한에 동조하는 사람들에게 남한에서의 모든 혜택을 끊고, 북한으로 추방하는 것이

맞다.

일본이 독도를 자기네 땅이라고 끊임없이 주장하고 있는데도, 이에 대해 속 시원하게 대처하는 정치인이 없다. 나라면, '독도가 일본 땅이라면, 일본은 우리 땅이다'라 하겠다. 역사를 아는 사람이라면 이 주장의 타당함을 인정할 것이다. 일본국민의 약 90%는 대화족(大和族)이다. 백제와 신라 등의 한반도에서 일본으로 건너 간 사람들을 도래인(渡來人)이라 하는데, 대화족은 도래인과 일본 열도의 북방계원주민과의 혼혈이다. 더구나 일본의 천왕은 비류백제의 후손이다. 이것은 헤이세이(平成) 천왕도 인정한 바가 있다. 이래도 일본이 우리 땅이 아니냐? 역사를 아는 정치인이라면 독도가 자기네 땅이라고 우기는 일본인에게 이렇게 타일러야 한다 '아우야, 그동안 고생했다. 이제 조국의 품으로 돌아오라.'

. . .

대한민국을 어떻게 바꿀 것인가?

대한민국을 어떻게 개조할 것인가? 아주 간단하다. 법 하나만 제정하면 된다.

"10인 이상 모든 사업장 고졸 채용 70% 이상 의무화"

이 법 하나면 대한민국의 모~든 문제를 해결할 수 있다.

대학을 졸업한 사람이 직장에 들어왔을 때, 고졸 후 바로 취업하여 4년이 지난 사람과 급여와 대우가 똑같고, 향후의 인사관리에서 전혀 차별이 없다면, 누가 돈들여 대학에 가려고 하겠는가?

고등학교까지 의무교육을 시행하면, 부모들에게 자식교육은 전혀 부담이 되지 않는다.

결혼을 늦게 하거나, 하지 않을 이유가 없고, 자녀를 적게 낳을 이유가 없다.

세계 최고 수준의 이혼율·자살률, 세계 최저 수준의 출산율은 금방 개선된다.

자식은 부모에게 효도하고, 부모는 자식에게 자애하며, 형제간에 우애가 깊은 오손도손한 가정에 행복이 만개한다.

초·중·고의 교육과정이 전혀 달라진다. 어릴 때부터 비싼 사교육비 들여서 과외를 시킬 이유가 없다. 학교에서는 입시위주의 과열 경쟁보다는 인성교육이 제자리를 찾는다. 스승과 제자 사이는 존경과 사랑으로 복원되며, 학부모는 더 이상 학교교육에 관여하지 않게 된다.

인성교육으로 인간의 존엄성, 인간관계의 중요성, 용서와 화합, 봉사, 희생, 사랑, 화목… 이러한 가치를 깨닫고, 공익성, 시민성, 준법성이 철저한 성인으로 자란다면, 스트레스로 인한 우울증이나 알콜중독자가 나올 수 없다. 낮은 인권의식(장애인, 인종, 저학력자, 저지위자, 여성, 성소수자, 노인, 왕따 대상 등에 대한 차별…), 비인간적인 범죄(살인, 강도, 강간, 유괴, 학대…), 비도덕적인 행위(부정, 비리, 사기, 뇌물, 사이비 언론, 내로남불, 떼법, NIMBY…) 이런 것들은 없어지는 게 당연한 게 아닌가?

대학입시 지옥은 더 이상 없다. 대학은 의사, 법률가, 연구개발자 등 전문직을 원하는 사람만 가고, 보통 사람은 대학에 갈 필요가 없어진다. 대학은 취업 잘 하기 위한 곳이 아니라, 전문적인 학문연구기관이 된다. 경쟁력 없는 대학은 퇴출되고, 대학은 학생선발권을 가지게 되며, 진짜 공부하려는 사람만 대학에 가므로, 대한민국의 대학은 세계 최고 수준이 된다.

인구가 서울로 몰릴 이유가 없다. 좋은 학교를 가기 위해 모든 것을 감수하면서 서울로, 서울로 모여들었다면 이제는 공기 좋고, 집값 싸고, 직장 가까운 곳에서 사는 것이 당연하게 된다. 따라서 수도권지역의 교통난, 주택난이 자연스럽게 해결되고 도시와 농어촌 간의 균형 있는 발전이 가능하다. 부동산 투기라는 말 자체가 없어지고, 물가정책, 인구정책, 주택정책, 교육정책 등등 되지도 않을 일에 매달리는 공무원 수를 확 줄일 수 있다.

지금은 사회문제가 많기 때문에 정치인이 활개를 치지만, 대한민국이 문제가 없는 사회가 되면 꼴보기 싫은 정치인이 없어진다. 싸움하기 위한 국회의원은 없어지고, 정말로 나라를 위해 법을 만드는 국회의원만으로 100명 정도로 줄어든다. 정치인 뿐만 아니라 경찰, 검찰, 공무원 등 이른바 서민을 대상으로 갑질하는 모든 계층이 목에 힘주기 대신 봉사와 희생정신으로 일하게 된다. 지자체 정치인들도 '정치화하는 순간 퇴출된다'는 사실을 알게 된다.

청년들의 구직난, 중소기업의 구인난이 있을 수 없다. 고졸 후 자기 적성에 맞는 직장을 찾아 일하면 되는 것이다. 군복무기간을 경력에 그대로 반영하면 병역비리가 발붙일 곳이 없어진다. 노사관계는 대립보다는 화합으로 진행된다. 더 이상 공권력을 무시하는 행위가 용납되지 않는다. 진보니 보수니 하는 구별이 모호해진다. 모두가 대~한민국으로 하나 된다.

대한민국이 이렇게 바뀌면 남북문제도 쉽게 해결이 된다. 북한 정권은 더 이상 유지할 명분이 없어진다. 이산가족 문제, 나아가 통일문제도 해결될 수 있다.

법 하나로 대한민국을 개조할 수 있다. 이 법을 시행하여 한 세대(30년)만 지나면 대한민국은 세계에서 가장 강하고, 살기 좋은 나라가 될 것이다.

일범의 평범한 사람 이야기

제2부 한국 생활 적응기

나의 경험

The Story of an Ordinary Man

밀성 손씨

밀성 손씨 (밀성이 현재 지명으로는 밀양이니까 밀양 손씨로 부르는 사람들이 있지만 잘못된 것인다. 밀성이 본향이다)는 신라 흥덕왕 때의 효자 손순(孫順)을 시조로 하고 있다. 그런데, 《삼국유사(三國遺事)》에 의하면 진한(辰韓) 육촌(六村) 중 무산 대수촌(茂山大樹村)의 촌장(村長) 구례마(俱禮馬)가 처음 이산(伊山)에 내려와 모량부(牟梁部) 손씨(孫氏)의 원조(元祖)가 되었다고 한다. 따라서 손순 이전에 밀성 손씨의 선조가 살았음은 분명하다.

그러나, 나는 성(姓) 얘기가 나올 때 마다 신라 때의 효자 손순이 시조라는 사실을 인정하지 않는다. 그 이유는 밀성 박씨, 경주 김씨, 김해 김씨, 전주 이씨 모두가 왕족인데, 밀성 손씨는 신라 시대에 효자로 이름난 사람의 후손이라는 설명에 동의할 수가 없어서다.

나는 밀성 손씨의 원조는 제천대성(齊天大聖, 하늘(제왕)과 같이 높은 성자(신선), 하늘나라 옥황상제와 동등한 위대한 신선을 이름) 손오공(孫悟空)이라고 주장한다. 제천대성의 후손이 아니고서는 그렇게 유명한 사람들이 배출될 수 있겠는가?

제천대성의 후손들은 동서고금을 막론하고 이름을 떨쳤다. 면면을 보자.

우선, 한국인 중에는, 3.1운동 민족대표 손병희 선생, 베를린올림픽 마라톤 금메달 손기정 선수, 기업인 손경식 씨, 김영삼 대통령의 부인 손명순 여사, 정치인 손학규, 방송앵커 손석희, 배우 금보라(손미자),

아나운서 손범수, 가수 손담비, 축구선수 손흥민, 체조선수 손연재, 연예인 손예진, 야구선수 손아섭, 방송작가 손영목 등등 이들 모두가 밀성 손씨이다.

중국에는, 『손자병법』의 저자 손무(孫武)와 손빈(孫臏), 오나라를 세운 손견, 손책, 손권 3부자, 중화민국 초대총통 손문(孫文), 사실 그는 한국의 독립 운동 지원과 대한민국 임시정부 창립에 일조한 공로로 대한민국 정부로부터 건국훈장 대한민국장을 추서받았다.

서양에서도 손 씨를 흠모하여 이름을 손으로 지은 사람들이 많다. 스웨덴에는 구드나손, 구스타프손, 안데르손, 윌손, 오스카르손, 헨릭손 등 유난히 손으로 끝나는 성(姓)이 많은데 모두 제천대왕의 후손일 가능성이 크다. 미국에서 흔한 성(姓)인 Johnson, Thompson, Wilson, Anderson, Olson, Jackson, Robinson, Richardson, Peterson, Henderson, Mason, Robertson, Furguson, Olson, Erickson, 이들은 왜 성(姓)에 son(孫)을 붙였을까? 역시 제천대왕의 후손일까? 혹시 원조 007 손 코넬리도 손씨를 흠모했을까?

• • •

집성촌

내가 중학교 졸업할 때까지 자란 고향마을은 밀성 손가(孫家) 집성촌이었다. 그 당시에는 일가 친척들이 한 마을에 모여 사는 집성촌이 많았다. 우리 마을에도 약 80호 정도가 되는 큰 마을이었는데 그 중 50호 정도는 밀성 손가였다.

　마을 주민의 대다수가 친척들이다 보니 손가 사람들은 똘똘 뭉쳤다. 때문에 이 마을에 사는 타성(他姓)들은 손가들로부터 많이 무시당했다. 파평 윤씨, 김해 김씨, 청송 심씨, 학성 이씨 등 양반 가문이 있었지만 손가의 위세에 당하지 못했다. 손가들이 대부분 지주(地主)인 탓도 있었던 것 같다. 나는 설날 아침이면 그 많은 손가 할배, 할매, 아재, 아지매들에게 세배를 다녔다. 손가 중에서 나의 아버지는 가난하였다. 고집 세고 정의감에 불탔지만 돈 많은 할배, 아재들로부터 무시당하기 일쑤였다. 나는 아버지와 그 할배들의 언쟁을 자주 봐 왔기 때문에 손가 어른들이 싫었다. '나중에 내가 크면 저 할배들에게 복수해야지'라는 생각도 많이 하고, 손가 친척들 대신 타성 친구들과 더 많이 어울렸다. 아이러니한 것은 '한 세대가 흘러간 지금 보면, 재산 많았던 그 할배들의 후손은 대부분 자손이 흥하지 못하고, 가난했던 우리집은 자손들이 모두 잘 살고 있다는 것'이다. 지금도 재산이 많은 집은 재산 때문에 형제 간에 불화하지만, 가난한 집은 형제간 우애가 깊지 않은가? 미국생활 20년을 청산하고 한국으로 돌아와 파주에 정착했는데, 여기는 청송 심씨 집성촌이다. 이장도, 노인회장도 모두 청송 심씨 친인척 간이다. 내가 어릴 때 경험했던 집성촌의 문제점을 회고하면서 이 사람들과 얘기해 보면, 옛날에는 여기도 청송 심씨의 위세가 대단했던 모양이었다. 내 고향의 많은 손가들이 도시로 나가버리고, 폐가로 변한 집들은 외지인이 새로 집을 지어 이사 왔듯이, 이곳 청송 심씨 집성촌에도 이제는 외지인이 반 이상이다.

누나의 삶

누나는 나와 두 살 차이다. 어릴 때, 누나는 누나라고, 나는 남자라고 서로 지기 싫어해 참 많이도 싸우면서 컸다. 아버지는 누나가 여자라는 이유로 초등학교만 보내고 중학교를 보내지 않았다. 누나는 초등학교 졸업 후, 장사를 하러 다니는 엄마를 대신해 집안 살림을 도맡아 했다. 고향에 사립 중학교가 하나 있었는데, 그 학교의 권혁호 영어 선생님이 야간 학교를 개강하였다. 배움에 목말라 있던 누나는 낮에는 집안 일을 하고 밤에는 야간 학교에 나가 영어를 배웠다. 내 생일이 칠월 칠석날 이었는데 아버지의 생신일은 7월 열나흗날이었다. 예전에는 같은 달에 아버지보다 생일이 빠른 자식에게는 생일상을 차려주지 않는 게 관례

였다. 누나는 내 생일날이 되면 아버지 몰래 흰 쌀밥을 퍼 주었다. 보리 쌀 90%, 쌀 10% 정도로 밥 짓던 때에, 내 밥그릇에 쌀밥을 퍼 주는 것은 여간한 정성이 아니었다.

누나는 스물세 살 때 밀양의 어느 부농의 막내 아들과 결혼을 하였다. 평소 부지런함과 야무짐, 알뜰함이 몸에 밴 누나는 신혼 때부터 집안에만 있지 않고, 조그만 구멍가게를 하나 차려서 장사를 했다. 신랑은 직장을 다니면서 농사도 짓고, 누나는 누나대로 농사일을 하면서 구멍가게도 꾸려 나갔다. 누나의 시아버지는 열심히 사는 누나가 귀여웠는지 자주 누나 구멍가게에 오셔서 소주 한 병 마시고는 꼭 그 값을 누나에게 주고 가시곤 했다.

엄마는 시골 5일장을 돌아다니는 보따리 장수였는데, 그 큰 보따리를 시골버스에 싣고 다니는 것이 여간 힘든 게 아니었다. 그 시골버스 회사의 직원이었던 자형 덕분에 큰 짐을 버스에 실을 때마다 많은 도움을 받았다.

누나는 아들 둘을 낳았다. 그러나 불행히도 둘째 아들은 태어날 때부터 양쪽 엄지 손가락이 기형이었다. 어릴 때 수술을 했지만 정상으로 돌려 놓지 못했다. 더욱 열심히 산 누나는 구멍가게를 제법 그럴 듯한 마트로 바꾸었다. 과일, 음료 등 무거운 물건을 취급하는 일이라 여자의 힘에는 많이 부쳤을 텐데 전혀 아픈 내색을 하지 않고 열심이었다. 원래 물려 받은 재산에다 자형의 직장 수입, 누나의 마트 운영 덕분에 살림은 부유했지만 자형과 누나 두 분은 1년이 가도 외식 한 번 하지 않는 구두쇠였다. 작은 돈은 엄청 아끼고 알뜰한 구두쇠였지만, 여동생이나 친정 오빠가 곤궁할 때 조건 없이 큰 돈으로 도와줬던 의가 넘치는 누나였다. 클 때 일 밖에 몰랐던 누나는 마트 운영을 하면서 많은 이웃과 친구를 사귀고, 불교합창단 활동을 하면서 사교성도 넓혀 나갔다. 나는 TV에 가수 하춘화가 나오면 되게 좋아했는데, 그 이유는 누나가 하춘화를 꼭 닮았기 때문이었다. 누나는 하춘화처럼 노래도 잘했다. 사귄 이웃들과는 시간이 날 때 마다 여행을 다녔다. 고생 밖에 모르던 누나가 어디에 여행을 다녀왔다고 하면 나는 괜히 기분이 좋았다. '내 누나여, 이제 삶을 꽃 피우는 구나' 하며 내 일처럼 좋아했다. 내가 미국에 있을 때, 자형과 누나는 엄마를 모시고 미국까지 온 적이 있었다. 눈물이 날 만큼 고마웠다.

누나는 운동을 참 열심히 했다. 마트 운영으로 몸이 피곤할 텐데 매일 아침 일찍 일어나 자전거타기 1시간과 수영을 2시간씩 했다. 내가 여동생으로부터 '말을 안 해서 그렇지 사실은 언니가 '골수형성이상증후군'이란 희귀질병을 앓고 있다'는 말을 듣고도 믿기지가 않았다. 내가 미국에 있을 때라, 골수이식은 누가 할 수 있는지 알아봐도 답을 찾을 수가 없었다. 누나에게 장거리 전화를 해서 물어보면, 누나의 대답은 '나 괜찮아, 아무 이상 없어, 운동 열심히 하고 있어'라는 대답만 할 뿐이었다. 여동생에게 물어보니, '서울에 있는 현대 아산병원에도 가 봤는데, 의사들도 신기해한다. 병이 저 정도면 정상적인 생활이 불가능할 텐데 어떻게 그런 운동을 하는지 이해가 안 된다'는 것이었다. 내가 치매로 요양병원에 계시는 엄마를 보기 위해 한국 나올 때면 항상 누나가 동행해 주었다. 누나에게 물어보면 '허리가 좀 아프다'라 말했다.

누나의 가장 큰 고민은 엄지 손가락이 불편한 둘째 아들이었다. 첫째 아들은 공무원이 되어 직장동료와 결혼해서 아들, 딸 낳아 잘 살고 있었지만, 작은 아들은 자신의 신체적인 핸디캡 때문인지는 몰라도 언행이 올바르지 못했다. 자주 가출을 해 서울로 가 버리기도 했고, 돈 떨어지면 다시 돌아오기도 했다. 고혈압과 당뇨가 있는 줄도 모르고 술을 너무 많이 마셔댔다. 누나는 아들이 결혼을 하면 좀 안정될까 싶어 사골 사과 과수원에 아들의 직장을 알선하고, 결혼하면 살 아파트도 하나 마련해 두었다. 절에 가서는 '아들이 제발 정신 좀 차리고 정상적으로 살 수 있게 해 달라'고 열심히 불공을 드렸다. 그러나, 2019년 설 이튿날, 누나는 경찰로부터 한 통의 전화를 받고 거의 실신을 하였다. 가출해 있던 둘째 아들이 서울의 어느 술집에서 급성 알코올성 심장마비로 싸늘한 시체로 발견된 것이었다. 누나에게 평생 단 하나의 바램이 있다면 그것은 작은 아들의 정상적인 삶이었는데, 결국 그 바램은 이루어지지 못한 꿈이 되어 흩어져 버린 것이다. 내가 생각하기엔, 그렇게 의지가 굳었던 누나는 이때부터 좀 흔들린 것 같다.

그로부터 약 1년 후 누나는 밀양의 작은 병원에서 허리 수술을 했다. 이왕 수술을 할 거면 서울 아산병원에 다닌 기록도 있으니, 그런 큰 병원에서 수술을 해야지, 조그만 시골병원에서 그렇게 큰 수술을 받은 것이 문제의 발단이라 생각된다. 시골 의사는 누나의 골수형성이상증후군이라는 병을 간과했던 것 같았다. 수술 후 염증이 낫지 않아 계속 약을 쓰고 결국은 재수술을 하고, 그래도 염증은 계속 몸 전체를 돌아다녀 손을 쓸 수 없는 상태가 된 것이었다. 골수형성이상증후군으로 백혈구가 제대로 작동하지 않고 혈소판이 모자라는 환자를 생각지 않고 단순히 허리 수술만 생각한 일종의 의료사고가 분명하였다.

액운은 연달아 온다든가, 2020년 삼월 삼짇날 치매를 10년 이상 앓아오던 엄마가 세상을 떠났다. 미국에 있던 나는 COVID 19 때문에 엄마의 장례식에 참석지 못했다. 10년 이상 누나와 함께 정성으로 엄마를 간호해 오던 두 여동생은 엄청 울었다. 누나는 아직 퇴원을 할 상태는 아니었지만, 엄마의 장례식 때문에 퇴원을 했다. 장례를 치르긴 했으나 이때부터 누나의 상태는 급격히 나빠졌다고 했다. 왜냐하면 몸속에 염증이 계속 돌아다녀 심혈관과 뇌혈관을 막히게 하였기 때문이었다. 결국에는 뇌혈관이 막혀 반신 마비가 되었는데, 누나는 재활병원으로 옮겨 재활치료만 하면 좋아질 것이라 생각했던 것 같았다. 재활치료를 하는 중에 염증으로 인해 또 다시 심혈관이 막혀 가슴이 터질 것 같은 상황을 삼성병원에서 혈전을 조금 떼 내어 겨우 피를 통하게 한 적도 있었다.

내가 한국으로 돌아온 것은 2020년 8월이었는데, 코로나 격리를 끝내고, 파주에 집을 하나 구해 놓고, 묘제 시기에 시간을 맞추어 밀양으로 내려갔다. 마침 형님이 가족묘를 완성한 시기여서 4촌까지 모든 형제 자매 전부가 모여 식사를 했다. 이때만 해도 누나는 고기와 밥을 먹을 수 있었고, 펜션을 하나 빌려 1박을 할 때는 노래도 한 곡 했다. 그러나 몸은 현저히 약해져 있었다. 누나의 의지력만으로 극복될 상황은 아닌 것으로 보였다. 누나는 재활병원에서 더 이상 받아주지 않아 삼성병원을 비롯해 혈소판 주사를 놓아주는 여러 병원을 전전할 수밖에 없었다
이때에도 두 여동생은 언니를 돌보느라 힘들었다.

2021년 여름, 누나는 창원 삼성병원에 있었는데, '마지막'이란 심정으로 서울의 현대 아산병원에 가고 싶다'고 했다. 자형과 여동생 내외가

누나를 부축해서 아산병원으로 왔다. 나도 아산병원으로 가서 누나를 만났다. 아산병원의 의사도 뾰족한 수가 있을 수 없었다. 그날 나는 누나를 모시고 우리집으로 왔다. 내가 한국으로 돌아와 새로 마련한 집을 누나가 볼 수 있다는 것에 눈물이 났다. 다음날 내 차로 밀양으로 모시고 갈 때에는 누나가 자형에게 '동생에게 집들이 선물해야 되니 돈을 좀 보내라'고 신신당부를 해서 또 눈물이 났다.

2021년 추석이 지난 며칠 후, 창원에 사는 여동생으로부터 누나가 위험하다는 연락이 왔다. 이때 창원 삼성병원에서 본 누나는 더 이상 말을 하지 못했다. 나를 알아는 보고 내 말을 듣는 것 같았으나, 더 이상 누나와 의사 소통을 할 수가 없었다. 어릴 때 그렇게 싸우면서 컸어도, 공부 잘하는 나를 항상 너무나 자랑스럽게 여겼던 나의 누나는 2021년 음력 구월 초하루 향년 68세의 짧은 생을 마감했다. 누나의 사진 중 가장 화사한 옷을 입고, 가장 환하게 웃는 모습의 사진이 누나의 영정사진으로 사용되었다.

· · ·

술의 역사

나의 아버지는 술을 엄청 좋아하셨다. 2리터 소주 한 병을 사면 혼자서 며칠 만에 다 비웠다. 안주는 술 한 잔에 멸치 한 마리 고추장에 찍어 드시는 것으로 충분했다. 우리 6남매는 아버지의 체질을 이어 받았는지 남녀를 불문하고 전부 술이 셌다. 새 식구로 들어온 자형과 두 매제도 보통 술꾼이 아니었다. 해마다 명절이 되면 엄마가 맥주 두 박스, 소

가족 이름이 새겨진 술

주 한 박스를 준비했는데, 통상 나와 작가인 동생이 양주 한 병씩을 가지고 왔다. 그 술들은 하룻밤에 다 마셔 버리고, 새벽에 국산 양주 캡틴 큐를 더 사온 적도 있었다.

내가 초등학교 3학년 때인 어느 날 우리동네에 두 집에서 잔치가 있었다. 나는 동네 친구들과 함께 그 날 단자를 했는데, 한 집에서는 소주, 다른 한 집에서는 막걸리를 주었다. 10살밖에 안 된 우리 친구들은 처음으로 모두 술에 취한 경험을 했다. 그런데 나는 술 취한 느낌이 어떤 것인지 몰랐다. 시골에서 중학교를 졸업할 때까지 동네 친구들과 자주 술을 마셨다.

부산에 있는 고등학교로 진학한 후에는 거의 술을 마시지 않았지만 대학에 가서부터 나는 내가 얼마나 술을 많이 먹는지를 알게 되었다. 한번은 술 좋아하는 다른 친구와 누가 더 센지 내기를 한 적이 있었다. 여기 이길 수 있는 비결을 하나 소개하겠다. 술이 너무 취해 더 이상 마실 수 없을 때는 조용히 화장실로 가서 모든 걸 토해내라. 그 다음 입을 헹구고 다시 마시기 시작하면 그 다음부터는 잘 취하지 않는다. 주량대결의 결과는 2박 3일 만에 내가 이겼다. 쉽게 이길 수는 없었다. 첫날은 비겼다. 둘째 날 아침에 친구가 먼저 '해장술 할까?'라 해서 하루 종일 또 마시게 되었다. 정말 취했던 나는 위에 언급한 비결을 사용했다. 셋째 날 아침에 내가 친구에게 '해장할까?' 물었더니, 친구는 '졌다'라 했다.

군대에 가서는 술 마실 기회가 자주는 없었지만, 한번 기회가 생기면 엄청나게 마셨다. 나는 레이다 기지에서 근무를 했는데, 야생 염소를 사냥한 날이나, 작전을 잘 해서 포상으로 돼지 한 마리를 받았을 때면 기지장이 술파티를 열어 주었다. 이럴 때는 아무리 마셔도 취하지 않았다. 군기 때문인지 주량 때문인지는 몰라도.

대학을 졸업하고 포스코에 취직을 한 후에는 아예 술 먹는 것 외는 주말에 할 일이 없었다. 오죽하면 아내를 소개받았을 때에도 아내가 술을 같이 마셔 주길래 우리의 만남이 계속 이어졌고, 결국 결혼하게 되었지, 만일 그 당시 아내가 술을 마시지 않았더라면 우리의 연연은 거기서 끝나지 않았을까 생각된다. 결혼 후에 얼마 동안은 자주 마시지 않았다. 간혹 한 번씩 술 마실 기회가 있어도 적당히 마셨다. 물론 취한 적은 없었다.

1989년 초, 나는 포스틴이라는 신설 회사의 공장장으로 가게 됐다. 공장이 하나뿐인 회사의 공장이기 때문에 소관업무가 상당히 광범위했다. 공장 건설, 조업대비, 전산시스템 구축, 인력충원, 관공서 상대

등 공장 가동 전의 일뿐만 아니라, 공장 가동 후에는 조업, 정비, 생산 관리, 품질관리, 출하, 판매지원 등 거의 회사 전 분야의 일에 관여하게 되었다. 신설회사이다 보니 그 만큼 조직간 단합과 결속이 중요했다. 당연히 회식이 잦았고, 오늘은 이 팀과 내일은 저 팀과 거의 매일 술을 마실 수밖에 없었다.

내 술의 절정기는 포스틴이 포스코로 흡수 통합된 후 석도강판공장 장 시절이었다. 그 당시 조업은 3교대 근무를 했는데, 한 근무조가 50명 정도 되었다. 문제는 포스틴에서 넘어온 직원들은 나이가 어리지만 설비를 돌려본 경험이 있는 반면 포스코 타 공장에서 차출되어 석도강판공장으로 온 직원들은 나이와 경력이 많지만, 설비를 돌려 본 경험이 없다는 점이었다. 당연히 나이 어린 포스틴 출신 직원들이 리더가 되어야 했지만, 팀내 단결과 융화는 무엇보다 중요했다. 방법은 회식뿐이었다. 조별로 단합대회를 하려면 한 근무조 50명이 함께 식사를 했는데, 당연히 술을 먹게 마련이었다. 같은 테이블에 앉은 Staff 직원들과 소주를 한두 병 마시고 있으면, 직원들이 공장장인 나에게 한 잔씩을 권한다. 대개 약 40명 정도가 내게 술을 권하는데, 누구 술은 받고 누구 술은 안 받을 수가 없어서 다 받는다. 물론 약간씩 몰래 부어 버리기도 하지만 적어도 소주 일곱 병 정도는 마셔야 1차가 끝난다. 1차 회식을 마친 후에는 일부가 2차로 맥주집이나 그 당시 유행하던 스탠드 바로 가서 또 한 잔 더 하고 헤어진다. 나는 2차가 끝날 때까지 전혀 흐트러짐이 없고 다 끝나면 직접 운전해서 집으로 돌아왔다. '공장장이 직원들 앞에서 흐트러진 모습을 보여서는 안 된다'는 정신력으로 버틴 것이지 실제로 몸은 이때 많이 상했다. 왜냐하면 차를 몰고 집에 도착한 후부터는 완전히 뻗어버리기 때문이다. 아침에 일어나면 머리가 깨어질 듯이 아파, 두통약 게보린을 두 알씩 먹어야 했다. 그리고, 어제 저녁에 마지막으로 누구와 술을 먹었는지, 어디서 먹었는지를 기억하지 못했다. 또한 몰고 온 차를 어디에 주차해 두었는지를 기억하지 못했다. 따라서 아침에 일어나면 제일 먼저 하는 일이 내 차가 어디에 주차되어 있는지 찾는 것이었다.

공장장이 술 먹었다고 늦게 출근할 수는 없는 노릇이고, 일찍 출근하긴 하지만 머리가 아프고 속이 메슥거리는데 책상에 앉아 있을 수는 없었다. 자연히 술도 깰 겸 현장으로 나가 작업도 점검하고 직원들을 만나게 되는데, 직원들은 놀란다. '아니 어제 우리 공장장이 A조와 새벽까지 술 마셨다던데 정말이야?'라고 놀란다. 점심을 먹고 나면 더욱 속이 불편해져서 대개 점심 식사 후에는 화장실로 가서 속에 있는 것을 다 토해낸다. 그런데 문제는 근무조가 3조라는 것이다. 월요일에 A조와 회식을 했으면, 수요일에는 B조와, 금요일에는 C조와 똑 같은 짓을 반복해야 했다. 일주일에 세 번, 한 번에 소주 일곱 병 이상. 이런 생활을 경험해 본 사람이 또 있을까?

2000년, 미국으로 가면서 더 이상 회식은 없어졌다. 한국서 술 취한 상태로 새벽에 귀가하던 내가, 미국 오자마자 말짱한 상태로 일찍 귀가하니 아내는 참 좋아했다. 하지만, 술 마시는 버릇은 버리지 못해 저녁 식사 때는 반주로 소주 한 병씩을 먹었다.
미국생활 20년간 회식은 거의 없었고, 반주의 양도 점차 줄여 나갔다. 대신 골프, 등산, 수영, 헬스 등 건강에 신경을 써 몸이 많이 좋아졌다.

2020년, 한국으로 돌아와 정착한 파주의 도감골에서 만난 마을 노인들의 주량도 보통이 아니다. 나도 옛날에 먹던 가락이 있어 대작은 하지만 이제 좀 버겁다. 뇌수술 때문에 2022년 9월부터 벌써 6개월간 술을 먹지 않고 있다. 항생제와 뇌전증 (발작)예방약, 그리고 30회의 방사선 치료로 술은 엄두도 못 내고 있다. 언젠가 건강해지면 술 맛을 보고 싶다. 과음은 말고 적당히.

• • •

보고 싶은 사람들

시골에서 어릴 때 함께 자란 고향 친구들은 언제 만나도 나를 가장 잘 이해해 주는 친구들이다. 이수태, 이수천, 이수오, 이주석, 이정석, 변종필, 변종득, 손일수, 손영준, 손영현 등. 제실에서 손득구 선생님과 함께 공부했던 손영달, 손영수, 손법현, 손제호 등도 그립다. 각자 사는 환경이 달라도 항상 안부 전하며, 건강하게 자주 만났으면 좋겠다. 이중에는 저승에 가야 만날 수 있는 친구들이 있어 안타깝다. 초등학교 다닐 때의 선생님들이 그립다. 1학년 유순자 선생님, 2학년 제상명 선생님, 3학년 김인기 선생님, 4학년 이종근 선생님, 5,6학년 이만곤 선생님 그분들은 지금 백 세를 누리고 계실까?

집안 할배뻘들은 모두, 아재뻘들도 많은 분들이 돌아가셨지만 오랫동안 보지 못한 아재들이 보고 싶다.

눈 감으면, 시골의 조그만 사립 중학교에서 함께 공부한 120명의 동기생들이 떠오른다. 부산진 시장에서 그릇상점을 하던 김진억, 내가 제대 후 함께 붕어 낚시를 했던 김해성, 부산에서 야채상을 하는 안창현, 유재준, 너무 일찍 결혼한 윤덕선, 헌병대에서 힘 좀 쓰던 손영적, 공무원으로 정년 퇴직한 민병주, KT에서 정년 퇴직한 배건수, 소방서에서 정년 퇴직한 손태목, 대우에서 정년 퇴직한 배종성, 포스코에서 함께 일한 적도 있는 손제정, 군인으로 정년 퇴직한 박수곤 등 '산동회'라는 모임을 통해 가끔씩 볼 수 있는 친구들은 다행이나, 중학교 졸업 후 한 번도 만나지 못한 친구들을 꼭 한 번 보고 싶다. 손명희, 서보금, 김정애, 손정애, 김향수, 김을수, 손필규, 김선옥, 김연옥, 박정련, 박춘희, 집안 아지매 손월현, 안낙현, 박정수, 이경옥, 이순자, 신화숙, 정윤련, 정채석, 이필순, 박봉자, 손영희, 손영의, 안병숙, 김 수, 조정순 등 여자애들과 이만희, 백태호, 박춘희, 박일근, 박영보, 하규태, 이태섭, 조대제, 안영후, 안위현, 김상도, 황석주, 박재돈, 이원희, 이충희, 이윤두, 이인세, 김성태, 김노출, 권정도, 최해석, 방진태, 이상찬, 장건수, 장삼수, 김한곤, 박재윤, 구상태, 김성로, 강종복, 곽주섭, 황종연, 김기수, 조영창, 손맹수, 박순혁, 최화열, 배주한 등 남자친구들 모두가 그립다. 벌써 20명 이상이 무지개다리를 건너갔다는 소식을 들으니 더욱 안타깝다.

이종형, 박상목, 유사근, 박문학 등 선배들도 생각나고, '늘 부지런 하라'고 가르쳐 주신 은사님들도 그립다. 황의중 교장선생님, 안택현 교감선생님, 신상두 국어선생님, 임명홍 영어선생님, 여환덕 수학선생님, 김태홍 실업선생님, 현정용 농업선생님, 안영조선생님, 이선자 음악선생님, 김영숙 미술선생님, 황의정 도덕선생님, 이런 분들이 그리워진다.

S는 나와 초·중학교 동기다. 어릴 때부터 참 예뻤지만 가까이 다가 갈 엄두도 내지 못했다. 군대생활 중 휴가를 나왔을 때 잠깐 만났 적이 있었다. 모 화장품 회사 미용사원으로 일하고 있었는데, 너무 아름답 고, 미소도 마음에 들었지만, 친구 이상으로는 생각해 본 적이 없었다. 나이 들어서도 그대로인지 궁금하다.

P도 나와 초중학교 동기다. 일찍 아버지를 여의고 어머니와 함께 생 활했는데, 집안교육이 너무 잘 되어 있어 보였다. 반듯하고, 예의 바르 고, 공부도 잘하고, 키도 훤칠했다. 잘 살고 있는지 늘 궁금하다.

시골에서 부산으로 유학 와서 기숙사에서 만난 의령의 전병재, 언양 의 노판규, 반성의 정춘환, 정사행, 울산의 이광우, 박성호, 김맹환, 하 동의 권해성, 초중고 동기인 학생회장 손윤탁, 또 김효철, 김상진 등과 는 지금도 가장 친하게 지내고 있다. 언제 만나도 부담 없이 흉금을 터 놓을 수 있어 좋다. 친구의 일을 내 일처럼 걱정해 주고 응원해 주는 심 성이 착한 사람들이다. 백 세 인생이니 오랫동안 건강한 모습을 보고 싶다. 기숙사에서 함께 생활한 권오량, 오세원, 박종식 선배들도 그립 다. 그 외에도 복싱선수 차능진, 봉사 활동에 열성이던 홍상태, 특이했 던 구도판, 남해 고구마 박철현, 출석 부를 때 1, 2번이었던 강명길, 강 호용, 기숙사 생활을 함께 했던 황철순, 박영만, 중학교 교장선생님의 아들 은종민, 고려호텔 사장 아들 김태성, 돼지라는 별명을 가진 김성 택, 태권도를 잘 했던 하원호, 야간학교 1등이었던 박용화 등의 소식도 궁금하다. 김경희, 최홍길, 남홍길, 진호선, 이정주 등 1년 후배들도 보 고 싶다. 남기열 이사장 겸 교장선생님, 최두순 교장선생님, 1학년 담임 김오현 지리선생님, 정경술 수학선생님, 허만기, 박병환 화학선생님,

강선대 기숙사 시절

허만웅, 박계동 국사선생님, 허일성 정치경제선생님, 조상호 세계사선생님, 우대식 생물선생님, 이식우 체육선생님, 안영환 유도선생님, 권영기, 이종찬 물리선생님, 이창원, 김종욱, 윤덕만, 김봉기 국어선생님, 황상우, 김민, 이옥우, 김학배 영어선생님, 이병혁 한문선생님, 이춘식 독어선생님, 박명옥 지학선생님, 원현욱 미술선생님, 조만제 상담선생님, 3학년 담임 최명호 수학선생님, 이분들이 보고 싶다.

대학에서 만나 서클 활동을 하며 젊음을 함께한 친구들과는 각자 직장을 잡아 떠난 후부터 연락이 끊겨 정말 안타깝다. 특히 권태일, 최순철, 이준국, 전병도, 송성태, 구용택, 방근제, 최희영, 강진헌, 이원수 등과 윤진숙, 김승희, 고영숙, 강옥숙, 김미애, 최송희, 노인숙, 조옥자,

이순자 씨 등 여자친구들도 보고 싶다. 결혼은 언제 했는지? 애들은 몇 명이나 있는지? 건강하게 잘 있는지 모든 게 알고 싶다. 김문생 교수, 최성철, 조세형, 이종갑, 심영인, 김응수 씨 등 서클활동 선배들도 그립다. 특히 나의 결혼식 주례를 봐 주신 김경환 교수님은 내가 미국으로 가는 바람에 찾아 뵙지 못해 죄송스럽다.

그 밖에도 같은 과의 친구들인 손영수, 손수홍, 서정국, 박갑원, 정석교 등의 소식도 궁금하다.

대학 시절 하계봉사활동

Y는 대학에서 만난 친구다. 몸이 가냘프고, 도수 높은 안경을 꼈다. 마음씨가 너무 곱고, 뒷정리도 잘하고, 애교도 만점이었다. 별명은 '엄마'였고, 축제 때 포크댄스를 하다가 파트너가 되면 가슴이 울렁거렸다. 좋다고 말하고 싶었지만, 내가 군 입대 후 한 번도 소식을 듣지 못했다. 지금은 건강한지, 행복한 인생을 살았는지 궁금하다.

K는 대학 때 만난 선배였다. 내가 제대를 하고 복학을 하니 그는 이미 졸업을 했었다. 나는 그의 봉사심, 희생을 두려워하지 않는 심성, 열정, 순수함이 마음에 들어 내가 나온 중학교 선생님으로 추천을 했다. 몇 년간 나의 고향 후배들을 잘 가르친 멋진 선생님이었다는 소식을 들었으나, 그 뒤론 알 길이 없었다. 좋은 분 만나 행복한 가정 이루었으리라 생각한다.

영어회화학원에서 만난 김경애, 학원교회에서 만난 김옥순, 송지현, 이정라, 애플 박, 한미애, 역사 전공 오용문 형님, 김용운 전도사, 장병호 목사, 진주교대에 다니던 정영애 씨, 야간학교를 세워 함께 청소년들을 가르쳤던 손영규, 손영숙, 이운용, 장갑덕, 이강성, 이옥수 씨 이런 사람들과 야간학교 학생이던 전효숙, 전민강이 보고 싶다.

J는 펜팔로 만난 친구였다. 서로 얼굴도 모른 채 편지로 많은 얘기를 주고받았다. 실제로 만났을 때는 그의 남자 같은 시원시원한 성격이 마음에 들었다. 남자에게도 무엇을 하든 지기 싫어하는 악바리였다. 후에 내 친구와 결혼했으나 남편과 일찍 사별했다는 소식을 들어서 안타까웠다. 남은 인생은 행복했는지 궁금하다.

H는 키가 훤칠하고 애교가 있었다. 누구에게나 친절했지만 나에게는 좀 특별히 대하는 것처럼 느껴졌다. 어느 날 나에게 '나는 너와 결혼하였다'라는 제목의 책을 선물해 줬다. '무슨 의미이지?'라는 생각이 들었지만 책 내용은 '나는 예수님과 결혼하였다'라는 것이었다. 다시 보고 싶은 사람이다.

야간학교에서 만난 L은 허리가 굵고, 덩치가 컸다. 평소에 나의 엄마가 '며느리감으로는 첫째 건강해야 된다'고 입버릇처럼 말씀하셔서 엄마가 좋아할 며느리감으로 생각되었다. 한번 잘 사귀어 볼까 얘기했더니, 의외로 수줍음이 많은 그가 '아이라예'라고 답했다.

K는 새침데기이고 내숭이 장난 아니었다. 손잡고 데이트도 해 보고 싶었지만 항상 두어 걸음 뒤에서 따라왔다. 결국 식사도 한번 함께 못 했다. 그래도 생각은 난다.

P는 교회 형님이 소개해준 간호사 아가씨였다. 키가 나보다 한 뼘이나 커서 몇 번 데이트를 할 때는 좀 불편했지만, 마음씨가 참 착했다. 간혹 '그와 결혼했다면 2세는 키가 어땠을까?' 생각 들 때가 있다.

논산훈련소 시절에는 김동철 내무반장과 취침 이후에 옥상에서 색소폰을 불어 훈련병들을 눈물 나게 한 조하사, 용두산 엘레지를 맛깔 나게 부르는 동료 홍순원 등이 생각난다. 동백꽃이 피어나는 금년의 고지레이다 기지에서 군대생활을 함께한 상관, 선배, 동료들도 생각난다. 윤승노 기지장, 이경식 경장, 김기대 순경, 전경 17기 김영진, 홍순협, 성남선, 박수대, 강길수, 하선학, 18기 장덕상, 박춘식, 최재호, 20기 이

포스코 입사 동기들

성훈, 김찬성, 김윤곤, 22기 조정호, 임창호, 이복선, 윤광석, 24기 동
기인 박영욱, 박경태, 이경락 그리고 후배인 신복성, 홍승표, 바둑을 잘
두던 최상휘, 대학동기이지만 늦게 군대 온 이성훈, 김창덕 등이 그립
다.

　졸업과 동시에 포스코에 함께 입사한 동기들과는 처음 관계부터 참
좋았다. 강인모, 오영석, 김갑열, 김태원, 김동호, 강영일, 강신환, 원천
수, 윤황영, 김태원, 이승주 등과는 지금도 가끔 만나 회포를 풀고 있으
며, 오랫동안 만나지 못했지만, 유철영, 여강연, 이석재, 김갑열, 김영
기, 김진우, 진정우, 박동완, 김성한, 김진우, 박재성 진철제, 신재철,
장인환, 박현민, 김현배 등과 일찍 퇴사한, 한정배, 엄흥섭, 하재근, 하
병후, 박성진, 임병술, 정경모, 박이훈, 김재명, 한재영 등이 보고 싶다.
엄흥섭의 친구인 배수상 씨와 술도 자주 마셨다. 우리 동기는 20기 2차
였는데, 20기 1차는 우리보다 한 달 반 먼저 입사한 김홍섭, 김준식, 백
승관, 이창수, 홍득식 씨 등이 있었다.

포스코에서의 첫 보직은 연수원 교수실 IE 담당 기술 강사였다. 과장급 이상은 교수, 계장급 이하는 강사라 불렸다. 나는 선배 강사였던 우창제, 우성정, 맹민덕, 이재우, 김윤곤, 박용범, 노연길, 김현철, 나승철 씨 등과 스스럼 없이 어울렸으며, 계장 고참이었던 양관동, 이인근, 황진곤, 위중환, 이광수, 최병한 씨와 나의 사수였던 박찬오 씨와도 잘 지냈다. 강종섭 교수실장, 이동춘, 황재광, 이상일, 박정길, 김규식, 이정소, 김주휘 교수 같은 분들이 시키는 일은 뭐든지 열심히 했다. 덕분에 권오훈, 서상달 연수 원장으로부터 인정도 받았고, 교무과에 근무하던 19기 김영헌씨와 잘 지냈다. 현장 경험이 풍부한 황동섭, 한신택, 손병열, 조원신 주임 등과도 매우 가까웠으며, 내 결혼식에 참석해 준 황동섭, 최학순 씨 등이 잘 있는지 보고 싶다.

연수원 근무 시절에 재포 배정고 동문회를 조직했는데, 1회 이영복, 10회 김선호, 14회 정정수, 신용조, 15회 이정국, 16회 이종복, 17회 배종주, 이병헌, 임정진, 신완석, 18회 오세원, 19회 동기생인 석대용, 우정린, 최병선, 임대웅, 김성태 그리고 전병률, 최홍길, 임광수, 박재현, 장병탁, 한형철 등 후배들도 찾을 수 있었다. 일부와는 지금 연락이 끊겼지만 아직 많은 분들과 연락하며 잘 지내고 있다. 모두 백세까지 건강했으면 좋겠다.

포스코에서 나의 두번째 보직으로 외자부 기재과 기술조사직이었다. 이대공 연수원장 시절, 외자부로 발령 내 준 박춘택 인사과장, 한형섭 인사계장에게 고마웠다. 당시에 외자부에서는 김철웅 부장, 김문규 차장, 신충식, 이정필, 최종을, 곽호정 과장, 강대식, 이광수, 유영선, 이명철 주무 그리고 팀원으로는 전흥조, 이문표, 안영철, 단복만, 김기환,

일본 연수 동료들

김명원, 김삼만, 이건수, 박문주, 안은엽, 야구선수 장효조의 형인 장효
준, 김병수, 박동우, 신기복, 이황구 씨 등을 만날 수 있었다. 외자 구매
업무에 생소했던 나에게 많은 도움을 준 분들이었다. 유명을 달리 하신
분도 있지만 다들 어디서 무엇을 하시는지, 건강하신지 궁금하다. 고려
대 경영대학원을 다닐 때 생산관리론을 강의하셨던 황규승 교수도 생
각이 난다.

　세 번째 보직은 포항 생산관리부 IE 전문 요원이었다. 이때 만난 분
들이 윤상규 실장, 이기용, 서태환 과장, 이광무 주무, 이해수, 이시정,
오성수, 김의연, 안동모, 이성국, 김봉렬, 윤종계, 이승재, 윤영식, 박진
서, 박규호, 이권열, 미스 김 등이다. 눈을 감고 그려보면 모두, 함께 했

던 추억이 새록새록 떠오른다. 생산관제모델을 개발할 때 함께 했던 서대석 박사도 생각난다. IE실에 있을 때 신치재 부소장과 권억근 부장은 나에게 일본연수의 기회를 줬는데, 일본서 만난 네팔인 Jha, 필리피노 Alvin과 Linda, 인도인 Kumar, 홍콩인 진준명, 싱가폴인 Chen, 그리고, 기차에서 만난 제일교포 김천곤 씨, 일본 가정으로 초대해 준 야타가이 씨 부부, 강의를 해 주신 카와세 교수, 호시 교수, 카나자와 교수, 미국의 Mundel 박사, 카와세 교수의 제자 Bob, 연수생들을 늘 뒷바라지해 준 카타오까 씨 등이 생각난다. 외국인들이지만 두 달 동안 너무도 친하게 지낸 사람들이다.

생산관제 Project를 완수한 나는 권억근 부장이 주도하는 CE-DSS라는 새로운 프로젝트를 맡았다. 리더는 신동익 과장, 팀원으로는 표준화 그룹에 백송학, 서정윤, 최석규, 현성진, 김우열 씨가 있었고, 시스템개발 그룹에는 카이스트 출신의 김쾌남, 김봉열 씨가 함께 했다. 공정 표준화 작업을 하면서 원가 시스템을 개발 중이던 강창균 씨와 인연을 맺었으며, 용선 모델을 개발하면서 철도관제를 담당하던 정동화 씨와 인연을 맺었다. 생산관리부의 여러 선후배들과 가깝게 지냈는데, 박세홍, 강대희, 박창남, 백송학, 조병옥, 김종민, 서영섭, 서정욱, 고운식, 박차영, 김충현 씨 등이 생각난다. 이 당시 포항공대 대학원에서 공부를 좀더 해 보려고 시도한 적이 있었는데, 김호길 학장과 산업공학과의 정무영, 홍유신, 전치혁, 정민근 교수 등이 그립다.

네 번째 보직은 포스틴 공장장이었다. 초대 사장은 장세훈 씨였지만, 서상달 부사장과 이동우 인사계장의 끈질긴 유혹으로 새로 생긴 자회사인 포스틴으로 가게 되었다. 2대 안정준 사장과 조병덕 상무, 송정

선 본부장, 이형재 부장, 전기강판부에서 온 문재승 씨, Davy Mckee의 Mr. Green과 Mr. Sands, 쥬몽 슈나이더의 르롱, 현대중공업의 김중영 부장, 포스콘의 조창흠 부장, 윤춘근 과장, 제철정비의 이인수, 정태진 부장, 포스코 공사감독 지보림, 윤종황, 정영만, 김종선, 권우택 씨 등과 힘을 합쳐 공장을 지었다. 전산부문은 Atworth에서 스카우트해 온 후배 박영철이 박용순, 한요안, 정영석 씨 등과 함께 완벽히 구축했다. 손진호 초대 감사, 서상기 부사장이 기억난다. 특히 전단설비 구매 시 미국의 이만형 씨와 문제가 생겼을 때, 큰 힘을 주신 김광일 감사께 감사를 드린다. 조업준비를 위해 미국 UPI에 연수를 가서는 여상환 부사장과 이춘호 부사장, UPI의 Mr. Lanstrom, UEC의 Mr. Karouf, 최재호, 박정민, 전현철 선배, 비서 Diana Mason 등에게 많은 신세를 졌다. 인력 충원에도 힘써 간부요원으로 판매에 포스코 출신 노재홍, 김진명 씨, 조업에 서울대 출신 반영삼 씨, 정비에 포스코 출신 이덕규 선배, 생산관리에 포스코에서 이연호, 최성권 씨, 동성철강에서 이도형 씨, RI 요원 서덕수, 홍성곤 씨, 안전 주임으로 구점룡 씨를 모셔왔다. 조업준비는 동양석판에서 온 이경희, 백철진, 정명동, 현대 중공업에서 온 홍이식, 포스코에서 온 윤병현, 박영태, 신두완, 이종복, 조영보 씨, 그리고 경력직 고상원, 오태석, 신입사원 문형국, 강신성, 박청용 씨 등이 큰 역할을 했고, 유박인, 김용백 관리상무와 김광노 판매부장, 김수영 관리부장, 신동옥 차장, 임필수, 성태기 관리 과장, 안호식 총무과장, 황후석 인사과장 등도 뒤에서 힘이 되어 주었다.

조업안정화에 기여한 김기동, 김기호, 이복우, 김해수, 김경훈, 양희성씨 등 반장들과, 강경호, 김욱동, 김성록, 김한걸, 박용인, 이상호, 전상우, 한정희 씨 등 조업요원들과, 조영보 계장을 비롯한 조창래, 김광연 씨와 오경희 반장, 황용화, 권중헌, 박동순, 나수태, 김영진 씨 등 정

포스틴 직원들

비요원들이 고맙다.

그 밖에 출하의 박효일, 관리부의 하순규, 박현우, 김해영, 이동원, 김진연, 최병욱, 안호준, 비서 우지은 씨 등이 생각난다.

조업이 안정화되었을 때 김만제 회장이 석도공장 순시도 하였으나, 나는 공장장에서 물러나 나의 다섯 번째 보직인 제2공장 추진 프로젝트를 맡았다. 이때 함께 고생한 문재승 씨에게 특히 고마움을 느낀다. 포스코의 유상부 설비본부장, 최종일 부장, 윤용원 과장, 정태원 계장 등과 함께 중국 상해공장을 추진했고, 광양에도 공장을 짓기 위해 layout 심의도 통과하였고, 광양의 최병조 공장장과 회의도 했으나, 박득표 사장의 결제는 받았지만, 김영삼 대통령과 갈등이 있었던 박태준 회장의 최종 승인을 얻지 못해 제2공장은 결국 무산되었다.

1995년 말, 포스틴은 포스코 냉연부의 석도강판공장으로 흡수 통합되었다. 인력 전환 과정에서 이형실 포스코 상무와 갈등이 있었지만, 이구택 제철소장, 한수양 부소장, 신성휴 사장 등이 잘 협의해서, 결국 나는 냉연부 석도강판 공장장으로 여섯 번째 보직을 받았다. 새로이 석도강판으로 온 조영봉, 박상욱, 김정호, 김무식 씨 등이 정말 잘 보좌해 주었다. 이동섭 냉연 부장, 안선환, 유광재 차장, 이중웅 기성보, 정순태, 배명호, 정철영, 김동호, 김효성, 이관도, 이균백, 장지수, 박성권 과장과 이시우, 이진수, 박창현, 배인교, 여원구, 이기수, 최환택, 강춘구, 김광수, 조영기, 한상욱, 정훤우, 김진형, 대학 후배 기을도, 조명래 씨 등과 친분을 쌓았다. 포항-광양 기술교류회를 통하여 광양의 황봉택, 최병조, 이옥산, 이덕민, 윤훈, 정범수, 이덕민, 유홍종, 한광흠 씨 등과 연구소의 홍문희, 정진환, 배대철, 김태엽, 정기조, 소재춘 씨 등과도 함께 일을 하였다.

냉연부 동료들

재포 배정고 동문들도 다시 만나고, 이상영, 이상홍, 조창환, 박일규 선배와, 후배인 남식, 조상호, 이기호, 배양해, 이성규, 안동일, 김장갑 씨 등 부산대 동문들을 만날 수 있어 좋았다.

김만제 회장은 스틸캔에 관심이 커서 나는 마케팅 본부의 최성종 씨, 최상현 씨, RIST의 손영욱 박사 등과 CMB 등 유럽으로 출장을 자주 다녔다. 석도강판과 석도 원판에 대한 포스코 경영층의 관심에 부응하여 설비능력 증감팀이 구성되었고, 유광재 차장, 손인석 과장, 문형국, 이태호 씨 등이 참여했고, 나도 RIST의 김태수 박사와 제어담당 박남수 씨와 함께 일본 출장을 다녀왔다. 때 마침 미국의 UPI에서도 석도 강판 설비합리화를 검토 중이어서 Sal Sbranti, Gorden Monroe, Rod Simpson, Randy Thompson 등과 회의를 했다.

조업이 안정화 단계에 접어들자 이동섭 부장은 후배 전병률 씨에게 석도강판공장장을 맡겼고 나는 도금기술팀장으로 자리를 옮겼다. 나의 일곱 번째 보직이었다. 이영기, 김영우, 김종호, 최진구, 대학 후배 서종 덕 씨 등 새로운 Staff들이 나를 도왔다. 중국 푸동에 석도공장 건설을 추

시카고 Home Stay 식구들

진하던 채희명 차장과 박상욱 씨에게 석도 노하우를 많이 전수해 주었다. 미국으로 어학연수를 다녀온 것도 이때였다. 최준용, 엄기춘 씨와 시카고로 간 나는 Home Stay 아줌마 Evie와 재미있는 날들을 보냈다.

도금기술팀장은 얼마 하지 못하고 선배인 박정민에게 물려주고 나는 설비개선팀으로 자리를 옮겼다. 나의 여덟 번째 보직이었다. 이관도 씨가 팀장이었는데, 황보정만, 권기하, 이영민, 최석욱, 정주한, 진성억, 김정하 씨와 함께 냉연부 환경관리시스템을 구축하였다. 열연코일 강제냉각장 설치를 검토하다 신수철 부소장과 다툼이 좀 있어서, 열연부의 조준길 부장에게 업무를 이관했다. 또 설비계획부 정성현 부장과, 문형국, 박우상 씨가 추진하는 석도설비합리화 사업에 관여했다. 이 즈음, 대우의 장병주 사장이 포스코 이구택 사장에게 중국 해남도에 있는 해우석판을 인수해 달라는 요청을 해 와, 나는 온경용 과장과 해우석판을 두 번 방문하여 이구택 사장에게 보고서를 올렸으나 내 뜻대로 되지는 않았다.

2000년 봄, 내가 UPI 파견 요원으로 선발된 후에, 기술교류회 차 냉연부를 방문한 Rod Simpson, Shane Gravid, Todd Kelstrom, Dimitri Hrovat, Dean Broglie, Mikal Brevig, Tim Deweerd 등 UPI 사람들을 친절히 안내했다.

원래는 Tin Division의 Quality Engineer였던 김준형 씨의 후임으로 가게 되었으나, Sal Sbranti는 나에게 Tin Division Production Assistant Manager라는 Title을 주었다. 차장 대우였다. 이것이 나의 아홉 번째 보직이었다. Division Manager는 Greg Isola였고, Lynnett Ziacobacci, John Young, Kevin Madsen, Markus Boro, Mike Otis, Tim Beasley, MD Amin, Marylin Isola, Jim Belton등 동료들과 함께 일을 시작했다.

1986년 UPI 준공식

　함께 UPI로 발령이 난 이박석(Paul), 고일석(Issac), 반점호(Jason) 씨 외에, 김경화 수석 부사장과 UPI에 먼저 와서 자리를 잡고 있던 많은 선배, 동료들을 만나게 되었다. 박종완(Chris), 김남식(Norman), 김종선(Jason), 노경숙(Kenny), 배인호(Inho), Janice Shin, 이승안(Sam), 김민동(Mike), 이창순(Charles), 김대혁(Dave), 이종관(James) 씨 등이었다. 우리는 자주 골프를 함께 치며 끈끈한 유대를 맺었다. 나보다 늦게 UPI로 온 장준형(Joon), 이수철(Charlie), 오상돈(Sean), 임성식(Sean), 김용건, 김용수, 김태남, 이세진, 노병민(Bryan), 조정호(John), 황영근(Kenny), 도한의(Henry) 씨 등과도 가족처럼 잘 지냈다.

　김경화 수석 부사장 후임으로 신충식 씨가 오셨고, 그 뒤에는 이문수 씨, 또 그 다음에는 동기인 김홍섭 씨가 왔다. 의견이 잘 맞았던 나와 김홍섭 씨는 유종완 MC 위원과 함께 UPI에 오랜만에 설비투자를 할

일범의 평범한 사람 이야기

UPI Korean Staff 2006년 송년회

수가 있었다. 김홍섭 씨 후임으로 온 김광수(Kevin) 씨는 UPI 역사상 처음으로 한국인 사장이 되었다. 김광수 씨 후임으로는 유영태(Tae) 씨가 또 그 후임으로는 선주현 씨가 왔다.

한편 나는 2006년 1월, 포스코에 사표를 내고 UPI에 현지인 신분으로 채용되었다.

사표를 내기 전에 다른 방법이 없을까 고민할 때에, 조성식, 최종두 전무, 이건수, 김태만, 박한용 상무, 인도 사업추진반의 정태현, 권춘근 씨, 동기생인 김준식 사장, 장인환 부사장과 유광재 부소장, 이건수, 김태만 상무, 김동호 냉연부장, 윤동준 인사실장 등과 접촉해 봤으나 결국 뾰족한 수가 없었다.

UPI 20주년

보직도 Technology Division의 Technical Support Manager로 바뀌었다. 나의 열 번째 보직이었다. 한국으로부터 많은 기자재를 수입하면서 범우의 윤명철 후배, 부공산업의 이재명 사장과 정우룡 전무를 비롯해 많은 기업인들과 교류를 했다.

현장 개선 업무가 많았던 관계로 Dave Allen, Frank Martucci, Dean Broglie, Mike Rowney, Jim Carthew, Kim Johns, Adam Krey, Linda Pico Alonza Lewis, Mike Checquer, Matthew Choi, Lonny Welker, Mark Brady, Bryan Afflerbach, Evan Abbett, James Yokel, Walter Nixson, Eric Bonaventure, Charles Bryant, Jesus Partida, Raul Susrtaita, Reed Rosenkranz, Ross Orduna, Herminio Delgado, Dave Hall, Darren Young, Lorenzo Barajas 등과 협업을 많이 했다.

2018년에 나는 마지막이자 열한 번째인 Administration & Finance 부서의 Senior Advisor가 되었다. 구매부서, 안전, Accounting 부서의 직원들과 주로 일을 했다.

Tom Blasingame, Cheryl Novo, Joycelyn, Erin Barrett, Susan Reich-muth, Freddy Repoli, Bob Bedoya, Julie Bedoya, Stephan Cusick, Kathleen D'Agostino, Travis Swanson, Minji Kim, Minkyu Kim, Jeanne Millecam이 그들이었다.

40년의 직장생활을 마무리하고 Retire할 때는 Korean staff 선후배 몇 명과 평소 친하게 지냈던 Frank Taylor, Tom Blasingame 부부와 함께 식사를 하고, 인사부서 Marla Radosevich에게 신분증을 반납하였다.

미국생활 20년 동안 가족 주치의(Family Doctor) 류성화, 이교득, Dr. Elyasi 그리고 카이로프랙터 Dr. An, 한의사 Dr. Kang 등도 생각이 난다. 내 영어공부에 많은 도움을 주셨던 개인교사 Sue Gibens, LMC의 Dr. Zhu, Disbrow, Nakaji, Proc 교수, GGU의 여러 교수들도 생각이 난다.

사회생활에서 가장 중요한 것은 인간관계이다. 현직에 있을 때는 잘되는 것도 못 되는 것도 인간관계에 의해 크게 영향을 받고, 은퇴 후에는 좋았든 안 좋았든 다 추억이 된다. 그런 의미에서 나의 인간관계는 성공적이라 볼 수 있다. 앞에 언급한 사람들 중에는 이미 유명을 달리한 사람들이 많다. 먼저 간 그분들은 나도 죽으면 돌아 갈 그곳에서 무엇을 하고 계실까? 다시 만나 회포를 풀까? 전혀 다른 새 생활이 시작될까? 나는 '사람이 죽으면 육(肉)은 흙으로 돌아가고, 영(靈)은 없어지며, 혼(魂)은 원래 있던 곳으로 돌아간다'고 믿고 있지만, 그 원래 있던 곳이 어딘지 궁금하다. 어쨌든 한 번 이 세상에 왔으면, 인간관계 잘하고, 거짓말하지 말고, 착한 일 많이 하면 사람의 도리를 다 하는 것이라 생각한다.

내가 만난 사람, Charles

내가 2000년 7월 UPI에 부임했을 때, Charles는 Rolling Division의 Quality Engineer로 있었는데, 나보다 5년 늦은 86년에 입사해, 전기강판부 근무를 시작으로 광양 냉연부로 가서 그곳에서 정정계장을 하다가 UPI로 온 지는 3년정도 되었다고 했다. 미국생활에 정착해 갈 동안 업무적으로나 개인적으로나 자주 만날 일은 없었다.

초기 미국생활에서 골프에 재미를 들인 나는 함께 UPI로 온 Paul, Jason등과 자주 골프도 치고, 저녁 식사 때는 술도 먹으며 여러가지 잡다한 얘기를 나누면서 시간을 보내곤 했다.

미국 온 지 1년쯤 지난 어느 날, Paul, Jason등과 저녁을 먹을 때 Charles가 동석하게 되었다. 여느 때와 다름없이 술을 마시면서 이런 저런 얘기를 하다 집으로 갔는데, 그 다음날 회사에 출근하니, 아침 일찍 Issac이 전화로 내 사무실로 오겠다고 했다. 잠시 후 얼굴에 시퍼렇게 노기를 띠고, 씩씩거리면서 나타난 Issac이 대뜸 "우리 집사람에게 뭐라고 했느냐?"라고 따졌다. 무슨 말인지 이해를 못한 나는 "무슨 일이 있었나? 왜 그러느냐?" 고 반문할 수밖에 없었다. Issac이 "손 부장님이 우리 집사람을 '소식통'이라고 했다면서요? 함부로 그렇게 말하면 안 되지요"라고 따지는데, 꼭 나를 한 대 후려칠 것 같은 태도였다. 언뜻 어제 저녁 술 먹을 때 한 얘기가 생각났다. 술자리에서는 '남자가 바깥에서의 일을 집에 가서 미주알고주알 얘기하는 게 아니다'라는 주제였다. 사실 Paul은 약간 덜 했지만 Jason이랑 나는 회사일이나 바깥일을 집사람에게 말해 주는 경우가 거의 없었다. 아내가 회사소식을 아는 것은 부인들 모임에 가서 듣는 게 거의 전부였다. 술자리에서 내가 Issac 부인을 소식통이라 한 것은 Issac 부인이 그만큼 똑똑하다는 뜻도 포함되어 있었는데, 주제의 분위기상 오해할 만했다는 생각이 들었다. Issac에게는 사과하고 끝났지만 Charles에게는 크게 실망했다. 개인적으로 처음으로 함께 한 술자리였는데, 저녁 먹고 집으로 간 시점부터 이틀날 아침 사이까지 그들 사이에 이루어진 전광석화 같은 Communication은 과연 놀랄 만했다. Charles는 자기 부인에게, 그 부인은 Issac 부인에게, Issac 부인은 다시 남편 Issac에게 이렇게 얘기가 전해진 것이 밤 사이에 다 이루어지다니….

2003년, Charles는 UPI 파견기간이 만료되어 한국으로 복귀하게 되었는데, 후임으로는 Mr. Oh로 내정되어 있었다. 그러나 이미 '한국으로 돌아가는 대신 미국에서 살겠다'고 생각한 Charles는 영주권 취득 등 여러가지 준비를 하고 있었고, Mr.Oh가 부임할 즈음에는 POSCO를 사직하고 UPI직원으로 채용되어 Rolling Division Quality Engineer 자리를 차지하고 있었다. 갈 곳이 없어진 Mr.Oh는 예정에 없던 Sheet Division Quality Engineer로 명령이 났는데, Division Manager인 Kelly McMahon은 Korean Staff에 대해 차별을 심하게 하던 사람이라, Mr.Oh에게 일을 주지 않아 Mr.Oh는 복귀할 때까지 마음 고생이 심했다. 그 후 Charles는 Boss였던 Kevin Cox가 6-Sigma 전담 Manager로 빠지면서 Rolling Division의 Quality Department Manager로 승진하였다.

몇 년을 함께 지내면서 업무적으로, 골프모임 또는 Korean Staff 모임 등을 통해 차츰 Charles에 대해 파악하게 되었다. 그를 한마디로 평가하면 '영악스럽다'라고 표현할 수 있겠다. 자신의 이익을 위해 약삭빠르고, 아첨하고, 최대한 아는 체하는 스타일이었다. 무슨 회의를 할 때면 자기가 아는 분야만 장황하게 떠들어 대는데 주제와는 거의 관계가 없는 경우가 많았다. 예를 들어 어떤 설비의 투자 필요성에 대해서 얘기하면, 그는 '무슨 강종은 탄소가 몇 %, 망간이 몇 %, 실리콘이 몇 %... 등등' Quality Manager로서 알기만 하면 되는 내용을 지루하게 얘기한다. Greg Isola등 대부분의 미국인들은 Charles가 하는 얘기를 자기들은 잘 모르는 분야이기 때문에, Charles가 참 많은 것을 알고 있다고 생각하는 것 같았다. 실제로는 주제와는 관계없고 다른 사람들은 깊이 알 필요가 없는 내용들인데 말이다. 그럴 경우 나는 대개 Charles가 계속 얘기하도록 그냥 두었다. 어쨌던 Charles도 Korean Staff이고 내 후배이니까. 나는 어떤 모임에서든지 앞에 나서서 사회보는 것을 잘 해 왔는데, Charles를 남에게 소개할 때, "UPI 최초로 POSCO 출신으로서 부하를 거느리는 Manager가 되었다"고 해 주면 Charles는 으쓱해했다.

UPI 설립 이래로 사장은 USS 측에서 맡고 수석부사장은 POSCO 측에서 맡아 왔는데, 역대 수석 부사장들은 사실상 경영에 큰 영향을 미치지 못해 왔지만, 2011년 Kevin이 수석 부사장으로 오면서부터 달라졌다. 정준양 회장으로부터 모종의 지시를 받고 온 그는 적극적으로 경영에 개입했고, 매너리즘에 빠져 있던 임원들은 크게 당황했다. 2012년 사장이 된 Kevin은 여러가지 조직개편을 단행했는데 그 중 하나가 Quality 부서를 독립시키는 것이었다. Charles는 Kevin 사장에게 자신을 Division Manager로 시켜 달라고 설명, 설득, 건의, 아부… 온갖 노력을 다 했으나, Kevin 사장으로부터 "인사권자는 나다. 니가 인사권자냐?" 라는 얘기를 들었고, 초대 Quality Division Manager는 Frank Martucci가 되었다. Department Manager는 Division Manager를 잘 보좌하는 것이 조직인데, 그러나 Charles는 달랐다. 이 때부터 Charles는 만나는 거의 모든 사람에게 Frank를 씹고 다녔다. '무능하다', '아무 것도 모른다', '내가 아무리 설명해 줘도 이해를 못한다', '없는 만 못하다' 등등 거의 매일 누군가에게 Frank를 깎아내리고 다녔다. 결국 1년후 Frank는 Technology Division으로 옮기고, Charles는 Quality Division Manager가 되었다. '니가 인사권자냐?'라는 말을 들을 정도로 Kevin 사장에게 밉보였던 Charles가 1년만에 사장을 자기편으로 만들었으니, 그의 능력도 대단하다 할 수 있겠다. 그러나 Kevin 사장은 2015년 1월, 한국으로 복귀할 때 '아! 내가 Charles에 대해 잘못 판단했다' 라며 뒤늦게 후회했다.

품질부서는 신제품개발에 주도적인 역할을 하게 되는데, Charles는 사장주재 Business Update Meeting에서 공식적인 보고를 할 때면, 'PLTCM에서 자동차용 AHSS (Advanced High Strength Steel) 생산에 성공했다, OCC(Ohio Coating Company) 향 BP생산 Trial에 성공했다, Easy Open End 용 Tin 제품 생산 trial에 성공했다'는 걸 단골로 보고했다. 대부분의 사람들은 Charles가 대단한 일을 하는 것처럼 이해하겠지만, 내가 보기에는 참 웃기는 얘기다. AHSS는 내가 잘 모르는 분야지만, BP와 Tin에 관한한 내 앞에서 아는 체하면 안 되지. PLTCM의 Flash Butt Welder로 AHSS 용접이 되는가를 물었더니, 아르곤 가스를 분사시키면서 용접하는 기술을 개발하여 아무 문제없이 용접할 수 있다고 했다. 기술교류회차 온 POSCO 직원들이 아르곤 가스를 이용한 AHSS 용접기술에 관심을 가져 자세하게 질문을 했을 때, Charles는 자세한 내용에 대해 전혀 아는 바가 없었다. 그저 현장에서 성공했다는 얘기만 들었을 뿐이었다. 내가 아르곤 가스 분사장치를 제작했다는 직원을 찾아내어, POSCO직원과 함께 Machine Shop으로 가서 직접 분사장치에 대한 설명을 들었다. '그런데 왜 용접기에 설치되어 있지 않고 Machine Shop에 방치되어 있느냐'고 물었더니 'AHSS를 자주 생산하는 것도 아니고, 또 사람이 수동으로 아르곤 가스를 분사하는 것 보다 불편해서 잘 사용하지 않는다'고 했다. 결국 AHSS를 용접할 때면 직원이 직접 아르곤 통에 연결된 호스를 잡고 용접기가 작동될 때 가스를 Spray시킨다는 얘기인데, 용접마저 완벽하지는 않다고 했다. 뿐만 아니라 AHSS 생산 실수율은 50%도 되지 않았기 때문에 Kevin 사장은 결국 자동차용 제품 생산을 포기했다. 그동안 Charles나 Kelly McMahon 같은 사람이 GM, FORD 같은 회사에 출장 다니면서 쓴 비용과 제품인증을 받기위해 투자한 시간과 돈은 허공으로 날아갔다.

Easy Open End용 Tin 제품은 내가 POSCO 석도강판 공장장 시절인 1995년경부터 생산해서 국내 제관사에 공급해온 것이다. 그런데 Trial 생산에 성공했다는 것은 축하할 만한 얘기이지만, Tin용 Hot Band는 POSCO에서 가져오는 것이고, PLTCM 조업기준은 포항 1냉연에 물어보면 다 있는 데 무슨 개발노력을 했는지 모르겠다. OCC(Ohio Coating Company)용 BP Trial 생산에 성공했다는 것은 더욱 웃기는 얘기다. 이것은 개발이라는 말을 붙일 수 없다. OCC도 주석도금설비이므로, Tin용 소재인 BP를 압연하는 것은 똑같고, BP Coil을 UPI에서 Ohio까지 운송 중에 Rust가 생기지 않도록 포장만 잘 해 주면 되는 사안인 것이다. 2006년 Technology Division으로 옮겨온 후부터, 내가 맡고 있는 일 중의 하나가 POSCO-UPI간 기술교류회를 주관하는 것인데, 매회 발표자료, 질의응답자료, 교환자료 등을 잘 정리해 두고 있다.

다만 Charles가 인솔해서 한국에 다녀온 2002년도의 13차 기술교류회 자료는 없다. Charles에게 물어봐도 가지고 있지 않다고 했다.

　Korean Staff들이 모여 2개월에 한 번씩 골프를 치는 한가족골프회라는 것이 있다. 그 회칙 중에는 '승진/결혼/졸업/취업/Jackpot 등 경사(慶事)를 맞은 회원이 Sponsor를 한다'는 조항이 있다. 스폰서는 골프 후 식사를 할 경우 술값을 제외한 밥값을 부담하는 것인데 통상 $100~$200 부담이 됐다. 1년반 이상 잘 유지되어 왔는데, Charles가 Division Manager로 승진하면서 문제가 생겼다. 통상 골프모임 회장인 Chris 선배가 "이번엔 누가 스폰서를 좀 해 주시요"라 얘기하든지, 내가 골프모임 총무를 할 때는 내가 Chris 선배 대신 당사자에게 "당신이 스폰서 할 사유가 있소"라 얘기해 왔다. 그러나, Chris 선배는 어느 날 회식 중에 농담 한 번 잘못 했다가 10년 이상 후배가 되는 Charles에게 크게 무안을 당한 적이 있어 스폰서 얘기를 하기 싫어했고, 나 또한 더 이상 총무도 아니고 'Charles 정도면 알아서 하겠지'라는 생각에 방관만 하고 있었다. Charles는 승진한 지 1년이 되도록 결국 스폰서를 하지 않았다.

　아무도 스폰서를 할 사람이 없을 때는 돌아가면서 스폰서를 했는데, 이 경우는 인당 부담액이 $100을 넘지 않도록 했기 때문에 통상 2명이서 부담했다. 어느 날 Brentwood에서 골프를 친 후에는 Jason 선배가 스폰서를 하겠다고 했다. Jason 선배는 그 전에도 몇 번 스폰서를 한 적이 있기 때문에, 내가 "아니, 왜 선배가 스폰서를 하려 하느냐?"라고 물었더니, "아무도 할 사람이 없는데 어떡하나? 나라도 해야지."라고 했다. 그 날 Charles가 속한 조에서는 내기가 크게 붙어 Charles가 돈을 많이 땄다고 했다. 사람들이 여럿 모여서 출발하지 못하고 웅성거리고 있는데, Charles가 한 마디했다. "어어, 빨리 밥 먹으러 갑시다. 배 고픈데 이거".

식당까지 와서, 또 마지막에 Jason 선배가 계산할 때까지 Charles는 밥만 열심히 먹었다.

Division Manager가 된 Charles는 가끔 내 사무실에 들러, Chris 선배와 함께 점심을 먹자고 했다. 물론 Charles가 한 번 사면, Chris 선배나 내가 반드시 한 번씩 샀다. 올 때마다 Charles는 "Rod Simpson이 어떠냐?", "Dean Broglie는 어떠냐?", "Butch Clay는 나이가 어떻게 되느냐?" 같은 것을 묻곤 했다. 나는 Charles가 Kevin 사장에게 'Rod Simpson은 나이가 많으니 retire해야 한다'라 말한다는 사실을 이미 듣고 있었기 때문에, Charles가 나에게 Rod에 대해 자꾸 묻는 것이 못마땅했다. 사실 Rod Simpson은 내가 느끼기에는 UPI 최고의 resource이다. Kevin 사장이 Greg Isola를 부사장으로 시키긴 했지만, Greg는 무조건 복종하는 충성심과 현장경험이 많다는 것 외에는 지식, 기술, 설비, 기획, 미래지향, Documentation, 표현력, 보고능력, 타사 또는 해외경험 등 모든 면에서 경영자로서는 자질이 부족했다. 사장이 무슨 지시를 내리면 제일 먼저 Rod에 와서 Rod의 의견을 들어본 후에 다른 Division Manger의 의견을 듣고 일을 추진해 나가는 실정이었다. Charles가 내게 와서 Rod에 대해서 자꾸 묻고, 사장에게는 'Rod는 retire할 나이다'라 하는 이유는 결국 Rod를 내보내기 위한 수순으로 이해되었다. 정말 Charles의 공작대로 Rod가 회사를 그만둔다면 UPI로서는 누구도 대체할 수 없는 가장 큰 자산을 잃는 것이다. Charles가 Dean Broglie에 대해 묻는 것은 Rod가 나간 이후 Dean이 Technology Division Manager가 되는 것을 우려해서일 것이다. Dean과 Charles는 서로 사이가 안 좋을 뿐만 아니라, Charles는 자기가 밀어낸 Frank Martucci가 Division Manager로 되면 '내가 너를 시켜 준 것이다'라 과시하고 싶었을 것이다. 얼마 후, 이번에는 Charles가 느닷없이 Sheet Division Manager인 Tim Kuzmicky를 비방하고 다닌다는 얘기가 들렸다. '현직 조업담당 부사장인 Greg Isola에 아부하고, Rod Simpson과 Butch Clay는 나이가 많다고 하고, Alonza Lewis와 Markus Boro는 아직 어리니, 유일한 라이벌이라고 할 수 있는 Tim Kuzmicky만 없어지면 Greg의 후임으로 조업담당부사장이 되어보겠다는 생각을 가진 걸까? 평소 "자기 교회에 다니는 사람 중에 벡텔사 부사장까지 역임한 사람이 있다"고 존경하듯이 말하곤 하던 모습이 떠올라 웃음이 나왔다.

한동안 뜸하던 Charles가 어느 날 점심을 사겠다고 했다. Chris선배와 나는 오랜만에 Mac's Old House에 가서 Steak를 먹기로 했다. '고기가 싸고 맛있었지만 Credit Card를 받지 않고 반드시 현금으로만 계산하는 식당'임은 한 번 가 본 사람이면 누구나 다 안다. 주문을 한 뒤 Charles가 "현금이 없는데, 여기 어디 현금인출기가 없나?"라고 했다. 마침 내가 화장실을 다녀오다 보니까 벽 쪽에 현금인출기가 보였다. "Charles, 저기 현금인출기가 있던데"라 했으나, 아무런 대꾸가 없었다. 한 참 후에 Charles가 "손 선배님, $100만 좀 빌려 주세요"라 했다. 결국 그날 점심은 내가 샀고, 그 후로 Charles는 '함께 점심 먹자'고 하지 않았다. 나로부터 더 이상 알아내고 싶은 게 없는가 보다.

Korean Staff 상조회가 있었는데, 축의금/조의금 외에 전별금이라는 게 있었다. UPI에 근무하다 복귀하는 직원들에게 상조회에서 전해주는 성의였는데, 상조회가 없어진 뒤로는 축의금/조의금은 각자 성의를 표할 수 있었지만, 전별금인 경우 POSCO YB에만 한정되는 사항이라 좀 애매했다. Comptroller로 4년간 근무한 Sean이 복귀하게 되었다. Chris선배가 "OB들끼리 돈을 좀 모아서 선물이라도 하나 사주자"고 제안해서, 내가 OB들에게 "동참할 사람은 $50씩 내라"는 Mail을 보냈다. Charles를 제외한 모든 사람이 동참했고, 우여곡절 끝에 선물을 사지 못하고, 대신에 전별카드에 앞날의 건투를 비는 문장을 하나씩 적어서 전별금과 함께 Sean에게 건네 줬다. Sean이 출국하기 하루 전날 Kevin 사장 주재로 환송회식이 있었다. Charles도 참석했는데, 사장이 있는 자리에서 Sean과 얼굴을 마주치자 좀 어색했는가 보다. Charles는 Sean에게 "아! 내가 너무 바빠서 깜빡했다"고 하고서는, 무엇때문에 바빴는지 한참 얘기하다가 마지막에는 "고생했다, 어디에서든 잘 하실 것이다"라는 덕담을 했다. 얼마 후에는 Mr. Lee가 복귀하게 되었는데, 이 때에도 Charles는 전별금에 동참하지 않았다. 함께 회식도 없었으니 그에게는 변명할 필요가 없어 다행이었으리라.

어느 날, Charles가 "토요일에 골프를 함께 칠 수 있느냐?"고 물었다. Charles가 나에게 먼저 '골프 치자'고 제의한 경우는 없었기 때문에 의아한 나는 "누구와 치느냐"고 물었다. '임군택 씨, Chris 선배, 나, Charles 이렇게 네 명'이라고 했다. 임군택 씨는 POSCO 7기로 나보다는 5~6년 선배인데 포항에 근무할 때 업무적으로 잘 아는 분이라 인사도 할 겸 함께하기로 했다. 골프장에서 "Charles는 임군택 씨와 함께 근무한 적이 없을 텐데 어떻게 임군택 씨를 아느냐?"라고 물었더니, '학교선배'라고 했다. '아하, 그랬구나. 학교 선배이니까 잘 모시다가, 마침 임군택 씨가 다른 곳으로 이사를 간다고 하니까, 떠나기 전에 임군택 씨와 안면이 있는 Chris선배와 나를 골프에 초대했구나' 이해가 되었다, 물론

Green Fee는 각자가 부담했지만, 라운딩 후 함께 식사를 하기로 했고, 식당에는 Chris 선배가 좀 늦게 도착했다. Charles는 Chris선배가 도착하기 전에 자기가 알아서 이것저것 여러가지 음식을 주문했다. 먼저 나온 안주와 술을 좀 먹고 나니, 밥과 찌개는 별로 먹을 생각이 없었지만 이미 먼저 주문이 되어 있었고, 찌개도 다 끓여진 상황이라 억지로라도 먹어야 했다. 식사가 끝나갈 즈음, 임군택 씨가 "오랜만에 이렇게 Chris 선배도 만나 즐거운 시간을 보냈으니 오늘 저녁은 제가 사겠다"라 했다. 이에, Chris 선배가 "그럴 수 있나, 선배인 내가 사야지"라고 했지만 Charles는 입을 꾸욱 다물고 있었다. 'Charles가 자기 선배를 위해서 우리를 초대한 것이 아니었던가? 봉급을 훨씬 많이 받는 Division Manager가 이럴 수 있나? 요리를 먼저 이것저것 주문할 때부터 자기가 계산하지 않겠다는 의도였던가?' 여러가지 생각이 들었지만, 결국 이날은 Chris 선배가 계산했다.

한국의 (주)범우는 냉간압연유 공급사인데, UPI에 압연유를 팔고자 수 년간 노력하고 있었다. 범우의 광양소장인 Mr. Yun은 Charles와는 광양에서부터 알고 지내는 사이였다. 나는 Charles를 통해서 Yun이 내 대학후배라고 소개를 받았다. 범우가 압연유 관련 회의를 하기 위해 UPI를 방문할 때면, Charles가 중간에서 연락도 하고 자주 회의에 함께 했다. 한 번은 회의 후에 Charles가 Yun 소장에게 "미국에 왔으니 미국 Steak를 한번 먹어줘야 할 것 아니냐? 저녁은 Steak를 먹으러 가자. 좋은 식당을 소개하겠다"라 했고, 그날 Yun소장은 저녁 값으로 약 $800을 결제했다고 했다. 이 얘기를 듣고 내가 "어느 식당에 갔는데 그렇게 비싸게 나오나?" 라고 물어보니, Walnut Creek에 있는 Fleming's Prime Steakhouse & Wine Bar에 갔다고 했다. 남의 돈이라고 비싼 Wine을 마구 시켜 먹었을 Charles의 미소가 떠올랐다. 나는 4명이서 Wine과 Steak를 다 먹어도 $80이면 되는 Mac's Old House같은 곳을 잘 가는 편인데, 어느 날 한국에서 온 손님과 Mac's Old House에 간 적이 있었는데, Charles는 다 먹지도 못할 Extra Cut Steak를 주문하던 광경이 생각났다.

아들인 자아린이 한국에서 결혼식을 올리게 되었다. 한국으로 떠나기 며칠 전 Korean Staff 회식이 있었는데, 신임 Tae 사장을 비롯해 많은 직원들이 참석했다. 어쩌다 자아린 결혼 얘기가 화제가 되었을 때, 사장 옆에 앉은 Charles가 "자아린이는 우리 아들 James에게 수학을 가르친 적이 있다. 참 성실하고 착했는데 결혼을 한다니 정말 축하한다. James에게 Card라도 한 장 써서 보내도록 해야겠다"라고 말했다. Korean Staff 직원 모두가 진심으로 축하해 주어서 고마웠다. 며칠 내에 모두들 나에게 와서 축의금까지 전해주었다. 다만, Charles는 끝까지 축의금에도 동참하지 않아서 정말 놀랐다. 결혼식을 마치고 돌아온 내가 Korean Staff들을 점심에 초대했을 때는 James만 참석하고 Charles는 오지 않았다.

Charles는 교회에서 한글학교교장을 한 적도 있고, 교회재정담당 등 핵심적인 역할을 하는 것 같았다. Korean Staff 골프 행사 시 Charles와 같은 조로 라운딩하는 경우가 많았는데, 모두가 '몸 컨디션이 별로다'라 얘기하면, Charles는 종종 "어제 저녁에는 무엇때문에 늦게 잤고, 오늘 아침에는 새벽기도를 다녀와서 잠을 제대로 못 잤다"라는 핑계를 대곤했다. 나는 이런 사람들이 기도를 할 때 무엇을 위해 기도하는지 늘 궁금하다. 성경에 묘사된 예수의 성품을 보면, 사랑, 희생, 봉사, 화목, 용서, 온유, 믿음과 같은 단어들이 떠오른다. 그런데 내가 만난 교회 다니는 사람들의 언행을 보면, 구복(求福), 이기(利己), 편견, 독선, 위선(僞善), 권모술수 같은 단어들이 떠오른다. 모든 것이 예수의 성품과는 정반대다. 남을 위해 자신을 희생하는 사람을 예수의 심성을 가진 사람(Christian)이라 한다면, 자신의 이익을 위해 남을 비방하고, 남을 이용하는 사람은 Anti-Christ, 즉 사탄이라 할 것이다. 스스로는 Christian이라 하지만, 성경에 묘사된 예수의 심성에 비춰보면 Anti-Christ가 분명한 이런 사람들이 교회에 새벽기도를 가면 무엇을 위해 기도하는지 정말 궁금하다.

냉연부장을 역임했던 이동섭 씨가 방문한다 하여 옛날 함께 근무했던 사람들끼리 저녁을 함께 하기로 했다. Paul이 Arrange를 했는데, 나는 Paul에게 '비용은 우리끼리 공동 부담하는 게 좋겠다'고 미리 얘기했다. 식당으로 출발하기 전에 참석대상인 Charles와 Kory에게 '비용은 우리끼리 부담하자'는 e-mail을 보냈다. Kory로부터는 '좋다'는 답장이 왔고, Charles로부터는 답장이 없었다. 식당에서 식사를 하기 전에, 이동섭 씨가 "오늘은 내가 사겠다"라 하자, Paul과 Kory가 "아닙니다, 저희들이 대접해야죠"라 하고, Charles가 "아니, 오늘은 제가 사겠습니다"라 했다. 나는 "이거 원 살 사람이 많아 좋구먼"라 하고는 잘 먹고, 유익한 얘기도 많이 했다. 계산할 때는 Paul이 계산서를 받아 결제 Card를 꺼내려고 할 때, 내가 Paul에게 귓속말로 "오늘은 Charles가 사기로 했지 않느냐?"라고 했는데, 이동섭씨가 '내가 사겠다'면서 계산서를 뺏으려 했다. 옥신각신할 때, Charles가 "아니 오늘은 제가 살게요"라 했다. 결국 이동섭 씨는 "다음에 올 기회가 있으면 꼭 사게 해 달라"고 했고, 그날은 Charles가 부담했다. 나중에 안 일이지만 Charles는 이 돈을 자신이 부담한 것이 아니라 회사에 비용처리를 했다. 혹시나 했는데 역시 그는 공(公)과 사(私)를 구분하지 않는 사람이었다.

조업담당부사장인 Greg Isola는 현장경험이 많고 추진력, 친화력, 조직 장악력이 돋보이는 사람이다. 반면에 현장 외에는 타경험은 부족하고, 경영능력, 기획능력, 기술지식 등이 많이 부족한 사람이다. 특히 Charles가 얘기하는 내용은 Greg가 잘 모르는 분야라서 Charles의 말이 중요한 내용인지, 별 의미 없는 내용인지를 판단하지 못하고 Charles를 무조건 믿는 경우가 많다. Rolling Division의 Division Manager와 Quality Manager로 만나 오랫동안 친분을 쌓은 Charles는 이러한 Greg의 장단점을 잘 이용하는 편이다. 자신이 좀 버거운 상대에게는 Greg를 먼저 설득한 후 Greg의 지위를 이용해서 자신의 목적을 달성하는 것이다. 기술교류회에 참가할 인원을 선발할 때였다. Charles는 Greg를 설득하여 입사한 지 1년정도 밖에 안되는 Sheet Quality Engineer Eric과 Tin Quality Engineer Mary를 기술교류회 인원에 포함을 시켰다. Leader를 제외하면 4명 중 2명이 Quality 담당인 파격적인 선발이다. Quality 부서의 사기를 생각해서 1명 정도정도 포함시키는 것은 이해가 되지만 2명은 너무했다. 그런데 더욱 문제는 Eric과 Mary는 부부 사이이고, POSCO는 Tin 설비가 없기 때문에 ETL에 관한 내용은 기술교류회 대상이 아니라는 것이다. Charles는 자기 부하들에게 UPI내에서의 자신의 Power를 과시하고, 'Greg도 내 마음대로 움직일 수 있다'는 걸 보여줬지만, 회사로서는 귀한 기회를 낭비하게 되었음은 물론이다. 경험이 일천한 Mary는 기술교류, 토론, 질의 응답 어느 부분에서도 아무런 역할을 하지 못했고, 그저 남편 따라 한국여행 잘 다녀왔을 뿐이었다.

범우가 다시 UPI에 압연유 Trial을 시도하게 한 것은 Paul이 추진한 UPI의 여러가지 개선 Project중 하나였다. 그런데, 범우가 UPI에 와서 회의를 할 때는, Yun소장과의 친분으로 Charles가 회의에 참석하게 되었고, 영어능력이 조금 부족한 Paul은 Charles에게 통역의 주도권을 뺏기고 있었다. 이것은 부장 Greg나 조업과장 Alonza에게는 Charles가 주도하는 것처럼 보였고, Charles도 Yun소장에게 'UPI와의 communication을 자신에게 경유'하도록 요구했다. Charles가 관여하고 있었기 때문에 나는 범우를 UPI의 신규 Vendor로 등록하는 행정업무를 도와준 것 외에는 전혀 관여하지 않았다. Trial에 대한 윤곽이 대략 정해진 2015년 9월경에, Paul이 나에게 "이제 대략의 계획이 잡혔는데, 실제로 범우의 Test가 진행되게 되면 손 부장님이 많이 좀 도와주십시오" 라고 해서 "내 도움이 필요하면 그러겠다"라 했다. 10월에는 Alonza가 범우와의 최종 가격협상을 진행할 때에 내게 통역 및 중재를 해 줄 것을 요청해 와서, 사실 이때부터 내가 이 일에 관여하게 되었다. 압연유 변경은 UPI 창사이래 첫 시도하는 대단히 중요한 변화인 반면, 준비 일정이 너무 빠듯하여 UPI와 범우와의 완벽한 Communication은 어느 때보다 중요했기에, 내가 좀 적극적으로 개입하게 되었다. 압연유 Trial을 위한 사전 준비사항, 소요되는 압연유량 산출, 환경영향분석을 위한 Oil Sample 요청 등 Thanks Giving 휴무 기간 중에도 계속 중재업무를 진행했다. 12월 초에 Test를 위해 UPI에 온 Yun소장은 나에게 "Charles가 자기를 경유하지 않고 일이 진행되는 것에 대해 기분 나빠 하더라" 라 하길래, 내가 Yun소장에게 "신경 쓰지 마라, Charles는 입으로만 일하는 사람이지, 몸으로 일하는 사람이 아니다. 실제 Test를 진행하게 되면 Mike Chequer, Matthew Choi, Darren Young 같은 사람을 상대하면 된다. Charles가 할 일은 생산된 제품에 대해 품질 Check이지, 그는 절대로 Test준비하는 현장에 가 볼 사람이 아니다"라 말해 주었다. Charles는 Paul 과 통화 중에 Paul에게 "범우 Oil Test는 현장부서에서 다 알아서 할 테니, Paul은 호텔예약 같은 것만 좀 도와주면 된다"라 했다. Sample Delivery와 Neat Oil Delivery에 대한 것은 통역만 하면 되었지만, Tank 와 Mill Stand 청소범위에 대한 쌍방 간의 의사소통은 직접 Mill Stand Drive Side로 내려가 신발과 옷이 기름 투성이가 되도록 몸으로 확인할 사항들이었다. 3일동안 Charles는 코빼기도 보이지 않았다. 회사사정으로 Test는 1월로 연기되었는데, Greg와 Alonza가 참석한 회의에 나타난 Charles는 잽싸게 Greg 와 Alonza의 말을 통역했다. Paul 이 Charles에게 왜 통역의 주도권을 빼앗겨 왔는지 이해가 되었다. 그런데 가관인 것은 Charles는 Greg나 Alonza가 한 말을 그대로 통역하는 것이 아니라, 자신의 의견을 말했다. 전체적인 내용은 같지만 Charles 는 자기 생각을 장황하게 말했고, Greg 나 Alonza는 Charles가 잘 통역해 준다고 생각했을 것이다. 그 자리에서 Charles에게 '통역은 말한대로 전해 주어야지, 니 의견을 말하지 말라'고 말할까? 라 생각도 들었지만 Charles의 체면을 생각해서 참았다. 통역이란 말하는 사람이 무슨 말을 하든, 설사 실수를 한다 해도 있는 그대로 전달하는 것이 생명이다. 말한 사람의 뜻이 아니라 자기 의견을 얘기한다면 말한 사람이 왜 필요한가? 지가 다 알아서 하면 되지. Test는 연기되었지만, 토요일에는 Mill Stand 청소와 Neat Oil Delivery 확인을 위해, 일요일에는 Sample 분석을 위해 출근해야 했다. POSCO YB 직원들모임에서, Shin 부사장이 "Oil Trial은 품질부서에서 주관하면 되지 왜 손부장이 관여하느냐?"라 했다는 얘길 듣고는 정말 어처구니가 없었다. '나에게 말하기가 어렵고 또 Tae 사장에게 얘기할 수도 없으니, 이제 Shin 부사장을 이용하려 하는구나' 하는 생각이 들었다. 압연유 교체가 얼마나 중요한 일인데, 누구든 일이 되도록 도와줘야 할 것인데, Charles는 내가 도와주는 게 왜 싫은 걸까? 어차피 실무적인 일을 하지도 않는 사람이, Shin 부사장에게까지 얘기해서 나를 밀어내는 것이 자신에게 무슨 이득이 있는 걸까? 참 이해되지 않는 심성이다. 이러한 Charles의 말을 믿는 Shin 부사장도 참 답답하다. 사람보는 눈이 그렇게 없을까?

Charles에 대한 기억들을 되살려, 이렇게 정리하고 있는 나는 지금 많이 고민하고 있다. '내가 자기 머리 꼭대기에서 내려다보고 있는데, 왜 저런 말을 하는지? 왜 저런 행동을 하는지? 그 속이 훤히 보이는 데, 나름대로 머리를 굴리는 그 모습이 안쓰럽다. Greg에게는 '네가 부사장이 되도록 내가 Kevin 사장에게 강력히 추천했다'라 말해서 자신의 영향력을 과시하고, Alonza 또는 다른 동료나 부하들에게는 '내가 사장까지 움직일 수 있는 힘이 있다'고 으스대고, 남이 한 일을 자기가 한 것처럼 Boss에게 약삭 빠르게 먼저 보고해 버리고, 실질적인 내용은 깊숙이 관여하질 않고 겉만 대강 아는 상황에서도 마치 잘 아는 것처럼 잘도 나서고…. 그렇게 인정받고 싶고, 승진하고 싶고, 과시하고 싶어하는데 '원래 그의 심성이 그려려니' 하고 그냥 내버려 둘까? 그런데 곧 POSCO로 복귀할 Paul을 왜 경계할까? 머지않아 Retire할 나를 왜 경계할까? 회사에 어떤 일이 생기면 모두가 힘을 합쳐 그 일을 성공시키는 것이 최우선인데, Charles는 왜 다른 사람이 관여하는 것을 경계할까? 혼자서 할 일도 아니고, 어차피 누군가가 도와줘도, 나중에는 자기가 주도적으로 한 것처럼 보고할 것이면서 말이다. Charles를 어떻게 할 것인가? 정말 고민이다. 이대로 두었다간 언제가는 회사에 큰 문제가 될 수도 있다. 지금 쓰고 있는 이 내용들을 영어로 번역해서 UPI 전 직원에게 뿌려서 완전히 매장시켜 버릴까? 안 되지, 그래도 한국인이고 (아니, 지금은 미국인이 되었지), 후배인데 차마 그럴 수는 없겠지? 불러서 솔직하게 대화를 해 볼까? 따끔하게 경고를 해 줄까? 내가 충고를 하면 내 진심을 받아들인 만한 사람인가? 아니다, 잠시 충격은 받겠지만 또 다른 꿍꿍이를 꾸밀 친구다. Tae 사장에게 살짝 Charles의 실체에 대해 얘기해 줄까? 그것도 치사한 행동이지? 내가 지금 이 나이에 후배와 싸우는 모습도 볼썽 사납다. 그래도 POSCO 후배인데 그냥 모른 체할까? 아니지, UPI를 살려야지. 이대로 두면 큰 일이 생길지도 모른다. K-Staff 간에 불화가 생길지도 모른다. UPI의 조직과 경영이 개판이 될지도 모른다. 무엇보다 저렇게 비양심적인 사람이 양심적인 사람을 짓밟고 올라서는 것은 용납이 안 된다. 뭔가 조치는 취해야겠는데, 어떻게 하는 것이 소리소문 없이, 모든 사람이 만족하는 결과를 얻을까?

2000년도에 Charles를 만나서 15년 동안 보고 느낀 그에 대한 요약은 다음과 같다.

- 입이 가볍다
- 배려심이 없다
- 약삭빠르다
- 세부적으로 잘 모르면서 전체를 아는 체한다
- 상관에게는 아첨을 잘한다
- 경쟁자를 헐뜯고 질투한다
- 부하에게는 힘을 과시한다
- 잘된 것은 과장한다
- 잘못된 것은 남이 한 것으로 포장한다
- 자신의 이익을 위해 거짓말을 한다
- 육체적으로 힘든 일은 회피한다

- 인간관계가 좋지 않다
- 공과 사를 구분하지 않는다.
- 공짜를 좋아한다
- 크리스찬이라고 말하면서 성품과 언행은 예수와 정반대이다
- 자신의 돈이 지출되는 것을 지극히 꺼려한다
- 남의 정보를 자신이 파악한 것처럼 잽싸게 먼저 보고한다
- 강한 사람에게는 한없이 비굴하다
- 대화에 진정성이 없다
- 변명과 핑계가 합리적이지 못하다

2016년부터 나는 가능한 일상생활에서 Charles와 어울리는 것을 의도적으로 피해왔다. 그가 무슨 목적으로 어떻게 살아가든지 내가 관여할 사항이 아니라고 생각했기 때문이었다. 그런데 2016년 1월부터 본격적으로 시작된 압연유 Test 때문에 자꾸 부딪힐 일이 생겼다. 나는 압연유 test가 성공적으로 되기를 바라는 마음에서, 영어를 잘 못하는 범우의 Yun 소장을 도와주는 것뿐이었지만, Charles에게는 다른 것 같았다. '압연유 교체업무도 내가 주도하고 있다'는 것을 Greg나 다른 사람에게 과시하고 싶어했고, '나중에 성공했을 때는 전부 나의 공이요 실적'이라는 것을 알리고 싶어했는가 보다. Charles는 범우의 Yun 소장에게 'Test에 관한 정보를 Paul이나 나에게 공유하지 말고, 자기와 Alonza에게만 얘기하라'고 끊임없이 요구했다. 그렇다고 나나 Paul이 하는 일을 그가 하는 것도 아니었다. 언제나 뒷전에 빠져 있으면서, 중요한 순간에는 다른 회의를 핑계로 현장에 나타나지도 않았다. '원래 그러려니' 생각하고 신경 쓰지 않기로 했다.

또한 Ricky Averion이라는 직원이 Charles 밑에서 Sheet QC 담당

Manager로 있었는데, 미국내 여러 철강회사 경력이 많아 경험도 풍부하고 아는 것도 많았다. 내가 보기에는 Charles보다 훨씬 QC 업무를 잘 수행할 능력이 있는 친구였는데, 어느 날 보니 회사를 나가 버렸다. 몇몇 사람들에게 왜 가 버렸는지 알아보니, Ricky의 의견이나 하는 일에 대해 Charles가 사사건건 트집잡고, 창피 주고 해서 그 Stress를 Ricky가 견뎌내지 못하고 회사를 그만 둔 것 같았다. Charles 성격상 자기보다 똑똑한 사람을 데리고 있는 게 불편하고, 자기 자리에 위협을 느껴 미리 잘라 버렸으리라는 생각이 들었다.

한편 Charles는 교회에서도 재정담당을 하면서 교회를 주도적으로 끌고 나가는 모양이었다. Charles가 롤모델로 생각하는 벡텔 부사장출신인 모인사와 함께 '교회는 목사를 위한 교회가 아니라, 신도들을 위한 교회가 되어야 한다' 라는 명분으로 몇몇 목소리 큰 신도들과 힘을 합쳐 교회의 모든 일을 마음대로 휘두르고 있어서, 다른 신도들이 불편해한다는 얘길 들었다. 특히 담임목사도 Charles때문에 엄청 힘들어 하고 Stress를 받는 모양이었다.

2016년 봄에 Korean Staff 골프모임이 있어, Charles와 한 조가 되었다. 속마음은 한 조에서 라운딩하기 싫었지만 내색할 수는 없었다. 그런데 함께 오랜만에 골프를 쳐보니, Charles의 Swing Power가 현저하게 약해져 있는 것을 보고 놀랐다. 원래 Charles는 체격에 비해 골프 비거리도 좋고 Single Handicap 수준의 실력이었는데, 이날은 Drive 거리가 150야드 정도밖에 나가지 않았다. '왜 이렇게 거리가 줄었느냐?'고 물어보니, Charles는 '요즘 왠지 힘이 없다'라 했다.

봄에 함께 골프 라운딩한 후로 거의 Charles를 만나지 못했는데, 2016

년 10월에 'Charles가 몸이 많이 안 좋다'라는 얘길 들었다. 오랜만에 그의 사무실로 가서 만나 보니, 이건 보통일이 아닌 것 같았다. 운동신경 전달체계에 이상이 생겨 근육이 점점 제 기능을 발휘하지 못하고, 말라가는 현상이라고 했다. 일종의 루게릭 병 비슷한 것이었다. 루게릭병 환자 얘기를 들어 본 적이 있는 나로서는 무슨 말을 어떻게 해야 할지 도무지 생각나지 않았다. Stanford 대학병원에 다니면서 여러가지 검사를 하고 있다고 했는데, 미국병원이라는 게 도통 믿을 수가 없는 곳 아닌가? 환자가 기다리다 죽는 곳이 미국병원시스템인데, 몇 달째 계속 검사만 하고 있는 모양이었다. 내가 생각하기에는 병의 원인이 스트레스 같았다. 회사일 뿐만 아니라, 집, 가족, 교회 등 주위에 있는 모든 것에 대해, 좋게 말하면 의욕과 열정이 넘치는 것이고, 나쁘게 말하면 분에 넘치는 욕심으로, 모든 것을 혼자 Control하기 위해서 추진하다 보니 감당할 수 없는 스트레스를 받았던 것이 아닌가라는 생각이 들었다. 과다한 스트레스 때문에 결국 몸의 어느 한 부분이 고장 나고, 이렇게 고장 난 몸은 원인불명의 불치병 또는 난치병이 되는 것이 아닌가?

사람을 상대할 때, 있는 그대로 대하지 않고 항상 어떤 목적의식을 가지고 상대하자니, 누구를 만날 때마다 (상관이든, 부하든, 동료든) '전에 이 사람에게 내가 어떻게 말했던가?' '이 사람에게 어떻게 하는 것이 나에게 유리할까?'를 생각해야 하니 얼마나 피곤했겠는가? 일을 추진할 때에도, 일 그 자체에 대한 순수함을 잃고, 항상 자신 목표를 달성하기위해 이 일을 어떻게 이용할 것인가를 생각해야 하니 얼마나 스트레스를 받았을까? 아이러니한 것은 Tae 사장으로부터 들은 얘긴데, Greg Isola의 Succession Plan에는 1번부터 5번까지 List에 Charles의 이름이 없다는 것이다. 뿐만 아니라, 스스로 독실한 Christian이라 생각하고,

교회에서 하는 모든 행위가 하나님의 뜻이라 생각하는데, 목사를 비롯한 많은 교인들이 싫어하니 이 또한 힘들지 않았을까? 그는 과연 자신의 말과 행동이 예수를 닮은(Christian) 것이라 생각했을까?

다시 건강해져서 함께 골프 칠 수 있었으면 좋겠지만, 솔직한 느낌으로는 건강을 회복하는 것이 힘들 것 같다. 모든 것이 자업자득이 아닌가라는 생각이 든다. 그래도 좋아지기를 진심으로 바란다.
그러나 Charles는 2017년 9월 16일 세상을 떠났다.

후일담: 1년이 지난 후, 그의 아내는 Tax 신고를 위해 회계사를 만났는데, 회계사로부터 'Charles가 주식에 투자해서 전재산을 잃었다'는 사실을 듣게 되었다.

· · ·
나의 투병기

미국생활을 하면서 골프를 너무 자주 치다 보니 몸이 아픈 곳이 많았다. 2016년에는 양쪽 어깨, 허리, 오른쪽 다리를 MRI 촬영을 해 가면서 치료했다.
2018년은 그 연도의 발음만큼 정말 재수없는 해였다.
캘리포니아주 브랜트우드 (Brentwood city, California)에 있는 시니어 하우스(Senir House: 55세 이상 거주)에 살 때다. 여름부터 피부 알러지가 생겨 알러지전문의사를 찾아가 여러가지 검사를 한 결과, 결론은 '진드기알러지'라 했다. 나는 진드기가 오래된 카펫 때문이라 생각되어, 몇 천 달러를 들여 카펫을 걷어내고 나무로 바닥을 바꾸는 한편, 청결을 위해 세탁기와 건조기도 아예 새것으로 교체했다.

가을에는 왼쪽 눈 주위와 이마에 부스럼 같은 게 생겨 패밀리 닥터(Family Doctor: 주치의)에게 갔더니 대상포진인가 의심을 하면서도 결국은 대상포진이 아닌 것으로 판단하여 연고를 처방해 주었다. 연고를 이틀 발라봤으나 낫지 않고 더 심해졌다.

집 근처 미국 피부과 닥터에게 갔더니, 보자마자 'Oh, Shingles' 하면서, 단번에 대상포진이라고 진단하고 약을 처방해 주었다. 그리고 '대상포진이 눈 주위에 오면 잘못되면 실명할 수도 있으니 빨리 안과에 가보라'고 했다.

안과 닥터를 만나 진료를 받으니, '눈에는 이상이 없다'고 했다. 나는 평소에 자전거를 탈 때, 간혹 물체가 두개로 보이는 경우가 있어, '눈에 이상이 없는데 복시(Double Vision)는 왜 생기느냐'고 물어보니, '눈에는 이상이 없고 혹시 뇌 쪽 문제일 수도 있으니, 뇌 MRI를 한번 찍어보라'고 했다.

즉시 패밀리 닥터를 통해 뇌 MRI 촬영을 했다. 결론은 큰 이상은 없고, 국소 빈혈(Mild chronic small vessel ischemia) 현상이 있는 것으로 나왔다. 패밀리 닥터는 아스피린(baby aspirin, 81mg) 복용을 권유했다. 이때부터 매일 아스피린을 복용하게 되었다.

미국병원에는 종합건강검진시스템이 없기 때문에, 주기적으로 한국에 와서 종합건강검진을 받아왔다. 2019년에 한국에 나와서 광혜병원에서 종합건강검진을 받았는데 건강에 큰 문제는 없었다. 다만 이때는 뇌 MRI를 촬영하지 않았다.

2020년에 은퇴(Retire)하고 한국으로 이사를 왔고, 2021년 7월에 광혜병원에서 다시 종합건강검진을 받았는데, 이때는 뇌 MRI를 해보니 '좌측 뇌에 뇌수막종으로 의심되는 2.3mm 크기의 종양이 보이니 큰 병원으로 가보라'고 했다.

며칠 후, 일산병원 신경외과로 가서 다시 MRI 촬영을 한 결과, 담당 의사는 '뇌수막종은 흔히 생기는 것으로, 평생 뇌수막종을 가지고 사는 사람도 있으니 일단 관찰을 해보자'고 했다.

1년 후 2022년 6월에 다시 일산병원으로 가서 MRI 촬영을 한 결과, 의사가 '1년 동안 2.4mm에서 2.8mm로 커졌다. 수술을 해서 제거하는 게 좋겠다'라고 했다. '수술을 할 경우 후유증은 없나'라 물으니, '말이 어눌해지거나 한쪽 몸이 마비될 수 있다'라 했다. 수술 후 '말이 어눌해진다 또는 반신마비가 된다'는 것은 상상만 해도 끔찍하였다.

나는 '일산병원보다는 신경외과에 권위 있는 세브란스 병원에서 수술하고 싶다'고 하였고, 의사는 그리하라고 했다.

7월에 세브란스병원 신경외과에서 다시 MRI를 찍었는데 결과는 일산병원에서와 같았다. '수술로 제거하는 방법이 최선'이라는 것이다. 다만 세브란스 신경외과 담당교수는 '비교적 간단한 수술이며, 수술 후 중환자실에서 2일, 일반병실로 옮겨 9일 경과하면 퇴원 가능하다'고 했다. 수술날짜는 9월 30일로 잡혔다.

나는 '간단한 수술이고 큰 문제는 없을 것'이라 생각은 했지만, '만일의 경우도 대비하는 게 좋겠다'는 생각이 들었다. 7월에는 미국을 방문하여, 옛 UPI 선후배를 만나고, UPI 직원들과 인사도 했다. 내년 말이면 UPI가 문을 닫는다고 하니 아쉬운 점이 컸다. 9월에는 형제자매들의 모임을 우리집에서 가졌다. 만나는 사람들에게는 내 상태를 설명하고 '큰 걱정은 안 해도 된다'라 했다.

9월 28일 세브란스 병원에 입원을 했고, 29일에는 혈관 촬영술과 가족과의 수술면담이 있었는데 담당교수는 '큰 문제는 없을 것이다'라 했다.

9월 30일에 뇌수막종 제거 수술을 했는데, 사실 이때부터 내 기억은 정확하지가 않다. 전신마취의 영향도 있었겠지만 거의 10일 정도는 혼수상태였던 것 같다. 후에 아내에게서 들은 상황을 정리해 보면 이렇다.

첫 수술을 마친 후, 내가 중환자실로 갔을 때, 아내는 병원에 있을 수가 없어 집으로 갔다가, 내가 중환자실에서 일반병실로 옮길 때 다시 왔다. 아내와 얘기를 하는데, 나는 상대방의 말소리가 들리지 않고 모기소리처럼 귓가에 왱왱거리기만 했다, 또 내 입에서 말소리가 나오지 않았다. '죽지는 않겠지만 죽음보다 더한 삶을 사는게 아닌가'라는 생각이 들었다. 아내가 종이에 글로 써서 의사소통을 시도했는데, 내가 쓴 글씨는 한글을 처음 배우는 어린 아이가 쓴 것처럼 삐뚤삐뚤했다. 마침내 '말도 못하겠고, 소리가 들리지 않는다'라는 의사전달은 되었고, 의사들은 재수술을 결정했다.

수술 전 의사는 아내에게 나의 살 확률과 죽을 확률은 50:50이라 했단다. 나중에 아내로부터 들은 얘기지만, 첫 수술 때 세균감염이 되어 패혈증이 되었다고 했다. 재수술 시 뇌 세척을 하기 위해 20리터의 소독액을 사용했다고 했다. 어쨌든 2차 수술은 잘 된 것 같았다. 왜냐하면 남의 말을 들을 수 있고 내가 말하는 데도 지장이 없었기 때문이었다. '이제 살겠구나' 생각되었다. 중환자실에서는 간호사가 계속 '이름이 뭐냐', '여기가 어디냐', '오늘이 며칠이냐' 등을 물었다. 나오는 음식도 거의 먹지 못했다.

중환자실에서 1주일가량 있다가 일반병실로 옮기니 아내를 만날 수 있었다. 아내로부터 위험했던 수술 전후 상황을 자세히 들을 수 있었지만 나는 대부분을 기억하지 못했다.

일반병실로 옮긴 후 약 1주일간은 귀속이 너무 아파 고생을 했다. 뇌수막종을 떼낸 왼쪽 머리에서 왼쪽 귀까지 심한 전기충격을 받는 것처럼 아파 죽을 지경이었는데, 의사는 쉽게 원인을 찾아내지 못했다. 이비인후과 의사와 협진을 했지만 이비인후과에서는 '귓속에는 아무런 이상이 없다'는 진단이었다. 결국 항생제를 바꿔서 통증이 줄었다.

의사들도 환자를 상대로 이것, 저것 약을 시험해 보고 맞는 약을 찾아내는 시행착오의 연속이며, 환자는 그저 실험대상일 뿐이라는 생각이 들었다.

지겨운 병원 생활이 계속되었다. 입맛이 없어서 병원식은 아예 먹지를 못했고, 아내, 아들, 또는 서울 사는 동생이 음식을 사다 날랐다. 그러나 외부 음식마저 대부분 짜게 느껴져 맛이 없었다. 아내는 '독한 항생제' 때문이라 했다.

병원에서는 코로나19에 걸린 노령환자가 죽어 시체로 실려 나가는 광경을 보기도 했는데, 어느 날은 나와 아내가 코로나19에 걸렸다. 나와 아내는 백신을 4차까지 맞았고 한 번도 코로나19에 걸린 적이 없었는데, 병원에서 걸리다니 참 황당했다. 나는 독방으로 옮겨졌고, 아내는 집으로 돌아가야 했다. 생각해 보면 병원에서 코로나에 걸리는 원인은 병원 시스템에 있는 것 같았다. 환자의 보호자는 단 하루를 외출해도 PCR 검사를 받고 음성확인이 되어야만 다시 병원으로 올 수가 있는데, 수천 명의 병원 직원들은 매일 출퇴근을 하지 않는가? 지하철로, 버스로, 때로는 걸어서. 그러나 PCR 검사를 매일 받는가?

1주일간의 독방 생활을 마치고 다시 2인실로 옮긴 후부터는 재활훈련을 시작했다.

손발자전거를 약 20분간 타는 것이었는데 나는 최고 강도(20단계)로 세팅해서 때로는 손을 놓고 발로만 자전거를 탔다. 트레이너와 간호사들이 '힘들지 않으냐?'고 했지만, 그 정도 해야 운동이 되었다. 간호사들은 '재활병원 역사상 가장 힘 있는 환자'라 말했다. 남자 트레이너들도 '나보다 힘이 더 세네'라 했다. 운동한답시고 병원 복도를 몇 바퀴 뱅글뱅글 도는 것보다 스트레스가 풀려 좋았다.

'시간이 약'이라 했던가? 입원 50일 만에 퇴원을 하게 되었다. 물론 집에서 항생제와 뇌전증(발작) 약을 계속 복용해야 하고, 추후 방사선 치료도 받아야 했지만 그렇게 좋을 수가 없었다. 50일 동안 감지 못했던 머리를 감을 수 있어 좋았고, 내 스스로 샤워를 할 수 있는 것이 너무 행복했다. 아! 행복은 멀리 있는 게 아니구나! 라는 생각이 들었다.

입맛도 차츰차츰 돌아왔고, 가벼운 운동부터 시작했지만 집 앞 산을 며칠 다녔더니 예상 외로 힘에 부쳤다. '아직은 정상은 아니구나, 여유를 가지고 천천히 해보자'고 다짐한다. 머리가 떨렁떨렁거리고, 띵~하다.

머리가 맑지 못한 것도 기분 나쁜데, 보험사들이 나를 더욱 화나게 했다. 한화생명에서는 나의 병원 서류 원본까지 다 가져가더니, '보험가입은 가능하고 보험료를 내야 하지만 보험금은 지급할 수 없다'고 했고, 삼성화재에는 진단비 천만 원, 수술비 2천만 원 조건으로 보험을 가입했는데, 수술비 2천만 원만 나오고 진단비는 나오지 않았다. 진단비를 달라고 이의신청을 했더니, 진단비 천만 원을 받으려면 수술비 2천만 원을 반납하라고 했다. 무슨 담보가 어쩌니 모르는 말로 핑계를 댔지만 도저히 이해가 되지 않는다. 보험사에게는 자칫하면 속기 쉬우니, 보험에 들 때는 조그마한 문구라도 꼼꼼히 확인하는 게 반드시 필요하다.

6주간 총 30회의 방사선 치료를 받았다. 방사선 치료의 부작용으로는 탈모, 어지럼, 구토 등이 있는데, 나는 원래 대머리였지만 얼마 남지 않은 머리카락도 거의 다 빠져 버렸다. 가발을 쓰니 친구들이 나를 못 알아볼 정도로 젊어졌다고 하니, 잘 된 건가?

어지럼은 잘 못 느꼈으나, 머리가 맑지 못하고 항상 지끈거리고 띵~하였다. 구토까지는 아니었지만, 모든 음식이 별로 맛이 없고 소화가 잘 안되었다. 먹기는 열심히 먹었지만 맛으로 먹는 게 아니라, 살기 위해서 먹었다고 할까? 엄마의 세 번째 기일을 지난 후에는 입맛도 돌아오고 여행을 맘껏 다닐 수 있기를 기대해 본다.

단학 수련일기

'93.10.26. 화 (1일째)

05:00에 일어나 선원으로 갔다. 두 손을 합장하고 고개를 숙이는 인사법이 낯설다. 그들은 내게 그렇게 인사했지만 나는 그냥 고개를 숙여서 받았다. 체조를 하는데 몸이 굳어 있어서 힘들다. (내 몸은 보통사람들에 비해 훨씬 굳어 있다. 아내는 나를 나무토막이라고 한다. 인정한다.) 단전호흡하는 법을 배웠다. 단전호흡이 아니라 장(腸)운동이라 하는 편이 옳겠다. 오랫동안 단학수련을 해 온 친구도 만났다. 열심히 해보라고 한다. 운동을 끝내고 집에 오니 07:00다. 평소에는 일어나지도 않는 시간이다.

'93.10.27. 수 (2일째)

또 05:00에 일어났다. 신기하다. 항상 07:00 넘어야 일어났는데, 그것도 아내가 깨워야. (돈이 아까워 일어난 건지 '건강하여야겠다'는 신념이 선 건지). 천부경(天符經)은 낯선 단어가 아니다. 지체부자유자인 금강(金剛)씨가 지은 '발해의 혼(魂)'에 나오는 비서(祕書)이다.

'93.10.29. 금 (4일째)

仙院에서 가르쳐주는 것은 아직 별로 없다. 단지 준비체조와 天符체조 동작요령인데, 내게는 전부 다 힘든 동작뿐이다. 직원 한 사람이 모친상을 당하여 왜관을 가야한다. '일찍 내려와서 내일도 선원엘 가야지' 생각한다.

'93.10.30. 토 (5일째)

어제 저녁에 상가에 갔다가 밤샘하는 통에 아침운동을 못 갔다. 나의 가장 큰 약점이 바로 이거다. 모임에서 먼저 일어서지 못하는 것, 건강을 해칠 줄 알면서도 술 마시고 늦게까지 노는 것, 단학은 마음공부인데…

＊선원에서 운동 마치고 나오면서 담배를 피워 물던 버릇을 없앴다.

'93.11.1. 월 (7일째)

아침 운동을 하면서, 인체의 경락과 맥에 대한 책을 몇 권 빌려 보고 있다. 12경락(經絡), 기경8맥(奇經8脈), 임, 독맥(任, 督脈)은 무협지에서도 많이 보던 용어이고, 백회, 태양, 단전, 명문, 견정, 용천 같은 혈도의 이름도 낯설지 않다.

'93.11.3. 수 (9일째)

준비운동 또는 수련 후 몸풀기 운동 시에 취하는 동작이 내게는 너무 힘들다. 나의 굳은 몸을 보고 친구는 "많이 굳었구나야, 계속 해, 꾸준히 하면 한 3개월 정도 걸리겠다"라 한다. 그래서 3개월을 목표로 정했다. 몸이 유연해지는 데까지 3개월, 그 다음 지감(止感), 氣체험, 축기(縮氣): 1년, 365혈 개혈(開穴): 6개월, 운기단법(運氣丹法): 2년으로 잡는다. '선원에서는 숨쉬기 운동하다가 집에 온다' 다른 사람에게는 이렇게 얘기한다.

'93.11.9. 화 (15일째)

엊저녁에 술을 좀 과하게 먹었는지 약간 되는 것 같은 단전호흡이 영 안 되었다. 친구 승주는 '술 과음하면 氣가 흩어진다'고 한다. '나야 뭐 아직 氣를 느끼지도 못하고 있는데 모아 둔 氣가 있나?'라고 대답하면 서도 '과음은 안 좋다'는 생각을 한다. 소설 丹(김정빈 저)을 빌려서 읽는다.

'93.11.10. 수 (16일째)

아내의 심기가 안 좋다. 주위의 아줌마들이 마음에 안 드는 모양이다. 아내가 '젊은 여자는 '자기 일'을 갖지 못해서 스트레스를 받고, 나이든 여자는 '돈이 없어' 스트레스를 받는다'고 했을 때, 내가 대답하기를 '당신은 둘 다 해당되겠네'라 한 적이 있다. 내가 도움 줄 수 있는 것은 한계가 있다. 스스로 빨리 헤쳐 나와야 할 텐데.

'93.11.12. 금 (18일째)

선원에 정경례라는 여자 법사가 새로이 왔다. 대구서 왔다는데 훈련시키는 것이 마음에 든다. 훨씬 이해하기가 쉽고 따라하기가 쉽다. 丹田에서 내는 소리라며 목소리부터가 다르다. 도인(導引)체조 시에 몸이 굳어서 뻣뻣한 것은 아마 내가 제일 심각한 것 같다. 승주에게 얘기했더니, '開穴수련 등 진도에 너무 집착하지 말고 기초를 튼튼히 쌓아라'고만 한다. 계속 丹田호흡만 하란다. 나도 그렇게 생각하고 있다. 남명이 법사는 나의 굳은 신체구조를 유연하게 하려면, '열심히 성실히 하는 방법밖에 없다'고 한다. 3개월 정도면 반쯤 풀리고 6개월이면 완전히 풀리리라 한다. 알 만하다. 남 신경 쓰지 말고 꾸준히 하자.

'93.11.15. 월 (3주째, 정확히 21일째, 수련한 날로는 16일째)

좀 특이한 날이다. 도인(導引)체조 시에는 남들이 다 되는 자세가 나는 안 된다. 남들이 다 느끼는 뭐가 있는 모양인데 난 아무것도 느끼지 못한다. 초조한 마음이 없지는 않지만 '내 몸이 워낙 굳어 있으니 느긋하게 생각하자'라 위안해 왔다. 그런데 오늘 아침 수련에서는 止感훈련 도중, 합장한 손을 약간 떼니 양 손바닥에 뭔가 느껴진다. 양 손바닥이 하나는 음극, 하나는 양극으로 된 약한 磁力 같은 것이 느껴진다. '이것이 氣의 일종인가'하는 생각이 들면서 양손의 거리를 넓혔다, 좁혔다 해 보았다. 이 磁力같은 것이 붙어 있어(끈적끈적한 풀을 바른 것 같기도 하다) 참 재미있다. 저녁에는 절하는 방법도 모르면서 보통 제사 때 하는 큰 절로 103배를 하고 잠든다.

'93.11.18. 목 (24일째, 수련 날짜로는 19일째)

'수승화강(水昇火降)'은 丹學의 첫번째 원리다. 그래서 丹田은 따뜻하고 머리는 시원하게 해 주게 되는데, 나는 항상 아랫배가 차다. 술만 먹으면 설사하고, 음식을 약간만 잘못 먹어도 배가 사르르 아프다. 아내는 내 배를 만질 때마다 그 차가운 감촉때문에 깜짝깜짝 놀라곤 한다. 아침 운동 시에 다시 止感훈련을 했는데 21일째에 긴가민가하면서 느꼈던 氣를 더욱 확실히 느낀다. 아무런 느낌이 없을 때는 온갖 잡생각이 다 들어 정신집중이 극히 어려웠는데, 이렇게 氣를 느끼기 시작하니, 그 氣(磁力같은 것)에 온 정신을 집중할 수가 있다. 신기하고 재미있다. 또 하나의 특이한 사항으로 단전호흡(아직 이것이 단전호흡인지 아닌지 확실히 모르지만)을 하는데, 숨을 들이쉴 때는 모르겠는데, 숨을 내쉴 때는 배가 좀 따뜻해지는 것 같다. 피부와 옷의 마찰에 의한 열인지, 아니면 火降인지 애매하다.

저녁에는 천제(天祭)와 開穴수련이 있다. 초보자가 수련에 진척이 없을 때 開穴을 받으면 훨씬 진척속도가 빨리 나타난다고 하는데 기대가 자못 크다. 손바닥으로 氣를 느끼면서 丹田에 뭔가 모이는 것을 느끼기만 한다면 정신집중과 마음수련에 크게 도움이 될 것 같다. 계속 열심히 해 보자.

저녁에 天祭에 참석했다. 처음 참석이라 호기심 반, 의지 반으로 참석했지만 약간 얼떨떨하다. '무슨 사교(邪敎)집단이 아닌가'하는 의구심이 문득문득 들기도 한다. 그런 의구심이 들 때마다 고개를 흔들며 마음을 진정시켰다. 숭배의 대상이 하늘과 조상이지 개인 교주(敎主)가 아니지 않는가? 염원의 대상이 나와 가정과 국가와 온 인류의 행복이지 구복(求福)이나 저주가 아니지 않는가?

1차 開穴수련이 시작되었다. 대단한 것으로 기대했는데 솔직히 실망도 좀 있다. 그러나 다시 냉정히 생각한다. '나의 정성과 노력의 결과로 나와 하늘이 하나가 되는 과정일 뿐, 누가 30,000원을 냈다고 그저 주는 것은 아니지 않는가? 길을 알았으니 그 다음은 내가 얼마나 한마음으로 노력하는가에 달린 것이다. 그래, 확실하다.'

월요일부터 느끼기 시작한 磁力같은 느낌(이것을 氣라고 부르자)이 훨씬 잘 느껴진다. 다른 사람에게 氣를 받을 때는 손바닥에 뜨거운 기운만 느껴졌으나, 내가 타인에게 氣를 줄 때는 뜨거운 중에 시원한 바람이 중간중간 스쳐가는 느낌이다. 바람이 불지도 않는데. 집에서 혼자 止感훈련을 해 보는데 눈을 뜨고도 잘 느껴진다. 내가 가져온 몇 권의 책만 읽어본 아내에게 氣를 보내 보니 아내도 뜨거운 것을 느낀다고 한다. 아내는 나보다 확실히 빠르다. 한 번의 연습도 없이 느끼다니.

'93.11.24. 수 (30일째)

감기가 점점 심하다. '이번에는 약을 먹지 않고 나아야겠다'고 생각한다. 저녁에는 신입회원을 위한 특별수련이 있다. 丹學의 기본원리에 대한 강의가 좀 있고 난 후에 단무(丹舞)를 추었다. 원래 '丹舞란 氣의 흐름에 따라 자신도 모르게 몸이 따라 움직이는 것'이라 하지만, 나는 처음 하는 것이라 그런 상태가 아니고, 그냥 음악에 맞춰 신명(神明)나는 한 판 춤사위였다. 나는 원래 나이든 어른들과 이렇게 춤추며 노는 것을 좋아하고 또 부끄럼을 잘 타지 않기 때문에 정말로 한 판 신나게 춤을 추었다. 땀을 흥건히 흘리도록…. 참 재미있다. 또 의식을 음악과 손바닥에 집중했는데, 춤추는 가운데서도 장심(掌心)에 氣를 느낄 수 있는 것이 가슴 뿌듯하다.

'93.11.29. 월 (35일째)

　토, 일요일을 푹 쉬고(운동은 못 했지만) 나니 몸이 좀 낫다. 새벽운동을 나갔다. 앞으로는 열심히, 정성으로 해야지. 지금까지 丹과 관련해서 읽은 책으로는 소설 '丹', 무협지 '발해의 魂', 단학총서 '丹學, 丹學人, 天地人, 神人이 되는 길, 단학수련체험기, 운기단법(運氣丹法)' 등이 있고, 현재 읽고 있는 책은 격암유록(格庵遺錄)을 번역한 '종말로부터의 구원'이라는 책이다. 앞으로 읽고 싶은 책은 '한단고기(桓檀古記)'이다. 성경을 공부해 본 적이 있는 나로서는 느끼는 바가 실로 크다. '인생의 목적이 성통공완(性通功完)에 있는 것이 아닌가?'하는 생각이 든다. 그리하여 '나와 가족, 민족, 세계인류를 구원해야 하는 게 아닌가?'하는 생각도 든다.

　* 우선 체험부터 하고 난 뒤에 생각해 보기로 하자. 103배를 드리고 잤다.

'93.11.30. 화 (36일째)

　아내에게 止感훈련을 시켜 보았다. '손바닥을 5cm 정도 띄운 상태에서 정신을 집중시켜 보라'고 했더니, '뜨거운 기운과 무언가 끌어당기는 것 같은 느낌이 있다'고 한다. 내가 3주일 만에 느낀 것을 이미 느끼고 있다. 회사 직원 몇명에게 꼭 같은 것을 시켜보니 따뜻한 기운을 느낀다고 한다. 난 정말로 엄청나게 몸이 경직되어 있고 정신이 분산되어 있는 모양이다. 선원에 나오는 사람들(道友들) 중에 나만큼 導引체조 시에 여러가지 자세가 안 취해지는 사람이 없다. 가장 힘들어하는 사람이 나다. 마음을 급하게 먹지 않으려 다짐을 해도 나 자신이 너무 한심하다는 생각이 든다. 빨리 될 수 있는 왕도(王道)는 없겠다. 오로지 정성껏, 열심히 노력하는 길 외에는.

'93.12.3. 금 (39일째)

아침에 좀 심하게 운동을 했다. 땀을 뻘뻘 흘렸다. 다른 道友들보다 나는 훨씬 더 힘이 든다. 한 자세를 오래 하는 것이 너무 힘든다. 체력이 남의 반도 안 되는 것 같다. 남사고예언서(격암유록)를 계속 읽으면서 神, 인간, 종말, 성인(聖人)들, 진리, 구원이 확실히 이해가 된다. 내가 어떻게 해야 되겠다는 생각은 들지만 직장, 가정, 사회의 속박들을 헤쳐 나가면서 이루자니, 시간과 돈과 사욕(私慾)의 문제가 가로 막는다. 수련의 진전은 더디고 초조해진다. 성통공완(性通功完)의 지름길은 없는가? 우선 開穴만이라도. 開穴이 되면 수련의 진전이 빨라진다고 하는데, 이렇게 경직된 몸으로는 남보다 몇 배 더 노력해야 할 텐데, 남만큼 노력할 여유도 없구나.

'93.12.11. 토 (46일째)

시내 서점에서 '桓檀古記(임승국 역)'를 구입했다. 역자 후기만을 읽고도 많은 느낌을 받았다. 내가 배우고 알고 있는 역사의 허구성과 우리 민족의 참된 뿌리와 배경… 가슴 찌르르한 뭔가를 느낀다. '격암유록(남사고예언서)'에서 말하는 것, 一指 단학총서에서 말하는 것, 소설 '丹'에서 말하는 것, 무협지 '발해의 魂'에서 말하는 것, 소설 반야심경에서 말하는 것, 소설 천자문에서 말하는 것, 그리고 성경과 불경에서 말하는 것, 내가 기성종교에서 느끼는 것, 이러한 모든 것들의 내용이 일치된다는 사실에 두려움과 환희를 동시에 느끼고 기대한다.

'93.12.14. 화 (수련시작 49일= 7주, 특별한 날)

2차 개혈을 받았다. 1차개혈은 1개월 전에 장심혈(掌心穴)을 뚫는 과정이었는데, 수련하는 요령에 대해 강의를 듣고 실습을 했었다. 그리고 1개월간 숙제를 내 주었는데, 이 숙제란 것은 정성으로, 열심히, 매일, 꾸준히 스스로 노력하는 것이었다. 첫째, 단학총서를 읽는 것은 열심히 읽었다. 느낌도 많았고, 인생의 새로운 의미를 생각하겠끔 했다. 이제는 단학총서는 아니지만 桓檀古記를 읽고 있다. 둘째, 체험을 일기형식으로 적어 두는 것은 처음부터 일기를 써 왔으니 다 했다고 본다. 그러나 세째, 다른 사람과 氣를 주고받는 것은 거의 하지 못했다. 1차 개혈을 받을 때 실습, 그 다음날 한 번, 그 뒤에 아내에게 한 번, 직원에게 한 번밖에 없다. 掌心穴이 뚫려야 다음 단계로 넘어 갈 텐데 '뚫렸구나'라 생각되지 않는다. 다만 혼자 止感수련을 해 보면, 처음보다는 훨씬 센 氣를 느낄 수 있다. 이러한 상황에서 2차 개혈을 받는 것이다.

2차 개혈은 전중(또는 단중)과 단전(丹田)을 여는 수련이라고 하는데, 가슴은 계속 답답하고 (차라리 아프다) 단전에서는 아무런 느낌도 없다. 개혈 수련하는 방법을 배우고, 느낌을 얘기할 때 나는 단전에 아무런 느낌도 없다고 대답했다. 다만 하나 특이한 것이 있다면 손바닥을 비빌 때 너무 뜨겁다는 점이다. 평소에 導引체조를 하거나, 와공(臥功)1, 1-2를 한 후 손바닥을 비비면 한참 비벼야 뜨거워졌는데, 오늘은 개혈 수련을 마치고 손바닥을 비비니 금방 아주 뜨거워졌고, 너무 뜨거워서 손을 더 이상 비빌 수가 없었다. 개혈을 지도한 사범은 '좋은 현상'이라고 격려하면서 '열심히 해 보라'고 하셨다.

　옷을 갈아 입으면서 돈에 대한 생각을 해 본다.(이건 평소에도 느끼던 사실이지만.) 첫 달에 입회할 때 127,000원, 뒤에 책 사는데 30,000원, 1차개혈비 30,000원, 둘째 달 회비 60,000원, 2차개혈비 30,000원, 현재까지 277,000원이 들어갔고, 앞으로도 매월회비와 특별수련비가 들어갈 것이니까 월평균 100,000원씩을 생각해야 한다. 운동하는데 돈이 너무 많이 든다. 돈 없는 사람은 하고싶어도 못하고, 부유한 사람만이 할 수 있는 것 아니냐? 아내와 애들도 시키고 싶은데 그렇다면 1개월에 40만 원이 든다. 봉급의 반을 넣어서 단학을 한다면 생활은 어떻게 하나? 목돈으로 200만 원을 내고 평생회원이 되면 좋겠지만, 목돈 200만 원이 어디 있나? 회비 60,000원도 비싸지만, 개혈 수련방법 단 한시간 가르쳐 주는데 (개혈을 시켜주는 것도 아니고, 개혈은 스스로 수련해서 시켜야 되는데) 30,000원이면 너무한 것 아닌가? 이런 생각이 든다.

　또 다른 생각도 한다. 황금을 산더미처럼 준다 해도 건강을 잃으면 아무것도 아니지 않느냐? 단학을 통해 지금까지 알고 있던 모든 지식이 허구이고, 참진리를 발견하지 않았느냐? 삶의 새로운 목표를 발견하지 않았느냐? 이렇게 거창한 얘기가 아니더라도, 지금 나는 변화되고 있지 않느냐? 생활이 즐거워지고, 세상을 긍정적으로 보고, 신경질부리지도 않고, 모든 사람에게 웃으며 대하고, 술, 담배량도 줄어들었고, 실제로 늦잠 버릇 고쳐서 아침에 일찍 일어나고 있지 않느냐? 가장 직접적인 것으로 어깨 아픈 것, 발목 아픈 것도 나았지 않느냐? 인생의 의미를 알고, 성품이 神化되고, 육신의 모든 질병이 낫고, 남도 낫게 해 주고, 인류를 구원할 수 있는 몸과 마음을 기르는데 돈 10만원이 문제냐?

재산을 다 팔아서라도 해야지. 돈을 받는 사람들이 다른 종교에서처럼 치부하느냐? 모든 인류를 구원하기 위해 사용되고 있는 것 아니냐? 현대사회에서 돈 없이 무엇을 할 수 있다는 말이냐? 내가 솔선해야지.

어느 생각이 옳은 것인지 아직은 단정하기가 어렵다. 그러나 단학선원을 꾸준히 다녀야겠다는 결심은 이미 섰다.

'93.12.15. 수 (수련시작 50일째, 특별한 날)

아침수련에서 어제 배운 2차개혈방법으로 수련해 보았다. 그런데 이게 웬 일인가? 단전에 뜨거운 기운을 느꼈다. 수련 24일째 되는 일기에 적은 적이 있지만 지금까지는 호흡 도중에, 숨을 들이쉴 때는 아무런 느낌이 없고, 숨을 내쉴 때는 아랫배가 따뜻해지는 느낌이 있어서 긴가민가 생각했었다. 그런데 오늘은 다르다. 숨을 들이쉴 때 단전이 뜨거워지고, 숨을 내쉴 때 오히려 식어진다. 권사범에게 얘기했더니, 옆에서 듣고 있는 이승주는 '축하한다'고 얘기하고, 권사범은 '더욱 열심히 노력하라'고 했다.

'93.12.21. 화 (56일째)

아침운동 중 겨우 단전에 따뜻한 기운을 느끼기 시작하는데 시간이 끝나고, 사범이 '행공 8번'이라고 한다. 친구 승주에게 얘기했더니, '시작할 때도 뇌파가 완전히 가라앉아 평온한 상태가 될 때까지는, 사범이 시작하라고 해도 여유를 가지고 시작하고, 끝마칠 때도 사범이 종료시키더라도 막 열기가 오르는 순간이라면 잠시 더 행공을 하라'고 한다. 또 내가 '와공2번을 할 때 단전(丹田)에 정신을 집중해야 할지, 아니면 장심(掌心)과 용천(湧泉)에 마음을 두어야 할지 모르겠다'라 하니, '어디다 마음을 두어야 할 지 고민하는 것 자체가 문제'라 하면서 '잊어버려야 한다'고 한다. '고요한 가운데 무념무상의 세계에서 단전호흡은 저절로 되는 것'이라고 한다. 꿈같은 얘기지만 틀린 말은 아니라는 생각이 든다. 나 자신의 존재를 잊어버리는 것, 그게 쉽냐? 그래도 노력은 해보아야지.

'93.12.22. 수 (57일째)

아침수련에서 사범으로부터 '천지기운(天地氣運)'을 받았다. 그리고는 비슷한 운동경력을 가진 道友와 천지기운을 주고받는 수련을 하였다. 내가 줄 때는, 처음에는 장심(掌心)에 열감만 느끼다가, 조금 지나니 마치 나 혼자 지감(止感) 수련할 때처럼 그 道友의 장심과 내 장심 사이에 끈적끈적한 자력을 느꼈다. 그 道友는 나로부터 氣를 받아 가슴(전중혈)과 단전까지 氣를 흘려보낼 수 있었다고 한다. 내가 받을 때는, 그저 장심에 열기만 느낄 뿐이었다. 이것은 내 몸에서 장심-팔목-어깨-가슴-단전으로 흐르는 脈을 뚫지 못했기 때문으로 느껴진다. 혼자 개혈 수련 (2차) 할 때도 마찬가지다. 손바닥에서 氣를 느끼는 것은 확실한데 이것을 단전까지 보내는 감각은 느끼지 못하고 있다. 좀 초조하고, 내 몸의 굳은 정도에 대해 안타깝다.

'93.12.28. 화 (63일째)

마음을 가다듬고 운동에 집중했더니 氣감각이 조금 살아난다. 저녁에는 직원 부친상이 있어 경산까지 다녀왔다. 집에 돌아오니 새벽 3시다. 덕분에 다음날 운동도 또 못 했다.

정말 불쌍하고 눈물이 핑 돌 정도의 가정환경이다. 뇌성마비의 큰 아들, 장인이 속았다고 하는 어린 처를 둔 둘째 아들, 회사 입사 때는 영양실조처럼 보였고, 말도 없고, 그러나 성실하고, 점점 생기를 찾아가는 막내 최창현. 어머니는 일찍 돌아가셨고, 이제 아버지마저 갑자기 돌아가시니, 상가에 두 아들과 며느리만 있다. 문상객은 우리 직원뿐이고, 큰 아들은 다락방에 가두어 놓았는지? '장지에서는 일꾼을 사야한다'는데 210만 원이 없단다. 장례 후 큰 아들은 누가 돌볼 것인가? 복지사회는 어디 갔는가? 대한민국의 도둑놈들(=도둑질해서 돈 많은 놈들)아! 재벌아들은 돌대가리인데도 30대에 회장이 되나?

'93.12.30. 목 (65일째)

아침운동을 다녀왔다. 저녁에 엄청난 술을 마셨다. 기억의 Film이 끊겨버렸다. 그런데 신기한 것은 다음날 화장실에 들락거리지 않았다는 사실이다. 예전 같으면 이렇게 술 마신 뒤에는 하루 5번 정도 변소를 갔었다. 배가 사르르 아프고, 설사는 아닌 것 같은데도 계속 화장실을 들락거리려야 했는데, 단전에 뜨거운 기운을 느끼면서 내 腸이 좋아진 것 같다. 나 자신도 모르게 몸이 좋아지다니, 정말 신기한 일이다. 天地氣運에 감사드린다.

'94.1.2. 일 (68일째)

집에 가훈(家訓)을 정했다. 「바른 몸 바른 마음」 이 말 속에는 엄청난 의미가 있는데 그 의미를 전부 다 설명할 수는 없다. 아내와 애들이 알아들을 수 있을 만치 가훈을 정한 동기를 설명했다. '내 몸은 세상을 구원하는 약이요, 내 마음은 세상을 구원하는 밝은 빛이다' 올 한 해는 精充의 해이다. 1월 3일부터 아내도 선원(仙院)에 등록하게 했다. 늘 신경통이 있고, 몸이 약한 아내가 氣를 통해 건강한 몸으로 회복되길 간절히 기원한다. 오후에는 甲戌年 개의 해를 맞아 애완용 개를 한 마리 샀다. 몰티스 종, 암컷, 애들이 너무 좋아한다. 한 식구가 추가된 것이다.

일범의 평범한 사람 이야기

이름은 '뽀삐'.

'94. 1. 3. 월 (69일째)

아침 5시, 아내와 함께 선원에 갔다. 아내도 회원으로 등록하고 단학 (丹學)에 입문하였다. 에어로빅체조를 얼마간 했기 때문에 導引체조 시의 여러가지 자세에 힘들어하지는 않는다.

'94. 1. 4. 화 (수련시작 70일째, 특별한 날)

낮에 책상에 앉아서 가만히 단전호흡을 해 보니, 아랫배에 뜨거운 기운을 느낀다. 숨 쉬는 것 자체가 한없이 즐겁다. 나로 하여금 이러한 현묘지도(玄妙之道)를 느끼게 한 천지신령(天地神靈)과 조상님께 감사를 드린다. 더욱 정진하여 天地人이 되어야 한다. 天地氣運이 내 기운이고 내 기운이 天地氣運이 되어야 한다. 천지마음이 내 마음이고 내 마음이 천지마음이 되어야 한다. 그리하여 홍익인간(弘益人間), 이화세계(理化世界)를 이루는데 한 몫을 해야 한다. 하루 종일 기운에 대한 생각을 했다. 걸어갈 때도, 회의를 할 때도, 앉아 있을 때도.

'94. 1. 6. 목 (수련시작 72일째, 특별한 날)

아침 운동 시에 天符체조 중 '始자세'라 하는데, 기마자세에서 팔을 자연스럽게 하늘로 받쳐들고 단전(丹田)에 의식을 집중한 상태로 있는 자세로 수련을 했다. 처음에는 팔, 다리가 아팠으나 어느정도 지나니 다리가 후들후들 떨린다. '힘이 들어가면 부르르 떨리는 것은 당연한 것 아닌가?'하는 생각으로 계속 자세를 유지했더니, 아! 이것은 힘을 주어 떨리는 현상과는 다르다. 힘을 빼도 떨리고 멈추어지지가 않는다. '이 것이 진동이구나' 생각하면서 계속 단전호흡을 했다. 그런데 뜨겁던 단전의 기운은 없어지고 명문(命門)에서부터 시원한 느낌이 오더니, 명문과 기해(氣海)로 이어지는 허리띠 메는 부위가 전체적으로 시원해진다. 머리부터는 땀을 비 오듯이 흘리며 하체는 계속 진동을 하고, 명문과 단전은 시원하다. 약 30분간의 수련에서 15분 정도는 이와 같았다. 수련 후 소감발표시간에, 사범께서 대맥(帶脈)이 유통되기 시작했다면서 축하의 박수를 보내주었다. 천지기운(天地氣運)에 무한한 감사를 드리고, 다른 사람에게 이 기쁨을 나누어 주고 싶다. 오늘 이제 3일째 단전호흡하는 아내는 하체 뿐만 아니라 팔, 어깨, 머리, 가슴까지 전신에 진동을 느꼈다고 한다. 정말 고마운 일이다. 천지기운 내 기운, 내 기운 천지기운.

'94.1.7 금 (73일째, 1000배 수련)

아침운동은 보통날과 다름없었으나 오늘의 Highlight는 저녁의 특별수련(절수련)이었다. 내가 단학을 시작한지 얼마 지나지 않아 집에서 혼자 103배를 해 본 적이 있다. 절하는 방법도 몰라서 그냥 집에서 제사 지내는 식으로 103배를 했는데, 대단히 힘들어서 중간에 두 번 쉬면서 103배를 마친 적이 있다. 그 후 선원에서 절수련을 한다 길래 몇 번 하는가 물어보니 1000배라고 해서, 나는 아예 도전조차 하지 않았다. 그 다음달에도 마찬가지로 수련에 참여하지 않았다. 이번이 세 번째의 기회인 셈인데 그동안 '절'에 대해 좀 느끼는 바가 있었다. '절'은 우선 자기자신을 낮추려는 노력이다. 가장 낮은 위치에 자신을 둠으로써, 겸손해지고, 남을 존경하게 되고, 만물을 사랑하게 되는 것이다. 이것이 바로 '下心'이라고 했다. 둘째로 절을 하는 것은 머리끝에서 발끝까지 전신운동을 해 주는 의미이다. 이보다 더 확실히 온몸의 신경과 근육을 단련시켜주는 운동이 어디 있는가? 셋째로는 단전호흡이 저절로 된다는 것이다. 꿇어 앉아 상체를 완전히 굽히면 呼가 되고, 다시 일어설 때 吸이 저절로 되는 것이다. 1000배를 하려면 2.5시간 정도 걸리는데 두 시간 반 동안 자연스럽게 단전호흡하는 것이다. 일단 도전하기로 했다. 103배를 하는데도 두번이나 쉰 경험이 있기 때문에 '해낼 수 있을까?' 하는 의심은 있었으나 '하고 말리라' 하는 각오는 대단했다. 150배정도 까지는 쉽게 했다. 300배까지는 대단히 힘들었다. 그러나 어느정도 힘 든 과정이 지나고 나니 약 700배까지는 그런대로 할 수 있었고, 800배 까지는 숨도 차고, 허리, 다리도 아파 겨우 따라 했다. 800배부터 1000 배까지는 제대로 자세를 유지하지 못했다. 어쨌든 해냈다. 원래부터 식 사만 해도 땀을 뻘뻘 흘리는 체질이라 1000배 하면서 땀으로 목욕을 한 것 같다. 몸 안의 모든 탁기가 빠져나갔으리라 생각하니 몸이 가뿐하 다. 두 시간이 좀 넘게 걸렸다. 성철스님께서 '3000배를 한 후에 자기를 만나러 오라'고 하신 의미를 알겠다. 1000배를 같이 수련한 道友들에게 '진동턱'을 냈다. 사범에게 명치부위가 아프다고 하니, '아직도 아파요? 2000배만 더 해야겠어요'라고 한다. 아내는 '불교식 절'에 대해 대단한 거부감이 있다.

'94.1.10. 월 (76일째)

단학총서 '神人이 되는 길'을 정독하고 있다. 지난번에 한번 읽었을 때보다 훨씬 느낌이 많다. 精, 氣, 神에 대해서도 그렇고, 天地人에 대 해서도 그렇고, 종교에 대해서도 그렇고, 한문화운동에 대해서도 그렇 다. 계속 읽기 때문에 빠져드는 것이 아니다. 조금씩 깨우쳐 가기 때문 에 계속 읽는 것이고, 점점 느끼는 바가 크다. 그러나 내게 한가지 문제 가 있다. 2차개혈을 한 후 단전과 전중혈을 열기 위해 계속 노력하고 있 는데, 단전에 뜨거운 기운을 느끼는 것은 대단히 기쁜 일이다. 또 실제로 차가운 腸때문에 생기던 병적현상도 다 나았다. 그러나 가슴(전중) 을 누르면 아픈 통증이 없어지는 대신, 명치부위가 계속 아프다. 호흡 을 할 때 좀 깊게 숨을 들이쉬어도 아프고, 누르면 더욱 아프다. 1000배 수련을 하면서도 명치부위가 아파 숨을 제대로 쉴 수가 없었다. 책상에 앉은 자세로 단전호흡을 해 보면, 아랫배는 따뜻해져서 좋은데, 명치는 점점 더 아파지는 것 같다. 임맥(任脈)유통수련을 받아야겠지만, 현재 도 임맥을 뚫으려고 하는데, 오히려 더 통증이 온다. 좋은 현상인지 나 쁜 현상인지 모르겠다.

'94.1.11. 화 (77일째)

어제부터 명치부위를 계속 꾹꾹 눌러 주었더니 아픈 느낌이 훨씬 덜 하다. 아랫배에 따뜻한 기운을 느끼는 것 외에 별다른 느낌이 없다. 오 히려 수련시작 50일째 처음 느꼈던 뜨거운 기운만큼 못하다. 방귀를 뀌 면 예전과 달리 냄새가 지독하다. 또 자꾸 잠이 온다. 낮에도 졸린다. 이것은 무슨 현상인가? '상단전의 비밀'을 다 읽었다. 반신반의다. 아니 어쩌면 좀 황당하다는 생각이 든다. 丹學의 이론이 처음에는 아주 '바 로 이것이구나'하는 생각이었는데, '神人合成 인공배양법'까지 오니 억 지로 끼워 맞추고 있는 느낌도 들고, 이상한 교파에서 끼워 맞추는 교 리와 비슷하다는 생각이 든다. 사이비교의 교리도 빠져드는 자에게는 절대 진리가 되는 법이다. 나는 겸손한 마음으로 한걸음 한 걸음 전진 해 갈 뿐이다. 나 자신을 위하여, 求道하는 마음으로.

'94.1.13. 목 (79일째)

천지기운(天地氣運)전달식을 가졌다. 지난번에는 백회(百會)를 통해 천지기운을 받았는데 그 때에도 별 느낌은 없었다. 다만, 두 사람이서 주고받을 때에 따뜻한 기운과 특히 내가 줄 때에 손바닥에서 마치 혼자 지감(止感) 수련하는 것과 같은 자력을 느꼈었다. 오늘은 내가 받을 때에 자력이 밀물처럼 파동을 가지고 쭈욱쭈욱 밀려옴을 느꼈다. 내가 줄 때에는 잡념이 너무 많이 들어서 제대로 되지 않았다. 단학지침서 '운기단법'을 읽고 있는데, 지난번에 읽을 때보다는 전혀 다른 새로운 느낌을 받는다.

＊ 아내는 천지기운을 전달받은 후 계속 진동을 했다고 한다. 내가 말하기를, "당신의 진척도를 보니 곧 포항선원에서 제일 가는 고수가 되겠다."

'94.1.18. 화 (84일째, 氣치료)

아침수련이 끝나고 권사범에게 명치부위의 통증에 대해 얘기를 했더니, '진작 말씀하시지'하면서 점검해 주었다. 누워서 가만히 단전호흡을 하는데, 손바닥으로 임맥(任脈)을 쭈욱 진단해 보더니 '호흡을 잘못하여 氣가 역상하게 되어 임맥이 꽉 막힌 현상'이라고 한다. 그리고는 장심(掌心)으로 몸의 탁기를 몇차례 빼 주었고 호흡법도 교정해 주었다. 그런데 이게 웬 일인가? 약 2주간을 계속 통증때문에 어떨 때는 숨쉬기도 어려웠는데, 氣치료를 받고 나니 통증이 완전히 없어진 것이 아닌가? '모든 병의 원인이 氣에 있고 氣에 의해 치료가 된다'는 사실을 절감했다. 그동안 수련의 진전이 늦어 초조한 나머지, 혼자 앉아서 하루종일 단전 생각을 하면서 행한 호흡에 문제가 있었다. 吸상태에서 너무 억지로 복부를 팽창시키려고 한 결과, 氣가 임맥을 타고 역상해 버린 것이다. '吸息 때는 氣가 독맥(督脈)을 타고 올라가고, 呼息 때는 氣가 임맥을 타고 내려간다'는 원리를 이용하여 치료가 가능하다. 氣에 대해 더욱 확신을 가졌다.

아침에 권사범에게 다시 氣치료를 받을까 했으나 호흡을 하고 나니, 통증이 훨씬 줄어든 것 같아, '혼자서 호흡을 통해 치료를 해 보자'고 생각하고, 권사범의 치료를 받지 않기로 했다. 仙院의 칠판에는 평생회원 모집안내문과 심성(心性)수련 참가신청자 접수안내문이 쓰여 있는데, 평생회원 등록 유자격자명단에 내 이름이 있고, 심성수련 참가 가능한 사람의 명단에도 내 이름이 있다. 그 자격과 대상선정의 기준이 무엇인지 모르지만 나는 아직 준비가 안 된 것 같다. 마음이야 평생회원도 되고 싶고, 심성수련도 받고 싶지만 경제적인 여유가 없다. 언젠가 단학선원에 다니는데 들어가는 '돈' 얘기를 쓴 적도 있지만, 이건 정말 갈수록 '가난한 사람은 단학을 할 수 없다'는 생각이 든다. 지나간 월간지 '丹'을 구입하려면 2,000원, 開穴수련 한시간 받으려면 30,000원, 심성수련 1박2일 받으려면 150,000원, 매월 수련비 60,000원, 책(단학총서 및 기타관련서적) 권당 5,000원, 진동하면 진동턱 5,000~10,000원, 또 지금은 모르지만 언제 무슨 돈이 필요할지? 평생회원이 되려면 한 번에 2,000,000원, 내가 매월 1,000,000원 남짓 봉급을 받는데, 아내와 나의 매월 수련비 200,000원 잡고, 애들 둘 태권도학원 70,000원, 애들 둘 컴퓨터 학원 50,000원, 애 하나 피아노학원 45,000원, 따라서 매월 학원비가 고정적으로 365,000원이 지출되는데, 1박2일 심성수련에 150,000원 여유가 어디 있나? 애들은 자꾸 커 가고, 집안에 큰 일 치를 일도 많은데, 매달 얼마 씩이라도 저축하면서 살아야 할 판에, 정말 저축 한푼 못 하고, 허급지급, 아둥바둥 살아가는 사람에게 150,000원이든 2,000,000원이든 목돈의 여유는 없는 것이다. 정사범은 '150,000원이 뭐 비싸요? 다른 데는 1,000,000원 받습니다'하면서 일본기업에서 한다는 무슨 심성교육사례를 든다. 아마 일본 기업에서 10년~15년 전부터 하고 있는 '지옥의 13일' 과정 같은 걸 얘기하는 것 같은데, 내가 듣기에는 철모르는 얘기다. 내 뜻은 150,000원 자체가 비싸다는 의미가 아니다. 150,000원 들여 중단전(中丹田)이 열리고 심성이 밝아진다면 그보다 더 싼 게 어디 있겠나? 그러나 대기업체 과장인 내게 부담되는 금액이라면, 우리나라에 나보다 가난하고 나보다 여유가 없는 수많은 사람들은 단학의 근처조차 갈 수가 있겠는가? 안타깝다.

'94.1.21. 금 (87일째)

가슴이 아직도 좀 아프고 답답하다. 계속 바른 자세를 유지하려고 하니 등뼈도 아프다. 어제 저녁에는 아내와 함께 반가부좌 자세로 단전호흡을 해 봤다. 아내는 약 10분 후부터 격렬한 진동을 했다. 나는 30분을 꼭 같은 자세로 있어도 잡생각만 계속 들고, 팔, 다리가 아플 뿐 진동은 없었다. 밥을 먹고 나면 속이 더부룩한 것과 등뼈가 아픈 것은 나아지기 위한 현상 같은데 좀처럼 진척이 없다. 굳어진 몸 탓이겠지. 사무실에서 체험기를 읽다가 의자에 앉은 자세에서 허리를 곧바로 세우고 단전호흡을 했다. 처음에는 의식집중이 잘 안 되었으나, 잠시 후 丹田이 뜨거워졌다. 다시 5분 정도 더 호흡을 하니 단전의 뜨거운 기운은 그대로 유지되고 命門으로 시원한 바람이 들락날락했다. 그러나 머리는 약간 열을 받는 것 같았다. 직원의 업무때문에 약 25분 만에 중지했지만 단전에 힘이 꽉 차고, 명문의 시원한 기운은 계속 남아 있어서 기분이 아주 좋다.

'94.1.26. 수 (92일째)

점심시간, 식사하기 전에 단전호흡을 했다. 天符체조 '始자세'(하체는 기마자세에서 무릎을 안쪽으로 굽히고 팔은 하늘을 향해 벌려 손바닥을 안쪽으로 향하게 한 자세)로 버티기를 했는데, 72일째 되던 날, 仙院에서 이 자세로 30분을 있으면서 진동(?)과 帶脈유통(?)의 感을 느꼈기 때문에 혼자서 해 보았다. 그 때의 기분이 아직 재현되지 않아, 좀 초조한 감이 있어서 일부러 해 본 것이다. 5분정도 되었을 때 가장 힘들었으나, 차츰 시간이 지나면서 다리가 아픈 것을 잊고 안정된 자세를 취할 수 있었다. 30분동안 그 자세를 유지했는데, 다리에 진동을 하고 (힘이 들어 하는 진동이지 氣의 교감이 이루어진 진동은 아니었다) 땀을 엄청나게 흘렸을 뿐 대맥유통의 感은 없어서 좀 실망했다. 다만 혼자서도 30분을 견딜 수 있었다는 데에 대해 기분 좋다. 육관도사의 풍수, 명당 이야기 '터' 상권을 읽었다. 原始反本이니, 天地人의 조화니, 배달민족에 대한 긍지니 하는 내용이 丹學과 너무나 똑같아 새로운 감명을 받았다. 우주의 원리와 인간이 무엇인지? 앞으로 이 세상과 미래가 어떻게 될 것인지 무언가 알 것 같다. 내 인생의 목표를 어디에 둘 것인지도.

'94.1.29. 토 (95일째)

어제 저녁에 업무상 과음을 했다. 새벽 3시30분까지 마셨으니, 잠도 자지 못했다. 과음하면 縮氣된 것이 다 흩어진다는데, 아직도 과음하는 버릇을 고치지 못하고 있으니 큰 일이다. 그런데 한가지 신기한 것은 설사도 나지 않고 머리가 옛날처럼 아프지 않다는 것이다. 술 먹은 후의 상태를 정리해 보면,

- 조금 먹었을 때, 과거, 화장실: 3번 정도, 머리: 아프다, 복통: 조금 있다.
- 현재, 화장실: 1번(정상), 머리: 안 아픔(정상), 복통: 없다(정상).
- 많이 먹었을 때, 과거, 화장실: 5번정도, 머리: 빠게 질 듯 아프다 (게보린 먹지 않고는 못 견딘다), 복통: 굉장히 아프다.

- 현재, 화장실: 2~3번, 머리: 약간 아프다(게보린 안 먹는다).
- 복통: 없다(정상).

'94.2.4. 금 (101일째)

아침수련 중 계속 가슴이 답답하고 명치와 복부가 아파서 호흡이 제대로 안 됐다. 권사범께서 호흡하는 방법이 아직도 잘못되었다고 교정해 주시고 가슴을 두드려 주셨다. 단학총서 8권 '행복을 창조하는 사람들'을 반쯤 읽었다. 심성교육을 다녀온 사람들의 체험 수기인데, 지난번 정사범이 심성교육참가를 권유했을 때는 망설였었다. 그리고 돈이 너무 비싸다는 생각도 했었다. 그러나 이 체험기를 읽다 보니, 여느 기업체나 교육기관에서 행하는 훈련과는 다르다는 생각이 든다. 또 하나는 체험기를 쓴 사람 중에 나와 비슷한 생각을 가진 사람도 더러 있다는 생각도 든다. 피해의식, 이기심, 자만심을 버리고 '참나'와 '참사랑'을 발견할 수 있다는 것인데, 내 경우에는 피해의식은 없다고 보지만, 이기심과 자만심이 없는지? 반성해 볼 문제다. 스스로는 '사랑을 베풀고 있다, 정의감이 있다, 진실하다'고 생각하지만, 그 사랑은 가식과 위선이 아닌지? 그 정의감은 불평이나 이기심이 아닌지? 내 판단기준으로 살아가는 것이 다 맞는지? 어느 기회에 '참나'를 찾아야지, 다음 기회에는 꼭 심성교육을 받아야겠다.

단학 수련 도우들

　설날이다. 차례를 모신 후 아버지께 활공(活功)을 해 드렸다. 아버지
는 가래와 천식으로 숨이 차서 걷기조차 힘든 상태이고, 양쪽 고관절을
절단하고 인공뼈를 해 넣은 후는 하체에 혈관, 신경, 근육조직이 전부
힘이 없는 상태다. 대신 상체만 비대해지고, 신약을 많이 드시기에 상
부와 얼굴이 많이 부어 있다. 변비가 극심하여 배가 개구리처럼 볼록하
고 건강상태가 말이 아니다. 금년 76세가 되신다. 정성을 다하여 전신
을 두드리고 주물러 드렸다. 좀 시원해지고 숨쉬기도 한결 편안하다고
하신다. 단전호흡하는 방법을 가르쳐 드리고, '변비는 1개월, 호흡도 6
개월이면 틀림없이 고쳐진다'고 큰소리 쳤다. 아버지의 성격이 한 곳에
집중하는 스타일이고 건강에 대한 욕심이 대단하시므로 좋아지리라 믿

는다. 나도 빨리 수련에 정진하여 의통(醫通)능력을 쌓아 효도한번 제대로 해야겠다.

'94.2.117. 목 (114일째)

어제저녁에 과음을 했더니, 아침에 일어나서 상태가 좋지 못했다. 소화가 잘 안되어서 배가 더부룩하고, 트림을 하니 엊저녁에 먹은 안주냄새가 난다. 은단 몇 알을 씹어 삼키고 '호흡이 잘 안되겠구나' 하는 생각을 하면서 새벽수련에 임했다. 그런데 예상외로 호흡이 잘 되었다. 와공 2번 자세를 취하고 있는데, 전에는 힘이 들어 자세 유지하는 것조차 어려웠는데, 오늘은 힘이 들지 않을 뿐만 아니라, 掌心(강하게)과 湧泉(약하게)으로 숨이 쉬어지는 것 같았다. 단전호흡을 계속하고 있는데, 새로 포항선원에 오신 김사범께서 복부에 活功을 해 주셨다. 그런데 이게 웬일인가? 더부룩하던 배가 씻은 듯이 나아지고, 늘 막혔던 것 같은 명치부위도 시원해졌다. 정말 신기하다. 김사범에게 몇 번이고 감사를 드렸다. 수련을 끝내고 차를 한잔씩 마시는 중, 권사범께서 '손바닥을 하늘로 향하게 하고 掌心에 의식을 집중해 보라'고 하셨다. 그렇게 했더니 '상태가 참 좋다'고 하신다. 뭘 보고 그러는지? 내 손바닥에서 氣가 뻗치는 것이 보이는지? 신기하기만 하다. 사실은 다른 부위보다 내게는 掌心穴이 제대로 살아있는 것 같다. 하루 종일 단전에 의식을 집중하고 있는 생활이다. 호흡도 거의 숨을 아랫배까지 들이켜고 내쉬는 호흡이 대부분이다. 오늘은 낮에도 계속 아랫배가 뜨뜻하다. 아랫배뿐만 아니라 명치부위까지 배 전체가 뜨겁다. 다만 명치부위의 통증은 약간 있다. 권사범에게 술과 담배에 대해 물어봤다. 겨우 모아 놓은 氣를 술 먹고 흩어져버리고 또 縮氣 좀 해 놓으면 술로 흩어져버린다고 했다. 한두 잔은 괜찮지만 과음은 금물이라고 했다. 담배는 탁기를 단전

161

까지 들이마시는 것이므로 수련의 진전을 방해한다고 했다. 그 말이 다 옳은 것 같다. 오늘이 수련한 지 114일째인데, 담배는 많이 줄였고 술은 먹어도 잘 취하지 않고, 술 먹은 뒤의 후유증이 없다. 그러나 술, 담배 다 절제해야지. '담배는 끊고 술은 한두 잔'

아내는 대구 동산지원으로 1차開穴을 받으러 갔다.

'94.2.23. 수 (120일째)

대구 성당지원에 3차開穴을 받으러 갔다. 두류공원 옆이라 꽤 시간이 많이 걸렸다. 開穴이라는 것이 어떤 것인지 이미 경험했기 때문에 당장 획기적인 일이 일어나지 않는다는 것을 알고 있었다. 다만 개혈을 받은 후 '얼마나 정성을 다하여 수련하느냐'에 따라 그 성과는 완전히 달라질 뿐이다. 내게는 掌心과 命門穴은 살아있는 것 같았으나, 가슴의 전중혈은 미심쩍었고, 百會와 湧泉은 전혀 느낌이 없다. 내가 운전을 하면서 옆에 앉은 변 정사와 오며, 가며 여러가지 얘기를 많이 했다. 집에 돌아오니 새벽 1시가 넘었다.

'94.2.28. 월 (125일째)

氣壯형 선원운영시스템이 시작되었다. 기초부터 다시 시작하는 각오로 하자. 수련체계가 좀 짜임새가 있고 기간도 길어졌다. 一地자세, 一天자세, 一十자세와 같은 하체단련운동은 그야말로 운동이 되었고, 腸운동 9형 (허공자세부터 8단계까지)도 대단히 기본적이면서도 내게 꼭 필요한 것이다. 運氣丹法 1진법은 가슴을 열고 심신을 안정시키기 위한 것이며 運氣心功 1단계는 모래부터 배운다. 정성수련은 계속하고 있으나 눈에 띄는 진척은 없고, 금연한지는 10일째가 된다.

'94.3.4. 금 (129일째)

선원에 가서는 땀을 많이 흘린다. 선원에는 아침에 나가는 경우도 있고 저녁에 나가기도 한다. 평생회원 신청을 했다. Visa Card로 할부가 된다고 하여 18개월 할부로 끊었다. 평생회원 29기가 되는 모양이다. 말 그대로 평생동안 理想人間, 한世界 건설을 위한 일꾼으로 변화되어야겠다. 3월 13일 평생회원 입회식이 천화원에서 있다고 한다. 기대가 된다. 금연한 지 2주째가 된다.

'94.3.5. 토 (130일째)

시골의 아버님을 가 뵈었다. 아버님은 천식기침이 몇십 년은 되었고 걸어다니기만 해도 숨이 차다. 변비가 워낙 심하고, 양쪽 다리는 수술하여 고관절을 인공뼈로 바꾼 상태다. 설날 때 와서 단전호흡하는 방법을 가르쳐 드렸는데, 숨이 가쁠 경우는 대단히 도움된다고 하신다. 반드시 뉘인 후 기점검을 해 보았다. 3차개혈 때 배운 대로 해 보니, 아내에게 할 때는 손바닥에 별다른 느낌이 없었는데, 아버지에게는 열감이 전해오는 부위와 냉기가 전해오는 부위가 현저히 느껴진다.

'94.3.12. 토 (137일째)

제29기 평생회원 입회식에 참석하기 위해 천화원에 도착했다. 산세에 대해 설명해 주시는 변정사의 말씀이 아니더라도 맑은 공기와 물, 사방으로 둘러쳐져 있는 산, 꼬불꼬불한 길이 전부 신령스럽게 느껴진다. 처음 보는 사람이라도 반가이 인사 나누는 모습도 좋다. 저녁엔 본부 총무과에 근무하는 한 사범의 지도로 특별 수련을 한 후, 단학에 들어온 동기와 평생회원에 가입하게 된 동기에 대해 나눔의 시간을 가졌다. 나도 경험과 포부를 장시간 얘기했다. 후련하기도 하나 설레기도

했다. 내 주위부터 알리고 이끌어, 한世界를 이루기 위해 나부터 理想
人間이 되도록 노력하겠다는 각오를 단단히 다짐한다.

'94.3.13. 일 (138일째)

제29기 평생회원 입회식을 가졌다. 仙院長의 축하메시지와 특별 천
지기운 전달식이 있었다. 여러사람이 가슴속에 응어리진 한을 풀고 눈
물을 흘리며 큰 소리를 지르곤 했으나, 내 경우는 그저 지금까지 내가
살아오는 동안 잘못된 여러가지 말과 행동을 깊이 되새겨보는 정도의
시간이었다. 이럴 때는 좀 감성적이 되고 분위기에 잘 젖어 들어야 하
는 건데, 내게는 끝까지 냉철한 이성적 판단과 이지적인 성격 때문에
참 좋은 기회를 제대로 살리지 못했다. 박순용 정사의 기타반주와 리드
로 기운풀이 시간을 가진 후 점심을 먹고 헤어졌다. 한마디로 이런 곳
(천화원)에는 와서 살고 싶을 정도로 분위기가 좋다. 자주 찾아오고 싶
지만 직장 생활하면서 시간적인 여유가 날 것 같지 않다. 어쨌던 평생
회원이 된 이상, 정말 죽을 때까지 理想人間, 한世界 건설을 위해 일로
정진할 것을 다짐한다.

'94.3.17. 목 (142일째)

며칠째 계속 오른쪽 목덜미, 오른쪽 어깨, 오른쪽 경추가 굉장히 아
프다. 얼마전에 명치부위가 아프던 현상이 요즘은 느껴지지 않아, 지금
등이 아픈 것도 독맥(督脈)이 뚫리려는 징조이거니 생각하고 계속 호
흡만 하고 있다. 그러나 이렇게 근본적으로 아파서는 운동 자체가 어렵
다. 또 회사에서의 설비사고 이후로 긴장과 스트레스의 연속이라 '신경
질을 내서 그런 가보다'라고도 생각된다. 水昇火降이 건강의 기본임은
확실한 믿음이 가는데, 그것을 지키지 못하는 마음자세가 안타깝다. 정

성수련을 중단한 지도 2주쯤이 된다. 정성과 노력없이 무엇을 성취한단 말인고? 회사의 여러 동료들에게 丹學에 대해 계속해서 얘기해 주고 있으나, 아직 확실히 丹學에 입문하겠다는 사람이 없다. 우리민족의 3대경전에 대해 정리했다. 그 중에서도 丹學의 기본원리가 담겨있는 三一神誥의 인간에 대한 가르침에 더욱 의미를 느낀다.

感 (僖懼哀怒貪厭) → 止感 (명상) → 명상수련

息 (芬 寒熱震濕) → 調息 (단전호흡) → 호흡수련

觸 (聲色臭味淫抵) → 禁觸 (마음) → 심성수련

'94.3.20. 일 (145일째)

아버님을 집으로 모시고 왔다. 내 기운이 아직 미흡하고 모자라지만 정성으로 아버님께 活功을 해 드려야겠다. 1주일~10일 정도 집에 모시면서, 나는 매일 活功을 해 드리고 아내는 매일 서암뜸과 수지침, 그리고 음식조절과 정성을 통해 치료해 보려고 한다. 아파트 한계단만 올라와도 숨이 차서 헐떡거리는 현재상태와 30년된 천식, 1주일에 콩알만큼 밖에 변을 보지 못하는 극심한 변비 – 병원에서도 속수무책이지만 – 양쪽 고관절을 인공뼈로 수술하신 후 양쪽다리에 신경과 피와 기운이 돌지 않는 상태. 상태는 대단히 심각하지만 오로지 정성과 효심만이 치료된다고 생각된다. 천하에 약이란 약은 다 드셔 보셨지만 차도가 없는 76세 되신 분. 천지기운이 아버님의 몸속 구석구석에 壯하셔서서 부디 이 기회에 낫게 되시기를 기원하며, 정말 많이 달라진 아내에게 너무나 고마움을 느낀다.

'94.3.21. 월 (146일째)

아침수련 후 권사범에게 活功을 받았다. 주로 오른쪽이 아프다면 腸

의 기운이 허해서 그렇다고 하면서 '縮氣 많이 해야겠다'고 하신다. 명치 부위는 한결 시원해졌으나, 목뼈와 어깨뼈는 아직 탁기가 덜 빠져나갔다. 의통능력에 대해 신기함을 다시 한번 느끼며, 나도 정말 열심히 수련하여, 내 주위에 기운이 모자라 아픈 사람들을 치료해 주어야겠다는 생각을 해 본다. 저녁에는 아버님을 모시고 선원에 갔다. 변 정사와 권사범께서 활공을 해 주셨다. 아버지께서는 모든 혈자리에 통증을 호소하셨다. 주무시기 전에 단학과 氣치료에 대해서 많은 말씀을 해 드렸다. 아버지는 단학과 氣치료에 대해 믿음보다는 의심이 더 깊다. 나는 '마음을 열지 않고는 치료가 되지 않음'을 누누이 설명해 드렸다. '내 몸은 내가 아니고 내 것이다'

'94.3.22. 화 (147일째)

선원에 안 가려고 하시는 아버지를 억지로 모시고 갔다. 권 사범의 정성스러운 氣치료를 받고 오신 후, 아파트 계단을 올라오실 때 '숨이 훨씬 덜 차다'고 하시면서 '거 참 신기하다'고 하신다. '아! 천지기운 감사합니다' 氣치료의 효과가 벌써 나타나는 것인가? 나 자신도 놀라고 있다.

'94.3.23. 수 (148일째)

요즘은 매일 아침, 저녁 하루 두번씩 선원에 가서 운동을 한다. 오늘부터는 103배 정성수련도 다시 시작했다. 깜짝 놀랄 일은 아버지께서 설사를 하셨다는 것이다. 낮에 약국에서 변비약을 사 드렸다고 아내가 얘기를 했지만, 이것은 약 때문이 아니다. 설사약 때문이라 하더라도 약이 효력을 발휘하게끔 氣치료를 했기 때문이다. 아내의 뜸(서암뜸)과 정성, 선원에서의 기치료, 나의 간절한 소망과 정성, 아버지의 열린 마음, 이런 것들이 어우러진 결과라 치자. 그러나 가장 중요한 것은 천지 기운임은 두말할 여지가 없다.

'94.3.26. 토 (151일째)

아버지께서 선원에 가서서 치료받는 것은 끝났다. 변 정사는 '상태가 워낙 중하기 때문에 한달 이상 치료를 받아야 한다'고 하셨지만, 아버지는 '1주일간 포항 있는 동안 먹던 약을 중단하였더니 두통이 심하여 만사가 귀찮고, 입맛이 떨어져서 먹는 게 없다'고 하신다. 경침을 하나 사드리고, 단전호흡과 腸문질러주기, 그리고 적당한 운동을 하시고 과식하지 않도록 주의를 단단히 드렸다. 아버지께서는 말씀은 대단히 부정적으로 하시지만 속으로는 긍정적임을 나는 안다. 형님, 형수와 조카에게 단학에 대해 말씀하시는 것을 들어보면 완전히 단학인이 되신 것 같다. 꾸준히 정성을 드리면 충분히 건강이 좋아지리라 믿는다. 정사, 사범의 정성에 감사드리고, 일주일간 정말 고생 많이 한 아내에게 고맙다. 밤12시까지 아버님과 대화를 나누다가 1시경에 103배와 정성수련을 드리고 잤다.

'94.4.11. 월 (167일째)

토, 일요일에도 정성수련을 쉬지 않고 했다. 103배를 매일 하니 불룩 나온 아랫배가 정상으로 들어갔다. 아랫배가 나오는 것이 중년 건강의 적신호라고 하던데, 많이 좋아진 것 같다. 오늘은 동료직원(반영삼 과장) 한 명을 仙院으로 인도했다. 계속 丹學을 알리고 모든 사람이 함께 天地氣運을 알아 건강하고 행복하게 살 수 있도록 功完에 힘써야겠다. 의연의료재단에서 성인병 검진을 한 결과가 나왔다. 76가지 검사항목 중 다른 것은 다 정상인데, 중성지방치가 높다. 육식을 금하라는 의사의 충고다. 시골서 자라 먹을 것이 부족해, 풀뿌리, 나무껍질 먹으며 컸는데, 과도한 육식으로 인해 동맥경화의 우려가 있다니, 세월 참 많이 변했음을 실감한다. 고기 덜 먹고 과일과 채소를 많이 먹어야겠다. 무엇보다 정성으로 天地氣運을 운용하자.

氣가 들어가는 단어

기운(氣運), 기백(氣魄), 기분(氣分), 기력(氣力), 기량(氣量), 기질(氣質), 기미(氣味), 기색(氣色), 기세(氣勢), 기지(氣志), 기합(氣合), 기급(氣急), 기진(氣盡), 기개(氣槪), 기후(氣候), 기우(氣宇), 기품(氣品), 기품(氣稟), 기절(氣絶), 기절(氣節), 기상(氣相), 기상(氣象), 기상(氣像), 기고만장(氣高萬丈)

혈기(血氣), 원기(元氣), 심기(心氣), 대기(大氣), 공기(空氣), 생기(生氣), 용기(勇氣), 화기(和氣), 화기(火氣), 수기(水氣), 패기(覇氣), 양기(陽氣), 양기(涼氣), 양기(揚氣), 음기(陰氣), 정기(精氣), 상기(祥氣), 상기(喪氣), 상기(霜氣), 상기(上氣), 객기(客氣), 천기(天氣), 심기(心氣), 의기(意氣), 오기(傲氣), 오기(五氣), 지기(志氣), 지기(地氣)

丹學의 원리

水昇火降, 精充 氣壯 神明, 心氣血精
精 = 米(地氣) + 靑(天氣), 日(陽) + 月(陰) = 丹(氣)
믐 = 몸 + 마음

내 몸의 穴과 이완정도를 점검해 본다.

掌心 : 정신을 집중하면 氣를 느낀다, 丹田 : 항상 따뜻하다, 命門 : 항상 따뜻하다,

任脈 : 막힌 곳이나 아픈 곳이 없다, 百會 : 잘 느끼지 못한다, 湧泉 : 잘 느끼지 못한다, 氣運 : 장심에서 곡지까지는 약간 느낀다. 명문에서 단전까지도 잘 느낀다. 다른 경락은 별 느낌이 없다, 腸 : 설사나 복통이 나았다. 두통 : 나았다.

경추, 흉추, 요추: 바른 자세를 유지하려고 하니 오히려 아프다. 등뼈 옆으로 나란히 있는 근육이 굉장히 단단하다, 진동: 억지로 힘을 줬을 때 부르르 떨리는 것 외에는 진동을 경험치 못했다.

丹舞: 약간 꼼지락거리는 것만 경험했다.

변화가 있느냐 없느냐가 중요한 것이 아니다. 그저 '편안하다'고만 생각하면 된다. 술, 담배가 수련진도를 늦추는 주요인일 것이다. 마음을 편안하게 갖자.

'94.4.20. 수 (176일째)

회사의 창립기념일이라 모처럼 평일 날 여유가 있었다. 오후부터 선원에 가서, 3 time 수련을 했다. 선원에는 천지기운이 가득 차서, 앉아 있기만 해도 마음이 편안하다. 평생회원에 대한 천지기운 회로수련이 있었다. 一指Power라는 것을 조금은 이해할 것 같다. 開穴수련이 4월 28일인데, 정성수련을 하고는 있으나 정성이 부족함은 내 자신이 잘 안다. 술을 마시고 103배를 드리는 날이 너무 많다. 회사생활때문에 어쩔 수 없이 술 마시게 될지라도 정성수련 중에는 과감히 끊어야 하는데, 그것이 안되는 것은 정성이 부족해서겠지. 한편으로는 '수련때문에 인간생활의 삶 자체를 구속한다면 그 수련의 의미가 올바를까?' 하는 생각이 든다. 어쨌든 마음수련은 몸수련보다 중요하다. 연초에 가훈으로

정해 놓고 아이들에게 강조하고 있는 '바른 몸, 바른 마음'이 나부터 실천해야 할 일이다. 마음, 마음, 넓고, 깊고, 밝고, 맑은 마음. 내 마음이 나의 주인이고, 천지마음이 내 마음이다.

'94.4.21. 목 (177일째)

애들(자아린, 세빈)도 선원에 등록을 했다. 네 식구가 함께 단학을 하니 너무나 기쁘다. 항상 가정에 천지기운이 가득하고, 천지기운으로 건강하고 행복에 넘치는 가정이 되기를 기원한다.

'94.4.26. 화 (182일째)

애들이 선원에서 기운점검을 받았다. 둘 다 간(肝)이 나쁘다는 결론이다. 큰애(남, 12세)는 평소 腸이 나빠 설사를 자주 하는 편이라, 식사시간 중에도 화장실을 가는 경우가 많고, 성격도 대단히 급하고 자만심이 강하여 친구와 잘 어울리지 못하는 편인데, 肝이 안 좋다고 한다. 작은애(여, 10세)는 알레르기성 체질이 심하여 육류나 생선을 먹으면 곧바로 두드러기가 발생되고, 코에 물혹이 생겨서 벌써 두번이나 수술한 적이 있으며, 숨소리가 고르지 못한데 肝이 대단히 나쁘다는 것이다. 결과는 좀 의외지만, 두 애를 일찍 선원으로 데리고 가 단학에 입문하게 한 것이 다행스럽고, 천지기운의 인도에 감사한다. 둘 다 천지기운을 통하여 몸과 마음이 건강하게 되길 간절히 기원하고, 많이 도와줘야겠다고 다짐한다. 아내는 심한 감기몸살을 앓고 있는데 氣몸살이라 생각하고, 약을 먹지 않고 견뎌내고 있다.

'94.4.25. 월 (181일째)

저녁수련을 마치고, 아내가 一指Power를 10,000원 주고 샀다. 도형을 아픈 곳에 붙이면 천지기운이 통하여 상처를 치료해 주고, 장심(掌心)이나 인당(印堂)에 붙인 채 수련을 하면 기운이 훨씬 잘 모이며, 수련의 진척도 빨라진다고 하였다. 그러나 나는 아직 거기에 대해서는 믿음이 덜하다. 아내는 신경통이 있는 곳에 붙인 모양이나, 나는 완전한 믿음이 생길 때까지 보류하기로 했다. 이러한 불신이 나의 수련진척에 방해가 됨을 잘 안다. 그러나 나는 원래가 비판적이고 理性的이며, 나 자신의 지식과 경험으로 판단하는 냉철한 이성주의자인데, 그 성격을 아직 고치지 못하고 있다. 반면 아내는 정말 감성적인 성격의 소유자라 수련의 진도가 나보다 훨씬 빠른 것 같다. 마음수련이 더욱 필요하다.

'94.4.30. 토 (186일째)

심성수련 (제17기) 입과를 했다. 회사생활을 15년 정도 하면서 비슷한 교육을 많이 받은 바 있고, 특히 연수원에 근무하면서 관리감독자교육을 통해 알고 있는 바가 많았다. 또한 어릴 때부터 엄격한 아버지 밑에서 자라면서 형성된 마음자세가 진취적, 적극적, 능동적, 도전적이며, 자신감과 용기, 진실, 추진력 등 나름대로 주인의식과 착한 심성을 가지고 있다고 생각한 것이, 어떤 의미에서는 자만심으로 굳어져 있었고, 교육과 훈련, 독서, 그리고 고민을 통해 쌓은 지식과 경험으로 인해 냉정한 비판의식과 理性的인 사고의 지배를 받고 있는 터라, 슬픈 연속극을 보고 눈물을 흘리는 감성적인 성격이 못되어서, 매시간마다 이루어지는 각 Game들에 대해 '-이 Game도 전에 해 본 것이다, -강사가 너무 감정에 호소하는구나, -분위기를 억지로 형성하는구나, -이 부분에서는 강의의 요령이 없구나, -저 사람도 너무 感傷的이구나' 하는 평을 했다. 스스로 마음을 열려고 하지 않고, 비판자와 채점자의 입장에서 진행과정을 지켜보고 있는 나를 발견했다.

역사와 종교와 철학 그리고 미래… 이러한 것들에 대해 나름대로 지식과 판단력을 가지고 있고, 합리적으로 정의로운, 옳은 판단기준을 가지고 있는 (그것이 바로 관념의 껍질이라 하지만) 나를 설득시키려면, 그 원리로서 믿음의 확신을 심어줘 봐라. 옛날 어머니들이 3류연속극을 보고 눈물을 흘리게 만들던 感傷的인 방법을 쓰지 말고, 이성적인 판단이 되도록 얘기해 보라고. 단학의 원리(水昇火降, 精充 氣壯 神明, 心氣血精)가 내게 확신을 심어 주었듯이, 그러한 원리로 확신을 심어줘 보라고. 이러한 반발심이 끊임없이 생겼다.

'사람마다 보는 시각과 관점의 차이가 다르다는 것을 알고, 자기기준으로만 판단하지 말고, 남을 이해하라.' – 그거야 당연한 것 아닌가? 이런 교육에 와서 그런 얘기를 듣지 않더라도 이미 다 알고 있는 상태이고, 또 실제로 그렇게 실천해 오고 있지 않은가?

'피해의식과 주인의식'–피해의식의 정의부터가 내 생각과는 다르다. 내 생각으로는 '칼자루 쥔 사람이 고기 한 점 더 먹는다'는 식으로, 경찰관 아는 사람은 교통법규를 위반해도 빠져나오고, 세무공무원과 친한 사람은 탈세를 하고, 환경청사람들을 잘 알면 폐수 버려도 괜찮고, 권력 있고 돈 있는 사람들은 온갖 부정과 부패를 다 저질러도 괜찮은 반면에, 우리 같은 소시민은 세금 10원 한 푼 떼먹지 않고, 악법도 지키고, 굽실거려야 하는 데서, 어쩌면 정의감이 투철한 사람이 불의를 보고 투덜거리는 것이 피해의식이라 생각하는데, 여기서는 그러한 말이 하나도 없다. 적극적이지 못하고, 부정적인 사고방식을 가지고, 용기가 없고 추진력이 없고, 진취적인 기상을 가지지 못한 것을 피해의식이라 규정하고 있지 않은가? 누구의 생각이 옳은가? 내 생각이 과연 관념의 껍질 때문인가? 이곳에서는 너무 주인의식의 반대개념으로 피해의식을 정의하다 보니 그런 것 같다. 그러려면 피해의식이라 하지 말고 종(하인)의식이라 해야지. 그렇다고 내가 주인의식이 없는가? 그렇지는 않다. 나는 누구보다도 긍정적이고 적극적인 사고방식을 가지고, 강한 의지와 책임감, 추진력이 있다고 자부한다. 그렇게 살아왔고 그렇게 살고 있고 또 그렇게 살아갈 것이다. 이것을 또 자만심에 빠져 있다고 평하겠지?

그렇다. 내가 자만심에 빠져 있는지도 모르겠다. 그러나 능력과 실력이 있고, 자신감과 추진력도 있고, 이해심과 포용력과 자부심도 있을 경우, 그렇다고 공정하게 평가를 받는 경우, 자신이 그렇다고 믿는 경우, 이것은 자만심에 빠져 있다고 해야 하는가? 잘 모르겠다. 만일 자만심이라면 더욱더 내 자신을 낮추고, 남을 이해하고 존경하고 사랑하는 마음으로 대하고, 그러면서도 일은 한치의 오차도 없이 주도 면밀하게 해 나가야지. '이것은 자만심이니까 앞으로는 이런 생각을 버려야지'하면서 틀린 생각, 옳지 못한 남의 의견에 동조하여 일을 그르칠 수야 없지 않느냐?

흑적(黑赤)Game도 그렇다. 게임의 규칙과 목적을 처음부터 자세히 설명해 주었다면, 누구도 赤을 택하지는 않을 것이었다. 오로지 이기고 지는 것을 강조한 다음, 나중에는 이기심 때문이라고 질책하는 것은 교육시키는 강사입장에서는 교묘했지만, 받는 사람입장에서는 속은 것 같은 기분이었다. 실제로 나와 남이 다 같이 잘되고자 하는 일에 반대할 사람이 얼마나 될까? 물론 나도 살아오면서 정말로 이해가 안 되는 파렴치하고 도둑과 강도 같은 인간群을 많이 보아왔다. 그런 무리들은 천벌을 받을 것을 알고 있다. 자기代에서 부귀영화를 누린다면 자손代에 가서라도 인과응보가 이루어지리라. 그러나 실제로 이런 부류들의 인간들을 제외하고 대부분의 사람들은 善하다는 생각을 믿는다. 일부러 함정을 만들어 놓고 강의 각본대로 유도하는 것은 바람직하지 못하다는 생각이 들었다.

밤 12시가 다 되어 1일차 수련이 끝났다. 감동을 받아 눈물을 흘리는 사람들(특히 여자분들)이 많았다. 그 사람들의 눈물을 이해할 수가 있다. 마음으로 이해되는 것이 아니라, '어려운 세상을 아등바등 사느라 이런 류의 교육을 평생 받아볼 기회가 없었을 텐데, 또 평생 이렇게 깊숙이 자기반성을 해 볼 기회가 없었을 텐데, 생전 처음으로 자신의 내부를 들여다보고, 말 잘하는 강사로부터 감정에 호소하는 일장연설을 들었으니, 눈물이 나올 만하다'는 수준으로 이해했다.

이런저런 사정으로 심기가 크게 안정되어 있지 못한 상태에서, 道友 한 분과 야식을 먹으러 가서, 소주를 한 병 마시고 와서 잠들었다.

'94.5.1. 일 (187일째)

어제 수련 중 낙법(落法)을 하다가 허리에 타박상을 입었는데, 아침에 통증이 심했다. 또 엊저녁에 먹은 술때문에 머리가 아프다. 단학 수련을 시작한 후, 음주후유증(두통과 설사)이 완전히 없어졌는데, 오늘 머리가 아픈 것은 웬일일까? 인과응보인가? 아니면 자아를 발견한다는 이번 수련의 목적이 나와 인연이 없는 것인가? 묘한 기분이 든다.

내부의식 속에서 여러가지 비판과 갈등이 있다는 것뿐이지, 수련 자체에 내가 소극적이거나 소심해서 남 앞에 나서지 못하거나, 마음속에 비밀을 꽁~하게 간직하는 것은 아니다. 누구보다 적극적이고 활발하게 참여하는 것은 사실이다. 대중 앞에 서서 발표하는 것을 부끄러워할 내가 아니다. 어느 모임이건 내가 주도적으로 분위기를 이끌어가는 것이 체질화되어 있기 때문이다. 오히려 내게 아무 역할도 주어지지 않는다면, 좀이 쑤셔서 못 있는 성격이다. 이곳에서는 정말 강한 기운을 느낀다. 쉬는 시간에는 많은 사람 앞에서 기운을 타고 덩실덩실 춤을 추었다. 남의 시선이 의식되지 않는다. 오히려 모두가 나를 쳐다봐 주니 더욱 신(神)이 났다. 나눔의 시간에 많은 사람들이 눈물을 흘리며 고백할 때는 나도 코가 시큰거린다. 파트너와 열린 마음으로 대화를 나누었다. 따뜻한 가슴으로 모두와 포옹을 했다. 이러한 Game은 가슴을 열고, 모두가 하나된다는 공동체의식을 심어주는데 대단히 좋은 Program으로 느껴진다.

진실로 내가 원하는 게 무엇인가? 목이 쉬도록 고함을 질러 보았으나 확실히 와닿는 게 없다. 막연히 '열림'이라는 생각이 든다. '365 穴도 열리고, 마음도 가슴도 열리고, 사랑도 열리고, 의통 능력도 열려서 나와 내 주위에 있는 모든 사람들이 육체적으로 건강하고, 정신적으로 깨달음을 얻어서 천화하는 것이 생활의 목표가 되어야 한다'고 생각된다. 고함을 쳐서 자아에게 물어봐도 그렇고, 냉정히 생각을 해 봐도 그렇다. 그러나 한편으로는 '이것이 욕심 아닌가? 내 사욕 때문에 열림을 원하는 것은 아닌가?'하는 생각도 든다. 그렇다고 '진실로 내가 원하는 것이 뭐냐?' 하고 아무리 물어봐도… '돈-아니다, 명예-도 아니다, 건강-어쩌면 그러나 아니다, 사랑-말은 좋지만 아니다, 열림-그렇다. 性通功完이다'라는 대답밖에 안 나온다. 관념과 지식이 그렇게 판단을 내렸는지, 내부의식으로부터 그렇게 외치는지는 모르겠다. 어쨌던 내가 원하는 것은 性通功完인 것은 확실하다.

피해의식, 이기심, 자만심에 대해 많은 생각을 한다.

- 돈과 권력이 있는 자가 부정, 부패하는 것은 불법으로써 바로잡아야지, 그렇다고 내가 피해의식을 가질 필요는 없지 않은가?
- '누구보다도 능력 있고, 완벽하게, 앞날을 내다보고 최대다수의 최대행복을 위해 의사결정을 내리고, 가장 정의롭고, 합리적으로 일을 처리한다'고 하는 생각이, 자만심에 빠져 있어 돌이킬 수 없는 오류를 저지르지 않는가?
- 솔선수범하고 功을 남에게 돌리고, 미안하다고 솔직하게 얘기하고, 화를 내려다가 한발짝 물러서서 참는 것이 이기심의 발로는 아닌가?

해답은 구하지 못했다. 그러나 앞으로도 지금까지 살아온 것처럼 그렇게 살 것이다. '단학의 원리를 모든 사람에게 나누어 주고, 정성과 열성으로 수련하여, 신선이 되어야겠다'는 마음자세는 변함이 없다. '내가 왜 사는가?'에 대해서 확실한 개념이 없이 살아온 것은 사실이다. 그러나 단학을 만난 이후부터 내 삶의 목적이 정해진 것도 사실이다. 그것은 性通功完이다, 천화다, 신선이 되는 것이다.

1주일 Vision으로는 매일 아침 일찍 일어나 360배를 드리기로 했으며, 1년 Vision으로는 5명 이상 단학에 입문시키는 것을 세웠다. 또 하나는 '운전 중에 욕하지 않겠다'고 다짐했다. 정 사범은 포항서 올라온 道友들, 특히 나와 문도우가 심성수련을 통해 큰 느낌이 없었는 걸로 보였는지 표정이 그렇게 밝지만은 않았다.

'94.5.8. 일 (194일째)

선원에서 단학을 열심히 수련하는 도우들이 모여 천성산으로 산행을 갔다. 학교를 졸업한 후 등산을 하지 않던 내게 산의 새로운 의미를 느끼게 해 준 하루였다. 산촌에서 자란 내게 산은 생활 그 자체였지 여유와 휴식의 대상은 아니었다. 그러나 오늘 산정상에 널리 어우러진 진달래와 철쭉, 정상에서 바라다보이는 사방 경치, 소나무 그늘 아래에서의 명상, 그리고 함께한 도우들의 인간미와 기운, 모두가 새롭다. 우리들은 하나의 모임을 만들었다. 나의 제안에 의해 모임의 명칭은 仙友會로 정해졌다. 신선이 되고자 하는 사람들의 모임이랄까? 우리가 이렇게 만남은 바로 신선 놀음이 되겠지. 仙友, 仙友, 신선, 神仙.

'94.5.9. 월 (195일째)

지난 주부터 명치부위가 아프고 갑갑했는데 오늘은 훨씬 심하다. 심성수련 가서 다친 허리도 계속 통증이 있다. 선원에서 도인(導引)체조를 할 때도 허리가 아파서 어떤 자세는 취할 수도 없고, 지감(止感)수련을 하는데도, 명치부위가 아파서 기감각이 둔해져서 도저히 느낌이 없다. 이 사범께서 활공(活功)을 해 주셔서 약간 시원해졌다. 그러나 근본적으로 이것은 위염이다. 단학을 시작하기전 신경성위염으로 아주 고생을 했는데, 단학수련 후 6개월간 전혀 그런 증세는 없었다. 지금 다시 위염이 재발하는 이유가 뭔가? 내 마음자세가 해이해져서 그런가? 술, 담배, 커피 같은 음식물 때문인가? 아니면 명현현상인가? '마음 장고리 합바지 똥 싼다'더니 수련의 욕심만 강하고, 자세와 행위가 따르지 못하니 나도 참 한심하다.

'94.5.16. 월 (202일째)

토, 일요일을 쉬고 나니 아픈 허리가 많이 좋아졌다. 금요일 저녁에 정사로부터 기치료를 받아서인지 금요일 밤에 찜질을 해서인지는 모르겠다. 저녁에 선원으로 가서 도인 체조를 했는데, 다시 또 통증이 온다. 호흡 중에 정사께서 다시 기치료를 해 주셨다. 점혈법으로 맑은 기운을 불어넣어 줬는데 손가락을 대고 있는 동안은 시원한 느낌이 들었다. 그러나 마무리 도인(導引)체조 시에는 너무 아파서 제대로 움직일 수도 없었다. 밤에 뜨거운 물로 찜질을 하고, 멘소레담으로 마사지를 했다. 며칠 간은 도인 체조를 하지 않는 게 좋겠다는 생각이 든다.

'94.5.17. 화 (203일째)

오늘부터 다시 아침에 일어나 103배를 하기로 했다. 허리가 좀 아팠으나 103배를 마치고 호흡수련을 한 후, 샤워를 하고 파스를 통증부위에 붙였다. 103배를 하면서 천부경을 외웠는데, 103배를 끝내고 호흡수련 중에는 정신이 집중되지 못했다. 잠도 오고 잡념도 들고 해서 단전에 숫자를 제대로 쓰지 못했다. 마음수련이 가장 중요하다는 걸 알고는 있는데, 마음이 이렇게 산란하니 내 몸이 제대로 되지 않는 건 당연할 거다. 내 자신에 대해 한심한 생각이 든다. 一切唯心造.

'94.6.8. 수 (225일째)

4월 30일 날 다친 허리가 이제 거의 다 나았다. 아직도 약간은 아픈 것 같으며 심하게 옆구리를 굽힐 수는 없지만, 약을 복용하지 않고 나을 수 있었다는 것이 기쁘다. 포항선원에 온 지 얼마되지 않은 이 사범(이호룡)이 서울로 발령을 받았다고 한다. 우리집 애들이 뚱땡이 아저씨라고 부르며 좋아했는데 멀리 가신다니 아쉽다. 단학을 하고 있는 한 어디서도 건강하리라 믿는다. 아침수련이 끝난 후 이 사범으로부터 활공(活功)을 받았다.

'94.6.9. 목 (226일째)

본부의 윤성균 정사(총무부장)가 오셔서 특별수련을 지도했다. 이론 강의는 단학총서를 통해서 이미 많이 알고 있었으나, 장심(掌心)에 천지기운을 열어 주실 때는 지금까지 와는 전혀 다른 아주 강한 기운을 느꼈다. 장심에 팽이가 돌아가듯 기운이 구멍을 뚫는 것 같더니, 마치 웅덩이의 물이 소용돌이치면서 조그만 구멍으로 빨려 들어가는 느낌이 들었다. 장심을 하늘로 향하게 하고 단전(丹田)으로 호흡을 하니 명문(命門)으로는 시원한 기운이 들락날락하고 손바닥으로는 강한 기운이 들어왔다 나갔다 했다.

'94.6.14. 화 (231일째)

축기(縮氣)반 승급을 위한 심사가 있었다. 현재 기초3반을 수련하고 있는데, 와공(臥功) 2번~4번 자세로 호흡을 하면, 장심(掌心)과 용천(湧泉)에서 아주 강하지는 않지만 기운을 느끼는 상태다. 그런데 심사 중에 갑자기 '기초1반 4번자세를 취해 보라'고 하는데, 생각이 잘 안나는 거 있지. 기초2반 4번자세를 취했다가 지적을 받고 난 뒤에 기초1반 4번자세가 생각이 났다. 또 운기심공(運氣心功)에서는 마음으로 기운을 움직여야 하는데, 이건 의지로서 몸을 움직이고 마음은 따라가는 상태다. 단공(丹功)기본형(연합형)은 그런대로 할 수 있었으나, 너무 기운을 쓰다 보니 몸의 균형을 잡지 못했다. 수기자세는 그런대로 했다. 가장 우스운 것은 단무(丹舞)였다. 기운에 의해서 저절로 춤이 나와야 하는데, 손바닥에 그저 미약한 기운을 느끼면서 몸동작(춤동작)은 억지로 했다. 아직 까마득하다. 더욱 열심 정진해야겠다.

'94.6.15. 수 (232일째)

천지기운잔치가 있었다. 이자리에서 나에게 청띠를 주며 축기반으로 승급이 되었다고 했다. 나의 기운이란 아직 너무나 미약하고 가슴이 아직도 많이 닫혀 있는 것 같은데 청띠를 받다니, 너무도 송구스럽고 더욱 수련에 정성을 다해야겠다는 생각이 들었다. 청띠 받은 사람들은 대개가 오랫동안 수련한 고참들인데, 나를 포함해서 함께 단무(丹舞)시범을 보였다. 나는 장심(掌心)의 기운만 가지고 자연스럽게 춤을 췄다. 도우들이 정성으로 마련해 온 음식을 들면서 재미있는 시간을 나누었다. 정사께서 백회(百會)로 기운을 주실 때는 찌릿한 느낌이 있었다. 이 기운을 잊지 말고 정진하여 빨리 백회(百會)를 열어야겠다. 자아린이는 며칠전에 장모님 생신에 갔다가 발목을 다쳐 깁스를 하고 있어 며칠째 선원에 나오지를 못했다.

'94.6.28. 화 (245일째, 8개월 5일)

포항지원에서 개혈(開穴)수련이 있었다. 나는 이미 4차까지 끝낸 상태였으나, 4차개혈후 숙제를 제대로 하지 않아서 그런지, 아니면 아직 수련의 단계가 미치지 못해서 그런지, 초보 의통능력이 없는 것 같고, 오히려 요즘은 기감각을 많이 잊어버린 것 같아서, 4차개혈을 다시 받았다. 윤성균 정사로부터 받았는데, 장심(掌心), 용천(湧泉), 명문(命門)의 기감각이 아주 좋다. 다만 백회(百會)가 열리지 않는 게 아쉽다. 운기심공(運氣心功)도 마음으로 몸을 움직이는 게 아니라, 의지와 이론으로 몸을 움직이면서 그저 장심(掌心)의 기운을 조금 타고 있을 뿐이고, 단무(丹舞)도 마찬가지다. 아내가 백회(百會)로 기운을 받으면서 저절로 진동을 하거나, 우아한 단무(丹舞)를 추는 것과는 전혀 다르다. 아내는 특별수련실에서 약 10분간 엉엉 울었다. 그런데도 정사께서 축기(縮氣)가 어느 정도 되었는지 test해 보실 때는 5분 이상 견뎌서 합격한 세 사람 중에 속했으니, 알다가도 모를 일이다. 어쨌든 이제부터는 더욱 열심으로 정진해야겠다.

'94.6.29. 수 (8개월 6일)

기초3반에서 축기반으로 올라가는 예비심사가 있었다. 이미 축기반으로 승급된 청띠 도우들도 함께 했는데 김동현 사범께서 나에게 잘 했다고 한다. 칭찬이 좋기는 하지만 오히려 부담스럽다. 실제의 기운에 있어서 나는 아직 어린애다. 기(氣)점검과 거사법(去邪法), 보기법(補氣法), 촉수요법, 점혈요법 등 4차개혈 후 숙제를 하고 있는데 전보다는 많이 좋아진 것 같다. 장심(掌心)에서 느끼는 감각도 좋고, 내게 기(氣)점검을 받은 사람도 느낌이 있다고 말하니 이제 뭐가 좀 되는 것 같다. 자만심에 빠지지 말고 겸손하게 항심(恒心)으로 정진하자.

'94.7.3. 일 (8개월 10일)

손기홍이라는 후배가 있다. 시골서 결혼하여 농사를 짓다가, 울산으로 나와 식당업을 했단다. 돈도 좀 벌었으나 음주교통사고로 인해 파산하고, 설상가상으로 복역 중 아내가 바람이 나서 집안이 풍비박산이 되었다. 포항으로 이사 온 후에도 아내의 바람기는 여전해서 국교 5학년의 딸을 두고 가출해 버린 상태다. 기홍이는 임시직으로 근무하던 직장에서마저 해고되어 실업자 신세로 아내 찾아다니기만 하는데… 일단 기홍이에게 직장을 하나 알선해 줬다. 입사에 필요한 서류를 떼러 고향으로 보냈다. 차비도 빌려주고. 딸(영은이)에게는 빵과 과자를 사 줬다.

내 주위에 이렇게 어려운 사람이 있다는 것이 마음 아프다. 다 같이 잘 살 수 있어야 하는데. 임시직으로 근무할 당시 환경이 너무 시끄러워 한 쪽 귀가 멀어져 있는데 이 일은 어이할까?

'94.7.6. 수 (8개월 13일)

백회(百會)를 통해 천지기운을 받고 단무(丹舞)수련을 하였다. 단무(丹舞)란 기운에 의해 저절로 몸이 움직여, 학처럼 우아하게 자신의 의지와는 상관없이 나오는 춤사위여야 하는데, 나는 그렇지가 못하다. 제일 문제가 되는 것은 백회(百會)인데 아직 뚫리지 않는다는 것이다. 정신만 말똥말똥해진다. 관념의 껍질이 워낙 두꺼워 기운줄이 연결되지 않는다. 자연히 나의 단무는 어색하기 이를 데 없는데, 그냥 옛날 시골에서 할머니들과 함께 어울려 춤추며 놀던 기분으로 추었다. '백회에서 가슴으로 고속도로가 뻥 뚫린 듯하다'는 도우가 부럽다. 어쩌면 저렇게도 순수한 마음을 가졌을까? 나야 말로 이렇게도 관념과 고집과 생각으로 가득 찼을까? 수련이 끝날 무렵에는 천부성(天符星)과 북두칠성과 一指대선사와 나의 백회(百會)를 일직선으로 연결시키고 마음을 집중했다. 백회(百會)에 약간의 열감이 발생되는 순간에 수련이 종료되어 아쉬웠다. 오늘부터 매일 백회(百會) 뚫는 수련을 개인적으로 해야겠다.

'94.7.12. 화 (8개월 19일)

축기(縮氣)반 행공(行功)을 시작했다. 좌공(座功)으로서 와공(臥功)에 비해 힘이 덜 든다. 정신집중하기가 훨씬 쉬운 것 같다.

'94.7.13. 수 (8개월 20일)

기초3반에서 축기반으로의 승급시험이 있었다. 나는 먼저 축기반으로 승급된 자로서 수기자세 시범을 보였으나, 수련이 제대로 안 된 상태여서 좀 창피하였다. 아내의 수련정도는 나보다 훨씬 낫다. 특히 아내의 단무(丹舞)는 대단하다. 백회(百會)의 기운이 온 몸을 타고 내려와 저절로 온 몸이 춤을 춘다고 하니 신기하다. 특히 여자들이 백회(百會)가 빨리 뚫리는 것은 그만큼 순수하다는 의미일 것이다. 내 머리 속에 가득찬 관념과 쥐꼬리만 한 지식의 틀 속에서 벗어나지 못하고 있는 내가 초라하게 느껴진다.

'94.7.15. 금 (8개월 22일)

천지기운 잔치가 있었다. 먼저 천지기운 받는 시간: 백회(百會)와 장심(掌心)을 통해서 천지기운을 받았다. 백회(百會)는 역시 깜깜이었으나 장심(掌心)으로는 아주 강한 기운을 느꼈다. 파트너와 기(氣) 주고받는 시간: 아주 강한 기운이 한 손으로 들어와 다른 손으로 나갔다. 나눔의 시간: 역시 여자들과 어린애들이 잘 되는 것 같았다. 함께 노래하고 Game한 시간: 김 사범이 여러가지를 준비해서 좋았다. 나는 단공(丹功)시범을 보였다.

'94.9.4. 일 (수련 11개월에 접어들면서)

'일본인의 한국인에 대한 콤플렉스 2000년'이란 책을 사서 읽었다. 일본과 한국의 고대사와 숨겨지고 왜곡된 역사의 일단을 바로 알게 되었다. 지금은 정사(正史)로 인정받고 있지 못하지만 언젠가는 역사의 진실이 밝혀질 것을 고대한다. 내가 그 일에 일조할 수 있다면 더 좋고.

'94.9.7. 수

농초 박문기 씨의 '맥이(貊耳)'라는 책을 읽고 있다. 우리민족의 웅장

한 옛 기상과 터전을 되찾아겠다는 다짐이 된다.

'94.10.2. 일

천모산 천화원에서의 개천기념행사에 참가했다. 개천 5892년, 단기 4327년, 서기 1994년이다. '우리 것은 세계의 것이고, 우리 역사는 세계의 역사'라는 생각이 든다. 긍지와 자부심을 가지고 혼 정신을 온 인류에게 알리자.

'94.10.20. 목 (360일)

김동춘 씨의 '천부경(天符經)과 단군사화'를 읽고 있다. 천부경에 대한 해석이 지금까지 내가 알고 있던 바와 좀 다르다. 단군사화(史話)및 제천(祭天), 우리민족의 이동경로, 인류의 역사 등은 내게 크게 도움이 된다.

'94.10.22. 토 (1년)

작년 10월 25일 처음으로 단학선원의 문을 두드렸으니 이제 만 1년이 되어간다. 그동안 게을러서 수련에 정진하지 못한 날도 많았지만, 역사와 진리를 만나고 숨쉬어 왔다는 사실이 고맙게 느껴진다. 단학에 입문하게 된 1주년을 기념하는 뜻에서 오늘부터 금연하기로 했다. → 2주 후 끝

'95.1.1 (乙亥 元旦 一凡 順天)

심고(心告): 기(氣)체험, 기(氣)축적, 기(氣)운용, 기(氣)활용,
천지기운 천지마음
마음의 문을 열고 모두를 사랑하자.
내 자신의 건강뿐만 아니라 주위사람들도 도와주자.

항상 웃으며 즐겁고 적극적으로 살아가자.

큰 뜻을 가지고 꾸준히 정진하자.

'95년도에는 마음수련과 몸수련 동시에 힘쓰자.

가훈(바른 몸, 바른 마음)의 실천에 모범을 보이자.

'95.1월 (우리말 속의 丹學)

알, 얼, 울 (한 얼 속에, 한 울 안에, 한 알이다)

기(氣)를 펴다, 기(氣)가 꺾인다.

기(氣)가 세다, 기(氣)가 약하다.

기(氣)가 죽는다, 기(氣)를 살린다.

기(氣)가 모인다, 기(氣)가 흩어진다.

기절(氣絶)하다: 기(氣)가 끊긴다.

화(火)가 난다, 화(火)가 머리 끝까지 치민다: 심장의 화기(火氣)가 머리로 오른다.

열이 난다, 열 받는다: 심장의 화기(火氣)가 머리로 올라 열이 난다.

얼굴이 붉어진다: 심장의 화기(火氣)가 머리로 올라 열이 난다.

얼굴이 뜨거워진다: 심기혈정(心氣血精)

뒤통수가 따갑게 느껴진다: 심기혈정(心氣血精)

몸이 확 달아오른다: 심기혈정(心氣血精)

냉정하다: 신장의 수기(水氣)가 머리로 올라 머리가 차갑게 된다.

얼굴: 얼이 드나드는 굴

얼 빠진, 얼이 나가다, 얼간이

뱃심: 아랫배의 힘 (下丹田에 氣가 모여)

뒷심: 명문(命門)호흡을 통하여 생기는 힘

신(神)나다: 상단전(上丹田)이 열려 神이 밝아진다.

신명(神明): 神이 밝아진다.

실신(失神): 神을 잃는다.

혼비백산(魂飛魄散)

가슴이 넓다, 가슴이 따뜻하다, 가슴이 두근거린다, 가슴이 뿌듯하다: 가슴은 전중혈(中丹田), 마음이 있는 곳, 사랑이 있는 곳.

홍익인간(弘益人間): 1. 건강하고 2. 양심이 회복되고 3. 사회적으로 능력이 있고 4. 정서적으로 성숙하여 5. 신령스러운 완성된 인간

나쁜 사람: 나뿐인 사람

좋은 사람: 조화로운 사람

건지 곤지 짝짝: 乾知 坤知

도리 도리 짝자꿍: 道理 道理

삶 → 살암 → 사람

절 → 저절로 되는 것 (감사하면 저절로 절을 한다)

저얼 → 저의 얼 → 나의 혼(魂)

'95.2.24. 금

정성수련 19일째, 500배 수련을 했다. 크게 힘든 줄 몰랐다. 몸이 많이 좋아진 모양이다.

'95.2.26. 일

21일 정성수련을 마쳤다. 21일간 담배 끊는 것도 성공했다.

'95.4.4. 화 (수련시작 1년6개월)

부산 본원에서 一指대선사를 뵈었다. 온화한 얼굴이었다. 사람이 감정(뿌리, 관념)의 기쁨을 추구하는 것은 끝이 없다. 감정(이기심, 자만심, 명예욕, 소유욕, 피해의식, 교만함…)의 벽을 넘어, 혼(魂)의 기쁨을 위해 노력하고 혼(魂)을 성장시켜 천화하자는 요지의 강천이었다. 가슴이 뿌듯한 사랑을 심고 키워 나가 인간완성의 세계로 나가자는 말씀, 옛 성현들의 가르침과 다를 바 없으나, 몸으로 느끼는 수련이라는 측면에서 단학의 특징이 있는 것 같다. 丹學人, 天地人. 내게는 자만심과 이기심과 명예욕이 없는가? 실제로는 있으면서 없는 체하는 것인가?

'95.4.10. 월

오늘부터 인시(寅時) 정성수련을 개시했다. 21일간 매일 4:30~5:30까지 103배를 하고 기운을 모아 혼(魂)을 살리는 수련이다. 이기심과 자만심, 명예욕, 물욕(物慾), 피해의식과 비교심, 모든 것을 버리고 가슴에 사랑의 꽃을 피우자.

'95.4.27. 목 (수련 시작 만 1년6개월)

700배 수련을 했다. 얼마전 부산에서 들은 대선사의 강천, '절은 저얼(즉 나의 혼)을 성장시키는 수련'이라는 말씀을 되새기며, 1배 1배마다 이기심, 자만심, 物慾, 명예욕, 교만함, 피해의식… 등, 내가 타파해야할 단어들을 되 뇌이며 하니, 크게 힘든 줄도 몰랐으며, 답답하던 가슴이 조금은 시원해지는 것 같았다.

'95.5.12. 금

천제(天祭)를 지내며 평생회원 특별수련이 있었다. '가슴에 꽃이 피어 난다'는 사람, '상단전(上丹田)에 거머리가 수십 마리 달라붙었다가 뻥 뚫린다'는 사람, 진동하는 사람, 흐느끼는 사람, 모두가 부러운 대상이 다. 나는 계속 명치부위가 엄청나게 아팠다. 수련 후 지원장이 가슴의 기운을 단전(丹田)으로 내려 보내려고 시도했으나, 너무 많이 막혀 있어 안된다고 했다. 시간이 많이 걸릴 거라고. 내 몸은 나무토막이다. 명문(命門)호흡은 잘 되는데 가슴은 왜 이리 아플까?

'95.5.20. 토

「한단연」입학식이 있었다. 벽운장의 특별수련도 있었다. 한단 연수원의 과목내용이 옛날 것과 조금 달라졌다.

* 사마천(司馬遷)의 《사기(史記)》: 기원전 100년 (황제시대~한무제)
  本紀(황제): 12권, 世家 (제후): 30권, 表(년표): 10권,
  書(문물제도): 8권, 列傳(유명인물): 70권

'95.6.17. 토

「한단연」에 갔다. 역사, 활공(活功), 음양오행 등의 강의가 새로운 관점에서 행해졌다. 유익한 내용들이었다.

'95.6.19

일본의 역사서 니혼쇼키(日本書紀)를 읽고 있다. 한일간의 고대사에 대해 진실을 알 수 있어 기쁘다. 얼마전에 읽은 만요슈(萬葉集)와 더불어 '내가 직장 퇴직 후에는 이 방면의 연구를 해야겠다'는 생각이 든다.

일본인 와따나베 미츠토시가 쓴 '일본천황도래기'를 읽었다. 일본천황
이 백제로부터 왔다는 사실(史實)을 기록은 했으되 강조하지 않았으며,
교묘하게 위장되어 있어, 日本書紀와 일본역사를 선전하고 있다.

'비류백제와 일본의 국가기원'을 읽었다. 고대 한일관계를 이제야 확
실히 알겠다. 역사를 바로 알게 되어 기쁘다.

'점성학이란 무엇인가'라는 책을 읽었다. 미신적이라고만 생각할 게
아니라, 우주의 질서에 대해 일견을 가질 수 있게 되어 기쁘다. 다 믿을
수는 없을지라도 정보로서의 가치가 있다.

'노스트라다무스'를 읽었다. 16세기 위대한 예언가, 우리나라의 격암
남사고 선생과 동시대의 예언가면서 미래에 대해서는 거의 같은 내용
을 예언하고 있다.

'NBC 특종 「충격 대예언」 일본이 가라앉는다'를 읽었다. 지금까지 공
부해온 역사, 종교, 철학을 종합 정리한 것 같다. 모든 예언서(성경, 불
경, 증산, 단학, 격암, 노스트라다무스)의 예언들이 하나로 일치하고 있
다.

'현대물리학이 발견한 창조주'를 읽고 있다. 내용은 좀 어렵지만 우주

와 지구의 생성, 역사, 미래를 과학적으로 접근해 놓은 책이다.

「한단연」에서 고대사를 공부하고 있다. '고구려, 백제, 신라는 한반도에 없었다'라는 책을 구하고 있다.

'95.10월

지나 서미나라 著 '윤회의 비밀'을 읽고 있다. 예언자 에드가 케이시의 Phisical & Life Reading을 연구하면서 인생의 본질에 대해서 말하고 있다.

'95.11월

북애의 '규원사화'를 읽고 있다.

미국 생활 중의 단학 수련

2001년 7월경 그리고 2003년 여름, 두 번에 걸쳐 미국 아리조나 (Arizona)주의 세도나(Sedona)를 방문했다. 세도나는 일지 대선사가 '지구상에서 기(氣)가 가장 센 곳'이라 하여 단학을 수련하는 사람들이 명상을 하고, 기(氣)를 받기 위해 많이 찾는 곳이다. 벨 락(Bell Rock), 성당(Cathedral Rock), 에어포트 메사 (Airport Mesa) 등 볼텍스(Vortex)가 유난히 강한 몇 곳이 있는데, 기를 받기 위해 가부좌 자세로 손바닥을 하늘로 향하게 하고 명상을 하면 기분이 참 좋아졌다. 기감각이 좋은 아내는 잠시의 명상 중에도 '몸에 큰 진동을 느꼈다'고 했다. 이곳에 있는 단학수련 센터를 찾아가 '평생회원'이라 소개하며 인사를 나누었다.

샌프란시스코(San Francisco)에도 단 센터(丹 Center)가 있으나, 너무 멀어서 다니지 못하고, 집에서 혼자 단학 수련을 하기가 쉽지 않았다. 103배 절 수련을 몇 번 해 봤지만 꾸준히 하는 게 어려웠다. 대신 한국에서 단학을 하면서 역사공부를 하였기에 미국에서도 틈틈이 역사책을 읽었다. 『나를 운디드니에 묻어주오』(디 브라운 저, 최준석 역), 『인디언의 길』(김철 저), 『아메리카 인디언의 땅』(필리프 자켄 저, 송숙자 역) 등을 읽고 미국의 서부개척사는 아메리카 원주민의 멸망사라는 걸 알게 되었고, 『우리민족의 대이동』(손성태 저)을 통해서, 마야문명도 우리민족의 한 갈래라는 것도 알게 되었다. 참고로 흔히 '아메리카인디언'이라 불리는 미국 원주민들은 모두 우리처럼 엉덩이에 몽고반점이 있다. 또 종교서적 『기독교 성서의 이해』(김용옥 저), 『요한복음 강해』(김용옥 저), 『성서의 뿌리』(민희식 저), 『법화경과 신약성서』(민희식 저), 『살아있는 반야경』(서경보 저), 『성약성서』(보병궁복음서, 리바이 도우링 저)를 읽으면서 종교적인 이해도를 많이 높였다.

단학을 만나면서 몸과 마음이 건강해지는 많은 체험들을 하게 되었다. 내 인생에서 단학을 만난 것은 큰 행운이라 할 만하다. 죽을 때까지 틈틈이 단전호흡을 하면서 건강을 도모하고, 명상을 통해 마음수련도 해야 하겠다.

. . .

단식일기

斷食은

1. 腸속에 쌓인 숙변을 제거하여 질병을 예방한다.

2. 외부로부터 영양이 공급되지 않을 동안, 체내의 병적조직이나 불필요한 영양물질을 태워 에너지를 만들어 냄으로써, 혈액이 정화되고 자연치유력이 높아져서, 여러 질병이 치유된다.

3. 과잉영양과 스트레스로 인해 산성화된 체액을 약알칼리성으로 되돌려, 건강체질로 변화시킨다.

4. 불필요한 기름기와 군살이 빠져 비만이 해결되고, 피가 맑아지기 때문에 피부도 고와진다.

5. 각종 수련을 통해 세포가 새로 형성되고, 체력이 강화되어 정력이 충만해진다.

6. 피로해진 臟器들에게 휴식할 수 있는 기회를 주어, 생명력을 축적하게 된다.

7. 피를 탁하게 하고, 뇌신경활동을 억제하기도 한 체내의 노폐물과 독소를 제거함으로써, 피를 맑게 하고 두뇌가 좋아진다.

8. 단식은 인내심과 극기심, 의지력을 필요로 하므로, 끝낸 후에는 강한 정신력을 갖게 된다.

9. 세포와 각 장기가 정화되고, 마음이 비워진 상태에서 명상수련을 함으로써, 정신력이 고양되어 감수성, 직관력, 포용력이 향상되고 잠재력이 개발된다.

＊ 단식은 몸과 마음을 완전히 비움으로써, 몸속에 있는 나쁜 기운을

제거하고 천지의 맑은 기운을 채워 넣어, 심신의 건강을 회복하고자 하는 데 목적이 있으며, 음식을 굶는 대신 욕심을 채워넣는 단식은 결코 단식이 아니다.

《단식일기》

일정 기간 동안 단식을 하는 것이 몸과 마음의 건강 유지를 위해 대단히 좋겠다는 생각을 늘 하고 있었으나, 실제로 회사생활하는 사람이 1주일 동안 휴가를 낸다는 것이 어려워서 좀처럼 기회를 갖지 못했다.

이번에는 우여곡절 끝에 7.17부터 7.23까지 연차휴가, 특별휴가, 공휴일, 일요일 등을 합쳐, 단식하기로 하여, 참가비 ₩350,000을 선불하였다.

단식 들어가기 전에 감식기간이 5일 정도 필요한데, 사실상 이 예비 단식 기간부터 어려움은 시작된다.

기간: 감식(減食): 7/13 ~7/16 (4일)
　　　 단식(斷食): 7/17 ~7/23 (7일)
　　　 보식(補食): 7/24 ~8/20 (24일)
단식장소: 충북 영동 천화원

감식(減食):

갑자기 굶게되면 공복감을 이겨내기가 어렵고, 알콜, 니코틴 및 육류가 몸속에 축적되어 있으면, 단식기간 중 몸의 산성화가 심해지므로, 본단식 전 미리 식사량을 줄이고, 금연, 금주 및 채식생활을 한다.

예비단식 1일자 (7/13/1998. 월)

감식(減食)하는 첫 날이다. 식사량은 평소의 80%로 줄이고, 육류, 어패류보다는 채식위주로 먹는 것은 별 어려움이 아니지만, 하루 한 갑씩 피던 담배를 끊고 하루 3~4잔씩 마시던 커피를 끊는 것은 대단한 어려움이다. 사무실에서 업무회의를 할 때, 음료수마저 마시지 않고 오로지 물만 벌컥벌컥 마시려니 힘들다. 하루 종일 낮에도 잠이 와서 죽을 뻔했다. 저녁에 선원(仙院)에 가서 수련한 뒤 일찍 잠자리에 들었다.

예비단식 2일자 (7/14/1998. 화)

감식(減食)하는 두번째 날이다. 減食 자체는 문제가 아니다. 담배, 커피, 음료수, 간식 등 모든 기호품을 끊은 데 대한 금단현상이 나타나는 것 같다. 눈이 빙빙 돌고, 머리가 띵~하고, 잠도 오고, 사물이 이중으로 보인다. 하루종일 냉수를 얼마나 마셨는지 모르겠다. 식사량은 평소의 60%.

예비단식 3일자 (7/15/1998. 수)

머리가 띵~하고, 잠도 오고, 눈이 빙빙 도는 현상이 계속된다. 물을 계속 마시고 따라서 오줌도 계속 눈다. 광양제철소장의 부친상으로 전북 익산시까지 갔다 오느라 운동은 못했다. 잠도 부족하다. 식사량은 평소의 40%.

예비단식 4일자 (7/16/1998. 목)

어지럽고 배고픔이 느껴진다. 식사량은 평소의 20%. 냉수먹기-오줌싸기 반복. 저녁 때 회식이 있어 식당엘 갔다가 생수대신 결명자를 달인 물을 많이 마셨는데 그게 잘못된 건지 저녁동안 설사를 했다. 설사

일범의 평범한 사람 이야기

가 차라리 잘된 것이라 생각하고, 구충제를 먹고 잤다.

본단식 1일차 (7/17/1998. 금)

아침부터 전혀 먹지 않았다. 배가 고플 때는 물만 마시고, 포항에서 영동 천화원까지 약 4시간 반 동안 차를 몰고 왔다. 머리가 띵~하다. 13:30경 천화원에 도착하여 수련이 시작되다.

담당강사: 교육부장 강순태, 조XX 부팀장,

　　　　　　박경옥, 권현진, 김미현, 강영주, 안승만

단식할 때 현상

- 공복감
- 脫力感, 피로감
- 체중 감소: 病조직 → 脂肪조직 → 근육 → 내장 without Food
- 수면시간 감소
- 설태(泄汰: 위장의 나쁜 것 배출)
- 소변: 혼탁
- 숙변(宿便) 배출
- 피부 활성화
- 후각 예민
- 하혈(女)
- 현기증, 빈혈, 구토, 미식거림(나쁠수록)

14:00~15:00 접수, 신체점검

15:00~15:50 수련(導引체조, 止感, 보조요법)

16:00~17:00 냉온수욕

17:10~19:10 Orientation

19:10~20:30 보조요법 및 주의 사항

20:40~21:20 나눔의 시간

21:20~21:40 청소

21:50~22:20 풍욕(風浴)

22:20~23:00 명상, 일지 작성, 마그밀 복용

23:00 취침

導引체조:

평소 잘 사용하지 않는 근육을 위주로 하는 Stretching 운동으로 단전 호흡 전후에 함.

止感수련:

감정(僖, 懼, 哀, 怒, 貪, 厭)을 그치기 위한 수련.

보조요법:

毛管운동, 붕어운동, 합장합척(合掌合脊)운동, 등배운동 등 腸운동과 蓄氣를 위한 운동들.

냉온수욕:

독일의 브라운 헬레 박사가 창안한 피부호흡방식으로, 냉수(13~14°C)와 온수(41~43°C)를 각 1분씩 번갈아 들어감. 반드시 냉수에서 끝냄.

풍욕(風浴):

프랑스의 과학자 로볼박사가 창안. 신선한 공기와 피부를 직접 맞닿게 하여, 피부의 본래 역할(흡수, 배설, 호흡, 보호작용)을 되찾아 주는 수련으로, 해 뜨기 전과 해 진 후에 실시.

담요 덮고 1분 → 담요 벗고 20초 → 1분 → 30초 → 1분 → 40초 → 1

분 → 50초 → 1분 → 60초

담요 덮고 1분30초 → 담요 벗고 70초 → 1분30초 → 80초 → 1분30초 → 90초

담요 덮고 2분 → 담요 벗고 1분 40초 → 2분 → 1분 50초 → 2분 → 2분 → 담요덮고 3분으로 끝낸다.

마그밀: 마그네슘(Mg), 설사제, 숙변배출에 효과 있음

KBS-TV에 방영된 천화단식 프로그램을 봤다.

이번 기회에 최대한 열심히 하여 - 몸과 마음이 건강한 사람, - 氣감각이 좋아 수련이 잘 되는 사람, - 금연, 이 세 가지는 꼭 실천하자.

본단식 2일차 (7/18/1998. 토)

05:30~05:40 기상

05:40~06:00 이동

06:00~06:50 풍욕

06:50~07:20 세면

07:30~08:20 아침수련

08:20~09:40 관장(灌腸)

09:50~11:20 건강원리

11:30~13:30 산책수련(맨발)

13:30~14:00 휴식

14:10~15:00 사랑주기(活功)

15:00~16:00 단식 강의

16:00~17:50 조별 산책

17:50~18:50 냉온수욕

19:00~20:30 거울깨기(나눔)

20:30~21:00 청소

21:00~21:40 풍욕

21:40~22:00 명상, 일지 작성, 마그밀 복용

22:00 취침

아침수련:

腸내의 숙변제거를 위한 腸운동 (단전치기, 腸 움직이기, 腸 쓸어주기 등)을 중심으로, 탁한 기운을 배출하는 운동과 맑은 기운을 받아들이는 훈련 및 단전호흡을 함.

관장(灌腸):

소금물 1000cc를 腸속으로 넣고, 10분이상 腸운동을 한 후 배설함.

사랑주기(活功):

두 사람이 교대로 서로의 몸을 運氣시켜 줌. (어깨와 등, 다리, 복부, 팔, 머리, 온몸 등)

거울깨기:

마음속에 흑, 백 두 개의 거울을 그리고, 흰 거울에는 바람직한 자신을, 검은 거울에는 버려야할 자신을 담아 넣고, 검은 거울을 깸으로써 거듭남.

간밤에 잠을 많이 설쳤다. 잠자리가 바뀐 탓도 있겠지만 심한 공복감, 속쓰림, 위(胃)의 통증도 동반되었다. 실제로는 아프지만 숨겨져 있다가, 치료가 되기 위해 아픈 현상이 나타난다는 이른바 명현(瞑顯)현상이라고 생각한다.

아침 05:30부터 하루가 시작되었다. 아침수련 시간에 장(腸)운동을 약 1시간 정도 하였는데 아랫배가 뭉친 곳이 아팠다. 관장도 하기 전에 아주 고약한 냄새가 나는 시꺼먼 변을 보았다. 관장하고 난 후에도 또 상당히 많이 나왔다. 腸이 풀리려나 보다. 地塔까지 맨발로 걸어가서 기운을 받을 때는 5년전 단학(丹學)에 처음 입문했을 때 지감(止感)수련이나 기(氣)주고받기할 때의 경험으로 되돌아간 기분이었다.

- 딱딱하게 불룩 나온 똥배가 말랑말랑해졌다.
- 몸무게가 1kg 줄었다. (어제 66.9 → 오늘 65.9)
- 아침까지 속쓰림과 胃통증이 있었으나 낮에는 느끼지 못했다.
- 점심시간에 다른 사람 밥 먹는 것 봐도 먹고 싶지 않았다.

본단식 3일차 (7/19/1998. 일)

05:30~05:40 기상

05:40~06:30 풍욕

06:30~07:10 세면

07:10~08:00 아침수련

08:10~09:00 마음보기

09:00~09:30 자리정렬 (찜질 준비)

09:30~13:30 된장 찜질

13:30~14:00 물건 정리

14:10~15:00 관장

15:00~15:50 냉온수욕

16:00~17:00 사랑주기(活功)

17:00~19:00 자기표현

19:10~20:00 조별 산책

20:10~21:10 나눔

21:10~21:30 청소

21:30~21:10 풍욕

22:10~22:30 명상, 일지 작성, 마그밀 복용

22:30 취침

마음보기:

마음속의 잡념을 털어내고 天氣를 받아, 자신의 마음 속에서 진실로 원하는 것이 무엇인지 깨닫는 수련.

된장 찜질:

배 위에 된장을 얹고, 뜨겁게 약 4시간 유지하면서 腸운동을 계속해 주면(장운동 3,000번 이상), 腸속의 숙변배출에 효과가 큼.

자기표현:

조별 장기자랑 시간임.

새벽 02:30에 일어나 설사를 했다. 아침에도 또 설사를 하고… 된장 찜질은 정말 구수하고, 따뜻하고, 시원하고, 힘든 과정이다. 마지막 남은 腸속의 숙변을 제거하는 과정이란다. 관념의 벽을 깨뜨리기 위해 갖은 애를 다 써 보았으나, 결국 오늘도 실패다. 머리 속의 생각이 너무나 복잡한 인생아.

속쓰림이 다시 나타나고, 아침 된장 찜질 중 腸운동할 때, 명치부위에 미세한 진동이 계속되었는데 그 때부터 명치부위의 통증을 느낌. 몸무게 다시 1kg 줄었음(64.7kg). 입에서 고약한 냄새가 계속 남.

본단식 4일차 (7/20/1998. 월)

05:30~05:40 기상

05:40~06:30 풍욕

06:30~07:20 관장

07:20~08:00 세면, 외출 준비

08:00~09:00 하산(下山)

09:00~10:00 온천으로 이동

10:30~10:30 냉탕 25분 수련

11:30~12:30 금촉(禁觸) 수련 (도마시장)

12:30~14:00 옥계폭포로 이동 (導引체조)

14:00~16:00 폭포수련 (테마 산책)

16:00~16:30 숙소 도착

16:30~17:20 휴식

17:30~18:20 사랑주기(活功)

18:30~19:20 체험담 소개

19:30~20:20 나눔

20:30~21:00 청소

21:00~21:40 풍욕

21:40~22:00 명상, 일지 작성, 마그밀 복용

22:00 취침

냉탕 25분 수련:

약 14~15 °C 정도 되는 냉탕에 25분 동안 들어가 있는 수련으로, 통상 20분간은 가만히 있고, 마지막 5분간 손발을 움직여 줌. 몸이 부르르 떨리는 현상은 몸속에 축적된 알콜, 카페인, 니코틴 등 탁한 기운들이 태워지는 현상이라고 하는데, 월 1회 정도 해 주면 좋다. 겨울철에는 더욱 효과가 크며, 25분 초과는 별 의미가 없다.

금촉(禁觸)수련:

聲, 色, 臭, 味, 淫, 抵의 觸을 끊는다는 뜻으로 禁觸이라 하는데, 오늘은 시장의 음식골목을 지나치면서 먹고 싶은 욕망(臭, 味)을 극복하는 과정이었다. 4일 굶겨 놓아도 별로 먹고 싶은 생각은 없다. 또한, 단식 및 보식(補食)기간 끝나고 나면, 절대로 어떤 음식이라도 투정부리지 않을 자신도 있다.

폭포수련:

폭포의 떨어지는 물을 맞으면서 몸과 마음을 씻어내는 수련으로, 어릴 때 폭포에서 물 맞으면 건강해진다고 해서 여름만 되면 물 맞으러 가던 생각이 난다. 폭포의 떨어지는 물을 흠뻑 두들겨 맞고 나니, 정신이 개운해진다.

胃의 통증이 한 나절은 아프고, 한 나절은 괜찮은 현상이 계속된다. 변소 가면 숙변이 약간 섞인 방귀만 나온다. 가부좌를 하고 앉아 있는 자세가 너무 힘들어진다. 트림이 간혹 나온다.

본단식 5일차 (7/21/1998, 화)

05:30~05:40 기상

05:40~06:30 풍욕

06:30~06:50 세면

07:00~07:50 아침수련

08:00~09:20 관장

09:30~10:30 특별수련 (五氣調和神功)

10:40~12:30 눈 감고 산책

12:40~13:30 補食 1

13:30~14:50 휴식

15:00~16:00 사랑주기(活功)

16:10~17:00 냉온수욕

17:00~17:50 조별 산책

18:00~19:00 補食 2

19:00~19:30 휴식

19:40~20:40 나눔

20:40~21:10 청소

21:10~21:50 풍욕

21:50~22:10 명상, 일지 작성

22:10 취침

五氣調和神功:

水(신장), 木(간), 火(심장), 土(위장), 金(폐) 등 五臟에 손바닥으로 기운을 불어넣어주기를 9회 반복함으로써 오장을 튼튼하게 해 주는데, 기운 주기 전, 후의 효과를 O-ring test로 확인할 수 있었다.

눈 감고 산책:

두 사람이 짝을 이루어, 한 사람은 눈을 감고, 다른 사람을 완전히 믿고 그 사람이 인도하는 대로 걸어서 산등성이 꼬부랑길을 넘어 감.

補食 1:

사람의 胃와 腸은 2일만 굶으면 3일째부터는 완전히 활동정지가 되어, 胃는 아주 조그맣게 수축된다고 한다. 따라서 4~5일 단식 후의 첫 補食은 입속에서 거의 소화를 시켜서 삼켜야 하는데, 현미+백미+보리+기타를 섞어 2시간 반 동안 끓인 미음 한 국자(120g)를 먹는 데 1시간이 걸렸다. 찻숟갈로 한 술 떠서 200번 이상 씹은 후 단전에 힘을 주고

삼킴(丹田식사).

補食 2:

미음 200g (미음:침 = 1:1), 간식 불가

胃의 통증은 계속된다. 명현현상으로 알고는 있지만, 그 동안 내가
너무 많이 과음, 과식을 해 온 결과가 아닌가? 補食表에 나와 있는 대
로 식생활을 한다는 것은 사회생활을 하지말고 혼자 절(寺)에서 살라는
것과 같다. 1주일 정도 (1차補食, 2차補食)만 補食하고 그 다음은 과음,
과식 하지말고 금연을 실천하면 충분할 것 같다.

본단식 6일차 (7/22/1998. 수)

05:30~05:40 기상

05:40~06:30 풍욕

06:30~07:00 세면

07:10~08:00 아침수련

08:10~10:00 마음보기

10:10~12:30 VTR 시청

12:40~13:30 補食 3

13:30~14:20 휴식

14:30~15:30 活功

15:30~16:20 편지쓰기

16:20~17:20 냉온수욕

17:30~18:20 나눔

18:30~19:30 補食 4

19:30~19:40 이동

19:40~22:10 율려(律呂)수련
22:10~22:30 청소
22:30~22:50 명상, 일지 작성
22:50 취침

마음 보기:

여러사람이 한 사람을 상대로, 자기가 가장 존경하는 사람으로 생각하고, 그 사람의 장점을 찾아 말해주며, 그 말을 들은 사람은 무조건 자신의 장점을 인정함.

補食 3: 묽은 죽 350g (간식: 과일 즙)

補食 4: 묽은 죽 450g (간식: 과일 즙)

율려(律呂)수련:

1주일 동안 쫄쫄 굶으면서 생사고락을 같이한 14차 단식동기생들이 여러가지 게임과 노래, 춤으로 氣풀이를 하는 과정으로, 굶은 사람들이 참 힘도 좋고, 노래와 춤에서도 지칠 줄 모른다. 마음을 완전히 Open하고, 상대방을 이해하고 사랑하는 것이 얼마나 중요한지 새삼 느낀다.

1주일 단식이 거의 끝나간다. 補食을 하고있기 때문에, 관장도 하지 않고 마그밀도 먹지 않고, 또 죽염과 물도 많이 먹지 않는다. 그래서인지 대변, 소변도 횟수가 줄어들어 정상화되어 간다.

- 풍욕과 냉온수욕은 단식 끝난 후에도 계속할만한 건강법이라 생각된다.
- 보식으로 주는 미음의 양이 너무 적다. 강사들은 '그렇게 먹어야만 한다'고 한다.
- 집에 있는 가족에게 편지를 썼다.

본단식 7일차 (7/23/1998. 목)

05:50~06:00 기상

06:00~06:50 풍욕

07:00~08:30 아침수련

08:30~09:20 냉온수욕

09:30~10:50 마무리 정리, 마음다지기

　　　　　　설문지 작성, 사진 촬영

10:50~11:50 대청소, 짐 정리

12:00~12:50 補食 5

13:00~13:10 마지막 만남

13:10 퇴소

7일간의 단식 정리

1. 胃와 腸을 완전히 비우고 청소했다. 腸의 숙변이 다 빠져나오고, 胃가 어린아이처럼 수축되었다.

2. 몸안에 쌓였던 毒氣, 濁氣들이 거의 몸 밖으로 배출되어 개운해졌다.

3. 몸에 Stress가 쌓인 부분이 풀려서 유연해지고 丹田에 축기가 상당히 되었다.

4. 정신이 맑아지고 피부가 윤택해졌다.

5. 담배를 끊을 수 있다는 확실한 자신감을 가졌다.

6. 술과 음식에 대한 욕심이 없어져, 앞으로 과음, 과식을 삼가할 수 있을 것 같다.

7. 앞으로 꾸준히 운동해 주고, 과음, 과식 삼가고, 금연을 계속하면 평생 건강하게 살 수 있을 것이다.

8.몸무게는 대략 평소보다 6kg 정도 빠진 것 같다.

9.목, 어깨, 허리, 고관절이 풀리는 것은 아직 멀었다.

10.氣를 느끼기는 하나 運氣는 안된다.

補食

1차 補食기간(~7/25/1998. 토): 미음과 죽만 먹음으로써 수축된 胃를 점차적으로 훈련시키는 시기로서 대단히 중요함. 술, 담배, 고기류 금물. 계속 대변을 보지 못함.

2차 補食 기간(7/26. 일 ~7/28. 화): 묽은 밥을 먹되, 평상식의 60%, 70%, 80% 수준으로 늘려가면서 胃를 훈련시키는 시기. 대변을 보았는데 그렇게 보드랍고, 이쁘고, 아름다운 변은 처음 보네. 온 몸의 근육(배, 허벅지, 장단지, 팔, 옆구리 등)이 말랑말랑해진 상태가 건강의 청신호로 생각된다. 이제부터는 운동을 열심히 해야지. 고기류, 술 금물.

3차 補食은 8/13까지 본단식의 4배 일수에 해당되며, 평상식의 80% 정도 먹어야 한다지만, 이제부터는 과음, 과식 안하고 금연하는 것만이라도 잘 지키자. 약을 먹어도 됨.

제4부

미국생활

미국 Chicago에서
어학 연수할 때(1997)
쓴 글들

My Favorite Pet

I have two dogs at my home. Their names are PPOPPI and BOM. I have had no pets before I got PPOPPI. PPOPPI and BOM know the surroundings at home. When my wife shouts or speaks loudly, PPOPPI and BOM drop their heads and hide their eyes. PPOPPI and BOM always like 'skin—ship' with people. Whenever I come back from work, they run to me and rub their bodies to mine. PPOPPI and BOM follow on their host's order. When they are left in home while people come out, they don't make dirt on floor. I like PPOPPI and BOM.

My Best Friend

My best friends are PANGYU and BYEONGJAE. PANGYU is a primary school teacher in Seoul and BYEONGJAE works at the Korea Land Corporation. We met in the dormitory while we were in high school. We had lived in the same room for two years 1st and 2nd grade. PANGYU's characteristic was nearly same as mine. He and I were very lazy to study. But BYEONGJAE was more diligent and preparer than PANGYU and I. all of us had taken high scores in exams. After graduation from high school, BYEONGJAE and I entered B University for becoming engineers, but PANGYU became a teacher. We are keeping in touch with each other even though we live far from each other. We were called triple pair when we were in high school.

PANGYU and BYEONGJAE are my best friends now and will be forever.

Pohang City

Pohang is a beautiful Korean industrial city located in the south-east coast of Korean peninsula. There are a lot of summer resorts and a charming housing area for POSCO employees. The roads along the beautiful seaside are quite suitable for car driving. Pohang was a small fishing town about 30 years ago, but it is a big industrial city now because of POSCO which is the second largest steel making company in the world. The people who live in Pohang are very proud of POSCO. POSCO also returns its benefits to the people who live in Pohang – such as the bridge construction, the presentation of foot-ball team to the city, the build-up of a university and etc. In conclusion, Pohang is a model city of newly industrialized cities.

American Foods

There are various kinds of restaurants in America: Italian, French, Greek, Mexican, Japanese, Thai, Vietnamese, Chinese, Indian, Korean, and so on. But, unfortunately I have never seen any restaurant with its name as American style. The only menu with the word "American" is

American style breakfast. What are the traditional American foods?

There are a lot of fast—food chains in America: Mc Donald's, Burger King, Jack—In—The Box, Wendy's, Subway's, In & Out, TOGO, etc. All of these chains have the similar menus: hamburgers or sandwiches and beverages (Coke or Pepsi). America, the biggest country in the world, has very strongly influencing to other countries politically and economically. And also, some American fast foods as mentioned above have spread all over the world. People in foreign countries think those fast foods are American foods.

I think there are no traditional American foods in America because most people who live in America are immigrants. American foods are, therefore, the mixtures of the food which had been in the immigrants' homelands. America was developed and modernized by the frontier spirit which was started from the gold rush in 1840s. So the fast foods might be very much required at that time for forty—niners, cowboys, and mountain men who were the symbols of American dreams. The dried beef, hamburgers and some other easy—handling foods might be developed to meet the requirements of frontiers.

Nowadays the meaning of American foods is much changed. In America, there are various kinds of foods from various countries. But those are not same in the original counties, but already very much Americanized. Chinese foods in America taste sweeter and saltier than in China, which can be called Chinese American foods. Like the previous, there are Indian American foods, Italian American foods, Japanese American foods, and so on. All kinds of foods in America can be called "American foods".

What Makes Me Happy

The bright sunshine makes me happy when I wake up in the morning.

The hot morning coffee, just poured out from the vending machine, makes me happy before I begin my work at office.

The good production result during the night makes me happy.

My secretary's thoughtful consideration for the day's meeting makes me happy.

The small souvenirs from visitors make me happy.

No pending tasks near the day-off time make me happy.

No traffic jam at rush hour makes me happy.

My wife's lovely smile and my two dogs' shaking their tails make me happy when I open the door from work.

My wife's talking "Thanks for your efforts today for family" makes me happy.

The calm music and a cup of coffee after dinner make me happy.

The history books about the old oriental ages make me happy.

I live everyday surrounded by happiness from morning to night.

Korea, South and North

Do you know the country which is currently divided into two? Yes, it is Korea, South and North. There are a lot of differences between South and North Korea. But there are still a lot of same qualities. South and North Korea are quite different politically, economically and socially at this time when almost 60 years has passed since Korea was divided into two after World War II ended.

At first, I'd like to mention about the political system. South Korea is a democratic country which was influenced by the U.S.A. and the president of South Korea is directly elected by the votes of the people. Whereas North Korea is a communist which was influenced by old U.S.S.R. and the president of North Korea, Jung—il Kim, is a hereditary ruler succeeded by his father.

My second concern is the economical point of view. South Korea has been continuously developed since the end of Korean War. The national income per person reached $10,000. Many South Koreans waste a lot of their wealth to entertainment and enjoying. Meanwhile, North Korea has not been developed under the planned economic policy by the government. And the national income per person is under $500. So most people in North Korea are starving nowadays, and many of them are trying to escape from their country.

Third, South and North Korea have quite different social situations. South Koreans, especially many students, seem not to obey their government even though they are living rich. South Koreans may have too much freedom in publication, assembly, speech, and so on. But North Koreans seem to obey their government despite their poor life and a lot of restrictions to their lives by the government.

However, South and North Korea have almost same history, geography, and anthropology. Historically, South and North Korea are the same race, have the same ancestors, and the same history which has been almost 9,000 years.

Geographically, South and North Korea have very similar mountains, rivers, and fields which are quite different from any other countries. When we are flying in the airplane and see the scenes which are spread below us, we can easily know where we are flying, over Korea or over other countries.

Anthropologically, there are about one million people who live separately from their family in South and North. They miss each other very much and want to meet them eagerly before they die.

Korea is the only one country in the world which exists divided into two. But the possibility of reunification is becoming greater and greater because a lot of the same qualities are still preserved in spite of many differences between them.

Something Valuable to Me

I like to study the ancient history about Korea, China and Japan. So I bought and read a lot of books of the ancient oriental history. But I don't know well about the modern times of the other countries because of my knowledge is limited only for history. About Japan, I have read a lot of Japanese history books and sure I know well about Japanese history better than any other person. But I always doubt "Why has Japan so highly developed even though Japan had been helped by Korea until 200 years ago?"

Recently I could find a book at the library of my company. The name of the book is "Here is Japan". I picked it up and began to read it. It was so curious to me. I could find out the answer of my long doubt when I finished reading it. The reasons of Japan's development were clearly described in that book.

I have many books which are valuable to me. But the book "Here is Japan" is the most valuable to me, because it made me solve my long doubt without any payment.

Money can't Buy Happiness

I agreed to this topic fifteen years ago but not now. Fifteen years ago, I thought that everything can be solved if I have the firm will. And I also thought that money causes a lot of problem.

However, this kind of my thought has been changed gradually since I have met some difficulties by the lack of money. I could not keep my happiness in my mind without money.

"If I had more money, I would be happier than I am." I frequently thought this.

I don't believe that money can solve every problem, but I must think that money is very necessary and sometimes essential for happiness. I am sure you have heard the proverb, "There is no one over and no one under." It means all men are equal. But you know that money can change your position, sometimes put you over the other people, or sometimes put you under the other. If some seeks for too much money, it can make troubles. But generally, the more money you have, the happier you will be.

Do You Have any Superstition? Why or why not?

Many Koreans have a lot of superstition. For examples, 1) The number 4 means death, 2) The cry of crow makes somebody die, 3) The cry of magpie shows a visitor's coming, 4) Whistling at night makes a snake come, 5) Eating raw rice makes your mother die, and so one.

I don't believe any superstition, because the superstition has been made by the people who wanted to make the surroundings be better for them. Some of the superstition may be made by the long—period experiences. I think that the most important thing in our life is the mind. If I don't believe it, it never comes.

I love this proverb: "Everything depends on the mind" "一切唯心造"

I Hear American Singing   written by Walt Whitman

I hear American singing, the varied carols I hear,
Those of mechanics, each one singing his as it should be blithe and strong,
The carpenter signing his as he measures his plank or beam,
The mason singing his as he makes ready for work, or leaves off work,
The boatman singing what belongs to him in his boat,
The deckhand singing on the steamboat deck,
The shoemaker singing as he sits on his bench,

The hatter singing as he stands,

The woodcutter's song, the plowboy's on his way in the morning, or

at the noon intermission or at sundown,

The delicious singing of the mother, or of the young wife at work, or

of the girl sewing or washing,

Each singing what belongs to him or her to no one else,

The day what belongs to the day – at night the party of the young

fellows, robust, friendly,

Singing with open mouths their strong melodious songs. (1860)

* Walt Whitman (1819–1892)

: A famous American poet. He wrote a lot of lovely poems about the

American country life.

Natural vs. Artificial

I prefer the natural to the artificial. When I finally escaped from the noisy, disordered, stifling building, the nature was waiting me. I felt cool, fresh air touching my nose. A few of trees were trying to compete each other in order to grow higher than others. A red moon was hanging over the top of those trees. Stars were struggling against the lamp lights.

I Want to be a Good Writer because...

When you start your job in a company after you graduate from university, you would know how much important the writing is. I have worked in a company for seventeen years. And I am sure that the most important thing for a good performance of your job is the writing ability. It's not enough how much you emphasize its importance.

If you have a wonderful ability to write, you must succeed in any fields. Without the writing ability, you never succeed whatever you want to do. Working in a company means writing something. For examples, Contracts for selling or purchasing, Reports of investigation, Specifications of any equipment, Regulations and obligations, Information of new ideas and so on. These must be written in very well-organized form and suitable expression in order to achieve their goals.

I have been taught by my seniors about how to write documents since the beginning of my job. And also, I have made a lot of efforts to be a good writer. But it is not enough for me to be the excellent writer. I must learn more to write everything to be perfect. Being a good writer is the best way for your success in your life.

My Reaction to Frida Kahlo's Story

She was so aggressive and strong that she could use the terrible situations for the turning point of her life. For examples, her polio made her outgoing, and her near—fatal car accident made her look inside her own life. Her story reminded me a Korean proverb, "Crisis has two meanings, one is danger, and the other is opportunity." Most people become depressed when they are faced to a crisis. But the crisis can also be a good chance if you accept it affirmatively and use it for the benefits of yourself. I think that Frida Kahlo is a very good example of positive way of life. Her story encouraged me to live more actively.

＊ Frida Kahlo (1907—1954): 멕시코 출신의 서양화가
＊ 危機: 危險 ＋ 機會

Does Society Need Artists in order to survive?

The answer depends upon the society. What kind of society?
Let's imagine a devastated island where nobody has livered before several people met with a disaster. The disasters group can also be a society. They will do their best for survival at the isolated island. In that case, the artist does not have any special reason for that society.

Now imagine the present society. The people who live in high—

developed society have various needs for their lives. So, artists are necessary for the society, but it is not privilege. Everyone has the same right.

Artists are not essential for survival in society, but they are necessary in order to survive.

Home Stay in Chicago

I live in a homestay which is located in Oak Park. My host father, Ernie, is a professor in Concordia University and my host mother, Evie, is an elementary school teacher. She also teaches children and adults dancing and swimming. For two weeks since I first came to Chicago, they had been travelling to Spain, so I had lived with another foreign student in the large house. After they came back home, I was very satisfied in living with them. Ernie and Evie are very busy every day, but they are so thoughtfully kind that they share their time for my English practice. They are not like general Americans. They understand Asian cultures well and do their best to talk with me about various kinds of topics which are very helpful to my English practice. One of my neighbors is an old man named Ken. I will have an interview with him someday about 'American policy for the old man'. Another neighbor is a housewife who has a dog-poodle. I also want to have an interview with her about 'Pets in America'. I love my home-family and I wish living at this home for years if possible.

If I could be a Famous Artist,
I would choose to be like …

My father was a farmer. He had worked very hard even though he had a small area of farm. I was grown up in the depths of the country where my father had his farm, sometimes helping him and sometimes disturbing him. I used to do a lot of funs with my friends. And I could learn many things about nature and human life at the countryside. I remember a picture hanged on the wall of my father's hut which might fall down soon.

When I entered a middle school, I recognized that the picture at the hut was a copy of "The Angelus" pained by Millet. I cannot escape from the country life in my mind after I moved to a city. If I could be a famous artist, I would be like Jean Francois Millet.

The World's Emphasis is on Sports is ...

"Do you know Chicago?"

"Yes, it's a terrible city with full of killings, violence, and drugs. You must be careful in Chicago."

"How do you know?"

"I have seen the movie 'God father' in which Mafia and Al Capone had a great influence in Chicago."

This was a conversation fifty years ago. Then, what conversation do you imagine nowadays?

"Do you know Chicago?"

"Yes, I know. Chicago is a very famous city for basketball. Chicago Bulls is the champion in NBA. I know many star players in Chicago Bulls, Michael Jordan, Pippin, Rodman···. I like Michael Jordan; his uniform number is 23 and I really want to see him."

"What changed Chicago from a notorious city to a famous one?"

"It's sports. Sports are so powerful that it can change every impression. Because of the importance of sports, many counties, cities, even companies are willing to have sports team such as football, basketball, baseball, tennis, hockey, marathon and so on."

"How can we live in this world without sports?"

The Controllable Is Better than the Uncontrollable

Who doesn't want to control his/her circumstances instead of adapting himself/herself to circumstances? Everyone prefers a higher position, an employer, and a master rather than a lower position, an employee, and a slave. Everyone wants to do his/her own ways if possible. This can be applied to artists. Cezanne, a famous the post—impressionist painter, preferred to paint still life rather than landscapes or human subjects, because still—lives allowed him to control the scene.

A landscape can be a good subject for artists because of its beautiful scenery, but it is very difficult for artists to select the right viewpoint for the uncontrollable landscape. The scenery which is good for artists may be unbalanced for painting. The landscape can show different meanings according to the viewpoint. Paul Cezanne, who was born at Aix, the ancient capital town of Provence on Jan 19, 1839, had also taken long trips in his youth to find landscapes suitable for his motif.

Portrait painting is also not easy for artists to control. It is very hard for human models to sit quietly and get along with the artist for a long time until the artist finishes his/her painting. Human models have needs of the body such as eating, sleeping and going to the bathroom. Therefore, artists often use the still—life for painting with human models. "Woman with Coffee Pot" painted by Cezanne in 1890 to 1895 is a good example of this.

Furthermore, the still life is easily controlled by artists. The viewpoint is changeable. So, artists can arrange the still-life's however they want: they may set one flower base or two flower bases, they may dispose apples or pears, and they may or may not use fruit dishes. The artist can control the objects to create the harmony. "Still-life with Fruit Basket", 1888–1890, clearly shows Cezanne's strong interests in creating order and harmony. He created "the impression of random composition", which says Richard W. Murphy in the book, The World of Cezanne by rearranging the objects suitable for his motif.

In conclusion, still life is better than others for painting. Paul Cezanne also preferred to paint still life rather than landscapes or portraits because he wanted to be the controller instead of being the controlled.

What Religious Faith Means to Me?

I have no religion, but I accept the teachings of any religion. I am sure that every religion teaches us the same thing. I can understand every religion's insistence, because I have diversified experiences of reading religious books and interacting religious people.

I have met a lot of people who have different religion, different positions and different ways of thinking. After all, I have reached to several conclusions: 1) Every religion except quasi-religion teaches the same thing. It is love. 2) Someone who insists that his or her religion is the truth, and the others are the false is not religious. 3) Human being is made of body, spirit, and soul. Death means separating the soul from the body. When a man dies, the body returns to earth, the soul returns to the original place where it had been before it was combined with its body, and the spirit is vanished.

I hate the fanatic and the people who are different between their words and behaviors. I know the meaning of Christian. It means "like Jesus Christ". But unfortunately, most Christians are not like Jesus Christ. They are corrupted and morally ruined more than non-Christians. I met a lot of Buddhist scriptures by their lips, but many of them are frauds to seek for their own profits. I read and heard many articles about Muslims who are terrorists to kill people. I know that most of wars from the beginning history until nowadays were begun because of religion. The said religious people have destroyed peace and love even though every religion has taught peace and love. Do you have the right to kill others by the reason they have different religion?

Have you ever thought about this? If Jesus were I, how did he do this? Would he do like I did? If Buddha were I, how would he do in this case? I am sure the religious faith is not in the book, not in the words, not in your knowledge, but it's in your heart. Don't say "I'm a Christian". Don't say "I'm a Buddhist". Don't say "I'm a Muslim". Instead of them, love others as Jesus did, give yours to others as Buddha did, and stop to kill Mohamed won't want it. This is my religious faith.

The Changing of the Seasons Means

When I was a child, I had been waiting Seol—Nal, January 1st, or Chu—seok, August 15th in lunar calendar which are Korean traditional holidays, because I could have got some new cloths or gifts from my parents on those special days. I had nothing to worry about. The only thing I did was playing with friends: playing at fields and hills, shuttlecock with the feet, spinning a top, swimming, and skating.

When I was a teen—ager, every middle school, high school and college had an entrance examination to select good students. I had to study very hard for entering a better high school and a better college over all the competition. School life was too tight for me to feel the changing of seasons. But I enjoyed my college life by going picnic in spring, swimming in summer, hiking in fall, and playing game in winter. Season by season and year by year was challengeable and full of expectation for the future.

After I got married, time passing has not been cheerful any more. I had to prepare or provide something suitable for my parents, my wife and my children every season. I have been too busy to have any allowance for feeling season's changing. If spring comes, I had to provide money for my children's tuition, maybe new cloths for my wife and children, and gifts for my mother's birthday. If summer comes, I had to provide money for summer vacation and gifts for my father's birthday. In fall money for Chu—seok, in winter, money for preparing cold season and for Seol—Nal. Everyday life has been tightened with struggling against money.

However, I do not complain about my burdens (someone say it is burden). I am happy because of these burdens. My family can be happy with me. I thank God to have given me a beautiful wife, clever children, and a positive thinking and a healthy body. Day by day and season by season means a tunnel to go to happiness. Without me, who can make them happy?

When I get older in the future, I may be waiting my children's coming to see me with gifts for me.

In conclusion, the changing of the seasons means to me: expectations in child, dreams in youth, happiness in adult, and expectation again in old.

Weekends Give Me Time to ...

I am enjoying my life here in America. My company dispatched me to Chicago for three months for the purpose of my English training. However, I think I came here not only for English training but also for experiencing American culture. I have been busy every day since I came here in Chicago and being busy would be continued until I return to my country.

I usually use the weekends for long trips which make me know more about America. I had a car–driving along the Lake Michigan for twenty hours at the weekend. During the driving, I saw "What the nature is." from the blessed country.

I also had a tour to Washington D.C. at the weekend. During the tour, I found "Why America is leading the world." from the government building and museum.

During my stay in America, I want to visit several other places such as Niagara Falls, Disney land, and a few of American national parks.

I am not sure when I can come again to America. This is the best chance for me to know more about America, Americans, American culture and nature. Weekends give me good possibilities to know about human and nature.

Everything depends upon one's MIND.

My favorite proverb is "一切唯心造" which means everything depends upon one's mind. MIND can save you and also can kill you. Someone say, 'Be positive' instead of 'Be negative". But MIND is a little different from the word 'positive' or 'negative'.

What is the difference between MIND and THINK? THINK is in your head. It can be changed by education and training. But MIND is in your heart. It cannot be changed. MIND is as it was from the beginning.

Who are you? Is your face you? Are your eyes you? Is your mouth you? No, those are not you, but yours. Mind is you. Yours are your slaves, while MIND is your master. Your mind is your soul which God gave you.

How can you find MIND? i.e., how can you find yourself? MIND can be grown up by love. MIND cannot be grown up without love. If you win a lottery, if you are promoted, if you pass an exam, or if you take delicious food and so on, your 'THINK' or your desire will be happy. But if you secretly perform good deeds, or if you give a love to others and tell none, your 'MIND' will be happy.

The more you do good things, the more your MIND is grown up. Everything depends upon your mind. Keep on loving.

SEOL-NAL, the Lunar New Year's Day

There are two New Year's Days in Korea, Solar and Lunar New Year's Day. Koreans have reckoned time according to the lunar calendar since the beginning of Korean history. The lunar New Year's Day is called SEOL—NAL which is one of the biggest traditional holidays of the year, even in modern times.

For thousands of years, many traditional events have been held on SEOL—NAL. One of those is New Year's obeisance which children make to their parents and grandparents and the younger people to the older people. Ancestral ceremonies are another one. After ancestral ceremonies, people visit the ancestor's graves and thank for their care for safety and richness with deep bows. Then, people go around the neighborhood to offer New Year's greetings to older neighbors.

In 1910, Korea became the first country invaded by Imperial Japan. For the first twenty years, the colonial rulers used a conciliatory policy for Koreans. SEOL—NAL could be maintained even though the traditional events were not faithful enough as a colony. In 1930, the rulers changed their colonial policy to a pressure policy in which Korean traditions barely kept in existence.

When Word War II ended in 1945, Koreans disappointed again to SEOL—NAL due to the western culture instead of the colonial rule. For four decades, the government has tried to replace the New Year's Day form the lunar to the solar calendar. Korean government made a law of three-day holiday for solar New Year and a working day for the lunar New Year. But people still held on the traditional lunar New Year Day. At last, in 1986, the government was forced to make the lunar New Year Day an official holiday.

Nowadays, Koreans gather at the eldest descendants' home on SEOL-NAL and perform the ancestral ceremonies which have been done for thousands of years.

SEOL-NAL, the lunar New Year' Day, is the biggest traditional holiday in Korea.

When Someone Important Dies...

Death is one of processes in life. I mean that LIFE in this case is not limited to the life in this world, but it is extended after death. Once you agree to my opinion, every death has the same meaning. You may have a bigger regret for an important person's death than a common person's one, because the important person would have performed the more important things for the world. Are you with me?

God made human being as his feature by using soils and gave him his breath. Then, it became 'living soul'. God called him Adam (Gen. Chapter 1). Human being is made of BODY (soils) and SOUL (breath).

If your soul is separated from your body, you die. Death means SOUL separating from BODY. What will happen after death? BODY will go back to soils, and SOUL will go back to the place where it came from… to God (Christians say), to the origin if it is completed (Buddhists and Zennists say).

SOUL is you and BODY is not you. BODY is yours while SOUL is in this world. You (SOUL) existed before you borrowed your body and will exist after your body is separated from your soul.

Once you accept my theory about death, you never feel sad about anyone's death. You would accept indifferently someone's death. You would think of his/her life in this world whoever he/she is.

Buddhists and Zennists say that SOUL cannot go back to the origin unless it is completed in this world. How to make it complete? The answer is LOVE. SOUL can be grown up by eating LOVE. If you do LOVE without telling it anyone, your soul will be grown up. Grown up, grown up, and grown up by doing love, love, love…. and finally, your soul will be completed.

In conclusion, when someone important dies, I will remind his/her life in this world and will imagine that he/she is with God or at the origin.

The Exit Writing Test Was...

It was not easy for me to write an essay within a limited time. But it was a good chance for me to measure my writing ability. I have learned very well about how to write an essay, and also learned the difference between essay and journal. I was surprised to know that Americans had been trained by the scientific ways of thinking from the childhood. As I know, Koreans are never trained by that way, and they don't know how to write essay unless they major at literature. In order to write a good essay within a limited time, we must have a wide knowledge about the various topics. The exit writing test reminded me the proverb: 'Knowledge is power'.

Guidance to Niagara Tour

A two−day tour for Niagara Falls was quite suitable for seeing a lot of views of the falls.

On the first day, we lodged American side of Niagara Falls. We went to Goat Island which was located at the just upper side of Niagara Falls. We enjoyed our trip by seeing the nature itself at the closest point of view and by walking along the walkway around the island.

On the second day, we moved to Canadian side and took a tourist bus which took us to the various places. We also took a ship, the Maid of the Mist, which took us to the nearest point of the falls.

If we visited Niagara Falls for only one day, we could not enjoy a lot due to the short time. I would like to recommend other people to take a two—day trip to Niagara Falls.

Different Kinds of Friends

I have many friends. My friend can be grouped to about five groups according to the time I made friendship with them.

The first group is my childhood friends. I can meet them on SEOL—NAL or CHUSEOK, because we usually visit our hometown to see our parents. I keep in touch with them continuously. The friendship shall be continued until I die.

The second group is my middle school friends. My friends have various kinds of jobs. A store owner, a mechanic, a postman, a government office, or a salesman···. We meet periodically in order to exchange friendship and help each other in difficulties.

The third group is my closest friends. I met BYEONGJAE and PANGYU at the dormitory when I was in high school. We three were roommates for two years. We can understand each other very well. I am sure we've already been beyond the normal friendship. We are in the status that our friendship is more important than our families. We can imagine each other's life without calling for long time. We can understand each other's feeling without any words. BYEONGJAE and PANGYU are my best friends.

The fourth group is my university friends. I had a lot of meaningful activities and enjoyed my university life with them. However, I have not had much relationship after I graduated from university. I hope I can meet them with their accompanying families – wives and children.

The fifth group is my company's colleagues. These friends are also important to me, because I have to do my works with these colleagues. When someone asks, "What do you do for living", this question implies "Job is for living". My job is important for me and my family's living. Therefore, my friends at the company are also important for my living. They can help me at any kind of situations. I must keep good relationship with them.

Friendship means the different meanings according to the time when I made friendship with them.

An Introduction to Korea

When Americans meet an oriental person, they usually ask "Are you Japanese?" If the oriental person says "No," they ask again "Chinese?" If the answer is still "No," they finally ask "Korean?" In spite that many Americans don't have much knowledge about Korea, Korea is a country which is traditionally courteous, economically developing, and politically facing problems.

Koreans are very proud of their unique race over the long history of 9,000 years. They have some special traditions which are quite different from other countries. The most staple food in Korea is sticky rice and some fermented side dishes such as Kimchi and bean sauces. The eldest son in a family is very important to succeed the family's traditions. Men are more powerful than women in many parts of society. Korean's desire for education is so strong that most people in Korea graduate college. The most honorable tradition in Korea is the act that younger people always respect older people.

After World War II ended, Koreans had been terrible for 20 years. However, Koreans made a successful development of their economy. Korea has been rapidly developing since 1960's. Nowadays the industries of semi-conductors and steel making are the leading group all over the world. And several industries such as automobile manufacturing, ship building, and electronics have good competitive power in the world. Koreans are willing to help people in Africa, Bosnia, Bangladesh, and even North Korea.

Meanwhile, Korea is the only one country whose territory is still divided into two. The people who live in North Korea are the same as the people in South Korea. However, North Korea's political leaders are so dangerous that other countries cannot rely on them. When Koreans and Americans helped them with some food which would be delivered to the starving people in North, the political leaders used the food for military soldiers. And they are still in the suspicion of developing nuclear weapons. South Korea is facing a different political issue which is the present government is going to the left—hand side. The political parties are divided in two opinions and debating every day without use: Which has higher priority, growth or distribution? Which is better, modification or abandonment of National Security Laws? Moving capital to a local area is constitutional or not constitutional? Most Koreans are now tired on their useless debates and not concerned about politics.

In conclusion, Korea has not been well known to western countries for many centuries. However, Korea will be a famous country within a few decades, because the highly educated Koreans are doing their best to establish their future to be a powerful country.

제4부 미국생활

LMC에서
영어공부를 할 때(2001)
쓴 글들

* LMC(Los Medanos College) : California주 Pittsburg 소재 Community College

Pittsburg Sea Food Festival

Corrupted Politics

Politics has been since the beginning of human history. But in the ancient times, even in the Middle Ages, politics did not have the meaning that it has. Politics was merely the relation of ruling and obedience and politicians meant only the ruling classes.

Politics as an actual meaning was begun from the democratic government in the modern ages. The government must be for the people in democracy. Therefore, politics must be for providing the happiness of the people. Nevertheless, politics has merely been for the people, but has mostly exploited the people.

Most of all politicians have been corrupted. The more undeveloped the country is, the more corrupted the politicians are. The politicians in undeveloped and under-developing countries are corrupted autocrats and liars. The politicians in developed countries are corrupted liars.

I can enumerate a lot of examples for proving it.

— Philippines former president Ferdinando Marcos and Indonesian former president Soeharto were ousted by the people because of their illegal accumulation of wealth.
— Korean former presidents Chun and Noh were jailed under the new government because of their profiteering.
— Peru former president Alverto Fujimori was dismissed from the congress by his corruption.
— Japanese former Prime Minister Tanaka was prosecuted by his illegal property.
— Do you remember how Chile's former president Pinnochette is?

I could find a lot of articles about politicians' corruption and lies in the recent newspapers.

— Philippines' president Estrata quit after besetting by scandal.
— Indonesian president Wahid censured because of involvement in two corruption scandals.
— Israel's president Weizman resigned due to the financial misleading

— Israel's prime minister dropped by his wrongdoing

— Russian ex—premier Chernomydin has a secret Swiss bank account

— Mexican president Zedill accused of corruption

I don't think it is necessary to make a list of politician lies. But I am sure above 90 % of politicians are not free from their illegal political fund—raising. These are a few outstanding samples of politicians' lies.

— Richard Nixon has lied to the American people time and time again of Watergate scandal.

— And also, Bill Clinton has lied to the American people time and time again of Monica Lewinsky scandal.

— French former president Miteran and religious leader Jessy Jaxon hided their concubine and daughter.

In conclusion, people in every country vote for the honest, the servant, the leader who can lead them to the place of happiness, health and peace. Because they believe that politics is for the people, by the people, for the people.

Thank you for your listening.

Family Name

I have a project meeting every other Wednesday.

I had a new member, Gary, last week. I made the minutes of meeting after the meeting and distributed it by e—mail to all attendees. After a while, Gary came to my office.

"Hey. Young. The meeting was good, in time, good discussion and can you correct my name Gary O'Brien, not Gary O'brian."

"I am terribly sorry to change your family name. I'll correct it right away."

"Oh, that's all right, it's not a big deal, not a big deal."

To write a wrong family name is a big mistake in Korea. You could change his/her root of family by using the wrong family name. I think it's the same case in the U.S.

I usually play golf with my Korean staffs every weekend. In case that I play golf with Americans by chance, I used to be diffident by American's long distance of drive shot.

One day I was playing with my Korean friends just by the green which was about 300 yards far from the teeing area. Suddenly a ball flied and dropped just nearly to me. If the ball hit me, I might be injured. When we were moving to the next hole, the American who hit the ball came close to us and spoke.

"I am very sorry."

"That's O.K, no problem."

일범의 평범한 사람 이야기

"I apologize for it"

"No problem, don't mention it."

You must be careful not to hit other players by the ball you hit.

Anyway, I envy American's power to be able to hit the ball so long distance.

Interview about American Football

I: Nice to meet you Gary, I am very glad to have an interview with you. I want to know about American football and American holidays.

My first question is: What is the age of American football player start football?

G: Ah—— they have differently, generally they have flag football with the kids starting with six years old. Um the clever kids have full contact with their hit their helmet. And past generally they have about 9 years old to get their full contact, so um they can start from 6 years old generally.

I: I see. Ah—— is it just for guys or girls?

G: Oh, that's changed recently. Primarily in the past to get half in all guys playing, but the more you hear you girls but whatever playing over the rear extra the college football in the division one triple A.

I: O.K, and is college team paid for the game?

G: Well I guess what the college administrator think of it as paid by getting the education what they get it Scholarships, and uh so but money in the pocket no there not supposed to anyway and sometimes you without about in discretion in certain colleges with players are gotten paid, but generally no, there is not supposed to get paid again to get uh a good brake on the education that is primarily what is set up in the education.

I: That is totally amateurism.

G: Yes, yeah totally

I: Could you explain the scoring system of American Football?

G: Yea, there is uh four ways, Let me count them. Now you have a touch-down that is won your team won of the other opponent goal line with the ball. That is won 6 points. A fewer go it when after the kick the ball through the upright um that won 3 points. You have an extra point and that's after touching down you actually a line up the ball line up kick uh the ball 1 point. There is also a uh defense of way of scoring point that's a safety uh and that is also won 2 points.

I: O.K, thank you. And how many players generally play one game one team?

G: Well on offense is 11, and defense is 11. Usually, they are likely to carry about 40 players and so on. a team. In high school, maybe a little bit more than that, but generally like to keep that the number around 40. In professional football they also have a uh what they call a people are reserved and those player that incase one of the players on the starting 40, not starting 40, but on the 40, get hurt connect call them up as a reserved and a play man.

I: O.K, and uh I want to know many people play in high school and how many percent of them go to the football player in college or pro team?

G: Um I remember read an article that generally what happens they say a half percent of high school players go to a 4-year college, and then I heard a half of percent of college players go in player of pro, and so start in high school you actually have a half of a half of half percent make a high school players, so not go many.

I: And the last question about American football. Why is American football so popular in America? Everybody is very crazy to watch TV and playing game.

G: Well, do you know they always say that the baseball in America past time, But I don't see that I think that because of violence of the ball, because of so many players in balls. In the game in the high school ranks about the people can probably relate the high school games. I think forth passes now baseball as America's #1 spectacular in sports. But I think a lot of must do of always action a lot of there are some violence on the field. Um people just willing to just watch them.

I: O.K, Thank you.

(보통의 미국인들은 발음이 불분명하고, 문장은 비문법적이라, 익숙치 않은 한국인들은 정말 알아듣기 힘들다. 그냥 알아들은 체하는 것이지.)

Interview about American Holidays

I: Nice to meet you again Gary, I just came here in America last July, so I am not so familiar about the American holidays. You know Feb.19th is the holiday in America as the president day. What the Presidents' Day means?

G: Yea, we celebrate the Feb.19 this year. Basically, that's a combination of George Washington who is our first president and Abraham Lincoln and combined days Feb. for Presidents' Day. Why is so good is that basically we get paid for stayed at home.

I: I see.

G: No, there are two for probably most uh important of the country, so we do celebrate again.

I: Besides the president day, what are the important holidays in U.S?

G: Important holidays. Um if you think of it, it will probably July 4th as far as what probably means when we get independent. Yea so independent day, so, probably as a holiday. Probably the largest holiday in a lot of good over, American Catholicism is probably American Christmas, as when uh people are lined up for day a month ahead of time. So as far as important in USA, it's the independent day July 4th.

I: And how many continuous holidays do you have? Two days holidays, three days holidays like that.

G: Yes, we only have one holiday, uh uh sometimes it's observed for two but of course Christmas 25th. If you're meaning by off work pay for the day that depends upon where you work in, here in POSCO we actually have to get pay for 24th, 25th of December, and also, I believe the day before thanksgiving and thanksgiving uh. But a holiday, Young, is one day.

I: O.K. So, on the Thanksgiving Day, we don't work for three days.

It depends on company.

G: It depends. If thanksgiving falls on Thursday, they don't work on Thursday, Friday, so we're four days weekend.

I: Do you have Father's Day, Mother's day or children's day here?

G: Well, we have Father's Day, we have Mother's day. And I remember asking my parent one time "When's the children's day?" They answered, "Every day."

I: Everyday?

G: Yea, we do have Mother's Day, Father's day.

I: O.K, we have children's day in Korea.

G: Is that right?

I: Yes.

G: That's good.

I: On that day every child wants to go play ground, as roller coaster.

G: Oh, well.

I: And some kinds of enjoy ————

G: Really? Do they day—off work so parents to do for their children——

I: Yes, off course. Presents must take care their children.

G: That's great.

I: Special day.

G: Do you know what day it is?

I: Yes.

G: What is?

I: 5th of May.

G: Here you go.

I: O.K, and what kind of holidays related to Christianity?

G: Um − Palms Day, some of the major ones is probably Easter, umm and I can probably Christmas.

I: How about Good Friday?

G: Good Friday also right, exactly that's off course right around Easter.

I: And what do Americans usually do on holidays?

G: Um huh huh huh, Yea to me umm, in summer, July 4th off course it's depend on the holidays. July 4th, Labor Day's another one. Generally, they like a 3 days weekend somewhat make a camping outdoor stuff. Christmas, New Year will safety program maybe have a drink too. Uh and but I would say about Christmas at mostly have a family time where family get together and thanksgiving. It's a time for family come together and umm appreciates each other's company, sometimes they have each other for a wild try to make a holiday and as far as family get together. Um I would like to probably Christmas and thanksgiving primarily will be for family make a big effort to try to come together.

I: So in any time we need a lot of money.

G: Oh. Money always, Yea money always helps for some family to take relaxes.

I: O.K, thank you very much.

G: O.K

Reflection about Social Relationships

In the book titled, American Ways, the writer, Gary Althen, explained that social relationships such as customer & service people, tenant & landlord, neighbors, co—workers, courtesy, schedules, gifts and friendship are very essential for people's life, and also suggested some general ideas for foreign visitors to be involved in relationships with Americans.

Americans seem very kind and friendly at first, but are so private and have the thick walls which protect themselves from others. It takes a relatively long time to break down the wall and open each other's mind. It is quite different from Korea. In Korea, the very personal questions such as "where are you going?" or "what are you going for?" are used as the common greeting like "Hello" or "Hi" in America. I totally agree the writer's opinion that Americans' relationship with other people is "superficial". But I disagree to the writer on what many Americans are too busy to have the time that is required to get to know another person well. As my opinion, Americans are to bound in their family to have relations with others.

American ways in customer, tenant and neighbor are spreading rapidly to other countries which are being industrialized. We have a proverb in Korea: "Neighbors are cousins". The neighbors nearby are much better than the relatives far away. The Americans' general rule among neighbors, "Mind your own business" is too terrible for me to accept it.

Korean workers generally spend their times more in company than in home. So, the company is home away from home and the co—workers are also family members. Therefore, we respect the president at our company as our father at home.

Saying "Please" and "Thank you" is probably oriented from the gun men during the western frontier age. If they hadn't said "Thank you", "You're welcome", "Please" or "Excuse me", they might have been shot.

Waiting patiently in a queue is very good courtesy which every people must follow. American ways of gifts is quite different from Korean's. Gifts in Korea often mean "Thanks for some favors" or "Bribes for expecting some favors", but gifts in America are always the symbol of love. We must imitate the American ways of gifts.

Finally, I appreciate to the writer's advice for foreign visitors like as me: "Take the initiatives, but go slowly", "Make notes" and "Patient, but persistent".

Making Friends with Americans

- Three techniques useful in making American friends
  1) Drop your negative judgments
  2) Work on your language and communication skills
  3) Convince Americans that you want to meet them

- How to convince Americans that you want to meet them
  1) Join a club at school or participate in a sport
  2) Join clubs and organizations outside school
  3) Demonstrate your skills and talents
  4) Smile
  5) Be yourself

- Some benefits of making American friends
  1) To increase the self-confidence
  2) To increase the understanding cultures
  3) To adjust more quickly to the new environment
  4) To improve the communication skills
  5) To gain a larger perspective

- I have felt that Americans are very friendly since I had come to U.S.A last year.

  Because they say "Hi" or "How are you doing?" to the foreigners at first with smile, and they are so kind that they try to explain completely to my questions.

- Difficulties anticipated in my attempt to make friends with Americans.

  1) Misunderstanding of their meaning

  2) Incorrect expression of my opinion

  3) Embarrassment by cultural differences

  4) My own characteristics may not seem as it is

American Slangs

Last Tuesday morning, I was hurrying to attend the morning meeting with my boss. I met one of my colleagues in front of the door of my boss's office and said, "Good morning, Lynnette". She replied, "Good morning, how are you?" "Fine, Thanks. How are you?" And she said, "Hanging inner". I was embarrassed because I could not understand what she said. But she explained immediately that 'hanging in there' means 'pretty good'.

I think I don't have many difficulties in everyday communication. But

일범의 평범한 사람 이야기

I am being stressed so much due to my poor listening comprehension at the meetings in my company in which a lot of slang and the chopped English are used.

In the afternoon, I asked one of my colleagues how he felt about slang. Most Americans use a lot of slang every day. It makes me be excluded from their conversations.

I bought a slang dictionary, but I could not use it, because I could not catch the correct spelling of it.

The following words are the slang I have heard since I came here in U.S last year.

- cool: very good (many years ago, 'hot' also had the same meaning)
- bad: very good
- It's gross: It's very bad
- kick down: give, permit
- kicked out: out of order
- kicked to the curb: discarded
- fire away: go ahead
- out of the blue: suddenly
- buff: clean
- buffed: muscular
- freeze: don't move
- cold: mean, agree

It may take a long time for me to be familiar with the various kinds of slang. But the best way to be Americanized is maybe to understand American slang.

Tips for the first visitors to Korea

Congratulations your first visit to Korea! I'd like to give some tips about Korean cultures for your good trip.

The Incheon international airport which opened three years ago is so big and convenient. You can rent a cellular phone at the stores in the airport building as soon as you pass immigration and customs. You can take bus or taxi to your hotel in Seoul which is the capital with a population of over ten million. Buses are more convenient and cheaper than taxi. The driver's seat is at the left in car which is the same as in the U.S.

When you meet someone, a slight bow is appropriate especially to the older person than you are. It is polite manners to comment to the good health of an older person. Koreans use their names, the family name first, the given name last. Calling first names is not common as well as in the U.S. Mr. or Mrs. So—and—so is good.

Korean's staple food is boiled rice. They normally take it three times a day, even breakfast. Many Korean foods are fermented such as Kimchi and Deonjang (a kind of fermented bean). Korean foods are very hot and sour. I'd like to recommend you try Kalbi (a beef) and Haejangkuk (a soup good after heavy drinking). Most restaurants serve all courses of a meal at once. However, eating foods in class or in a meeting is not polite.

Koreans are very kind to foreigners, but their English are very poor, except some people. If you ask their helps for your directions, please write and show them instead of only speaking. Their reading comprehension is much better than their listening ability. If you speak clearly and slowly to students, they would highly appreciate to you.

Nose blowing is rude in public. If you are invited to a person's home, be sure to remove your shoes before entering the person's house inside. And also, be sure to take a modest gift (such as flowers), offering the gifts with both hands. Bear in mind that it is considered polite not to open a gift in front of the person giving it.

Korean peninsula is divided in two. The south is democratic, and the north is communist. The political situations are not so good. Health, family, hobbies and America are the recommendable conversation topics.

The consumer price is higher than the U.S. but the currency of Korean won to U.S. dollar is around 1,100 to 1. So, you can enjoy your trip very cheap.

Have great days in Korea!

LMC에서
영어공부를 할 때(2004)
쓴 글들

(ESL Conversation / Pronunciation II)

Attention to Neighbors

When I came to LMC, located E. Leland Road, Pittsburg, last week, I couldn't find the campus building. Because the scene that I was seeing was very different from that I had seen three years ago. There were a lot of groundbreaking areas for constructing something. I asked a man who looked like a student where LMC campus building was. He was not sure either, but he knew which building was gym. Walking along a narrow road to the campus, I found a map which showed the general layout for the future LMC campus in 2007.

I took a class at LMC three years ago. I have lived in Antioch, a neighboring city to Pittsburg, I have worked at USSPOSCO in Pittsburg for last four years. Furthermore, I have used Loveridge Road and E. Leland Road almost every day. But I didn't know what's going on LMC. How have I so unconcerned to my neighbors? Have I focused only to my own interests for last several years? I was not a heartless man in Korea. Is living in America so stressful enough for me not to have concerns about my friends and neighbors? What did I do in America last four years? Is my English improved a lot? – No. Is my knowledge about my job upgraded to the higher level? – No. Did I make many new American friends? – No. Can I understand American life culture better than before? – No. And then, do I play golf much better than before? – No. What have I done in America for last four years?

Coming back to LMC campus was a good momentum for me to

look back my life. I think having attentions to my neighbors can make my life more valuable. I pledged myself to have concerns about my neighbors more than I have had so far.

A Friend's Visit

B.J, my best friend, who lives in Korea, has had tours to foreign countries almost every year. I asked him to come to America when I visited Korea last year. He and his family finally came to America and visited me last July. I made a well—organized tour schedule for his family before they arrived here. Reservation of hotels and tickets, meals plan, driving distance per day, and sightseeing points for each day were included in the tour schedule.

On the first day, I took them from SFO and led them to see Pacific Ocean, Golden Gate Park, Golden Gate Bridge, Bay Bridge, Twin Peaks, China town, Pier 39, and Tilden Park in Berkeley. They enjoyed the beautiful San Francisco even though they were not adjusted themselves to the time difference between Korea and America.

On the second day, I took them to Lake Tahoe and rent a motorboat. We enjoyed speedy boating for about two hours. Boating at Lake Tahoe is cool enough to recommend to the first visitors to America because the package tour of any tour company does not have this activity.

On the third day, I took them to Yosemite National Park not only to

Yosemite village but also to Glacier Point and Sierra Nevada Mountains. B.J and his wife drove a rent car during the journey to Sierra Nevada Mountains. Any package tours never guide the tourists to Glacier Point and Sierra Nevada Mountains because tourist buses cannot reach there.

For a week from the fourth day, I took them to Las Vegas, Grand Canyon, Walnut Canyon in Flagstaff, Sedona, San Diego, and Los Angeles. I showed them the great nature, the history of the Native Americans, the development of America, and every possibility in America. I also tried to lead them experience American life and feel American culture as possible as I could.

I had several calls from him after he returned to Korea. He always said that he never forgets my treatment to him, it was totally different from any package tour he had ever before. He appreciated to my endeavor for him and his family. But I would say it's my duty, because I am his friend living in America. It was my pleasure to guide them for better tour in America.

The Watcher at the Gates

Summary of "The Watcher at the Gates"

In the article titled, "The Watcher at the Gates", the author, Gail Godwin, claims that many writers have an inside critic who restrains their creative thinking and explains how he could free from his inside critic. The inside critic which he called "The Watcher at the Gates" will go to keep you from the pursuing the flow of your imagination and grow self—important eccentricities. Watchers can appear in various ways: sometimes it makes you wastepaper, sometimes it makes you stop wring in the middle of your work, and sometimes it leads you to do something else which is not required for your work. The author suggests various ways of overcoming or outdistancing the Watchers: writing too fast to meet the deadlines, disguising what you are writing, looking for situations which look urgent, having the common inspiration with your Watcher, and keeping your Watcher in shape and he'll have less time to keep you from shaping. These are all helpful for you to free from your Watcher and keep your work done well.

My response to "The Watcher at the Gates"

When I previewed Gail Godwin's "The Watcher at the Gates" and even after I reread the article carefully, I could not understand what he wrote about. I read and read again the article with the help of English

Korean dictionary, but I still had some difficulties to understand the author's intention on his article. First, it was not clear for me the relation between "The Watcher" and Freud. Secondary, it was also unclear why he quoted Schiller. Third, why he named the inside critic "The Watcher at the Gates" was not clear. Forth, I have still some words of which meanings been unfamiliar even though I looked up dictionary, for examples, looker-uppers, run dry, clothesline, off-guard, dustheap, and dash off. I have tried to write the summary and my response every day since the last class, but I had failed every day with some excuses: leave it until tomorrow − today is the first day (Thursday), I have my vocabulary problem − I tried to do it − but I can't (Friday), I'll do it after golfing (Saturday), and American ways of thinking is so different from mine − I can't understand their expressions (Sunday). I finally could finish my writing on Monday afternoon just before I came to class. I think I understood how "The water" works inside me.

A Family Tradition

The lunar New Year Day called 'SEOL−NAL' is the biggest holiday of the year in Korea. For thousands of years, many traditional events have been held on SEOL−NAL. The first one is New Year's obeisance. Every son and daughter make a deep bow to his/her parents and grandparents and the younger people make to their older relatives. Parents and the older give good words to their children and the younger for another blessed year.

The second one is the ancestral sacrifices. The relatives gather and perform ancestral sacrifices to their ancestors. People visit to their ancestors' graves after the sacrifices and have peaceful times, feeling the nature and planning the future. Then, they go around the neighborhood to offer New Year greetings to the older neighbors. According to the industrialization and the success of population policy in Korea, it has been difficult for many relatives to gather altogether on SEOL-NAL. But there are still millions of people who visit hometowns on SEOL-NAL in Korea.

However, everything was changed after I moved to America. The Lunar New Year Day is not a holiday in America. I must work at company and my children have to study at school. I come out of home before my children get up in the morning. New Year's obeisance and the ancestral sacrifices are physically impossible.

I and my family are gradually being Americanized year by year. It is good for living in America, but I am worrying about my children in the future when we return to Korea. The good memory of SEOL-NAL is remained in my mind.

일범의 평범한 사람 이야기

Summary of "Shawshank Redemption"

Red came to Shawshank prison twenty years old for murder. At the prison, he met Andy Dufresne who was unjustly charged with murder of his wife and her lover and sentenced to life imprisonment. Andy has been a vice president of a large bank on the outside. Shawshank was like hell where only hideous, heinous criminals were confined. Red, Andy and other prisoners were treated like beasts under the incredible suppressions and barbarous guards. The inadaptable prisoners can easily be killed by guards and some prisoners were raped by the violent gay prisoners. One day, Andy helped Hardley, the chief warden, to solve tax problem. After that, Andy became to work as an accountant for the prison and as a secretary for the chief warden. After 19 years in Shawshank prison, Andy met a new prisoner whose name was Tommy. Andy heard from Tommy of the real criminal who murdered his wife and her lover. Andy tried to have a chance to be judged again by the fair justice, but the warden denied Andy's request and killed Tommy instead because of worrying about his secrets be opened by Andy. Andy made up his mind to escape from prison after a lot of afflictions and despairs since Tommy killed. Andy finally escaped from prison with indescribable hardships and exposed the absurdity of the prison which led to the guards' restraint and the warden's suicide. Andy left to Pacific oceans with 'Hope of Freedom'. Red also left to the city of hope to meet Andy when he was paroled after twenty years in prison.

LMC

Los Medanos College (LMC) is the best college for me to improve my skills required for living in America. One advantage is its location. LMC is located near to my company in Pittsburg and also near my home in Antioch. Ten minutes is enough to go to class from my office, while it takes over thirty minutes to Diablo Valley College (DVC) in Pleasant Hill or Golden Gate University (GGU) Walnut Creek campus. I am taking an English class at LMC by using lunch time every Monday, Wednesday, and Friday. Another advantage is its chief tuition and fees. I paid $1,744 for a three−unit class last semester for my MBA at GGU. But I paid only $108 for a three−unit class this semester at LMC. The other advantage of LMC is its curriculum. LMC has a lot of open classes which are not degree applicable. Many part−time students including me can take any class for improving their skills without an obligation of degree. I am willing to take two classes every semester in the field of English, citizen, and business administration. The more I take classes, the more my skills are improved.

Analysis:

Unified paragraphs: focused on why LMC is the best college for me to study.

Well−developed paragraphs: Topic sentence (LMC is the best college for me to improve my skills required for living in America), Three Supporting ideas including examples and explanations.

Conclusion Coherent paragraphs: One advantage, while another, but, the other.

Father's life

My father's life was a model of people's lives in Korea during the last century. He was born in 1919. Korea became the first country invaded by Imperial Japan in 1910. Most Koreans except some betrayals were in poverty due to the Japanese rulers' pressure policy.

My father had been unhappy during his young ages. He never had the time to go to school. However, he could read and write Korean and Chinese character by the results of studying by himself.

"If I had graduated only an elementary school, everything would have changed. I would have been richer, higher, and more powerful," he used to tell me.

During World War II, he was forced to work at a mine in Japan without pay. The war ended on August 15, 1945, with the unconditional surrender of Japan. Nothing but poverty was waiting when he returned to his hometown.

"The only thing I could do was working hard every day. The earnings were not enough to feed my family, because I didn't have my own land. I had to tenant a farm." My father used to recollect the time when he had taken care of his family's meals as the eldest son.

After Korea achieved independence from Imperial Japan, It was divided into two, South and North. South Korea had a democratic government by the support of America and North Korea was taken by the Soviet Union and became communist country.

"There should be no one like me. I lost my father and wife on the same day. My father died in the morning and my wife died in the evening. Can you imagine how I felt when I buried my father and wife on the same day?" My father used to tell me about his miserable past when he was drunk.

The Korean War was the war between Democracy and Communist and was continued for three years in early 1950s. My father married again in the terrible disaster after the war. My father was fifteen years older than my mother. The difference of age generated the difference of thinking and behavior. My father and mother had the continuous struggles during their marriage. My father never overcame the generation gap with my mother until his death.

From 1960s to 1980s, Korea has been economically developed a lot. People in Korea had worked very hard to build a new wealthy country.

They never wanted to hand over the poverty to their next generation. My father also worked day and night to escape from the poor life.

"Escaping from poverty was my priority at that time. When it was solved but not satisfactorily, my next goal was educating my children. That's because I thought that both wealth and high position are necessary for my next generation." My father used to emphasis his endeavors.

My father sacrificed himself in order to educate his children, three sons and three daughters. He expected to be rewarded for his sacrifice. He thought that his children would give back to him some of things when they have grown up. But the world was not changed as he expected. Most of the family which might consist of three generations had lived together in a home when the country was an agricultural society. Industrialization, however, has changed the concept of a family. Children had to be independent from their parents. They couldn't live with their parents at the same home anymore. Children were so busy trying to survive in the competitive world that they could not have much time to be with their parents. My father had the same situation as other families.

"I had starved a lot due to the lack of food. I had never come to school because of no money. But I have done my best to feed you, to educate you, and to support you. Now you are not so poor and do not lack of education, but I am alone. I need someone to talk with. I need some of you to be with me. But none of you, my kids, want to be with me. I am all alone." He used to tell his children when we met him on New Year holidays or Thanksgiving holidays.

My father committed suicide at the age 80. His country is developing based on his generation's hard working. His children are living with wealth and with happiness by the results of his sacrifice. My father's life had many ups and downs during the modernization period of Korea.

Business Trip to Korea

I had a business trip to Korea last week with nine Americans. The purpose of our trip was attending the technical exchange meetings which consisted of presentation and panel discussion at Dongbu steel and POSCO. I was the guide for our team. Going abroad was the first time for many of the participants. I had to spend many hours for preparing the trip before we left: checking the presentation materials, reserving hotels and transportations, daily meals plan, establishing every day's time schedule in detail, exchanging information with Korean partners about schedule, buying and wrapping gifts, and so on.

My role was started when we arrived at Incheon airport on Saturday evening. First, I rented a cellular phone and contacted to the rental bus driver to wait us at the exit gate. When we walked out after we exchanged us dollars to Korean money, it was rainy. The minibus was not big enough to carry ten people and their baggage. The bus took two and half hours from airport to our hotel which was the distance normally taking one and half hours. The bus driver had problems to find the main gate of our hotel in the rain. I had to apologize to our members for the inconveniences due to the bus driver. I complained to the tourist company about the inconvenience and asked to change the bus and the driver. But unfortunately, they could not arrange a new bus and driver available from Sunday. On Sunday, I guided our group to the Korean folk village where people could find out a lot of Korean traditional houses and customs. We also went to Etaewon which is the famous shopping street for foreigners. We enjoyed the first day in Seoul with shopping, drinking, and taking outback steak.

From Monday to Tuesday, we visited Dongbu Steel located in Asan Bay. The technical exchange meeting was very helpful to each company. We and Dongbu people had a lot of common issues as the Cold Rolling Mill. All our members had good experiences to take various kinds of Korean food. Two companies agreed to have not only the technical exchanges but also the cultural and managerial exchanges every year. From Wednesday to Thursday, we had the technical exchange meeting with POSCO which is in Pohang, southern east coast. I was very busy every day for checking flights, arranging schedules and meals, translating presentations and discussions, guiding tours, and meeting my old friends. Our members were very impressed to the state—of—the—art facilities and the clean & green steel works. Our group should be very proud of their mother company's technical leadership in the iron and steel manufacturing industries in the world. I learned a lot about Buddhism and temples from a tour guide at Bulguk temple on Thursday. It was a new experience for me.

On Friday, we had a site tour at Gwangyang steel works located in the southern coast. Gwangyang is the biggest iron and steel manufacturing works in the world. It has a lot of world records in capacity, operation, and facility reliabilities. Our group returned to Seoul on Friday evening and went to Etaewon again for enjoying the last night in Korea. There was a drinking house with darts and pools. Everybody drank too much and was hang over the next morning.

Many of us bought some gifts for their family at the duty—free shops in Incheon airport before we landed off. I slept during the most of flight from Incheon to San Francisco in order to adjust the time difference in America. When we returned the San Francisco International Airport safely, everybody appreciated to me for my arrangement and guidance for them during our trip. I also had a good experience of how to prepare the meetings, how to arrange the schedules, how to guide people, and how to take care of foreigners. When I came to my company the next week, they gave me a thanks—card with a gift certificate for golfing at Shadow Lakes Golf Course.

Golfing with My Wife

Golf is not an easy game but is one of my favorite sports. Because golf is not physically demanding as soccer or tennis, golf appeals to people all of ages. While in Korea, I used to go hiking with my wife. Since I came to the U.S.A. four years ago, I have played golf every weekend. That's because the green fees here in America are much cheaper than in Korea and there are no good mountains for hiking near here. Seeing how golf appeals to people of all ages, I started to push my wife to practice golf. This was done with the idea that playing golf with my wife would be fantastic.

It was almost one year ago when I went to a golf course with my wife for the first time. It was beautiful for golfing. The sun was shining. The breeze was. There were wild geese on the green fields eating grass. My wife looked very happy even before we started to hit the ball.

"I almost forgot what I learned from my Golf Instructor," my wife said, practicing swinging at the tee box of the first hole.

"There are only two rules in golfing: 'relax your shoulder' and 'keep your eyes on the ball', "I said.

At her first attempt to hit the ball, she swung her driver and hit nothing but air.

"Watch your ball until you finish your swing, don't raise your head until you hit the ball," I said.

Then she swung a second time and hit nothing but air again. On the third attempt, she hit the ground instead of the ball. Several players were waiting for their turn behind us, watching my wife's swing. I began to feel impatient.

"Golf is etiquette," I said nervously. "You must not delay the game for other players."

"I am not delaying the game intentionally. I also want to hit well," My wife said.

"Hit one more time. If you miss the ball again, we will place your ball at the position where my ball is." I spoke.

She finally hit the ball, but it flew only twenty yards ahead.

"Good shot!" I spoke.

Our first game took almost five hours. I pressed her to play quickly many times and she had to pick up her ball without hitting in order to keep the pace.

Golf is not an easy game for me, because I started it at my age 45 when my body was not so flexible. I have played for four years and my wife only for one year. My handicap is 22 and she usually hits around 110 strokes. But she looks to have the more carriers than I when we play golf. She is very self-possessed, and I am too short-tempered. She knows how to keep composure in a bad situation, while I lose my temper easily. My wife can enjoy golfing, but I am very strict and cruel to myself. My wife and I have had a lot of quarrels during golf.

"Damn it! Shit! Si—pal! How stupid I am!" I shouted when I hit the ground first, topped the ball or made a terrible slice / hook.

"Why do you say bad words?" She asked. "Your shouting can be a disturbance to other players".

"I'm not shouting to others, I'm angry to myself, I'm a donkey!"

"Take it easy! Getting angry can't solve the problem. How does shouting help you to make a good shot?" My wife tried to make me calm down.

"I know, but I am so stupid! I have played for four years, two or three times a week. How much money and time have I invested to golf? I'm almost same as I was when I started. My poor ability makes me get angry."

"We play golf to enjoy life, enjoy the fresh air, enjoy the green field, and enjoy the time we are together! These are the reasons we play golf every weekend, aren't they?"

"I know, but I'm …" I mumbled.

"Whenever you get so upset, I really feel like not playing with you again," My wife said with a disappointed look.

After my wife and I started to play golf together, we have played every weekend.

We try to play at different golf courses every time. There are hundreds of golf courses in Bay area. I have played at approximately fifty different golf courses for the last four years and my wife maybe about thirty. Every course has the different view, different points of interest, and different points of challenge. I like playing golf which is my only hobby and exercise in U.S.A. I can be refreshed by golf during weekend, and I can start the new week on Monday with energy. I specially love playing golf with my wife, because we can make happiness together and enjoy our lives.

My First Impression to American Steel Company

It was April 1990, almost fifteen years ago when I visited America for the first time. It was my second experience to visit foreign countries. The first one was three─ months' living in Tokyo, Japan in 1986. I had only good things in my mind about America: the most powerful and richest country, vast nature, freedom and equality, and the economic aids to the poor countries. The purpose of my visit was taking a technology training of Tin Plating at the electrolytic tinning lines in USS─POSCO Industries located in Pittsburg, California.

The training program consisted of a general plant tour, lectures, and detailed plant inspections. After the general plant tour on the first day, I thought that some of the facilities were too old to run efficiently. The lectures for one week were very impressive and helpful for me to understand the basic theories of Tinplating. The instructor, Mr. Kharouf, an expert in Tinplating from UEC was excellent. He had an ability to explain easily something complicated. He had so many experiences in teaching foreigners that he had no difficulties communicating the trainees who were poor in English. I thought America could not help being strong with this kind of powerful manpower.

Detailed plant inspections for two weeks surprised and confused me. UPI (USS—POSCO Industries) had two Electrolytic Tinning Lines, one established in 1958 and the other in 1962. The main power for the lines was generated by AC—motor generator which was too old technology to apply to modern steel facility. It was my first time to see that AC—motor generators were still working for generating DC power. There were rooms for operators on the line. All operating controls were being performed manually at the local panels located in the facility. Most panels were covered with thick dust, so I could not see the panel status clearly. Some panels had broken knobs and missing buttons. Labels on some panels were replaced with the bad handwriting. Nobody except the experienced workers at the line knew what switches/knobs for what were. A worker who wore a long—sleeve stripes T—shirt and dark jeans was pulling Tin anodes in the plating tanks by using a hook. Tin dust adhered to the DC—motors and the solidified tin—solutions flooded from the edges of the plating tanks. I couldn't breathe easily due to Tin—oxidation gas and Sulfuric acid gas which smelled like a rotten egg. When an over—head— crane ran running, the building was shaken and thundered.

The basement was worse than the process. The basement floor was so greasy that I had to be very careful not to slip. The solution circulating pipes were too entangled and no labels of arrows identified the flow of solution. Sludge accumulated in a pit showed how long ago the pit was pumped out.

Upstairs, a pair of inspection mirrors was located outside, not in a room. They were too dirty to inspect any defects on the strip surface. "How can you see the defects in these mirrors?" I asked to an inspector. "Experience!" he answered. A micron oiler was installed for oiling on the strip surface. The sight glasses through which operators could see the oil mist inside were too worn out. "How do you know the oiler is working properly?" I asked an operator. "Experience!" he answered again.

When the line was stopped for changing a roll which caused scratches on the strip surface, operators were doing nothing but resting on chairs. "What are you doing now? The line is stopped." I asked an operator. "Changing rolls is the maintenance guys' job, not the operators." He said.

I checked the quality of Tin coated steel product. Surprisingly, it was not so bad. The shape qualities such as wavy edges, coil sets, cross bows, and build—up pockets were good enough to be fed to the can manufacturing facilities. The surface qualities such as stains, dents, scratches, and brightness were also acceptable to customers even though they had some smudges.

I had to compare the competitive power between POSCO and UPI. POSCO had state-of-the-art facilities and well-organized teamwork. While UPI had the skilled operators and the strong technical background, they helped the old facilities to run well. Operators in POSCO wearing uniforms were manipulating control desks and watching Industrial TVs for sites in the air-conditioned rooms. Operators in UPI wearing jeans were sweating due to hard work at the inferior working conditions such as high noise levels and impure air.

The conditions in American steel companies were quite different from my expectation. However, the product qualities in UPI were good. I realized now that the competitive power of American steel industries is coming from the manpower like Mr. Kharouf and the experienced operators.

My Wife's Care

Check List

When my family goes to travel, I and my children usually are ready to depart in a car and wait my wife coming.

"Hurry, Honey. What makes you be late every time?"

"How you —man and children— understand me! I must check everything what you never do before we leave. I take every laundry box from our bathroom, children's bathroom, and the 1st floor and put them into the washer. I check if any light or electric devices are on in every bedroom, living room, and bathrooms. I check if the refrigerator door is open or any gas valve open. I have to make everything be arranged at its original place including books, newspapers, chairs, even pen or pencils in your room. And I also must go to restroom."

"Thank you, Honey. Come on, let's go."

Before going to school

I have an English class every Monday and Wednesday evening. My wife prepares my dinner around six o'clock. When I was taking dinner last Monday, I saw a fly flying here and there in the living room.

"How can a fly come in? Don't we have screen doors?" I spoke.

"Maybe the food smell made it come in." My wife said.

The fly was so fast that I could not see it continuously. It was in and out my sight. My wife got a fly catcher and tried to catch it. I had to twinkle according to its movement.

"When it gets tired, it may sit on a wall, then, you can catch it." I spoke.

I hurried to finish my dinner and took my books. When I was leaving home, I heard from back.

"I got it."

Why am I so Poor in English?

I think English is the most difficult language for me as a non-native speaker to learn and use as native speakers. I have been studying English since I was 13 years old (I am 49 years old) and I have been here in America for four years. But I still have a lot of difficulties to understand others well and express myself satisfactorily.

There are several reasons of my poor English. The first is I do not use English all the time. I try to memorize the meanings of English words every day, but I forget the meanings of words as many as I memorize every day. My memorizing ability may be poor, but the more important reason is that I do not use the words I memorized in my everyday life. I speak Korean in my home, and I use Korean to talk with Korean staffs. When I need to tell something to Americans, I think my idea in Korean first then translate it to English. I live in America with absent minded.

The second reason is Americans speak too fast. I can hardly understand the news program in radio and television. If I had been grown up in America, I would have been accustomed the expressions they speak fast, but their real speaks are unclear beyond my understanding. If somebody speaks very fast "I'm sorry if Anthony thod I w'z int'rested 'n 'im, b'd 'e w'z off—base when 'e thod 'e could kiss me", I cannot understand what he/she says unless I have the translation. I am not accustomed to listen to that kind of English—speaking speed.

The third reason is Americans use too many slangs in their everyday talking. It's very difficult for me to enjoy sit—coms or drama in television and any talks show in radio. Slang is actively efficient to communicate between Americans, but is an absolute barrier for my understanding. I was very embarrassed when I heard 'kicking ass, make money', 'hooked up', 'hanging in there', 'what's up, doc?', 'kicked out', or 'bull shitter' for the first time. I try to ask the speaker the meaning whenever I hear an unclear word, but how can I do about radio and television?

The fourth reason, the most significant reason, is I am lacked of vocabulary. If I had plenty of information and knowledge of any fields, I could understand others' talking more easily and express my opinions

일범의 평범한 사람 이야기

more fluently. Vocabulary about American football would help me understand co—workers' talking. Vocabulary about the procedures of prosecution would help me to understand the news of Scott Peterson's trial. I need to have information about baseball teams and players for talking with American friends, and need to have knowledge about American politics, economy, tax, military, social security, and Iraq for better understanding the presidential debate.

Many Americans recommend me to read, listen, and speak more and more. I am trying to read, listen, speak, and write as possible as I can. However, reading is boring when I must look up words in a dictionary too frequently, listening makes me sleep when I cannot catch what they are talking, and I hate myself when I cannot express my idea well enough. Isn't there a royal road for conquering English?

Golfing in America

Golf is my favorite sport in America. I used to go to hiking with my wife on weekends in Korea, but I have played golf every weekend since I came here in Bay Area in 2000. Golfing in America has several advantages, compared to golfing in Korea.

The first one is that green fees are much cheaper than Korea. You must pay over $200 a game in Korea based on a weekend fee. But you can enjoy golfing approximately within $30 in Bay Area, even though the fee varies according to the course. Playing golf means making money in the viewpoint of opportunity cost. For Koreans, the more frequently you play golf, the more money you can make.

The second advantage is that tee time reservation is much easier than Korea. Korea cannot build enough golf courses due to its limited lands. The population density per unit area of land is very high. People who want to play golf on weekends are overflowed the course capacity. So, making reservation for tee time on weekends is as difficult as picking a star in the sky. But here in America, especially in Bay Area, there are a lot of public golf courses enough to accommodate all weekends' golfers. You can reserve tee times any time if it is prior to a week.

The third advantage is all public golf courses in America are opened to everyone. Most of the golf courses in Korea are private. The membership price is too high for common people to buy it. So, there are a lot of social senses of incongruity between the rich people who enjoy golfing and the poor people who cannot afford to play golf. Inviting someone to a golf game can be often a bribe. But here in Bay Area, a golf course is a kind of community fields for citizens. I have met various kinds of players in golf courses: husband and wife who are enjoying as if they are dating, little kid who his father is teaching how to play golf, adolescent teens who are taking lessons from an instructor.

I play golf every weekend. It is a blessing and a special favor for me to play golf so frequently. I can keep good relationship with my colleagues by playing golf with them. I can enjoy my life with my wife by playing golf together. I will try to play golf as many as possible until I return to Korea, because golfing in Korea is impossible for me.

Human Being

God made human being as his feature by using soils and gave him His breath. Then it became 'a living soul'. God called him 'Adam'. This is from Genesis chapter 1. (Rsv. Bible, Gen. 2-7: "then the Lord God formed man of dust from the ground, and breathed into his nostrils the breath of life, and man became a living being")

Human being is made of body (soils) and soul (God's breath). If soul is separated from your body, you die. Death means separating soul from body. Then what is spirit? Spirit automatically came to you when soul and body combined. When you take a dream during sleeping, your spirit can separate from your body, go around everywhere, and take journey by itself. But soul cannot separate from your body unless you die. After death, what will happen? Body will go back to soils, soul will go back the place where it came from – to God (Christians say), to the origin (Buddhist and Zennist say), and spirit will be disappeared without any trace.

Who are you? Is your face you? Are your eyes you? Is your mouth you? No, those are not you but yours. Body cannot be you. Your body is moved by your will. Your body is your slaves. Mind is you. Mind is your master. Your mind is your soul that God gave you. Your soul had been before you borrowed your body, and your soul will be after your body is separated.

What is the difference between 'thinking' and 'mind'? Thinking is in your head. It can be changed by education and training. Thinking is based on your spirit. Spirit comes in your head and comes out of your head. But mind is in your heart. It cannot be changed. Mind is as it was at the beginning, because mind is soul. Some expressions such as 'Heart is pounding' or 'Heart leaped with joy' imply that soul is in your heart.

How can you find your soul? When you eat delicious food or when you see beautiful flowers, your body (eyes, nose, or mouth) will be happy. When you win a lottery or when you are promoted, your mind (ego or desire) will be happy. But when you do a good deed without notice to anyone or when you give even a small love to others without telling anyone, your soul will be happy. The reason is it is love.

Buddhist and Zennist say that soul cannot go back to the origin unless it is completed in this world. How to make it complete? The answer is love. Soul can be grown up by eating 'love'. If you do love, your soul will be grown up. The more you do good things, the more your soul grown up. Grown up, grown up, and grown up by doing love, love, and love. Finally, your soul will be completed.

Parking Citation

I have been working at USS—PSOCO in Pittsburg since July 2000. I have tried very hard to improve my English for better communication at work. I registered two English classes at LMC this fall semester. One is English vocabulary class from 1:00 to 2:00 p.m. every Monday, Wednesday, and Friday, and the other is English reading, writing, and thinking class from 7:00 to 10:00 in the evening every Monday and Wednesday. I bought textbooks, a good English dictionary, and a parking permit when I registered in August, 2004. I remember I paid $30.00 for the parking permit.

I could not hang the parking permit to be always displayed, because I had to park at my work, my home, or other places for longer hours than at LMC. So, I have tried not to forget to hang the parking permit to be displayed when I went to school. In the evening of September 20th, 2004, I had a long international call from Korea. So, I left home for school a little later than a normal day and unfortunately the traffic was really bad. I was hurrying in order not to be late for the class. I was barely on time for the class. When I returned to my car after the class was finished, I found a parking ticket on my car. "Oops! I forgot to hang the parking permit in my hurry!"

Since the day I got parking ticket, I have not been comfortable to find out how to settle this citation. I went to the security office to ask what I must do to settle the case. I filled out the review form which was given by the security office and mailed it to Office of Revenue Collection (ORC). The citation was upheld by the Police Agency at the first level agency review. I wanted to go to the second level review before a parking commissioner. So, I returned the second level review form to ORC with my declaration and $35.00 cashier's check. I paid $6.00 fee for the cashier's check. It is not settled yet. If the commissioner upholds the citation, my deposit will be applied to the citation. If the citation is cancelled, my deposit will be refunded.

By this experience, now I can understand the processes of a citation review which takes a long time and costs a lot. But I am still wondering why the processes are so complicated. I think the law makes the simple be complicated and it wastes time. I know I must follow the laws but hopefully the laws can be improved to have more flexibility.

Anyway, I did not know 'forgetting is guilty'. However, I have been more careful not to forget to hang my parking permit to be displayed since then.

* Levels of Parking Appeal

1st Police agency— (Upheld citations)

2nd Administrative Hearing— Parking Commissioner

3rd Superior Court— Last level

Requirements:

1. If citation not paid on levels 1+2, pay citation first to ORC.

2. Pay $25 court fees to superior court— if dismissed, a) + b) will be refunded.

America's Election

Yesterday, November 2nd, was the election day of the United State of America. I am not familiar with America's election system, but I remember the 2000 U.S. presidential election which more Americans voted for Gore, but Bush won the presidency. I came here in America July 2000. Therefore, I didn't have much information about America's election system four years ago. I understood the Electoral College as a cyber school and confused propositions with prepositions when I heard them for the first time. So, I tried to learn more about America's election system this time. Now I can understand how the President of the United States of America, the only strongest country in the world, is elected.

America's Election Day is on the Tuesday following the first Monday of November every four years. You can think of the election for President as 51 separate elections (one for each state and Washington D.C.). Each state has 2 electors plus the number of its representatives which varies according to the state's population. Therefore, states with the more population have the most electoral votes. To win a state, a candidate must win the majority of the people's votes which is called the popular vote. The winner of the state's popular votes takes all of that state's electoral votes. This year, the total number of electoral votes from all the states is 538. To become President, a candidate must win at least 270 electoral votes. This is why it is possible that a candidate who won more votes overall could not be elected.

In America, Republican Party and Democratic Party are not the only two political parties. There are also American Independent Party, Green Party, Libertarian Party, and Peace and Freedom Party.

On the Election Day, you vote not only for U.S. President and Vice President but also for U.S. Senates, and U.S. House of Representatives. There are many other candidates you can vote for your State Senate, your State Assembly, and your local government, such as country supervisor, city council or school board.

Another interesting thing for me was "Propositions". Propositions are proposed laws presented to the public to vote on. Voters can choose "for" or "against" for each proposition. I think this system is the evidence of providing people the more chances for participating directly to the legislation.

A Lucky Day

It was a cold night in December. Highway 4 was slippery due to the rain during the daytime. A motorcycle followed for a while and passed me, but my head was filled with thoughts of the quarrel between my two colleagues after dinner. I had had a hard time conciliating between them. I thought: Alcohol makes people brave and impolite. Maybe the Chinese liquor and those cocktails after dinner caused the quarrel. I must arrange a place for them to settle the dispute tomorrow.

Focusing again on my driving, I realized the motorcycle which had passed me was once again in my rear mirror. What a strange auto—bike it is! I stepped on the accelerator to go fast. Suddenly, the motorcycle behind me made flashing lights and something like warning was listened to me. Oops! Was it a cop? What an unlucky day today! I pulled over, waited for a while, handed over my driver license and insurance, and got out of my car following the cop's order.

"What's wrong with me?" I asked so in a carefully casual tone.

"Speed, you drove too fast," he said in a matter—of—fact way.

"No, I didn't, my speed was same as the previous cars."

"Your speed was eighty."

"I don't know how fast I was because I didn't see the dashboard, but I drove at the exact same speed of the previous cars. I didn't pass any car."

"You didn't pass any car, but had I given you a warning?"

"Did you? I didn't know about that, but uh you know, the traffic must flow like a stream of water. Every car has to move at the same speed. I think keeping the same speed is safe driving," I tried to prove my innocence.

"Did you drink?" he changed the topic suddenly. I was startled at his abrupt question. I had thought a lot of scenarios in short seconds. Oops! This is a big problem. This is the case that trying to escape a wolf comes to face a tiger. Oh, my god! I hadn't have tried to excuse myself. What can I say right now? If I say 'No, I didn't drink,' can he believe me? He must already smell alcohol from my breath. He may guess me to tell a lie.

"Yes, I did," I said, trying to appear nonchalant.

"How much?"

"Two glasses of bear."

"Large one or small one?"

"Small glass."

"You need to be investigated, but I don't have the test equipment. Wait here! I'll call a back-up," He looked like he didn't believe me. While he was calling somewhere, I looked around the circumstances. I was on Highway 4 between Somersville Road and L Street. The motorcycle was marked 'Highway Patrol.' Many cars shot by us. My watch was indicating its needles to 00:30 after midnight. The cold and fresh air might help for my sobering up. I breathed deeply in resignation.

After a while, two police cars arrived with their flashing lights. One parked in front of my car, and the other behind of my car. Three big cops got out of the cars and were standing around me. The highway patrol motorcycle left after he handed over something to one of the cops. I was shivering with cold and fear. I bit my lips, making sure of "I have to insist that I didn't drink much."

"You are on the suspicion of drinking and driving, we will have several tests with you," a cop said.

"O.K.," I said as if nothing is the matter with me.

First, he ordered me to touch the top of my nose with my index finger. I did so. After that, he ordered me to follow his finger with my eyes and investigated my eyeballs with a lantern. I passed two more test successfully to be checked my physical balancing: I raised both hands and was standing on one foot for a while, I counted one to ten with bending and unbending my fingers. Finally, he asked me to blow my breath into a tube. I became aware of what he was trying to do. Now he is trying to measure the alcohol percentage in my breath. I may be arrested and kept in custody. What will happen after that? My heart was pumping rapidly. I blew my breath into the tube two times. He measured the data on the tester. The short period while they were talking among themselves looked very long to me.

At last, one of the police officers said, "You are not arrested, but you can't drive." I breathed a deep sigh of relief when I heard it and I felt cold. They asked me where I live and ordered me to get on a police car. I still didn't know what was going on. They took me to the parking lot at a Shell gas station located at Hill Crest exit which is close to my home. They also drove my car to there. They asked me my home phone number and called to my home.

"This is a police officer. We are with your husband right now ⋯.," he asked my wife to come to the gas station. After a while, my wife and my son arrived. The police officers took over me and my car to my wife and disappeared.

"What's happened?" my wife was still abstracted.

"Nothing," I was totally sobered off.

"Can you imagine how much I was frightened when I heard you were with a police officer?"

"Sorry," I explained the incident briefly.

I had thought that driving after a little drinking would be no problem before I had this experience, because I was confident, I would not lose my control for driving. But I realized the idea of "I can drive well after a little drinking" is dangerous. Drinking and driving may cause a significant accident: may hurt you or someone else, may destroy your car or someone else's property, or even may kill someone. Drinking and driving can change everything of your life and your family. I learned the most valuable lesson from my experience: that is "never drive after drinking". Drinking and driving can cost an arm and a leg.

A Fortune Number

A birthday has a special meaning in Korea. The year, month, day, and hour of birth which is called "the four pillars" in Korea has been used the horoscopic data. Koreans have been traditionally thought that person be born with his/her fortune or misfortune predetermined by the four pillars. I had not believed that kind of superstition until I got an interesting number.

Many Koreans still celebrate their birthdays by lunar calendar instead of solar calendar. This tradition has almost gone in today's generation. My father's birthday was July 14th and my mother's is March 14th in lunar calendar. I was born on July 7th in lunar calendar. My wife's birthday is April 6th in solar calendar. My son was born on September 4th and my daughter on May 16th in solar calendar.

One day, I converted my family's birthdays to lunar calendar, and I was very surprised at the results. All men were born in July, all women in March. My parents were born on 14th, my generation on 7th, and my children on 27th. The following chart shows my family's birthdays in lunar calendar.

Father	07−14	Mother	03−14
Me	07−07	Wife	03−07
Son	07−27	Daughter	03−27

Since I found this wondering combination, I have continuously thought the meaning of the numbers. My father was 15 years older than my mother. Fifteen years age gap was very abnormal in those days in Korea. But they married and I was born between them. I and my wife had some difficulties to get married, but we married anyway. My son was born nine days earlier than his expected date and my daughter three days earlier than her expected date. Are these all coincidences? Isn't there a family's four pillars? I could not feel free from this numbers' doubts.

When I came to the United States four years ago, I thought the number might hint a fortune for lottery. I tried to find out a number by making combinations of the numbers 3, 7, 14, and 27. 3+7=10, 3× 7=21, 14/7=2, 27/3=9 and finally I got a combination of the numbers for Supper Lotto. That was 3, 7, 14, 27, 37 and mega number was 7. I have been buying Supper Lotto with this number very frequently hoping to get a great fortune. It seems ridiculous, but I may be in the temptation of a superstition.

Ancestral Sacrifices

Traditionally, Koreans have performed ancestral sacrifices for thousands of years. There are three ancestral sacrifices: the first on the anniversary of death, the second held in front of the grave, and the third performed in each season of the year. The anniversary of a person's death has a special meaning in Korea. The descendants come together at the eldest son's home and perform an ancestral sacrifice. Even though many Christian families recently have a simple worship instead of an ancestral sacrifice, Korean traditional ancestral sacrifices should be interesting to foreigners and young people who are not familiar with the traditions. An ancestral sacrifice is an extension of the filial piety, a religious ceremony in a family, and a spiritual culture in Korea. An ancestral sacrifice consists of three parts: preparation, performing, and partaking.

Preparation of an ancestral sacrifice enables the descendants to keep in intimate relations with family members. Korea has an extended family system in which family means not only parents and children but also grand-parents, grand- children, uncles, aunts, nieces, nephews, and cousins. All family members gather at the eldest son's home on a sacrifice day. The menfolk write a ritual paper and an ancestral paper tablet, and the women prepare offering foods in the kitchen while the kids are in some other room, watching TV or playing games. Offering foods include cooked rice, broth, beef, pork, chicken, fish, cooked greens, and fruits. Powdered red peppers and garlic sauce cannot be allowed because those drive out spirits. Peaches, scabbard fish, and tuna are not allowed either. All family members should be clean themselves and change to ceremonial dresses before performing an ancestral sacrifice. There are some rules for setting foods on the table. A folding screen is set up at the north side of the sacrifice table. The ancestral paper tablet in which man's name is written at west and his spouse at east is set at the center of the folding screen. Offering foods are usually set in five rows on the table. In the first row, boiled rice is set at west and soup at east. In the second row, meats are set at west and fishes at east. In the third row, broth is set at the center. In the fourth row, dried fishes are set at west and cooked greens at east. Fish heads must toward east. In the fifth row, white fruits are set at west and red fruits at east. Setting the sacrifice table is done by burning two candles set at east and west.

Performing an ancestral sacrifice has rigid sequential processes for invoking the souls of the deceased, communicating with them, praying devoutly, and seeing the souls off. An ancestral sacrifice is performed just after midnight to meet the time for the ancestors' souls. It is started by opening the house gate. The eldest son invokes the souls by burning incenses and pouring wines into a bowl with sands in it. After the souls sit, all members make two deep bows for greeting the souls. The eldest son presents the first wine−cup and a butler opens covers of foods and set spoons and chopsticks. After the first wine−cup presented, one of the family members reads a ritual paper. The eldest son sits on his knees during reading the ritual paper and makes two deep bows after reading finished. The second and third wine—cups are presented by the different members of the family, each with two deep bows. Then, all members come out of the room, close the door, and wait for ancestors' eating, sitting on their knees. After 3 ~4 minutes, all members come in the room following the eldest son and a butler changes soups to teas. When the souls finish taking teas, spoons and chopsticks are taken back and all members see off the souls by making deep bows two times. Finally, the ritual paper and the ancestral paper tablet are burnt in the sand bowl.

Partaking of the sacrificial foods and drinks means sharing the ancestors blesses with all family members. After performing the ancestral sacrifice, all members sit at a round table with the foods and drinks which had offered to the ancestors' souls. They usually talk about family matters, ancestors, and the future plans for family members, taking foods. They believe their ancestors give them a good harvest and help them to keep healthy and happy. On the next day, the eldest son delivers some offered foods to his neighbors in order to share the blessings.

No trees without roots, no descendants without ancestors. An ancestral sacrifice makes people review their roots and remind them of the origin of life. It is a history, a tradition, a culture, and a custom which has lasted thousands of years. Through the ancestral sacrifice, people can wish blessings from their ancestors, learn the family's tradition, and strengthen the harmony among family members. An ancestral sacrifice is not performed to show others. Therefore, the attitude of mind is more important than the complicated forms. It is an inevitable duty for descendants to devote to their parents who gave birth and fostered, and to the ancestors who were the origins of the present being.

제4부 미국생활

4장

LMC에서
영어공부를 할 때(2006)
쓴 글들

(Integrated Reading, Writing, and Critical Thinking)

Reading Short Article

I found out myself again "How I am lacked knowledge about American society and culture". I could get the general idea of this column but could not understand a lot of expressions in the short column.

That's because of my poor vocabulary and my lacks understanding American life.

These are the expressions that I could not understand the meaning very well.

1. Those women on the Titanic who passed up dessert at the dinner that fateful night to "cut back".
2. We live on a spare diet of promises we make to ourselves
3. When we get Stevie toilet—trained
4. Skip an elevator for a bungi cord
5. The other day I stopped the can and bought a triple—decker. If my car hit an iceberg on the way home, I'd have died happy.

The first step and the most important thing I must do for better speaking and listening to English is "the understanding" of American way of thinking. English structure is quite different from my language. It's more non—directive and complicated. Too many synonyms are used for describing a situation. I am confused every day.

Seize the Moment

I generally agree her opinion "Seize the Moment", but I do not agree that her opinion is applied to everyone. Let's think about a person who is starving. "Food" is the most valuable for him. He may have other desires such as trips, watching plays, having date and so on, but he must think about his pocket first. Ha must seek job and work for his living. What can he do without any money?

During the early age, I had lived every day based on "Seize the Moment". I drank when I wanted to drink, and I traveled to the counties when I felt to go somewhere. I was single at that time, and I didn't have so many restrictions for my behaviors. However, now I can't do like that anymore. I must save money for my family, and I have to make plan for my expenses. In other words, I must prepare for the future, for the rainy days. I can't go out for dinner whenever I or my family members want, and I can't go golfing whenever I want to play. All activities are very much related to money. I must control my expenses for surviving in this world.

"Seize the Moment" is good word for teaching and for the people who have enough money.

One Being a Real Westerner

Pre—reading

I had watched a lot of American western movies when I was young in Korea. Cowboys and mountain men were the most favorite heroes in those movies. Most of the movies have a defined subject – that is 'good persons finally overcome bad persons". A real westerner in this article reminds me a good person in a western movie that I have watched, as John Wayne.

Free writing

Actually, I couldn't understand the exact meaning of this story due to my poor vocabularies. I need to read carefully with the help of a dictionary for better understanding. Did the writer shoot the squirrel and kill it? And did he lie to his mother? It was not an honest behavior. Young boys are so curious that they can make mistakes something. The writer tells us two things. One is everybody can make mistakes, and another is "Be honest" like a real westerner.

Focused Response

For a week, he kept his promise of not going out with rifle without his mother and Roy. But the process of breaking his promise is interesting.

The first step is " Just cleaning", then marching around, striking brave poses, army uniforms, drawing a bead, and finally shooting. Curiousness is the most key factor which leads the boy to be brave. The writer tells us about how we can be "a real westerner", how we can educate our children to be "a real westerner" by using an example which is not so like "a real westerner".

A View from Mount Ritter

Pre—reading

What is "Ritter"? Is it the name of a mountain? Or is it a word meaning knight? If it is the mountain's name, it makes sense. Many people go hiking during weekends. Why do they climb mountain? When they step on the top of a mountain and look down the scenery below their feet, they feel like birds and their stresses piled during the weekdays will be gone.

Free writing

There is not a description about the beautiful views which I had imagined before I read it. Instead of the beautiful views from the top of a mountain, the writer explained his experiences of the hard fighting against the rainy storms. At the second part of his article, the author wrote about his school life. It looks like there are no firm relations between the first part and the second. He had some bitter struggles during his mountaineering last summer, and he is becoming a better student this year. What is this?

Focused Response

I had an intensive reading the article with the help of a dictionary. And I could understand the writer's intension about what he would like to tell the readers. In the morning after the storm came down, he saw sunlight overhead streaming over the mountains wiped out the dark clouds. He saw not only the orange-red sun but also his future. He found out the dark clouds which blurred his physical vision and the dark clouds which led him to be stubborn and rebellious. He started his new life with the brilliant sun.

Without Emotion

Pre-reading

"Without Emotion" means no feeling about something. Maybe it refers to a judgement by a law without any involvement of human emotion, or it may refer to a person who is so flat as if something has not a bit of relation to him/her.

Free writing

This article shows us how much a person can be changed from tender-hearted to cruel or ruthless. A person can be trained by repeating something, and finally can be an automatic machine or a robot. If the repetition is about killing the living creations, the person will become a killing machine which has no feelings of joy, anger, sorrow, and pleasure. We often hear about an uncommon devilish murder who has no guilty conscience. The repeat of killing would make him not to feel guilty.

Focused Response

The last part of the article: I was satisfied: when it came my turn to go to war, I would be ready, I could kill as I could run – like a machine.

I had served in the military for three years. I can remember that I was trained to have no fears of shooting, knifing, and killing enemies by repeat and repeat. I think every soldier taking part in the combat operations should be trained as I was. I had heard a sermon in a church about five years ago. The pastor said: "There was a random firing at a peaceful primary school in a state of America on the day when American Air Forces were bombing thousands of bombs to Iraq during Gulf War, and seven innocent children were killed at the peaceful village on the same day nobody were killed in the Gulf War". It took time for a while until I understood that his meaning "Nobody killed" means "No American killed". Isn't it an irony that 90 % of wars in the history were because of religion?

The Pie

Pre-reading

One of my friends is called "Pie man", because he makes pie good. There are not many people in my company who has not eaten his pie. He also made a pie for me, and I enjoyed it with my family. But frankly speaking, I don't like pie. It's too sweet for me. I don't understand why American foods are usually too sweet and salty which are not good for health.

Free writing

Stealing is always bad. There is no excuse for stealing. Everybody knows it, because we have been taught that by education. However, young kids may not know that the stealing is a sin. They may put more importance to get their wants than to judge what's wrong. I had also some experiences to take other people's fruits during my childhood. At that time, stealing was a kind of play and enjoyment to me and my friends. But a habitual stealing is a big problem. There is a proverb,

"As a boy, so the man". It is difficult for a man to give up his old bad habits.

Focused Response

In paragraph 5, I felt bad not sharing with cross-eyed Johnny, a neighbor kid. He stood over my shoulder and asked, "Can I have some?"

"Get away" I had answered.

What a great boy he was! His behavior was just like a child. A cross-eyed is a handicapped. The cross-eyed boy might have got a lot of ribbing by other boys. We need to share love to all handicapped people, and religion is valued.

Freshmen Blues

Pre-reading

Freshmen are the first-grade students at college. Blues is a kind of dances. So, this may be about the story of college festival in which the freshmen are participating and enjoying their party, dancing blues with their partners.

Free writing

In the business world, customer satisfaction is a very important value for surviving among the competitive society. College or university is also faced to a serious competitive situation. School consists of students, teachers, and buildings. Without any one of them, it is no more school for teaching. If the students are not satisfying the courses of college programs and then quit or transfer from the school, the college or university cannot be survived. America is more serious than Korea at this point, because people without college degrees have no problem to get jobs for living. Meanwhile, in Korea, it's very hard for the people without college degrees to get jobs.

Focused Response

Paragraph 31: "To keep class sizes small and to have senior professors to teach students, the university is spending several hundred thousand dollars to hire more faculty and staff members". If this college is a private school, I really respect the owner. And if this college is a national or public school, I want to give my full supports to them mentally and physically. I have heard many college owners who think the college as a way of earning money. Many of them were prosecuted because they had used the students' tuitions to their private purpose. It's embezzlement.

Never Again

It was the New Year Day in the lunar calendar last year which is the biggest traditional holiday in Korea. I had a big party with Korean people working at my company, USS-POSCO Industries, at a marvelous Japanese restaurant in Martinez. I had quite a few drinks with delicious foods such as raw fish and Sushi. After the party was ended by singing along and congratulating each other for the New Year, I and a few of my colleagues moved the banquet place from the restaurant to the home of one of my friends near the restaurant and were continuing the celebration with drinking and playing poker. The party was finally over after midnight, but I never dreamed what a miserable fate was waiting for me that night after all the fun of the days.

I used to drive after I drank alcohol. I had always been confident in my drinking and driving, because I had thought I had a "drinking driver license". There are a few rules for a drinking driver license. Keep speed limits, yield any time, do not hurry, and be stricter to traffic rules than usual. But on that fateful night, I had no memory of how much I drank and what the drinking driver's rules were. As soon as I took Highway 4, a police car tailgated me with brilliant flashing lights and noisy siren.

"Oh! Shit! What's an unlucky day" I pulled over and handed over my driver license and insurance, but it took quite a long time to find my insurance documents.

"Speed, you drove too fast," the cop said in a matter-of-fact way.

I could not say anything, because I did not recognize how fast my speed had been.

"Did you drink?" the cop suddenly asked me.

I was startled at his abrupt question.

"Oh! My God! I may look like drunk due to my affected manners and alcoholic smell from me." I tried to pretend I was sober.

"Yes, I did. But it was five hours ago. I think I'm all right." I was not too embarrassed but smiled because I recalled my experience about a year ago. I had been investigated on the suspicion of drinking and driving. After I successfully had passed several physical balancing tests and breathing tests, the cop had said, "You are not arrested, but you can't drive." They had taken me and my car to my home.

"This time also will be no problem." I consoled myself.

First, the cop ordered me to follow his finger with my eyes and investigated my eyeballs with a lantern. After that, I raised both hands and was standing on one foot for a while, I walked along a straight line, and I counted from one hundred to ninety with bending and un-bending my fingers. I tried to take every action as naturally as possible. I thought I passed the physical balancing tests successfully. But the situation was not as simple as I had expected. After I blew my breath into a tube of a tester, the cops handcuffed me and got me in a police car.

While they were driving me to the police station, I was awfully worried about what would happen after that. "I'm arrested. I may be kept in custody. How much fine? I may need a lawyer. How can I explain this to my wife? How much will my wife be disappointed? How often has she asked me not to drive after drinking since the experience last year?"

In the police station, the cops handcuffed me to a chair and asked a lot of questions about my personal information. When they asked me which way, I would choose for re—checking the alcoholic percentage, I chose a blood test instead of a breathing test which I already had failed on. While waiting for the blood test, they allowed me to phone my wife. My watch was indicating 01:30 in the morning.

When my wife, Mu—young, arrived at the police office to take me home, I tried to hide my handcuffed left hand from her sight. I signed on a few sheets of documents without reading them. I couldn't read them carefully because of my poor English and too small sized letters under dimmed lights. When I returned to my home, I found the cops had not returned my driver license to me. My wife drove me back to the police station by my request, and I asked to the cops to return my driver license. How foolish I was! I was totally absurd. My driver license was confiscated by the police and one of the sheets they gave me was a temporary driver license valid for one month. The reason why I didn't know about it was that I was still drunk and out of my senses until all the investigation for me was finished at the police station. I did not realize what a serious crime I committed until I was sober the next day and read all the procedures I must do from now on.

I was awakened to the gravity of Drinking and Driving day by day for the next nine months. I was convicted to be imprisoned for two days, to pay a fine of about $ 2,000, and to attend a 3-month First Offender DUI Program. I had to do a 2-day Work Alternative Program for picking up garbage along Freeway 80 instead of imprisonment. Mu-young had to drive for me to commute until I got a restricted driver license. My insurance company terminated my car insurance contract, and I had to pay an additional $2,000 per year for my new insurance. And the car rental companies may not rent a car to me for the next few years.

I had thought that driving after a little drinking would be no problem before I had this experience because I had been confident that I would not lose control driving. But I realized the idea of "I can drive well after a little drinking" is dangerous. Drinking and driving may cause a significant accident, may hurt you or someone else, may destroy your car or someone else's property, or even may kill yourself or other people. Drinking and driving can change everything in your life and your family. I learned the most valuable lesson from my experience: that is "Never drive after drinking".

Being Mindless

In the essay titled "Are You Living Mindlessly?" Michael Ryan argues that being mindless means doing something without thinking, and we all have been mindless. According to Ryan, mindlessness can cause accidents whether trivial or serious. He interviews Allen Langer, a professor of psychology at Harvard, who explains that our teaching system at school lacks flexibility and creativity so that we are rarely taught conditionally to the different possibilities. Langer gives us other examples, such as a habit which has been passed down for generations mindlessly although the need has gone. Langer insists that "There is more than one way of looking at things." And different results can be achieved by having different perspectives. Then Ryan gives us his own examples that overconfidence in technology without mindfulness can cause accidents with injuries. And he says that "mindlessness can help to destroy people's lives" as Langer found in nursing homes where the people with mindfulness have lived longer than the people without mindfulness. Langer also explains that being mindless can cause people to judge others prematurely and irrationally. Finally, she suggests that we should be mindful in any situation in order to succeed against challenges caused by mindlessness are sometimes trivial enough to be a laugh and sometimes serious enough to be a tragedy.

In my own life, being mindless has led to wasting time and losing money. A few years ago, I had visitors from Korea who had come for

320
일범의 평범한 사람 이야기

sightseeing to America. They dropped by my company to have a site tour of the production lines. On that morning I found that I had left my cell phone at home for charging battery. My cell phone was essential for me to ask their tour schedule. Before I headed home to pick my cell phone, one of the visitors wanted to see my home. In the car with him, I explained the difference between American life and Korean life to him. It took about thirty minutes for go—home and return—work. When I returned to company, I found myself still without my cell phone. How absent minded I had been! I had no idea where I put my cell phone. I didn't have much time to go back home because the site tour is almost closing. I rushed and drove home again faster than the speed limit. I found my cell phone on the table unplugged from the wall outfit. The only thing I did during my first come to home was unplug the cell phone. If I had been stopped by a police officer because of speeding during my second come to home, I would have wasted more time and money.

Being mindful and being mindless can also cause different results in business: both failure and success. In 1990, as Production Manager in POSTIN, a Tin Plating Company, I was responsible for purchasing and installing a shearing line. Littell Shear was the most famous facility for shearing Tin Plate, so most of all Tin Plating Companies in the world have at least one Littell Shear. However, Mr. Ahn, the president of my company, tried to buy a shearing line from Kobayshi in Japan because he had some connection with Kobayashi People.

Unfortunately, Mr. Lee, who had offered a Delta Brands Shear, was the lowest price bidder among three quotes. There were a series of serious argument and mindless disputes between Mr. Ahn and Mr. Lee since the quotation. Both were too narrow-minded to accept the other's opinion. In addition, the bigger issue was that neither Kobayashi nor Delta Brands were good as Littell Shear. As production Manager, I had to find a solution to settle down the dispute between Mr. Ahn and Mr. Lee which was on the brink of becoming a lawsuit. In response to the terrible situation, Mr. Kim, the Standing Auditor, called me. Mr. Kim has a lot of experiences in business and mindful of human relationships. He gave me a bright idea to help me with the issue. He explained to me, "Mr. Lee's purpose is not supplying Delta Brands Shear but getting money, Mr. Ahn's desire to choose Kobayashi Shear cannot be achieved because the quotation results were already opened to everybody. And what do you want? Is Littell Shear the best one for Tin Plate? Then, why don't you buy Littell Shear from Mr. Lee?" I could solve all issues with one shot and install the most proper facility for my company. And I understood how the flexibility of perspectives is important for decision making in business world.

More seriously, being mindless can lead to terrible accidents. Last December, there was a tragic accident at a hospital in Deajeon, Korea. The thyroid of patient A, whose stomach was to be operated on, was removed. And one-third of the stomach of patient B, whose thyroid was to be operated, was cut out. According to the articles in Chosun

Daily News, patient A, a 64-year-old woman, had been scheduled to have stomach cancer surgery at the hospital on Dec.29th. Patient B, a 62-year-old woman, had been scheduled to have thyroid surgery at the same hospital on the same day. The doctors and nurses at the hospital found that two patients' charts had been switched after the two surgeries had been finished. Patient A, whose thyroid had already been removed, had to have stomach cancer surgery. And patient B, whose stomach had already been cut, had to have thyroid surgery. Because of this, both patients need to have further medical treatment and to be careful of their food intake until they die. How could this kind of accident occur? The reason was mindlessness. Nobody among the three doctors, a surgeon, an anesthetist and a resident, or the nurses or others had checked the patients' charts before the surgery stared.

In conclusion, Ellen Langer has explained about mindlessness and its opposite, mindfulness, and how switching from one to the other can enrich our lives. I totally agree with her opinion. Being mindless can cause forgetfulness which can lead to losing or wasting time and money in our daily lives. Mindlessness can cause problems and mindfulness can solve the problems in business. Being mindless can cause a behavior which can cause terrible and unrecoverable accident. We all have been mindless, but we all need to be more mindful in order to make our lives safer and happier.

『Kindred』 독후감

『Kindred』는 미국 작가 Octavia E. Butler의 소설인데, 현실세계에서 혼절하면 과거의 세계로 돌아가 자신의 선조들을 만나는 예기로 전개된다. 현실 세계에서 흑인인 주인공은 과거에 자신의 할아버지의 할아버지의 할아버지가 백인이었음을 알게 된다. 아래에 이 책을 읽은 후의 독후감을 정리해 보았다.

Kindred (1)

In the first four chapters of the novel titled "Kindred", Octavia E. Butler describes the lives of black people in the era when Negro slavery was still in existence. Dana Franklin, a twenty-six old African American woman, who lives in Los Angeles in 1976, is ripped violently and suddenly backing time 150 years ago in Maryland.

During her first trip back to the fast, she meets a boy, Rufus, and his parents beside a river. She saves Rufus, who is nearly drowned, and returns to the modern days when she is threatened to be shot by Mr. Weylin, Rufus' father. But she does not know who Rufus is.

During her second trip back, Dana saves Rufus again by extinguishing the fire spreading to the drapery of the house. And she guesses that Rufus is her several times great grandfather. She meets her ancestors: Alice, her great, great, great, grandmother and Alice's mother. Dana wants to stay with Alice for a while and Alice's mother permits Dana to come in her house. But unfortunately, Dana is found by the patrollers who are white young people organized to keep the blacks in line. The patrollers think Dana is a runaway and hit her several times with their fists. Dana escapes the dangerous situation by hitting the patroller with a heavy tree limb and comes back to 1976 almost unconsciously.

Kevin, Dana's husband, a white man, does not understand Dana's trip back during her disappearance. He thinks Dana has a hallucination and tries to take her to hospital. However, Dana goes back to 1815 with Kevin on her trip. This time Dana and Kevin help to rescue Rufus with broken leg. Due to the help of saving his life, Rufus asks his father let Dana and Kevin live at his house. Me. Weylin hires Kevin as a reading and writing teacher for Rufus and Dana works at cookhouse helping Sarah, the cook, But Rufus's mother. Mrs. Margaret Weylin, hates Dana very much because Rufus prefers to be with Dana rather than her, and Dana can read and write better than she. On the other hand, Mr. Weylin permits Dana to read only for Rufus and prohibits her to read anywhere else. But one day Mr. Weylin finds Dana is teaching Nigel, a black slave boy, in the cookhouse. Because of this, Mr. Weylin gets so angry that he whips and beats Dana. Dana passes out by the whipping of Mr. Weylin.

By the trips to back in the 18th century, Dana, the protagonist, learns the life in those times. The whites always call black people niggers and often whip them as they do to horses. All blacks are slaves unless they have certificates of freedom. The blacks are prohibited to learn reading, writing, or calculating. The whites often sell their black slaves to get money to buy things such as furniture which they don't even need, and the black parent have nothing to do about the selling of their children. Personally, Dana meets her relatives, her ancestors, and tries to find ways to survive among the horrors of slavery in order to save her family.

The slavery is the worst humiliation of American history. The black slaves were treated as animals by the white slaveholders in those times. But the slave's children didn't understand that they were born as slaves. One day when Dana and Kevin saw a group of slave children gathered around and were playing some game in which, they were selling and buying slaves, Kevin said. "The kids are just imitating what they have seen adults doing." (99) They didn't understand that the games they played were preparing them for the future. It required a long struggle and a lot of sacrifices for the blacks to have the civil rights equal to the whites. After all, the slavery history has extremely contributed to build today's America as the model of democratic country.

Kindred (2)

In "Kindred", Octavia E. Butler continues to describe Dana's experience back to the past. Dana finds out that she came back home at the same date as she left. It took only a few hours in the present time even though she had gone away for nearly two months to the past. Healing her scars, Dana prepares for her next trip back such as putting clothes, shoes, comb, tooth paste and toothbrush, knife, the map of Maryland, a history book, and etc. in a canvas bag. After eight days at home, she goes back again to Rufus' time and rescues from a fight with Isaac, Alice's husband. While taking care of Rufus, Dana asks Rufus to mail her letter to Kevin who left Mr. Weylin's house for the North. But Rufus asks Dana to put her history book and the map of Maryland in a fireplace, because he worries that Dana may leave to find Kevin. At the same time, Alice and Isaac who went away are caught. Then Isaac is sold to the South with his eras cut off, and Alice is bought by Rufus and forced to live with him. Mr. Weylin gives some presents to Carrie and her husband Nigel who had a baby. But Nigel says to Dana with bitterness, "Cause of Carrie and me, he's one nigger richer." Returning to Dana's story, Rufus lies to Dana that he sent her letter to Kevin because he wants to keep Dana to be with him. Rufus's lie causes Dana to try to escape from Me. Weylin's house to find Kevin. But Lisa, the sewing woman, tells Mr. Weylin about Dana running away. So Dana is caught and beaten seriously by Mr. Rufus. Meanwhile, Kevin receives a letter from Mr. Weylin that Dana is back. At last, Kevin comes back to Dana after five years by Rufus' time. And they leave from Mr. Weylin's house with saying" good—bye" to Alice. As soon as they leave, they meet Rufus on the road. Rufus tries to kill Dana, because he doesn't want Dana to leave from him. Dana and Kevin come back to the present time when Rufus is going to shoot.

Dana learns more about the slavery during her fourth trip back. One example is that np slave marriage is legally binding yet the slaveholders like their slaves to get married and have babies. Once the slaves have family, they won't try to runaway anymore due to their family. Another example is that educating slaves is illegal. It is dangerous to educate slaves at the slaveholders' point of view. Education makes blacks dissatisfied with slavery, spoils them for field work, and makes them disobedient.

Although Mr. Weylin is cold-hearted and ruthless to his slaves, he has his own rules not to spoil the whites' dignity in his era. In other words, he is kind of a fair man. For an example, he is not grateful to Dana for her saving his son's life, but he writes to Kevin about her after he learned that Rufus hasn't sent her letters. One day while Rufus and Dana are eating together, Rufus describes his father to Dana, "He's a fair man. I said fir, not likeable." (134) Mr. Weylin shows his fairness once more when Dana is caught from her trial to escape. Mr. Weylin whips Dana but doesn't hurt her nearly as much as he's hurt others. He is easy on Dana because he thinks her running away is Rufus' fault.

Kindred (3)

In "Kindred", Octavia E. Butler continues to describe Dana's experience back to the past. After a few hours at home, Dana goes back to Rufus' time and saves an unconscious Rufus lying face down in a puddle. But a few hours for Dana are six years for Rufus. At this time, Dana finds out that Alice has lost two babies and the third one, Joe, is looking more like Rufus than Alice. While Rufus is getting well, Tom Weylin dies due to a heart attack. Rufus decides to punish Dana for letting his father die and let her work in the field. The overseer, Fowler, lashes and whips Dana hard across the back during the field work. When she was almost passing out, Rufus stops Fowler whipping and asks Dana not to walk away from him again. After that, he asks Dana to take care of his mother who is coming back home. He also tells Dana that Alice will be having another baby in a few months. Dana expects this time the baby would be Hargar, her great, great, great, grandmother. During her stay at Rufus' home, Dana disappoints Rufus because he sells some of his slaves despite her strong argument. One day, Alice asks Dana if Rufus has taken her to bed. Dana answers her that neither of them wants each other. Finally, Hagar is born, and Alice is satisfied that her daughter takes after her. Alice makes up her mind to leave from Rufus someday, and Dana plans to stay on the Weylin plantation long enough to see Alice leave. However, on day, Sam a slave, asks Dana to teach his brother and sister to read. Rufus thinks that Sam and Dana had a sex, so he sells Sam. When Dana tries to explain her innocence and pleads Rufus not to sell Sam, Rufus hits her.

Being disappointed with Rufus, Dana cuts her wrists to kill herself. Fortunately, cutting her wrists get her home. Kevin says that Dana has gone for about three hours which was eight months for Dana. After fifteen days at home, Dana goes back to Rufus on the fourth of July.

This time Dana finds out that Rufus is not in danger, but Alice hangs herself. Dana hears why Alice hung herself: Alice tried to run away from Rufus and was caught. So Rufus sent his children to his relatives without any notice to Alice. Alice thought her children were sold. After Alice's funeral, Rufus allows his children to call him daddy instead of master and writes certificates of freedom for them. But suddenly, Rufus tries to take Dana with brutal force. Dana sinks the knife into his side and brings it down again into his back. Rufus's body goes limp and leaden across her and Dana comes back home.

Dana has the scar Tom Weylin's boot had left on her face and the scars Fowler whipped across her back. Dana cannot be sure whether she has gone back to the past, saved her ancestor's life several times and finally killed her ancestor. No one, if they hear the story, can believe Dana's trips back either. Dana and Kevin want to reassure themselves that they are sane. So, they fly to Maryland and try to find solid evidence that those people existed. Finally, they find a clue, an old newspaper article — a notice that Mr. Rufus Weylin had been killed when his house caught fire and was partially destroyed, and in later newspaper, notice of the sale of the slaves from Rufus Weylin's estate in which Joe and Hager were not listed. Because of the articles, Dana thinks that she really had connected to her ancestor's survival and death.

During her fourth trip to back, Dana has a lot of talking with Alice about Rufus. And she finds out that Alice never believes Rufus despite having children between them. When Dana tells her that Rufus will write certificates of freedom for their children, Alice says, "When he does, and you read them to me, maybe I'll believe him. I'm tellin' you, he uses those children just the way you use a bit on a horse. I'm tried of havin' a bit in my mouth." (236) Without love, Alice cannot be happy in living with Rufus. Therefore, Alice constantly tries to escape from Rufus for freedom. In contrast, Dana realizes that her love and need for Kevin is continuously increased throughout the story. In other words, living with her master without love is just like a hell to Alice and living with her husband with love is a paradise to Dana.

The Relationship between Rufus and His Lovers in "Kindred"

In the novel Kindred, Octavia E. Butler describes realistically the briefs and behaviors of the principal characters: Rufus, Alice, and Dana. According to Butler, the era when slavery is still in existence has many restrictions for the people to keep relationship with the different colored people. For example, 'niggers' cannot marry white people, the whites often whip the slaves as they do to horses, and even the slaveholders can sell their slaves any time. All those examples are legal and proper at those times. Likewise, Rufus, Alice, and Dana have several insurmountable obstacles to their relationship although they love each other.

Rufus loves Alice very much, but he cannot marry her because of the law. Rufus and Alice have friends since they were young. When they grow up, Alice marries Isaac, a slave. Rufus is so jealous of Isaac that he begs Alice not to go with him and finally rapes her. For the white man, there is no shame in raping a black woman, but there could be shame in loving one. Rufus confesses to Dana after he bought Alice, "If I lived in your time, I would have married her, or tried to."(124) Rufus thinks that Alice is his property and he can take better care of her than any other field hand can. But Alice lives with him, having a grudge just to kill him until she hangs herself.

As a master, Rufus has to keep his dignity by punishing Alice or Dana when they try to do something wrong although he still loves them. On the other hand, when Tom Weylin died due to his heart break, Rufus decides to punish Dana for letting his father die. Because of his decision, Dana is seriously whipped and beaten by an overseer during the field work and finally she is out almost unconsciously. And when Alice hung herself, Rufus explains to Dana why he sent his children to his relatives without any notice to Alice, "To punish her, scare her, and make her see what could happen if she didn't⋯ if she tried to leave me." (251) In addition, Rufus loves Alice and their children, but he does not write the certificates of freedom for their children in front of Alice. Rufus also apologize to Dana many times and in many ways, but his apologies are always oblique with saying "sorry".

As a slaveholder, Rufus sometimes has to sell his slaves, which gives sorrow and pain to the slave family. Dana cannot put up with the selling and trading of slaves when she sees the situation of a coffle with her own eyes. When Dana tries to hold back Rufus to sell a coffle, Rufus says to Dana, "They are my property! Look, this sale is something my father arranged before he died. You can't do anything about it, so just stay out of the way!" (222) After Alice's funeral, Dana tries to push Rufus towards freeing a few more his slaves. But Rufus is still bound his times' rules and customs although he allows his children to call him daddy instead of master.

In conclusion, the institution of slavery is a great wall for an individual to overcome. Rufus loves Alice so he does not allow Alice to be free. And Alice lives with Rufus as a master may be not her husband, so she constantly tries to escape from him. Dana also can accept Rufus as her ancestor not as her lover, so she saves his life several times only for her family's surviving. The relationship between the white and the black cannot be realized as an equal under the slavery.

Alice and Dana in "Kindred"

In the novel titled Kindred, Octavia E. Butler describes the complicated characteristics of the principal characters: Dana, Rufus, and Alice. According to Butler, Dana takes trips back to the nineteenth century and saves Rufus, her ancestor's life several times. During her trip back, Dana meets Alice, her several times great grandmother and tries to help her surviving in the slavery era. With each trip back, Dana meets Alice as a little child, as Isaac's wife and Rufus's lover, as Joe and

Hagar's mother, and as a dead body. Although Alice is like Dana in appearance, will, independence, and a desire for love, her life is not happy like Dana's because of her slavery.

The appearance of Alice is just like Dana. When Dana meets Alice for the first time during her second trip back for saving Rufus form a fire, Alice is little, thin, frightened child. At that time, Dana thinks that Alice's mother looks like herself. But when Dana meets Alice again during her third trip back to save Rufus from the fight with Isaac, Alice is tall, slender, bareheaded, and dark — a lot like her. During Dana's fifth trip back, Dana has a lot of time with Alice, expecting a baby due. One day Alice talks about Rufus to Dana, "he likes me in bed and you out of bed, and you and I look alike if you can believe what people say. Anyway, all the means we're two halves of the same woman — at least in his crazy head." (229) When Hagar is born, she looks like Alice with darker skinned than Joe. Dana finds out the generic inheritance of her family which have been transmitted from Alice' mother, Alice, Hagar, and finally to herself.

The more important similarity between Alice and Dana is their strong will and independence, able to survive difficult situations. For instance, when Alice is brought by Rufus and becomes a slave, she has no choice except going to him with revengeful thoughts of killing him. But she does not kill Rufus. Meanwhile, Dana learns how to cook which she has never done before, teaches slaves to read despite Tom Weylin's threat, and pleads Rufus not to sell slaves in the slavery times. In addition, both have experienced trying escape from Rufus. When Alice shows Dana's letters to Kevin not sent but left in Rufus' bed chest, Dana tells Alice, "Thanks. Be careful when you put them back." And Alice says, "You be careful too." (170) What they talks means Dana's runaway. They understand each other by communion of mind with mind. After all, Alice becomes strong enough not to be frustrated when she loses her two children and independent enough to hang herself. Dana also becomes strong enough to endure the pains of whippings by and overseer during field works and independent enough to kill Rufus.

The most important similarity between Alice and Dana is their love for their men. Alice has a sincere love for Isaac as Dana does for Kevin. Although Alice lives with Rufus and has children, she always thinks, loves, and misses Isaac, her husband, sold to the South with his ear cut off. Like Alice, Dana always misses Kevin and wants to hear from him when they are separated from each other. Finally, WHEN Kevin comes back to Dana from his lonely wandering to the North, Alice says to Kevin softly, "Get her out of here while you can. No telling what our 'good masters' will do if you don't." (184) Alice watched Dana and kevin dry-eyed but with a pain on her face, thinking that Kevin has come to Dana finally, but Isaac will not be coming to her. Alice pledges to run away to get free whenever she is raped by Rufus, and Dana calls Kevin to help her whenever she is faced to dangers.

Although Alice and Dana look like, are strong and independent, and have sincere loves for their husbands, Alice is a slave, yet Dana is free. Alice is born free and has been friends with Rufus until she belongs to him. Rufus' taking Alice is rape which is legal in those times. However, Kevin and Dana are husband and wife. They make love because they love each other. When Alice is pregnant, Dana asks Alice," You're still think about running?" and Alice replies, "Wouldn't you be if you didn't have another way to get free? When I'm strong again after I have this baby, I'm going." (233) Because of slavery, Alice cannot live with her father and her husband, cannot learn reading and writing, and cannot marry Rufus, a white man. But Dana teaches people to read, marries Kevin, a white man, and lives with him as an equal.

Alice's life with Rufus is unhappy, yet Dana's marriage is happy. For example, Alice's father is sold by Tom Weylin when she was a little girl. She is raped by Rufus after she married Isaac. In addition, her husband is sold, and she becomes a slave. She is forced to live with Rufus and raped whenever Rufus wants to have her. She loses her first two children and tries to run away from Rufus with her two babies. As a result, she is caught, whipped, and becomes sick. And finally, she hangs herself because she thinks Rufus sold her two babies. On the other hand, Dana is well educated and writes novels. She meets Kevin while working. Kevin thinks he can have Dana work for him at first, but he finally proposes her to marry as an equal. They marry and move to a bigger house in Los Angeles. And Kevin takes care of her whenever she comes back home with scars from her trip back. Dana and Kevin find out that they really need and miss each other when they are separated from each other. When Rufus buys Alice, he confesses to Dana, "If I livered in your time, I would have married her, or tried to." (124) Rufus loves Alice as Kevin does Dana. However, there is a big difference between Rufus' time and Kevin's. Rufus sees almost the same woman in Alice and Dana. But he does not consider the slavery: Alice — a slave in the 19th century versus Dana — a free woman in the 20th century. When time passes, Alice's life becomes worse and Dana's better.

In conclusion, Dana and Alice look alike and need each other tied as family. Externally, both are tall, slender, bareheaded, black women. Internally, they are strong, independent and sincere. However, Alice has a critical disadvantage as a slave compared to Dana. So she consistently tries to escape from Rufus to get free. And finally, she hangs herself with overcoming her fate as a slave while Dana and Kevin's love has been strengthened. Although Alice and Dana have a lot of similarities, they have fundamental differences because of slavery.

Comprehensive Immigration Reform

President Bush proposed what he termed a "comprehensive" approach to immigration that consists of securing the border, strengthening enforcement inside the country and creating a temporary worker program. People may have different opinions about the new immigration proposal according to their own perspectives. The U.S. citizens who are suffering from the illegal immigrants may ask tougher enforcement borders, but the employers who must compete with foreign companies may continuously need the cheaper workforces from the illegal immigrants. Therefore, there are many controversial issues about the illegal immigration. However, because the U.S., as a law-governed country, has to keep its national security and to improve its industrial competitiveness, Congress should approve President's proposal in its original form.

The U.S. is a law-governed country, so all illegal behaviors should be punished at law. John J. Miller states in "Border Blues" that illegal immigrants have destructed the whole region near the border. For example, they are usually littering everywhere, busting waterlines when they're thirsty, killing barking dogs, robbing ranchers, and threatening women by making obscene hand gestures. Ranchers have to fight against property damage every day, and the Border Patrol has to struggle continuously to "catch and release" illegal immigrants. In addition, local hospitals cut services to keep from going broke, because federal law requires hospitals to provide medical service to even illegal immigrants (1). What the government can do are increasing agents for policing the border, supplying high-tech equipment to Border Patrol, and allocating millions of dollars each year to cover the cost of the illegal aliens (4). However, the crossers who are caught go back to their home countries and try to cross again. Miller asserts "Anybody who really wants to make it into the U.S. is going to succeed, even if it takes a few tries" (2). Why are the U.S. citizens badly damaged by the illegal immigrants, criminals? The U.S. government must secure its citizens' safety and property from crimes and to use no more budgets for the sake of criminals. Therefore, Border Patrol should be strengthened for securing the border tighter than ever before.

In addition to securing border tougher, the U.S. government must take proper actions for preventing the threats caused by illegal immigrants. There is always a possibility that illegal immigrants are infected with some kind of contagious disease and carrying germs. And nobody knows whether susceptible terrorists against America hide among them. Since President Bush took office, funding for immigration enforcement has increased by 42 percent. These resources have helped agents bring to justice smugglers, terrorists, gang members, and human traffickers. For example, through Operation Community Shield, Federal agents have arrested nearly 2,300 gang members who were in America illegally, including violent criminals like the members of the "MS-13" gang (Whitehouse News Release 2). The U.S. is the country for people who observe American values including liberty, civic responsibility, and equality under God. The U.S. is not the country for criminals and potential terrorists. Therefore, the U.S. government has to strengthen the laws in order to root out any crimes which defame American values.

With tougher border and laws enforcement, the U.S. government needs to create a guest—worker program in order to keep its industrial competitiveness by using the cheap labor forces of the aliens. According to the Bear Sterns report, the nation's illegal immigrant population is closer to 20 million and it is unbelievable statistic that "Mexican nationals working in the U.S. sent home $13 billion last year, the second—biggest source of funds for Mexico after petroleum exports" (McHugh 1). Roberto Hernandez, the Mexican consul in Nogales, Ariz. says that "we cannot resolve the immigration phenomenon with more agents, we have to find more creative and imaginative ways; ways that address the need of workers in the U.S. and the lack of good opportunities in Mexico" (Thompson 2). Miller also suggests that one alternative worth considering is a new guest—worker program that would make it possible for illegal aliens to legalize their status on a temporary basis and work in the U.S. (5). Many American manufacturers try to reduce costs to compete with foreign companies. And it is true that off—the—books immigrant labor is somehow contributing to the U.S. economy especially to the prices of the necessaries of life. Without the cheaper labor forces, the living cost would be increased a lot. But it is nonsense to allow illegal behavior because of the prices. Therefore, a guest—worker program is the best way to satisfy both the U.S. employers, looking for relatively cheaper work forces, and alien workers, looking for jobs with more money than in their own countries. A guest—worker program can also reduce the struggles occurring along the U.S. – Mexican border.

Opponents of the strict laws to illegal immigrants argue that the underground economy in the U.S., mostly made up of illegal immigrants, is almost $1—trillion—a—year and is growing faster than the legitimate business. Furthermore, any increase in regulation against the underground economy would threaten industries such as agriculture, apparel, construction, and hospitality, which depend on immigration labor. And the result could be further losses of business to overseas competition, coupled with escalating costs at home (McHugh 1, 2). According to the Immigration and Naturalization Service, 369 immigrants have died trying to cross the border since last October. Most of the deaths were caused by hypothermia, dehydration and drowning. Human rights advocates say that the desert death is increased because of the tougher U.S. border enforcement which has caused crossers to cut new channels through more perilous areas (Thompson 1, 2).

In conclusion, there may be a lot of contradictions about President Bush's new proposals for immigration. But the fundamental principle of finding out the optimal solution is prioritizing the controversial issues. Because the U.S. is the law—governed country, the punishment for an illegality is prior to the forgiveness on human rights and the law observance is more important than the unlawful competitiveness. Therefore, securing border and strengthening the internal laws are proper ways to keep the U.S. from illegality and creating a guest— worker program is the only way to satisfy the U.S. and aliens. Congress has no other way but approval of Bush's "Comprehensive Immigration Reform".

Appearances Are Destructive

In the essay titled "Appearances Are Destructive", Mark Mathabane claims that dress code is a good way to curb school violence and to promote learning. He enrolls his sisters, come from South Africa to American schools which are highly advanced than African schools. But his sisters cannot adapt to American school life because of their cloths. They become so distracted that they want to transfer to different schools. Mathabane investigates the clothing situations at several public schools in the country and finds out that famous brands clothing is the general tendency in schools. According to Mathabane, students pay more attention to dress than study and rate their parental love by how much money their parent spend for the students' dresses. Those parents without enough money for students' expensive outfits are considered uncaring. The students explain that clothing is more important than academic performance for boasting themselves and being attracted by boys. Mathabane refutes against civil libertarians who explain that dress codes infringe on freedom of expression. He argues that dress codes have no diminution of our freedoms in many aspects of our lives. He also explains that school dress codes are helping for students to focus on their studies in many other countries. Mathabane finally concludes that Americans have to realize that dress code has more benefits than curtailment of freedom.

In paragraph 8, Mathabane explains that "Those parents without the money to waste on such meretricious extravagances are considered uncaring and cruel". I totally agree his explanation because I have seen the very similar situations many times in Korea. When I was young, everybody was poor and had not enough money to think about dresses. According to the country has developed and industrialized for the last several decades, people have been richer and westernized. Finally, schools introduced free clothing instead of a school uniform. Free clothing looked good at first, but gradually a lot of negative effects showed up: the disparity between poor and rich, school violence, sexual problems, academic attainment declining etc. many schools returned to dress code after they experienced the problems of free clothing in school. I also had strongly asserted for dress code at a meeting of parents of students. A school uniform will be helpful for student to be safe, effective, and student-like.

GGU에서
MBA 과정을 공부할 때(2002~2004)
쓴 글들

＊GGU (Golden Gate University): California 주 San Francisco에 소재한 대학교

샌프란시스코 금문교(Golden Gate Bridge)

345

GGU course Summary

	Course No	Calendar	Course Name	Professor	Grade
Admission requirements	TOEFL	7/19/02(Paper 527), 1/29/03(CBT 203), 4/18/03(CBT 217)		550, 213	217
	GMAT	7/31/02(490), 2/05/03(450), 3/E/03 Waived		600	Waived
Credit	MATH 30	1981	College Algebra		Credit
Foundation Program (18 units)	ACCTG 201	01/07 – 03/09 2002 Spring I	Managerial Accounting	Gene Bucciarolli	A
	CIS 225	03/11 – 05/18 2002 Spring II	Computer Information System	David Fickbohn	A
	ECON 202	10/11 – 12/13 2001 Fall II	Economics	Said Haimor	A
	MGT 204	05/20 – 07/27 2002 Summer	International Business	Matthew M. Timbo	A
	MGT 210	10/14 – 12/12 2002 Fall II	Management Theory & Application	Lee Robbins	A-
	MATH 240	08/04 – 10/11 2003 Fall I	Data Analysis for Managers	Gene Sellers	A
Advanced Program (Core course) (18 units)	FI 300A	07/29 – 10/06 2002 Fall I	Managerial Finance	Joseph H. Labrie	B+
	OP 300	01/08 – 03/12 2003 Spring I	Operations Management	Nabil Rageh	A
	OP 303	05/31 – 08/02 2003 Summer	Innovation & Technology	Mohan A. Raj	A-
	MKT 300	10/13 – 12/20 2003 Fall II	Marketing Management	William Hess	B+
	MGT 300	08/04 – 10/11 2003 Fall I	Managerial Analysis and Team Dynamics	Anthony Constantouros	B+
	MGT 362	10/13 – 12/20 2003 Fall II	Developing Strategies for Competitive Advantage	Thomas Heimoth	A-
Advanced Program (Concentration course) (12 units)	OP 302 (Directed)	2/21,28 3/6,13 2004 Spring I	Quality Management	Gary Clapper	A
	OP 323 (Cyber)	01/12 – 04/26 2004 Spring I	Supply Chain Management	Robert Amos	B
	OP 320 (Directed)	03/15 – 05/17 2004 Spring II	Purchasing Management	Richard Dawe	A
	OP 340 (Cyber)	01/05 – 03/13 2004 Spring I	Project & System Management	Homer Johnstone	A-

일범의 평범한 사람 이야기

An Essay to Introduce Myself

have been working at USS—POSCO Industries, a joint venture between US Steel and POSCO –A Korean steel manufacturer–, located in Pittsburg, California since July, 2000. It was a great opportunity for me to come to the United States. My company might select me as the most appropriate specialist to work for UPI because of my work experience. As a production assistant manager in my organization, I need to be an excellent communicator and an effective interdepartmental coordinator. But I have had a lot of difficulties in performing the managerial roles due to my poor English.

Taking MBA courses at Golden Gate University is very helpful for me to achieve my objectives in the organization. Learning management theories, economics and financial statements was the new experiences to me as an engineer. The discussions and e—mail communication with other students to complete team projects enabled me to understand American education system and to remind the importance of team power. And the variety of case analysis with instructors who have a lot of experiences trained me to be qualified to the higher management position.

America is the land of dream. It has the unlimited possibility. I could understand the importance of family, neighbors and community by participating in outreach programs. Through the Seafood Festival in Pittsburg, Habitat for Humanity, Juvenile Diabetes Research Foundation

Walk at Heather Park, Family Holiday Celebration, my children's school activities, and many other forms of outreach. Participation in AISE golf tournaments which is impossible in Korea was also another experience to me.

I may return to my country after three more years. My dream is to be dispatched again to a new production line in another country as a superintendent who is responsible for every process for construction, organizing, financing, production, and sales. So, I need to be prepared as an excellent manager for every possibility. Fluent English speaking, master's degree of MBA, and better understanding of foreign cultures would be very helpful to my successful management.

Youngjing Sohn

Statement of Purpose

1.Job experiences

Dates	Jobs	Company
02/1976 ~ 07/1978	Military Service in Korean Army	
04/1984 ~ 02/1989	IE Instructor	POSCO in Korea
03/1983 ~ 04/1984	Purchasing Engineer	
04/1984 ~ 02/1989	IE Engineer	
03/1989 ~ 04/1991	Production & Technical Manager	POSTIN in Korea
05/1991 ~ 07/1992	Quality Assurance Manager	
08/1992 ~ 07/1993	Team Leader for New Plant Construction	
07/1993 ~ 11/1995	Production Manager	
12/1995 ~ 06/1997	Superintendent of Tin Plate Mill	POSCO in KOREA
07/1997 ~ 09/1998	Section Mgr. of Coating Technology Team	
09/1998 ~ 07/2000	Technical Mgr. in Facility Investment Team	
07/2000 ~ Present	Production Assistant Manager	UPI in CA,

2.How Obtaining an MBA Degree Will Assist my Future Goals

I may be here in USS—POSCO Industries for three ~ four more years, and then return to my country. The most important goal for me to achieve during my American life is becoming a fluent speaker in

English. I have a lot of difficulties in communicating with Americans. I cannot fully understand what's going on the meetings. My vocabulary does not allow me to express myself as I want. If I were at the fluency at with English, all other weaknesses would be covered and improved spontaneously.

I want to go to China as a superintendent in a subsidiary company within one or two years after I returned to Korea. If I go to China as a superintendent, I have to manage the whole process from construction, organizing, financing, production and sales. So I need to be prepared as an excellent manager for every possibility. I need to have a good command of English and Chinese. And master's degree of MBA and better understanding of foreign cultures would be very helpful to my successful management.

After I retire from my company in China, I would like to have my own office where I can read books, write my life story, invite friends for funny talks, and teach the younger generations the value of history, I am happy because I have a dream.

Youngjing Sohn

American Expressions

Good evening, I am Young Sohn. Glad to have a time to make a speech in front all of you. Tonight, I'd like to talk about American expressions that have been embarrassing me a lot since I arrived in the United States.

I have been here in America over 2 years. The two years' life in America looks happy in its appearance, but it was really hard time for me. I have maintained day by day with the heavy stresses by the English. I work at USS—POSCO Industries that is a joint venture company between U.S Steel and POSCO, a Korean steel company. It produces and sells Cold Rolled Steel, Zinc Coated Steel and Tin Coated Steel. I am Production Assistant Manager in Tin division. I have supported Division Manager and Department Managers with investigating and resolving a number of issues in the field of Operation, Maintenance and Quality.

The most difficult thing for me to work with Americans is communication problems — Listening or understanding others, expressing or speaking myself. I have learned English in my middle school and high school in Korea. The English education was focused at the normal, standard language. But based upon my experience, the American expressions used in the real life are quite different from what I had learned at school.

Let's take an example. I learned "How do you do, Mr. Smith?" and "How do you do, Mr. Kim?" as the greeting at the first meeting. But nobody said that. Instead of "How do you do" or "Mr.", everybody said "I'm Mike, nice to meet you" or "I'm Linda, good to see you". I knew that calling first name at the meeting for the first time is not courtesy, it's rude. But everybody introduced himself or herself only his/her first name.

Let's take another example. I think Americans prefer the expression "How are you doing?" to "How are you?" At the first time I heard "How are you doing?" from someone whom I came across on the road, I tried to reply to him. "I am doing well, how about you?" But he already has walked far away before I finished my reply.

Here is one more example. Someone asked me a lot of question to confirm my understanding during her explanation about a situation. "Do you know what I mean?" "Do you know what I am saying?" But she did not wait my answer and continued her talking. So I could not intercept and answer of "Yes, I do" or "No, I don't". It took many days for me to understand that was a meaningless pet phrase.

We have some same or similar expressions between America and Korea.
"One stone kills two birds" and "No news is good news" are the exact same proverbs in Korea. And there are some different expressions for the

same situation. "White elephant" in America means something which is regrettable to throw it away, but not valuable to keep it. We in Korea call it "Chicken rib" instead of "White elephant". "The squeaky wheels get the grease" is the similar expression of "More cake to the crying child" in Korea. This may be because of the cultural difference.

The expressions using among the workers in the steel making companies are more difficult to understand. They speak a lot of slang, unfamiliar terms and also bad words. Here are some examples.

"When was it hooked up?"

"Top entry rectifier #2 kicked out."

"Kicking ass, make money."

"What's the scoop ruddy poop?"

"Frozen roll"

"Chilling like a villain" yadi yadi yada.

They speak very fast, and their pronunciations are not clear at the noisy surroundings. So, I could hardly catch their meaning when they said.

"It's better to pissed off than pissed on."

"I came to kick ass and chew bubble gum, but I am all around bubble gum."

"What's up, doc?"

"This is kuku"

There are some CB radio talks being used in the steel company. I was so confused to understand what they were saying.

"Mike Ortiz, do you copy?"

"What's your 20?"

"10, 4"

I don't want to arrange in a row the expressions that I have collected. Perplexed by these unfamiliar sayings, I began to document them with their Korean translations. This is the note that I have catalogued in my quest to record new idioms. It's almost twelve pages and growing.

I think I have been an excellent manager in terms of understanding others, communicating effectively and developing employees for last ten years in Korea. However, everything was changed since I began my assignment at USS—POSCO as Production Assistant Manager. The problem was communication in English. I have never had any problems for shopping, making journeys, attending seminars, or even business trips to foreign countries. But the communication with the people who work in the steel making company is quite different from those kinds of outside activities.

Without the English ability of understanding others and explaining my ideas, how can be a good coordinator? How can be a good director? How can be a good mentor? How can be a good facilitator? And finally, how can be a good manager? Unnatural smiles cannot explain the proper responses and the poor body languages cannot replace the proper verbal explanation. Understanding the situation in advance is helpful for better communication, and preparation for talking also works. But the most important thing for a foreigner to be an American in listening and speaking is no other ways but "Listen, listen and listen" "Speak, speak and speak".

Leading With Soul

(이글은 미국 작가 Lee G. Ballman과 Terrence E. Deal이 함께 저술한 『Leading with Soul』이라는 책을 읽고 난 독후감이다.)

Basically, I agree with the authors' approach for leadership with soul. I would like to tell it by 'leading with love' instead of 'leading with soul'. 'Love' is the more common word for people's understanding than 'soul' that seems to be religious. Leading with soul can be accepted by readers as a new, fresh, and heart—oriented approach within the Americanized organization, but it is a kind of general and common leading approach in Korea and Japan. Leading with soul is a new approach for taking some advantages from oriental spiritual values.

1. Soul and spirit

The authors have their own ideas of soul and spirit. They explain.

'Soul and spirit are so interconnected that the two words are often used interchangeably, but we see an important distinction. Soul is personal and unique, grounded in the depths of personal experience.

When each of us plunges into the depths at the core of our being, there we find soul. Spirit is transcendent and all embracing. It is the universal source, the oneness of all things: God, Jahweh, Allah, and Buddha. Soul and spirit are related in the same way as peaks and valleys, male and female. Hey are intimately connected. Each needs the other'.

I have a different idea about soul and spirit. This means that my start line for managerial leadership is different from the American authors.

God made human being as his feature by using soils and gave him His breath. Then it became 'a living soul'. God called him 'Adam'. These are from Genesis chapter 1. (Rsv. Bible, Gen. 2–7: then the Lord God formed man of dust from the ground, and breathed into his nostrils the breath of life; and man became a living being.)

Human being is made of body (soils) and soul (God's breath). If soul is separated from your body, you die. Death means separating soul from body. Then what is spirit? Spirit automatically came to you when soul and body combined together. When you take a dream during sleeping, your spirit can separate from your body, go around everywhere, and take journey by itself. But soul cannot separate from your body unless you die.

After death, what will happen? Body will go back to soils, and soul will go back the place where it came from – to God (Christians say), to the origin (Buddhist and Zennists say). And spirit will be disappeared without any trace.

Who are you? Is your face you? Are your eyes you? Is your mouth you? No, those are not you but yours. Body cannot be you. Your body moves by your will. Your body is your slaves. Mind is you. Mind is your master. Your mind is your soul that God gave you. Your soul was before you borrowed your body, and your soul will be after your body is separated.

What is the difference between 'thinking' and 'mind'? Thinking is in your head. It can be changed by education and training. Thinking is based on your spirit. Spirit come in your head and comes out of your head. But mind is in your heart. It cannot be changed. Mind is as it as at the beginning, because mind is soul. Some expressions such as 'Heart is pounding' or 'Heart leaped with joy' imply that soul is in heart.

How can you find your soul? If you take delicious food, or if you see beautiful flowers, your body (eyes, nose or mouth) will be happy. If you win a lottery or if you are promoted, your mind (ego or desire) will be happy. But if you do a good deed without notice to anyone or if you give even a small love to others without telling to anyone, your soul will be happy. The reason is it is love.

Buddhist and Zennist say that soul cannot go back to the origin unless it is completed in this world. How to make it complete? The answer is love. Soul can be grown—up by eating 'love'. If you do love, your soul will be grown up. The more you do good things, the more your soul grown up. Grown up, grown up, and grown up by doing love, love, and love. Finally, your soul will be completed.

2. Diagnosis of present organization and leadership

Too many workplaces are almost devoid of meaning and purpose. They are ruled by technology, efficiency, and the bottom line, with little regard for what human beings need in order to experience personal fulfillment and success. Over time, this takes a heavy toll on motivation, loyalty, and performance. It is a road to crisis and decay—unless we find ways to reinforce the workplace with passion, zest, and spirit.

Across sectors and levels, organizations are starved for the leadership they need. Two misleading images currently dominate organizational thinking about leadership: one the heroic champion with extraordinary statue and vision, the other the 'policy wonk', the skilled analyst who soles pressing problems with information, programs, and policies. Both these images emphasize the hands and heads of leaders, neglecting deeper and more enduring elements of courage, spirit, and hope. Leaders who have lost touch with their own souls, who are confused and uncertain about their core values and beliefs, inevitably lose their way or sound an uncertain trumpet.

Most management and leadership development programs ignore and demean spirit.

3. How to solve it

It is easy to go astray when we forget that the heart of leadership is in the hearts of leaders. We fool ourselves, thinking that sheer bravado or analytical techniques can respond to our deepest concerns. We lose touch with the deepest and most precious of human gifts—soul and spirit. To recapture spirit, we need to relearn how to lead with soul: How to know ourselves and our faith at the deepest level. How to breathe new zest and buoyancy into life? How to reinvigorate the family as a sanctuary where people can grow, develop, and find love? How to reinforce the workplace with vigor and élan? Leading with soul returns us to ancient spiritual basics—reclaiming the enduring human capacity that gives our lives passion and purpose.

More and more people are working to recapture the essence of what soul and spirit can bring to the modern workplace. Life and livelihood ought not to be separated but to flow from the same source, which is Spirit, for both life and livelihood are about living in depth, living with meaning, purpose, joy, and a sense of contribution to the greater community. A spirituality of work is about bringing life and livelihood back together again. And spirit with them.

Leaders with soul bring spirit to organizations. They marry the two so that spirit feeds soul rather than starving it and soul enriches spirit rather than killing it. Leaders of spirit find their soul's treasure store and offer its gifts to others.

Management and leadership development programs desperately need an infusion of spiritual forms such as poetry, literature, music, art, theater, history, philosophy, and dance.

Our journey is a search, often arduous, for our spiritual center. Once we find our own light within, we can share it with others, offering our own gifts from the heart.

POSCO Strategy

Issue: POSCO expands its Chinese stainless-steel operation

Date: 10/21/2003

Contents: POSCO's Board of Directors resolved, during the October 17, 2003, meeting, to expand the company's stainless-steel operations in the Chinese province of Jiangsu. The company will construct stainless steel making plant and STS hot rolling mills on the site of Zhangjiagang POSCO Stainless Steel, with an annual production capacity of 600,000 tons. The construction is scheduled to begin early 2005 and be completed by the end of 2006.

It is expected that some 700 million US dollars will be invested in this expansion project. About 290 million US dollars will be raised through POSCO and Jiangsu Shangang Group's capital investment in Zhangjiagang POSCO Stainless Steel. The two companies, according to their equity ratio, will respectively invest 82.5% and 17.5% of the 290 million. The remainder of the 700 million will come from borrowings in China.

With China's demand for hot rolled stainless steel increasing by an average of 20% annually, major steelmakers in China have been aggressively attempting to expand their stainless—steel production facilities. However, it is expected that the deficiency in the supply of hot rolled stainless steel, will continue. Under these circumstances, POSCO's decision to expand its Chinese STS facilities will give its Chinese operations a stable supply of hot rolled stainless steel. This hot rolled stainless steel will be supplied to Zhangjiagang POSCO Stainless Steel, which produces 360,000 tons of cold rolled stainless products, and Qingdao Pohang Stainless Steel, which is scheduled to enter operation in January 2005 with an annual production capacity of 180,000 tons.

This enhancement of stainless—steel facilities will enable POSCO to meet a rapid increase in Chinese demand for steel and maintain its competitiveness against European and Japanese steelmakers, some of which are merging to become larger companies.

Crown Cork & Seal in 1989

Five firms dominated the $12.2 billion U.S. metal can industry in 1898, with an aggregate 61% market share. The county's largest manufacturer － American National Can－ held a 25% market share. The four firms trailing American National in sales were Continental Can (18% market share), Reynolds Metals (7%), Crown Cork & Seal (7%), and Ball Corporation (4%). Approximately 100 firms served the balance of the market.

The major trends characterizing the metal container industry during the 1980s included: (1) the containing threat of in－house manufacturer; (2) the emergence of plastics as a viable packaging material; (3) steady competition from glass as a substitute for aluminum in the beer market; (4) the emergence of the soft drink industry as the largest end－user of packaging, with aluminum as the primary beneficiary; and (5) the diversification of, and consolidation among, packaging producers.

In 1957, John Connelly took over the presidency of Crown Cork & Seal which was teetered on the verge of bankruptcy. Connelly's first move to rescue the company was to pare down the organization. The second step was to institute the concept of accountability. The next step was to slow production to halt and liquidate $7 million in inventory. Connelly emphasized cost efficiency, quality, flexibility and quick response to customer needs as the essential ingredients for Crown's strategy in the decades ahead.

In the early 1960s Crown concentrated on the beverage cans and the growing aerosol market and produced exclusively steel cans through the late 1970s. Crown spearheaded the conversion from steel to aluminum cans and investment on two—piece can equipments in the early 1980s. From 1976 through 1989, Crown had 26 domestic plant locations versus nine in 1955. By 1988, Crown's 62 foreign plants generated 44% of sales and 54% of operating profits.

However, it is not the right time for William Avery, the successor of Connelly, to bid on for getting any regional division of Continental Can Co. because Continental Can is one of the largest manufacturers of rigid plastic containers whose business is quite different from Crown's. Avery had better to wait for getting a chance to consolidate Carnaud Metal Box in Europe whose business is also metal cans in near future.

Honda (A) and (B)

The Honda Motor Co. was founded by Sochiro Honda, a visionary inventor and industrialist, in 1948. At that time, postwar Japan was in desperate need of transportation. Honda had experienced a lot of fails and difficulties during its initial stages. In 1958 the 50 cc Honda Supercub was introduced — with an automatic clutch, 3—speed transmission, automatic starter, and the safe, friendly looking. It was an explosive success. It was an important turning point for Honda to become the world's largest motorcycle producer. Honda increased its production 3,587 thousand units (41% of Japanese total) in 1981 from 531 units (only 7% of Japanese production) in 1952.

In 1959, Honda entered the U.S market. Honda established a U.S subsidiary company instead of distributors, offered very small lightweight motorcycles, and developed the market region by region, from the West Coast to eastward. Honda's motorcycle was superior to the Sears lightweight and easier to handle. Honda's machines sold for less than $250 retail, compared with $1,000 ~ $1,500 for the bigger American and British machines. Honda addressed its appeal primarily to middle-class consumers and claimed, "You meet the nicest people on a Honda" which was the fruit of a sales director's strong assertion. This marketing effort was backed by heavy advertising.

The market approach of Honda can be described as a "marketing philosophy".

Honda's emphasis on market share as the primary objective led to high production volume, improved productivity, low costs, and in the long term to higher profitability than its competitors. The Honda prices in the U.S are so much higher than those of the same products in Japan. This means that cost reductions have indeed taken place in parallel with real price reductions.

일범의 평범한 사람 이야기

The fundamental cause for Honda's success was its higher productivity. The motorcycle industry was exhibiting the effects that differences in growth rates, volume, and level of capital investment among competitors can have on relative costs. The high rate of levels of production achieved by Japanese manufacturers resulted in their superior productivity. In terms of value added per employee, Honda outperformed Western competitors by as much as five times.

Can Chinese Brands Make It Abroad?

China dominates global manufacturing because its labor is cheap. For now most Chinese companies are content to be original—equipment manufacturers that build products for Western brands.

But some are feeling pressure from the government and competitors to leave behind the anonymous OEM role and become branded players in developed markets.

While many Chinese manufacturers deliver quality that matches that of competitors from other countries, most lack a comparable marketing expertise.

Can Chinese Brands Make It Abroad?
The answer is yes, but it won't be easy.

Mckinsey have identified two business models that would help a Chinese consumer products company move its branded goods quickly into developed markets while taking the time to become familiar with them.

The primary model is a step—by—step procedure in which products exported from China penetrate overseas markets through independent distributors serving discount channels. This gradual process would permit Chinese companies to gain an understanding of customer behavior and to build brand recognition.

In the second model, Chinese companies buy an established brand that has fallen on hard times and then move its production to China to benefit from lower labor costs.

A Hundred–Year War: Coke vs. Pepsi, 1890s-1990s

Hyper-competition	Coke	Pepsi
Vision of disruption -Stakeholder Satisfaction -Strategic Soothsaying	-Dominated the consumer's taste (1886~1940) -Protected its secret formula -U.S. Market share: 50% (1950) -Advertising 1955: "American Preferred Taste" 1960: "No Wonder Coke refreshed Best:	-Began as small brand (1893) -Developed its own formula -Almost bankruptcy in 1923 and 1932 -U.S. Market share: 10% (1950) -Advertising 1950: "Beat Coke" 1963: "Pepsi Generation" 1974: "Pepsi Challenge"
Capabilities for disruption -Speed -Surprise	-Introduced new flavors: Fanta (1960), Sprite (1961), low-calorie Tab(1963), Diet Coke (1982), New Coke (1985) -Introduced 11 new soft drinks brands (1980s): Cherry Coke, etc -Purchased Cadbury-Schweppes (1998)	-Countered with Teem (1960), Mountain Dew (1964), Diet Pepsi (1964) -Introduced 13 products (1980s): Cherry Pepsi, etc -Purchased Tropicana (1998)
Tactics for disruption -Shifting the rules of competition -Signals -Simultaneous & Sequential strategic thrusts	-Fought against imitations and counterfeits in court (~1920) -Built nation-wide franchised bottling networks -Introduced vending machines(1930s) -Announced plans to acquire Dr. Pepper (1986) -Dominated fountain sales -Food restaurant business Wendy's, Burger King Overseas Market -Built bottling plants to supply American troops (1942~) -Steadily Expanded (1950s) -Primarily focused on overseas market (1960s) -Built brand presence in developing market -Appointed anchor bottlers -Major overseas markets: Western Europe, Latin America, much of Asia	-Followed to develop parallel network of bottlers -Price: 20 % lower than Coke (1960s) -Announced its intension to acquire Seven-Up (1986) -Focused on retail outlets -Food restaurant business Pizza Hut, Taco Bell, KFC Overseas Market -Followed to enter Europe in 1970s -Battled aggressively in the United States (1960s) -Utilized niche strategy with well-executed blitzes. -Formed alliance with local bottlers -Major overseas markets: Middle East and Southeast Asia

Marks and Spencer Ltd.

Resource-based Analysis of Marks & Spencer Ltd.

Competitive Advantage

Organizational Capabilities

Resources		
Tangible	**Intangible**	**Human**
-Charge-card services contributes profit	-New information technology (EPOS) increases efficiency	-Strong leadership fosters good human relations with customers, suppliers, and staff
-Long leasehold properties enables the lowest rent/sales rate	-St. Michael brand identifies quality and value	-Well-above-average benefits motivate employees to devote

Overseas expansion efforts and new overseas market in the future
- Canada and France were the concentrated markets and the other overseas market in Belgium, Ireland, and U.S have nor good performance.

- The highest potential market to growth is China, because of its population and high economic growth rate every year.

Successful transferring from clothing to food
- St. Michael brand of clothing are accepted as very high quality and moderate by the customers
- M&S food also was priced moderate to high with its superior quality

Less successful transferring from Britain to overseas
-The clearance of non-St. Michael goods and high tariffs in Canada
- Target customers are loyal to competitors (Peoples and D'Allaird's) chains
- Independent stores and hypermarkets have higher market share than multiple chains in France

A Surprise Ending At Hanaro Telecom

South Korea has the world's highest broadband Internet penetration in its population. There are three major telecommunication rivals in Korea — KT, Hanaro, and SK.

KT Corp. is the country's largest fixed-line telephone operator and Internet service provider. And Hanaro is the second-largest broadband company in the nation. Hanaro controls 27% on the high-speed internet market in Korea.

Hanaro Telecom has long been afflicted by the short-term liquidity problem and its debt-to-equity ratio of 156 percent.

On Oct. 21st, Shareholders of Hanaro Telecom voted overwhelmingly to sell a controlling 40 % stake to a U.S. group led by private equity firm Newbridge Capital Inc. and insurance giant American International Group Inc. Following the approval by shareholders, Hanaro will receive $500 million in equity from the AIG-Newbridge consortium, in exchange for 39.6 percent of Hanaro's stock as well as handing over managerial rights to the investment groups.

The loser was LG Group, one of the mightiest Chaebul in Korea. LG, as Hanaro's largest single investor with an18 % stake, wanted to fold Hanaro into its own telecommunications business to integrate online and wired services as well as broadcasting.

By the improvement of financial conditions, Hanaro can make a long-term business strategy to invest in next-generation high-speed Internet businesses and engage in new sectors as well. And LG may have to change its strategy by giving up its telecommunications business.

(Source: Business Week, November 3, 2003)

Charles Schwab: A Category of One

Has Schwab effectively balanced the old and new world of stock trading?

- Yes, Schwab was positioned between deep-discount online and full price, full service brokerage firms.

How will Schwab remain a leader between giants like Merrill Lynch and Internet pure plays like E-trade?

- Schwab developed a niche between low commission online firms like E★trade and Datek, and full-service brokerage firms with investment banking operations like Merrill Lynch and Morgan Stanley. In contrast to former, Schwab was not a price/performance leader. To the latter, Schwab was neither full brokerage nor an investment bank

How has Schwab remained a competitive player?

- The Schwab brand was synonymous with discount brokerage, customer service and longevity.
- Being first to market in discount brokerage and early to market in online brokerage contributed to the popularity and value of Schwab brand.

— Schwab offered an analogous mix of products and services to both discount and online clients for example SchwabAlerts, Schwab AdvisorSource, and Schwab Signature Service)

— Schwab was among the top three distributors of mutual funds in the nation

Has Schwab 's unique status as a discount brokerage began to wane?

— Not yet Schwab remained the popular brand of discount and online brokerage firms even though the market value of online firms, and that of most full service brokerage firms, declined as well due to the rising interest rates.

— But Schwab could not rely too heavily upon its unique competitive status because more powerful and resourceful mergers in the online brokerage community are challenging to Schwab by dropping trading commissions to $4.95. per trade.

What Schwab should do to sustain its competitive advantage?

Schwab also should join hands with other companies or banks which have enough resources to gain a strong competition to strengthen its competitiveness.

Procter & Gamble Europe: Vizir Launch

1. Issues:

    (1) Should Vizir be launched or delayed?
    (2) Should it be positioned as Eurobrand?

2. Evaluation of alternative approaches:

Issues	Pros (Should be)	Cons (Should not be)
Should Vizir be launched?	-The new HDL product won a blind test against the leading French powder, Ariel, in 1976 and German market leader, Persil, in 1977. -Procter's Formula SB won a blind test against the main competitive powders (France, Germany, U.K) -Prepared for 7 years -Superior cleaning performance at lower temperatures -Companywide supports	-In 1977, Colgate closed the test market and withdrew Axion even though it showed excellent initial results. -Vizir may not make sense to launch with the proposed market positioning and copy strategy. -Vizir would not cannibalize Ariel's sales -New competitive entries with lower price: no effective barriers to entry -Limited HDL market potential due to the different European washing habits -Counterattack from Henkel
Should it be positioned as Eurobrand?	-It can foster coordination of marketing strategies of brands in Europe -The market data indicates converging trend in consumer laundry habits -Standardization of brands and market strategies across Europe -To go to a single formula, standard size packs, and multilingual labels can save great money in mold costs, line downtime for changeover, sourcing flexibility and reduced. inventory levels	-It may conflict with the existing philosophy allowed to country. subsidiary managers -The differences in washing habits still overweighed the similarities. -Differences other than consumer preferences -Greater coordination is needed to protect subsidiaries' profit opportunities. -To establish a new brand is incredibly expensive -Cannot even be breakeven in blind test -Different detergent market according to each country

3. My Suggestion

A national launch of Vizir should be delayed because it is to risky to invest in a major launch based on only three or four months test results. Vizir should not be positioned as Eurobrand because every country has its own culture and habits. Product standardization probably results in cost down without any sales.

Meet Ted, New Low-Fare Service

United Airlines confirmed that Ted is the name of its new low-fare service that will bring travelers a quality experience with simplified low fares.

While the mainline remains United's core product, Ted expands the relevance of United's brand portfolio, capturing an opportunity in a high-growth segment of today's airline market.

"Customers want low fares, especially in our leisure markets," said Sean Donohue, Vice President — Low-Cost Operation. "In order to meet that need and seize the opportunity, United offered an operation that is competitive with other low-fare carriers. Ted is supported by a profitable and sustainable plan, with higher aircraft utilization, a simplified schedule and fare structure, and more seats per aircraft."

"Ted isn't just a low-cost initiative, it also creates more revenue opportunity in leisure focused markets," said John Tague, Executive

Vice President — Customer. "Although Ted will be a United branded product, it has been designed with a unique name and personality all its own. United chose the name Ted to emphasize that the service is an essential, integrated part of the company — it's the last three letters of the company's name."

Ted will begin flying customers in February 2004 with service from Denver to Reno, Las Vegas, Phoenix, New Orleans, Tampa, Orlando, Ontario (California) and Fort Lauderdale, a new Ted market not previously served by United. Beyond Denver, Ted will also offer service between Las Vegas and Los Angeles, Las Vegas and San Francisco and San Francisco and Phoenix.

Ted offers a compelling alternative to the current crop of low-fare carriers.

(Source: United.com Press Release, November 12, 2003)

Matching Dell

1. Issue

How should the newly combined HP/Compaq PC division go about competing with Dell?

2. How and why the personal computer industry has such a low average profitability?

There has been strong competition in the personal computer industry. Throughout the 1980s and 1990s, PC performance improved, and prices fell at a rapid slip.

In 1992, Compaq reduced prices by 32% in response to Dell price policy.

In the mid-1990s, PC prices continued to decline.

In 1997, Compaq offered a powerful PC for less than $1,000, and other companies rushed to offer similarly inexpensive PCs.

The declining prices of components and the financial crisis in Asia contributed to the faster decline in prices.

In 1998, IBM cut its server prices sharply by cost-saving at distribution.

3. The Keys to Dell's success and Dell's actual competitive advantage

Direct orders from customers → Higher margins than Retail

Customized PCs and no finished goods inventory

→ No inventory turnover

One day delivery from order entry to shipping → High ROI

Just-in-time delivery of parts procured.

Lined-up products.

Better service and support than competitors

Performance metrics for monitoring inventory and examining margins.

4. Competitors' attempts to respond to Dell by industry rivals and the resulting impact on Dell's competitive advantage.

일범의 평범한 사람 이야기

IBM:

Ambra (1992, mail order), AAP (1995, customized PCs), Web site (1998, direct order)

Compaq

—Production system by channel members forecast (1995, inventory 60→30 days)

—ODM (1997, total inventory 25 days)

—DirectPlus (1998, customized PCs)

Hewlett—Packard

—ESPP (1997, customized PCs→reduce price 5~15%)

—Web (1998, direct sales)

The reactions taken by the competitors increased the threats to Dell's gross rate and profitability.

5. My recommendation

Integrate the main office to reduce the administration cost.

Enlarge the Web services to its partners to shorten delivery.

Launch global advertise campaign for HP+Compaq's synergy effects.

More alliance with larger companies.

Where Cisco Is Looking for Growth

Cisco Systems doesn't want to be positioned as a networking company. Beyond its networking stronghold, it's targeting six promising new markets. These include network security, Internet telephony, wireless networks for homes and corporations, storage networking, and optical switches for big phone carriers.

With the exception of storage networking, the news is all good.

For years, Cisco has been the driving force in the market for voice-over-Internet-protocol (or, VOIP) phones. Now it leads in both the home market and in the corporate market.

Take Internet telephony. Cisco's is all-digital. That means companies basically need to scrap their existing systems to move to Cisco's approach. Cisco offers to cut prices or even throw products in for next to nothing along with its other gear.

Since Cisco failed to get phone companies to use its gear in the "converged" network in the 1990s, Cisco has changed its attitude, its strategy, and its technology to win over the telecom giants. Rather than tell these carriers to throw out decade's worth of phone equipment, the new plan calls for gear based on Internet technology that would work with their old-style networks.

Cisco isn't just relying on deal-making. It's also making substantive progress in increasing the reliability of its products. Also, Cisco is solving a problem that has held up progress with carriers.

일범의 평범한 사람 이야기

However, Cisco hasn't been able to land knock—out blows against competitors across the range of these businesses. Now, those rivals such as NetScreen, Airespace, Nortel, Avaya have made it through their darkest days and are also poised for a rebound. They aren't laying down. In fact, some are getting off the mat and grinning.

I will be interesting to see what's going on these battles.

(Source: Business Week, November 24, 2003)

Merck-Medco: Vertical Integration in the Pharmaceutical Industry

1. Issue

What should Merck do with the health management business in the future?

2. Merck—Medco in the pharmaceutical industry
• What was the rationale for PBMs?
  — Claims processing and adjudication
  — Pharmacy network management
  — Formulary development and management for clients
  — Rebate negotiation with pharmaceutical manufacturers

• Does Medco fit with Merck's strategy?
  — Yes, Merck wanted to integrate the functions of R&D,

manufacturing, and distribution in order to become the world's first coordinated pharmaceutical care. Medco could eliminate key information gaps in the drug delivery system by its strong data linkage. to patients and physicians.

• What are the advantages and disadvantages of the merger?
 − Advantages: Increase of drug spending, prescriptions filled, and covered lives
 − Disadvantages: The strong reaction from retail pharmacist by substitute Merck drugs to others.

• What does Medco bring to Merck, and what does Medco get from Merck?
 − Medco brought to Merck the strong linkages to employers, plan sponsors, and managed care organizations.
 − Medco got from Merck the strength on medical, clinical, and science side.

• Why is vertical integration so attractive a strategic option in this industry?
 − Because PBMs typically had the role to negotiate with the drug manufacturers to keep their customers' cost down, so the integration on pharmaceutical manufacturer. and distributor can limit the available choices of customers. From the other point of view, the integration can not only give the merger a good margin,

it also can reduce. health care cost significantly, so it can be a win-win for all.

3. My recommendation
• Focus more on health management program.
• Invest more in its information system.

4. Basis of recommendation
• It has potential for much larger profit margins than claimed management and mail service for the company and it also can reduce sponsors' healthcare cost.
• The rapidly changing business environment in pharmaceutical industry requires closer communication among patients, doctors, and pharmacists for providing better health management.

Corning Incorporated: A Network of Alliances

1. Issue
What should Corning do with its proposals for its Laboratory Sciences, Fiber Optics, and TV Glass Divisions?

2. Corning's business strategies
• Corning's stated corporate and business unit strategies.
  - The purpose of Corning Incorporated is to deliver superior,

long-range economic benefits to its customers, employees, shareholders, and to the communities.
- Corning has four global business sectors: Specialty Materials, Consumers Housewares, Laboratory Sciences, and Communications. Binding the four sectors together is the glue of common values, a commitment to technology, shared? resources, dedication to total quality and management links.

• The appropriateness of each partnership in achieving Corning's overall strategy
- Corning's joint ventures have achieved good results by bringing the products to the market much faster with its own culture and procedures independently from Corning.

• The effectiveness of Corning's "evolving network".
- The people responsible for sector strategies are more directly involved.
- The organization has come to be more team oriented.
- People rely less on formal power and share more information.
- Corning could increase its revenues helped by a shared core of technology, expertise, and values.

3. My recommendations

	Laboratory Sciences	Fiber Optics	TV Glass Divisions
Recommen-dations	Approve Gibson's proposal without amend. -Purchase the three laboratory testing companies and sell its share of Ciba Corning	Approve Dulude's proposal with amend. -Expand the optical fiber capacity gradually for 3 Years -Sell PCO to IBM instead of partnership	Approve the proposal with amend. -Sell Asahi 51% of Corning's U.S. TV Glass business instead of 49%
Basis of recommen-dation	-Corning would become the dominant firm in each of the three segments of the laboratory testing industries. -For Ciba Corning, investment needs are high, and profitability continues to be very poor.	-Optical fibers has a great growth potential for telecommunication and home video soon, and Corning must keep the position of market leader by developing tough new fibers. -PCO business is incurring operating losses and more invest needed.	-Corning cannot compete Japanese manufacturers in terms of the cost and quality of TV Glass. So, it's better for Corning to differentiate its focus on developing liquid crystal display. -Corning also can recover the links with Asahi.

GE's Two-Decade Transformation: Jack Welch's Leadership

1. Issues

Has Welch created a "new model of strategic management" and in what way should it be imitated by other companies?

2. Welch's principal initiatives

Strategic Change

Since Jack Welch became CEO of GE in April 1981, he performed the transformation of GE step by step for twenty years such as business restructuring in the 1980s, changing organizational culture and globalization by late the 1980s, stretch target building and focusing service business into the 1990s, and implementing six sigma quality program and performance appraisal system the late 1990s, and finally launching e—business for the new millennium.

Organizational Structure and Management system

The number of hierarchical levels in organization was reduced from nine to four, and the number of employees declined from 404,000 in 1980 to 292,000 by 1989.

The core elements of the organizational culture were characterized by speed, simplicity, and self—confidence through the "Work—Out" and "Best Practices".

The skill sets and mindsets of human resources were continuously developed focused on creating an environment in which people could be in their best. 360°feedback process was backed up this commitment to the new leadership criteria.

Focusing of "boundaryless" company enabled to remove the barriers among organizations and regions and to share new ideas.

A performance appraisal system helped leaders to maintain A players with "Four E's" (energy, ability to energize others, edge, and execution)

Corporate Strategy

Business Restructuring: Between 1981 and 1990, GE freed up over $11 billion of capital by selling off more than 200 businesses and made over 370 acquisitions, investing more than $21 billion in purchasing.

Globalization: By 1998, international revenues were $42.8 billion, almost double the level just five years earlier. And the business outside was expected to be almost half of its the United States by 2000, compared with only 20 % in 1985.

Building Stretch Targets: In stretching for achieving impossible targets, people could learn to do things faster than the doable goals and could have enough confidence.

Focusing Service Business: Revenues was consisted of selling products 80% in 1980 and service business 75% in 2000.

Six Sigma Quality program dramatically improved quality, lowered costs, and increased productivity.

e-business was introduced as the new initiative in 1999.

3. My recommendations

Based on the Welch's leadership for twenty years, Today GE is the most admired company in the U.S. and the most respected company in the world. GE operates in more than 100 countries and employs more than 315,000 people worldwide. Many companies such as Honeywell, Texas Instrument, Kodak, Citibank, AIG, and POSCO have imitated Welch's new strategic models and introduced Business restructuring, Stretch target concept, and Six Sigma program. However, every company which imitates Welch cannot be successful. The companies which don't have the strong system infra, high leveled management and standardized processes cannot achieve the successful transformation. All CEOs who want to change their companies successfully should lead the organization step by step from developing infra structure to introducing Six Sigma as Welch did in GE.

Project Paper 1:
Investment on Tinning Line at Hainan, China

1. Introduction

A. Company Profile

POSCO, the largest iron and steel company in the World, has been trying to seek new foreign markets as an investment of strategy abroad. POSCO assigned its project to our team with some guidelines of investments as follows.

- New market which is near to home country to reduce transportation expenses for raw materials
- Potential demand for iron and steel, especially Tin plate and Black Plate
- Preferred Joint Venture rather than company owned corporation to void risks in foreign markets
- New emerging country

Based on this guideline, we investigated several countries and markets from various points of view. As a conclusion of our team, we selected China to investment on an existing company, Haewoo Tin Plate, that are operated by several companies.

The major stockholders are Daewoo corporation, Dong-yang Tinning company from Korea and Hainan color company, Nissho Iwai.

Even though this company has capacity to produce 100,000 tons per year, its operation ratio is around 10~20 percent. Also, this company has been struggling with low quality and sales difficulty in local markets.

⟨Table 1⟩ Tons produced and Operation Ratio

	1997	1998	1999	2000
Tons produced	7,272	7,310	6,950	6,678
Operation ratio	21.1%	21.2%	16.7%	14.2%

• Source: POSCO's special report on Haewoo Tinning company

According to our investigation, this company is in Hainan Dao area that has many can-manufacturing companies because lots of fruits are produced there.

As our conclusion, it is the best location to invest with easy access port for raw. materials from Korea. And Hainan Doa government supports manufacturing. companies with giving some incentives like non-tariffs to revitalize local economies.

We decide to buy the portion of Korean companies' stocks and manage it as a majorstockholder.

B. Why China and Hainan Dao

China has undergone a massive economic boom in the last twenty years—and it shows. The coastal mega—cities such as Shanghai now boast neon advertising and chicly dressed shoppers. Privately owned firms have sprung up across the country,churning out everything from fridges to cars to CDs. Foreign investment has poured in, and firms with foreign investment now account for half of all exports. These changes have brought more wealth to millions of Chinese and even a tad more freedom—though no challenge to the Chinese Communist Party's political monopoly is tolerated.

■ Key Factors of China (1)
- Capital City: Beijing
- Population(2001): 1,273 million
- Capital City: Beijing
- Government Type: People's Republic
- Head of state: President Jiang Zemin
- Head of government: Premier of the State Council Zhu Rongji
- Language: Mandarin Chinese, based on the Beijing dialect
- Ethic Composition: Han Chinese are the largest ethnic group. Over 90% of Population and 55 other ethnic groups are there.

According to Peter Marcus of WSD (World Steel Dynamic), China's steel demand will rise 5.1% annually until 2005 and, consequently, China will become the driving force of the global steel economy. (2)

Hainan Dao is an island of China. It is located in the further south of China.

Traditionally this island plants lots of fruits because the weather in there is almost tropical. Because of this feature, can—manufacturing companies are doing business there. However, they have been ordered raw materials for their business to Guangzhou, and some cities in continental areas. Also, the local government of Hainan does not allow can—manufacturers to import raw material from abroad. Usually, the local government imposes high tariffs on imported goods and services.

But, we can get some benefits from the local government when we invest directly.Also Hainan has some ports for exports and imports. That means it is easy for us to transport our raw materials as industrial materials.

We think these points and decide to invest directly on the Haewoo Tin plate company as a type of joint venture.

C. What products and why foreign market?

As we discussed above, the area we choose has lots of fruits and can—manufacturing companies that have been struggling with purchasing of raw materials. We focus on this situation and market size. Based on these circumstances, we will produce Black Plate and Tin Plate for targeting local can-manufacturing market.

■ Black Plate and Tin Plate as our major products

In POSCO, Black plate is produced at world-class facilities with cutting-edge. technology. Black plate is used to manufacture different types of cans as it has fine surface quality and outstanding workability. It is usually used for container of food, beverage, and electrical parts. (3)

Tin plate has outstanding corrosion resistance, weld ability, and appearance, unrivaled by other metal plates. It is used to make a variety of containers, including beverage. It has recently become useful as materials for electrical parts. Due to the quality of products and purchasing of raw materials in Haewoo Tin company, we can easily make the contract with all parties.

Main Contents of Contracts

1. The portion of stocks for POSCO is 68%

2. POSCO has the authority of purchasing raw materials.

3. POSCO provides financial, technical, and managerial skill.

4. The local government gives non-tariffs on raw materials.

5. New company has the authority of distribution and use the existing distributors.

D. All parties relating to this contract make efforts to grow the new company.

■ Why foreign markets?

In Korea, even though POSCO can make black plate and tin plate with high quality, it is very hard to sell our good products in home market. Traditionally there are many small-sized can manufacturers. That makes very competitive markets in home country. They import raw materials from abroad and make black plate and tin plate very cheaper than POSCO's. Customers usually are willing to purchase their raw materials at cheaper price if raw materials meet its production requirements. Even more, POSCO had invested R&D to develop high quality black plate and tinplate by itself. It causes POSCO to rise its price more than others' and brings lower margin than its other products. Also, home markets for black plate and tin plate are full enough. There is no room to be expanded otherwise POSCO sell its products to electricity companies or automobile companies. Actually, POSCO has been trying to provide its products to those companies over years, but it is very difficult because when those companies were established they had long-term basis contract with several suppliers. Under this circumstance, POSCO has been seeking outside market to produce its high-quality products.

2. Environmental Analysis

■ Political Issues

There are some political issues in China. Taiwan is still big story. Taiwan broke away from China 1949. If Taiwan declare independence, China will invade. That is the basic message coming out of Beijing about Taiwan, which it regards as a breakaway province. Tensions have remained high since Chen Shui−bian, the pro−independence candidate, and Beijing's worst nightmare, was inaugurated as president on May 20, 2000. The inauguration was followed by a week of live fire military exercises close to Taiwan. However, the current crop of top Chinese leaders, grouped around President Jiang Zemin and his prime minister, Zhu Rongji, take a moderate stance on Taiwan. (4) Also, China has most of boundary with India in dispute and disputes over at least two small sections of the boundary with Russia remains to be settled. Despite 1997 boundary agreement, portion of the boundary with Tajikistan are indefinite. (5)

And China has lots of disputes with several countries which share boundary or sea. But we think political situation is relatively stable. The reasons are even though Chinese economic policy used to orient closed system however over past decades China has been changes its economic policy to survive in new global economic era.

Chinese government established special export or economic zone in which it gave foreign companies incentives to invest, provided that half of output was exported, and the rest was sold in China. If there is no threats to Chinese political systems, we think political environment for multinational companies is stable.

■ Economic Issues

China is the world's third largest country in area and largest in population, which makes it attractive to market—seeking foreign direct investors. The provinces have considerable autonomy in approving FDI. (6)

Since the introduction of market—oriented reforms in the late 1970s, China's economy Has performed remarkably well. Neither the regional financial crisis in the late 1990s nor the present global slowdown appear to have done much to dent the pace of economic growth. The opening of coastal zones led to a surge in foreign investment and an export boom, while many Chinese went on a spending spree, splashing out on goods such as TVs and fridges. Several years of double—digit GDP growth followed.

But alarmed by the property and banking bubbles that went sour across Asia in 1997—1998. China began a cleanup of the banks and state sector. The resulting shakeout has been painful, with millions losing their jobs and many unfinished reforms. But the rate of GDP growth in 2001 stood at around 7.5%, down only slightly compared to previous years. The growth rate is 2002 looks set to be broadly similar.

The compound annual growth rate of GDP in the period 1990 to 2000 was 10.16%. The following table shows percentage of the real growth.

〈Table 2〉 China GDP (US$ Mn), 1996~2000 (8)

	1996	1997	1998	1999	2000
Real GDP	869,093	945,573	1,019,327	1,095,777	1,184,535
% Growth	9.6	8.8	7.8	7.5	8.1

However, beneath the benign statistics some imbalances are evident. The fiscal deficit has been creeping upwards in recent years, and now stands at little short of 4% of GDP. The exports are unlikely to last, so an increase in investment and consumption is vital. The government has already cut interest rates repeatedly, with little result. So, to make sure growth does not sag any further, the government has resigned itself to further heavy state spending this year, pouring billions into road and rail, dams and bridges. This should keep the headline growth figure up.

〈Table 3〉 China Interest Rate (%), 1996~2000 (9)

	1996	1997	1998	1999	2000
%	6.6	5.7	3.8	2.3	3.2

The key economic issue facing China is how to restructure the ailing state owned enterprise (SOE) sector, the largely bankrupt remnants of the old command economy. These firms, which offer steady employment and social security benefits to millions of workers in depressed areas, have built up huge debts to state—owned banks.

Unwinding the bad debts in the financial sector and restructuring the SOEs without causing massive social dislocation are the twin headaches facing policymakers. (10)

In Hainan Dao area, the local government impose high tariffs on imported goods and services to protect their industries. Can-manufacturers in this area are suffering from lack of raw materials. But there are some exemptions for certain imported goods and materials. Especially, if imported materials is used to make finished goods and services, the local government does not much impose tariffs than others.

We are going to take of this advantage with investment on Haewoo Tin Company. As some multinational companies do, we also can take advantage of the dampened economy to improve our workforce quality. This can be achieved by replacing poor performers, through training, or by reviewing the systems for aligning and evaluating work. (11) With this labor market, we can hire employees who have qualified skill for making iron and steel at lower wage or salary than Korea.

■ Cultural Factors
■ Market characteristics

Chinese markets have been transmitted form seller−market to buyer−market over years. In the past, without special marketing or promotion for goods and services, companies could their goods and services not because companies made high quality goods and services but because there were always lacks necessities. After the government took open−market oriented policy, numerous multinational companies entered

China to take advantage of lots of merits there. This resulted in the flood of goods and services in coastal areas not in the central area. This situation causes companies to have to recognize customer's needs before launching new products to markets. (12) The result of lots of FDI gives opportunities to customers and markets are more than hot. Also, foreign companies not only export their well-known products but also use OEM in China and sell them in host markets.It makes Chinese people prefer famous brand products to common products. In general, Chinese people fell although domestic products are cheaper, but quality is not as good as famous brands.

■ Human Rights

In China, religion plays a significant part in the life of many Chinese. Buddhism is most widely practiced, with an estimated 100million adherents. Traditional Taoism also is practiced. Official figures indicate there are 18 million Muslims, 4 million Catholics, and 10 million Protestants. While the Chinese constitution affirms religious toleration, the Chinese government places restrictions on religious practice outside officially recognized organizations. Unauthorized organizations sprung up in many parts of the country and unofficial religious practice is flourishing. (13)

After 1979, the Chinese leadership moved toward more pragmatic positions in almost all fields. The government encouraged artists, writes, and journalists to adopt more critical approaches, although open attacks on the government were not permitted. Reform policies brought great improvements in the standard of living. Literature and the arts blossomed, and Chinese intellectuals established extensive links with scholars in other countries.

China has acknowledged in principle the important of protection of human rights and has taken steps to bring its human rights practices into conformity with international norms. This positive steps notwithstanding, serious problems remain. The government restricts freedom of assembly, expression, and the press and represses dissent. (14)

■ Labor Characteristics

The population of China is over 1273 million in 2001 and annual population growth rate is about 0.88%. The age structure of population is shown in table 4.

⟨Table 4⟩ Age structure of population in China (15)

	0~14 years	15~64 years	65 years and over	Total
Male	166.8 Mn	445.4Mn	42.5Mn	654.7Mn
Female	151.6 Mn	419.0Mn	48.0Mn	618.6Mn
Total	318.4Mn	864.4Mn	90.5Mn	1273.3Mn
%	25.0	67.9	7.1	100

After Asian economic crisis, Unemployment is also growing concern, with the urban unemployment rate standing at 3.5%. Some analysts expect this rate to double in the next few years, as economic adjustment to a more open trading environment impacts on the labor market.

Chinese laws allow people who are 16years and over to work and regulate retirement age when female workers are 55year-old female and for male workers at 60year-old male. Companies can hire retirees but cannot contract employment with them. (16)

Recently, companies in China are increasingly faced with industrial and community relations issues. Not only the Labor Unions beginning to be more demanding but individual employees have become more litigious and downsizing or restructuring in very often accomplished by labor unrest. Combined with the increasing sensitivity to public opinion and share value of both multinationals and listed Chinese companies, it becomes urgent for companies to ensure they implement change well and communicate thoroughly. (17)

E. Target Market

According to our analysis about Chinese political, economic, and cultural environments above, if we invest in China, we can take economically advantages. From this point, we will talk about our target markets in China. We are initially going to focus on Hainan area. Then as our final goal in China, we will pursue to sell our products to the automobile markets.

As the first step, we find out which segment of market will be our target. In Hainan area, many can-manufacturing companies are operated. Every year, they need raw materials over 100,000 tons for their business. Because of lots of fruits produced, their major businesses are making beverage and need Tin plate or Black plate to do that. Also, some companies make lit for bottle products. We invest and take over management power from the previous company that capacity to produce Tin and Black plate are 100,000 tons per year.

⟨Table 5⟩ Tin and Black Plate Demand in Hainan

	For beverage	For lit	Total
Tons/Year	104,000	1,000	105,000

We will have more competitiveness than other companies because we purchase raw material at low price from parent company, POSCO in Korea and lower tariffs on that. So, at the first stage, we set our target market in Hainan. After raising our presence in there, we will expand our market to the west coast where automobile companies are operating. One of largest markets for a steel company is an automobile market. Even though there is no major Chinese auto-manufacturing company, other foreign companies do business in China. We will try to get contract with them. As we know already, Transportation expenses from America to China are very high and it makes the price of final products high.

3. Entry Mode

When pursuing international business, any company must decide how to carry out its business. As we explained above, we decided to invest directly on the existing company, Haewoo Tin company. And most of raw materials come from POSCO in Korea. We take over 68% stocks from existing Korean side stockholders and operate it with Chinese side stockholders as Joint Venture.

The reasons we choose joint venture are as follows.

First, to minimize initial risks in foreign markets. Generally, when a multinational company invests in foreign country, a company sometimes face with unexpected risks or does not have chances to investigate all aspects of factors. Sometimes these factors are critical for doing business there.　Second, in order to take advantage of promotion and providing raw materials.　We think there are some companies that are owned by the local government should be our customers. As we invest in there to vitalize its economy, we expect to promote our products by using the existing distribution paths. Also, POSCO, our parent company, provide raw materials at the lower price than competitors do.

Last, Chinese laws allow foreign companies to business as joint venture rather than company-owned by foreign company. Foreign company can establish joint venture with Chinese company to sell to the Chinese market. However, the government scrutinized proposals and approved them only if they served a top-level national priority for which China had to seek outside help. Chinese market-serving investments were generally made to improve an existing Chinese product or industry.

Under this situation, we can improve not only the local market but also Chinese finished products like canned goods. In the long-term strategy, we will take over the rest portion—38%— of stocks and operate. It by us if Chinese laws allow to do that. From this operation as a bridgehead, we try to develop new markets in southern Asian area.

4. Resources of Cooperation

Competitive Environment
Supply of Back plate
The excessive production capacity has become a problem for steel makers worldwide. This means a lot of facilities which are not competitive should be shut down. But if we see the capacity of Black plate and Tin plate in Asia, each country is not self-supporting and self-sufficient for Black plate. Japan, Taiwan and Korea are the only countries to have excess capacity for exporting Black plate. Table 6 shows the capacity of Black plate and Tin plate in Asia.

⟨Table 6⟩ BP and TP capacity in Asia

(Unit: thousand tons)

	BP Capacity	TP Capacity	Excess BP for Export
Japan	5,469	3,880	1,589
Korea	1,490	1,050	440
China	400	1,310	- 900
Taiwan	600	320	280
Thailand	250	550	- 300
Philippine	250	300	- 50
Indonesia	80	130	- 50
Malaysia	0	240	- 240
India	0	150	- 150
Pakistan	0	120	- 120
Total	8,339	8,050	

Kawasaki steel company in Japan has supplied Black plate to Haewoo Tin Plate co. via a Chinese company, Hainan Color co. which is 37 % owner of Haewoo and has a firm relationship with Kawasaki by the former business. TongYi industry in Taiwan doesn't have an excess Black plate enough for selling to Haewoo. So, in terms of Black plate supply, Japanese mill specially Kawasaki is the only competitor against POSCO.

Selling of Tin plate

In China, there are eleven Electro Tinning Lines which have already operated or under construction. Most of them are located near the south-east coast where is special economic zones in China. These are not so much as the industrialized areas compared to the population, but excessive by considering less developed and food culture in China.

Chinese people prefer fresh food to the canned food. Table 7 shows the Tin Plate capacity in China.

⟨Table 7⟩ Tin Plate Capacity in China (18)

(Unit: thousand tons)

Company	Capacity	Started	Black Plate	Owners
Shanghai Shichang	20	1972	From Japan	Chinese
Woohan	100	1979	Self-supply	Chinese
ZhungSan	120	1989,1994	From Japan	Chinese
Shanghai Richang	100	1996	Self-supply	Chinese
Fujian TongYi	150	1996	From Taiwan	Taiwan, TongYi 65%
Jiangsu TongYi	150	1996	From Taiwan	Taiwan, TongYi 58%
Guangzhu Pacific	120	1997	From Japan	Japan, NSC 25%
Haewoo	100	1997	From Japan	Korea Daewoo 43%
Dongyang 15%				
Baosan	200	1998	Self-supply	Chinese
Fujian Zhungri	150	1998	From Japan	Japan, NKK 15%
Shenyang Zhungyi	100	Under construction	Not decided	Hong Kong, Pomona 49%
Total	1,310			

Yesu, can-manufacturing company in Hainan Dao, had purchased some Tin plate products from Zhungsan company in Guangdong and TongYi indistry in Taiwan. But the quality of Zhungsan did not meet the requirements of Yesu which was used for canned fruit. Yesu is still importing some amount of Tin Plate from TongYi which has same culture and language. The other Tin plate manufacturers are not qualified to sell tin plate to Haunan in terms of quality, cost and services. So, TongYi is the only competitor against POSCO in that area.

B. Strength of my Company

With an initial investment on Haewoo Tin company, we must need to innovate some parts of operation and management because we took over the insolvent business. We will delegate management of operation to local manager. However, in order to recover our position in the local markets, our parent company, POSCO, send some experts to new operation including engineers. They will be an expert or specialist in production, maintenance, and employee educational program. Not only human resources but will

POSCO support new operation with several aspects of management. POSCO, one of largest steel making company, recently is selected the best company among iron & steel companies in the World. According to WSD (World Steel Dynamic) announced that the best competitive steel making companies is POSCO and released the result of evaluation on steel companies. Table 6 shows as follows:

일범의 평범한 사람 이야기

〈Table 8〉 An analysis of 13 steel companies in 7 out of 21 total categories (19)

	POSCO	Nucor	Baosan steel	CSC	CSN	Nippon	Arcelor	USS
Labor Produtivity	10	10	5	8	6	10	8	8
Location	10	4	6	10	6	6	7	4
Operation Cost	9	8	9	8	10	6	6	2
Domestic Demand Growth	6	3	10	5	7	2	3	3
Legacy Cost	7	10	9	6	8	4	6	4
Financial Stability	8	10	6	8	5	3	5	5
M&A Joint Venture	3	10	7	4	7	8	10	10
Weighted Point	7.44	7.19	6.30	6.21	6.05	5.29	5.26	4.71

With supports of POSCO, we innovate our new operation to be more competitive than before. Technologies relating to Black plate and Tin plate will be transferred to Haewoo from POSCO with expertise. Of course, it will take one year or over to be competitive making our products at lower cost. More than anything else, we can purchase raw materials without any concern. It is very important for new operation to do business. Based on lots of experiences in the field of steel making industry, we can train our employees to adapt themselves to new management styles. They will learn how to reduce production cost, how to improve their skills and so on.

For these reasons, we are sure this new joint venture will be competitive and stronger.

Major strengths
- Financially strong
- High quality and technology
- Sufficient raw materials
- Lots of experiences in making steel products
- Hainan Government's supports for distribution

5.Problems and Opportunities

■ Problems
Poor Profitability

The existing facilities of Haewoo Tin plate company are not the newest equipment but pretty good for producing Tin plate for food and beverage cans. Table 8 shows the total cost of Haewoo Tin Plate company in case of full operation. And Table 9 shows the selling price to customers.

〈Table 9〉 Total Cost in case of full operation

(unit : U$ per ton)

Item		Cost
Main material(Black plate) Sub-material(Tin, Other materials, Water treatment)		594.3 40.7
Utility (Gas, Water, Electric)		15.8
Labor		6.0
	Maintenance Pay, Insurance Expence Depreciation Technical supervising	3.6 7,171/month 16,265/month 312,300/month 6,667/month
Manufacturing		46.2
Sales		20.0
General		12.5
Interest		28.0
Total cost		763.5

〈Table 10〉 Selling prices.

(Unit : U$)

Customers	Application	Price
Yesu Can Manufacturing co.	TP for Fruits can	860
Yepung Can Manufacturing co.	TP for Fruits can	790
Hungtai Industry	Printed TP for Fruits can	1,100
Huangguan Closures	Printed TP for closure	1,089
Export	TP for various use	610

The critical problem of Haewoo is high cost. The demand increase has not been so steep as the initial forecast since the completion of the facilities. And the sales amount is too low due to the small market share. The operating ratio of Haewoo Tin Plate company was below twenty percent during last three years. Therefore, the low operating ratio increases the operating cost which is higher than the selling price as a result. If the market share is not improved, the loss amount will be about nine million dollars annually.

But we will set up new policies to save cost first and replace old equipment by new one. In order to improve productivity, we invest continually on automation equipment in plants.

Weak Management Power

Daewoo is the biggest stockholder of Haewoo Tin Plate co., and it has the right to supply 60% of Black plate by the Joint–venture agreement. This means Daewoo would supply 60,000 tons BP for the full operation. But Daewoo had never supplied Blake plate to Haewoo, all the Black Plate supplied by Chinese partner, Hainan Color Co., which has 40% right. Haewoo needs to improve the management skill for market enlargement, sales management, and business services at marketing wise, and to improve the managing ability for production scheduling, quality control, operation and maintenance at production wise. Specially, the team power integrated by the harmony of each.

■ organization shall be quite needed. And the good communication between organizations and between top—management and employees are also necessary. Initially we authorize management to the local managers who know better about legal system, characteristics of trade in markets, cultural features and people.

Weak Human Capital

Most of the employees are high school graduated and almost no experiences of operating the automated facility for steel making. They lack responsibility, devotion and organization—oriented mind. They are also lazy, negative and slow motioned. Simply speaking, it looks like no vision for them without any evolutionary changes. So, we will start to train employees how to operate properly automatic equipment and improve their skills intensively.

B. Opportunities

Black Plate available

The most critical issues of all Tinning lines over the World are how to purchase Black plate at reasonable price and at the right time. Because many emerging countries are trying to build Tinning lines with the steel maker who can supply black plate. Years ago, POSCO could not export $40,000 \sim 50,000$ tons of Black plate Annually because Korean government enforced POSCO to supply its products to domestic market preferentially. But now POSCO is available to supply $40,000$ tons per year because Dongbu that was one of the Black plate customers built its own cold rolling mill. The quality, delivery, and technical services of POSCO for its customers are almost same (or better) as (than) any other Japanese mill.

Haewoo's entreaty

Two Korean countpartners of Haewoo Tin Plate co. have 68% of the whole stocks. Daewoo has 43% and Dongyang 25% in detail. At this stage, These stockholders want POSCO to take over their portions because they cannot manage Tinning Lines by themselves without Black plate and experiences of steel sheet manufacturing.Instead of steel company, one of them is willing to enter Automobile project in Hainan Dao. The other one already stopped to supply raw materials. Therefore, at this situation, it is the just time for POSCO to enter Hainan Dao. Otherwise, Japanese mill may take these golden chances to enter in China.

Assistance of Hainan province government

The government of Hainan province wants to support the domestic manufacturing companies in Hainan Dao and have an automobile plant in Hainan Dao.

One of Korean stockholders already expressed their opinion about the new automobile project to Hainan province government. So, Hainan province government has a policy to abolish tax—free on imported Tin plate from next year and ask local can— manufactures to use domestic tin plate. Yesu Can manufacturing co., the biggest one in Hainan Dao has imported a lot of Tin plate from TongYi of Taiwan.

Win—Win policy

POSCO has win—win management philosophy. This means; Like any other company, POSCO could not be existing without customers. This win—win management philosophy makes POSCO listen to and respond to customers immediately and brings its priority in innovative, cost—effective new ways. POSCO's entry to Haewoo Tin Plate company in Hainan Dao can contribute not only to the maximum profit of Haewoo but to the local markets and industries. Haewoo's employees and their family, Hainan province government, Can—manufactures in Hainan Dao can enjoy vitalizing economy there.

Also, POSCO supports the best technical, timely supply of black plate, high operation ratio, better quality & services, lower cost raw materials, family—like organizations and makes the maximum profit at Hainan Dao in China.

6. Summary

We made direct investment in China by taking over some portions of stocks of the existing company. We investigated carefully many factors which might affect our business there. As advantages, we can enjoy huge supports of the local government and POSCO, we can sure that the new company as Joint Venture will be one of the best steel making company. Because we replaced and invested on automation to improve productivity. Also, we trained our employees what they need to be an employee. We can make the local government, employees, customers and all of people who live in the local improve their quality of living together. But sometimes we may face with invisible and unpredictable factors that are critical to operation.

Even more we know well this direct investment in the foreign country is not easy project and will take long time to be successful there.

However, under careful evaluation on various factors, using the right management structure, and giving incentives to motivate our employees will result in our success.

■ References

1. www.datamonitor.com
2. http://weekly.posco.co.kr   World Steel Dynamics' 17th Steel Success Strategies Conference, June 17~19, New York
3. www.pocso.co.kr
4. www.datamonitor.com
5. www.cia.gov the World fackbook—China, Page 10
6. International Business—Environments and operations 9th edition, John Daniels and Lee Radebaugh, Page 374, Map 11.1
7. www.datamonitor.com
8. www.datamonitor.com
9. www.datamonitor.com
10. www.ljaconsult.com

11. www.korea8848.com

12. www.state.gov Page 7

13. www.state.gov Page 12

14. www.cia.gov the World factbook—China Page 3

15. www.korea8848.com

16. www.ljaconsult.com

17. www.steel.com Quality agreement between POSCO and Yesu &
    Yepung

18. http://weekly.posco.co.kr

Project Paper 2: Jamayka Dust Powered Beer

presented by Kenneth Koerner, Andrew Van Noy, Marina Pekelis, Youngjing Sohn and Jeomho Ban

I. Executive Summary

Jamayka Dust is a small start—up company, which will manufacture a beer flavored powdered alternative beverage in its headquarters in Dublin, California. We have leased a 40,000 square foot facility there, which will house our management offices, along with our R&D segments, our sales and marketing offices, and our production unit. Financially, we have an aggressive, but realistic, plan to become profitable during our third year of operation and to erase negative retained earnings by our fifth year of operation. During year three and year five, we plan to hold limited public offerings, which will increase our capitalization and diversify risk.

With regards to production, we possess patented technology from Purdue University, which we have licensed to a major beer manufacturer in order to produce the essentials of our product. We have signed a five—year non—competition agreement with this beer manufacturer for the use of our technology. We also have an outsourcing arrangement with Ultimate Shaker to produce our packaging vessels. However, we plan to acquire Ultimate Shaker or a close competitor in 2006 in order to bring those operations in-house. At present, we plan to do our own label design and production.

Our product line of beer flavored non-alcoholic alternative beverages exemplifies our company culture. Our company is deeply rooted in the Bay Area, and has a strong interest in health consciousness, ecological conservation, and nature. Our current products represent a healthy, nutritious, safe alternative beverage for consumers seeking great beer flavor, while also desiring nutritional benefits, an energy boost, and safety. Some of the unique features and benefits of our products include the following: 1) they are easy to carry and transport, 2) they are easy to make with simple instructions, 3) they have a long shelf life, 4) they represent a stark contrast to the dominant beer culture because our line is healthy and nutritious, and 5) they offer the consumer a high degree of safety when compared to alcoholic alternatives.

Our target market is primarily males aged 21-50, who are active people who enjoy athletics and the outdoors. However, we also hope to reach the teenage market and eventually expand into Asian and other Third World markets. Our customers will enjoy convenience, active lifestyles, and probably represent the more affluent urban segment of North America. Initially, we will focus geographically on the Bay Area, but will hope to expand into new markets in other major U.S. urban centers. Our direct sales via the Internet will help create marketing channels towards other parts of the country.

Our pricing plan is to use a markup model based on the cost of goods sold. That will put us at about 25% total price above most of our competitors, but our unique and innovative product should still find enough market share. We plan to focus our distribution efforts on boutique liquor stores, gourmet food stores, exotic product stores, health clubs, and sports stores. We will try to engage the selective model of distribution in order to balance the priorities of affecting perceived value and the other objective of reaching as many markets as possible. Later, if our product line is well received, we may introduce more intensive distribution in order to reach more markets.

In sum, we are an eager startup company with an innovative product, a well-conceived marketing plan, and a realistic set of financial objectives and projections. We will not realize immediate profitability, but we will become profitable in year three. As our profitability continues, we will expand our marketing activities, product line, and distribution into new geographic regions and towards new target markets.

II. Mission, Vision, and Value Statements

Mission Statement:
"To use the most advanced technology in order to deliver a convenient, healthy, delicious line of powdered beverage products to our valued customers."

Vision:

"To manufacture a product line of ecologically conscionable, natural, organic alternative beverages in order to add new benefits to markets in the Bay Area, North America, and the rest of the world, while bringing value and satisfaction to our customers.

Our Guiding Values:

integrity to our customers, our employees, our other stakeholders, and our production process to promote ourselves through the delivery on the promise of genuine value to protect and conserve nature and promote an environmentally sound production process. adding convenience and simplicity to the lives of our fellow citizens and consumers to honor a commitment to teamwork while also recognizing individual initiative striving for excellence and accountability in everything we do.

III. Introduction

1. Company Overview

Jamayka Dust is a small start-up company, which has established its headquarters in Dublin, California in order to realize the advantages of recent favorable corporate tax legislation introduced by the city of Dublin. Organizationally, the company will consist of five departments initially, with room for the creation of additional overhead and executive departments in the future. Each one of our start-up team members will occupy the position of a department head. First, there is the operations department, which will house the production, materials management, operations, distribution, and new products functions. Jason will be our operations department manager.

Second, we have a procurement department headed by Youngjing, which is tasked with the functions of supply chain management, purchasing, inventory management, and vendor relationship management. We also have a marketing department, which houses the functions of brand management, market research, forecasting, sales, and customer relationship management. Marina is our marketing department manager.

Finance will become an important department for us, even if it isn't so initially. Acting as our finance department manager, Andrew will help Jamayka Dust establish a credit line, control cash, manage our accounting and finance, and help us make budget decisions. Finally, our research and development department, headed by Ken, will be engaged with new product development, existing product improvement, and strategic planning.

With regards to company culture, Jamayka Dust will strive to mold itself along the lines of new startups in the era of globalization and increased competition. More specifically, Jamayka Dust will do its utmost to keep decision making a consensus operation and attempt to promote democratic decision-making processes. Eventually, as revenues increase, and budgetary amounts correspondingly increase, we may have to create positions for a CEO and a CFO, in order to consolidate decision—making responsibilities. However, initially we will strive to promote a democratic atmosphere based on the equality of departments, and therefore, the equality of competing opinions.

Our company culture will be marked by a strong commitment to environmental preservation and harmony with nature. For instance, our headquarters interior design will feature floral patterns and nature scenes from northern California. In line with modeling ourselves as a less rigidly hierarchical organization, we will promote the free flow of ideas, and reward innovations, good ideas, and initiative. Some of our rewards may include all expenses paid trips to national parks or scenic areas where nature and ecological preservation are highly valued.

Our corporate persona will also feature a strong sense of health consciousness, which will hopefully bolster our brand image as a leading health—conscious alternative powdered drink provider. We may try to do some cross branding with Reebok, or Nike, as well as Gatorade, because we are promoting ourselves as a nutritious health drink.

As such, our executive compensation packages will feature memberships to health clubs. We will also use athletic events to promote our corporate image.

Operationally, Jamayka Dust will endeavor to produce an outstandingly delicious, healthy powdered beverage alternative in the form of powdered beer at our Dublin plant. Our production plant will occupy the main part of our headquarters establishment, with management offices on one side. We will initially lease our production equipment with a FMV buyout option in order to help cash flow. We will also attempt to succeed at a modified form of JIT, so that we can realize different types of savings on inventory, and inventory management.

Ultimately, our strategic plan calls for setting up branch office and distribution in the Portland, Oregon area, and in several major cities in the state of Washington. If these ventures go well, we will turn our attention towards the Pacific Rim, especially China and Japan, and Hispanic markets in southern California, and the Southwest, especially Texas.

2. Product Description
Jamayka Dust offers a healthy, delicious alternative powdered beer beverage.

Product Attributes: we produce non—alcoholic powdered beer for those consumers who like to drink beer but have health and safety concerns. The non—alcoholic nature of our beverage allows consumers to enjoy it anywhere, at any time. Our powdered beer is refreshing, rather than depressing, and allows drinkers to continue to socialize, exercise, or study, depending on their interests.

Our powdered beer product will be convenient, because of the small individual packets, easy to mix with simple instructions, and very portable.

Jamayka beer is not simply an enjoyable beverage; it is also nutritious. The components in Jamayka beverages are characterized by the fact that the beer is produced from a natural product, i.e.malt. Our beer beverages contain no preservatives.

Vitamins and microelements:

	mg/8oz	% of daily requirement
B1 (Thiamine)	0.02	2
B2 (Riboflavine)	0.10	6
B6 (Pyridoxine)	0.13	7
Niacin	1.50	8
Panthotenic acid	0.23	4
Folic acid	0.03	17

	mg/8oz	% of daily requirement
Potassium	100	*
Sodium	20	*
Magnesium	25	8

* There is no recommendations for the daily requirement of these minerals

Magnesium is important for the energy transformation in the muscles.

Nutrition content:

Jamayka beverages are naturally fat free.

Protein − 0.3g per 100g

Carbohydrate − 2.7g per 100g (4 times less than a soft drink)

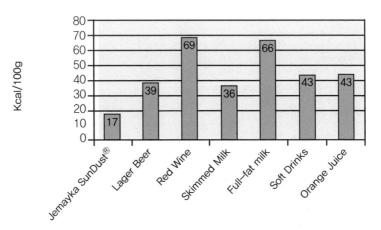

Energy level(Kcal) in beverages

Additional health benefit:

Jamayka beer derived beverages have high content of flavinoids, antioxidant compounds. Flavinoids are effective in preventing heart attack and other cardiovascular problems. They help arteries to dilate, which improves blood flow and blood pressure.

Current Products: We currently produce three types of beer flavored powdered beverage products: (1) our Gun Powder™ Stout, (2) our Sun Dust™ Lager, and (3) our Moon Lite™ Blond Pilsner.

Our Gun Powder™ Stout is for the more stalwart drinker who favors a stronger, heavier dark beer.

Our Sun Dust™ Lager is for those drinkers who prefer a beer with a medium body and medium density.

Our Moon Lite™ Blond Pilsner is for those consumers who prefer a lighter, crisper beer.

Our products are produced based on our patented technology through the use of proprietary raw materials.

Packaging: All three products varieties are available in two packaging options:

a) in individual 28 oz UltimateShaker plastic jug and

b) 5 oz plastic barrel with easy-to-hold, finger-grip moldings designed for greater moister protection and convenience.

UltimateShaker jug has a unique design that has an internal screen that breaks up any lumps or clumps in the mix. It is manufactured out of high-quality plastic; it is both durable and practical and calibrated in both imperial and metric measurements. The shaker allows the user to drink a smooth mix right from the bottle. The 28 oz plastic jug will come with 12 packets of Jamayka Dust beverage (Gun Powder™ Stout, Sun Dust™ Lager or Moon Lite™ Blond Pilsner). One packet of Jamayka Dust powder mixed with 8 oz of water produces ounce serving of Jamayka Dust beverage.

Reusable plastic barrel holds loose Jamayka Dust powder (any of the three varieties) and contains a measuring cup. One cup of powder mixed with 8 oz of water produces one serving of Jamayka Dust beverage. The barrel contains 150 g of Jamayka Dust powder, servings per container is about 12.

All the materials used in our packaging will either be biodegradable or recyclable. The recyclable containers will carry a recycling message on the container.

We plan to outsource the production of all plastic packaging (shaker jugs for packers and barrels for loose powder) to UltimateShaker Company (www.ultimateshaker.com), with which we have negotiated a favorable long-term contract. They have agreed to meet our specs for a custom barrel shaped container and affix the labels, which we will supply to them. All of our barrels will also carry mixing instructions

일범의 평범한 사람 이야기

which will be no more than two sentences.

Products in the Pipeline: in our next stage of product development, we plan to introduce an Ultimate Amber™ Ale, and a Delicious Deal™ Double Bock Beer during the winter season. If our seasonal bock beer succeeds, we might introduce other seasonal powdered beers, such as a spring Fasching beer or a powdered wheat beer. Eventually, we plan to penetrate the spice market with a beer—flavored spice, but that might be ten years out.

Warranty: we plan to offer a conditional money back guarantee to dissatisfied customers. Our only condition is that the customer must tell us in writing why they were dissatisfied with the product. We believe that thoughts committed to paper exhibit more clarity and carry more weight.

Service: we plan to offer a 1—800 line for ordering, complaints, and customer feedback. Initially, this 1—800 number will probably only be equipped with an answering machine. However, we hope that one day we may be able to staff a customer service desk with a knowledgeable company employee to handle telephone calls for sales, service, and complaints.

We also plan to have two exterior email address, which will be feedback@jamayka.com for complaints and feedback, and ordernow@

jamayka.com for sales orders.

IV. Current Market Situation

1. Macro—Environment Situation

Regarding the immediate target market, which is demographically the Bay Area, and males who enjoy outdoor activities such as camping, the prospects for our powdered beer product are favorable. Initially, in the wake of the 9-11 terrorist attacks, three trends have become noticeable within the Bay Area, and more broadly within the United States: 1) consumption of alcoholic beverages is up, 2) internal tourism within the United States has increased, and 3) disaster planning for potential terrorist attacks and other threats has increased the consumption of preparatory materials such as bottled water, flashlights, canned goods, and powdered substances, including powdered beverage substances.

With the decrease in international travel based on the existence of real and perceived threats from terrorist organizations, more and more members of our target market(s) are seeking travel and entertainment options within the United States. Since one of our primary target market constituents is the camper, our product should sell favorably within the current environment. Even when international travel begins to increase, our product should continue to enjoy strong sales because it can be safely and easily taken to international destinations as a non—alcoholic beverage, which can be conveniently transported.

California continues to be a leader in the areas of health consciousness and environmental preservation. Because our corporate culture and image promote environmental conservation and natural theses, our product should make substantial inroads into the Bay Area beverage markets. We will feature packaging with a strong environmental motif, which will naturally blend with such outdoor activities as camping and hiking. Additionally, our focus on the healthy attributes of our product should effectively tie into the California health consciousness that is especially strong in the Bay Area.

The broad proliferation of the Internet over the last ten years also affords our company a genuinely plausible channel for selling our product. We can sell directly to the consumer and then take advantage of any of a number of shipping media to satisfy the distribution of our product. Also, the Internet will assist us as an advance marketing vehicle for gaining market penetration into other geographic markets outside the Bay Area. If we experience a high volume of Internet sales in a particular part of the country, we will probably explore the option of distribution and retail sales in that region. In addition, regulatory issues should be reasonably easy to deal with, because we do not produce alcoholic beverages. Thus, we should be able to eventually operate in several states, by simply applying for the appropriate business licenses.

Ultimately, the new world order of globalization in the post—Cold War world will be beneficial to the promotion and sales of our product.

More specifically, rising standards of living in much of the third world could mean more per capita consumption of boutique beverages, such as powdered beer. Although distribution networks in much of the third world are inadequate, our product may fare more favorably because of its convenient size, weight, and packaging.

An excellent example of a rising potential third world market is China. China is now the world's number one beer producer, surpassing the United States. Since China already has the tradition of using water to mix tea, the China market might be very receptive to non-alcoholic powdered beer. Additionally, since Chinese apartments are generally small, powdered beer could become popular based on the amount of storage space required.

In sum, the mixture of elements in the macroenvironment tends to favor the introduction of our product. The combination of trends following the 9-11 terrorist attacks in conjunction with the possibilities of internet marketing provide us with an exciting environment within which to begin producing a powdered beer beverage.

2. Competitive Situation

Jamayka Dust is attempting to penetrate the powdered beverage market as a nutritious beer flavored alternative beverage. We are an innovative product, and hope to tap new market segments by creating programs that represent cross strata approaches to target marketing.

More specifically, we are hoping to target males in the 21–50 age range, but also hope to attract teenagers and people who love the outdoors. Part of our innovative nature is that we are attempting to invert the dominant beer paradigm by promoting a nutritious, healthy powdered beer beverage.

Another one of our strengths is that our company culture exemplifies some of our product attributes, e.g., conservation of nature and strong Northern California motifs. Our product packaging is scintillating and attractive in a humorous fashion, and we hope, that somewhat like Mad Magazine, we can produce a product that is humorous, but wholesome, and accessible to a range of age groups, interest groups, and market segments.

Our opportunities also include catering to upscale health markets, and perhaps even health clubs. We may give away free samples in Bay Area health clubs during our promotion efforts. We also hope to make strong inroads into disaster preparation markets in the wake of the 9–11 terrorist attacks and continuing global terrorist activity. While we initially hope to create new market segments within the Bay Area, we will employ the internet and our 1–800 number to seek out new markets in other geographical parts of the country.

One of the primary threats we face in the competitive arena is from other boutique, niche market beverages, such as Snapple, Arizona Iced

Tea, Soba Tea Drinks, and other types of soda pop, bottled water, and fruit drinks. Snapple has been largely successful based on its advertising campaign, while Arizona Iced Tea has been successful because of its unique bottle packaging. Our unique feature is the inversion of the dominant beer paradigm along with a company culture that embodies many of our product attributes. Our packaging will also be attractively alluring.

One of the other threats we face is from other types of powdered beverages, such as powdered tea, Kool Aid, instant coffees, Hawaiian Punch, powdered Gatorade, and Tang. We feel there is still room for us though, because we are targeting markets that cut across different strata. In addition, we initiate some cross branding opportunities with Gatorade and Nike.

Thus, even though the beverage market seems over-saturated with beverage possibilities, we still feel that we bring something new to the market with our nutritious, powdered beer. As the CEO of Coca Cola once noted, it wasn't only Pepsi that was the competitor, it was water, milk, other types of soda pop, and essentially any type of non-alcoholic beverage. We believe the same applies to the competitive situation surrounding our product. In other words, we believe that our competitors broadly consist of all beverages, and more narrowly consist of those more direct competitors mentioned above. Nevertheless, we still believe that there is room for our innovative product.

V. SWOT Analysis

1. External SWOT

Strengths:

Unique Product

Product can have long shelf life and long storage life.

Product is light and easy to pack and carry.

Product will be easy to make.

Volume growth and product differentiation potential

Weaknesses:

Introducing a new product to new markets will be expensive.

Introducing a new product to new markets will also be risky.

Will be primarily a regional presence.

Lack of established brand image or brand identity—lack of public

awareness

No established distribution system at starts up.

Possible consumer skepticism

If product is not carbonated, may face market apathy.

Opportunities:

Unfulfilled need in beer beverage concentrate market for non—

alcoholic powdered beer:

non—alcoholic beer for teenage consumers adults concerned about alcohol consumption due to cultural or health reasons.drivers and machine operators who feel deprived of the beer drinking experience. athletes and sports enthusiasts people who enjoy outdoor activities such as camping, hiking, and traveling.

Cross brand marketing opportunities with Kool−Aid and Tang, and perhaps Gatorade.

Winning government or NASA contracts for non−alcoholic powdered beer as a nutritious drink for military troops and astronauts.

Potential to grow towards mass production and economies of scale.

Penetration of Asian markets and parts of the developing world

Growth towards the food flavoring market

Product novelty

Price competitiveness

Threats

Long tradition of liquid alcoholic beer beverages and existing European based beer culture

Competition from new and existing kinds of boutique non−alcoholic beverages such as Snapple, Arizona Iced Tea, fruit drinks, etc.

FDA non−approval for non−alcoholic powdered beer sales to teenagers, and other types of government regulations

Opposition from groups like MADD who may argue that powdered beer may encourage underage consumption of alcoholic beer and other alcoholic beverages.

2. Internal SWOT

Strengths:

Patented technology from Purdue University

Cost advantages of proprietary manufacturing process

Solid management team of five GGU MBA graduates

Momentum in R&D to branch out beyond powdered beer into new areas and develop new product varieties and extensions.

Innovative image and innovative position in the market

Entrepreneurial mission and solid core values

Small startup with lots of flexibility and agility

New dry—freeze technologies combined with automation and robotics will reduce production and packaging costs.

Low overhead costs and low fixed costs

Weaknesses:

Initial Cash Flow

Lack of an initial brand image

Lack of mission critical expertise, such as food and beverage production, marketing, etc

Initial and continuing capacity definition—how much to invest, and how much to produce.

High R&D costs

Finding determined employees, and then training them.

Undefined market share

Opportunities:

Opportunities for employee fast promotion and advancement

Opportunities for scientists to work on interesting, and hopefully profitable, R&D projects.

Entrepreneurial opportunities in creating national presence and brand image.

Patents and proprietary manufacturing process

Easy advertising through the Internet

Quick decision making by GGU MBA management team.

Potential growth by firm and employees

Strong, vested interest by members.

Threats:

High employee turnover if losses persist beyond initial time period.

Best scientists may not want to work for us because of the risks involved.

Dependence on core group of people for their skills and expertise

High startup costs

Insufficient cash flow

Possibility of hostile takeover by existing competitors

VI. Financial Objectives

Jamayka Dust has a five-year financial plan to become profitable.
Initially, our operating capital will come from venture capital and debt
sources. We plan to open a revolving credit line with Washington
Mutual Small Business Services. Our five-person management team
has already met with the senior loan officers at Washington Mutual and
they have agreed to open a credit line of up to one million dollars that
will automatically renew each year. Andrew oversees maintaining our
relationship with the bank.

Furthermore, we plan to hold a limited stock offering in 2006 in
order to decrease our reliance on revolving credit. Currently, we plan
to offer the stock for five dollars a share. In 2007 we plan to issue more
stock, which is currently projected to sell at seven dollars a share.

In terms of earnings, we expect to become profitable in 2006 and
slowly erase the negative retained earnings. By 2008 we expect to
have positive retained earnings and possibly issue a dividend to our
stockholders.

With regards to cost, initially executive salaries will be low, but we
expect that profitability in 2006 will help motivate people, because our
executives will receive handsome bonuses once we reach the stage of
positive earnings. In addition, we may institute a system of awarding

executive stock options in coming years.

Apart from salaries, we intend to help control cost by purchasing a major bottling manufacturer in 2006. Bringing this part of production operation in—house will allow us better control and also afford us some cost savings. We only plan to have two company vehicles initially: one pickup truck for general errands and one Buick LaBaron for meeting with clients, sales calls, and general management use. We may eventually invest in a yellow Hummer, not only because it presents a powerful marketing image, but also because its gross axle weight allows us some tax advantages.

We also plan to be demanding with our suppliers, but to treat them well. We will allocate budget each year for golf retreats and awards dinners to our major suppliers. However, we plan to negotiate demanding contracts and hope that our suppliers will meet our demands with regards to price and specifications.

In sum, we face two to three years of projected losses before we become profitable, but when we do become profitable, we plan to remain profitable, and continue to expand our product lines and target markets.

VII. Marketing Plan

1. Target Markets

 Demographics

Mainly males aged 21—50

Trailing Edge baby boomers

Teenagers for non—alcoholic brand

Higher Income

Middle to Upper Class

Bay Area

Middle and Urban America (in cultural orientation)

Asian American Markets

Latin American Markets

 Psychographics

Active lifestyles

Sports enthusiasts

Outdoorsy people

Rush/thrill seekers

Trendy, concerned with fads and fashions.

Into convenience

Easy going at home.

Like to eat snacks.

Novelty and innovation are key.

Into chemistry and concoctions

Attracted to packaging with a flair.

2. Positioning

Our product is the first beer tasting, healthy energy drink in the market. We can benefit as the first mover. So, we would state our positioning statement as follow:

"To active beer-loving customers who love outdoor activities, Powdered Beer gives you more happiness than other alcoholic beverages since it delivers not only alcoholic taste, but also a healthy and safe mood. With Powdered Beer, you can enjoy your life wherever you want to be."

We are not trying to build a brand by appealing to everyone because sometimes a product that seeks to be everything to everyone will end up being nothing to everyone.

Therefore, our main message for the target market customer is:

You've consumed beverages that you felt needed more, and Jamayka Dust has created the beverage for you. Now enjoy non-alcoholic powdered beer that serves you whatever you want, whenever you want.

We will focus the selling efforts of our powdered beer-tasting beverage on the active lifestyle people who enjoy outdoor activities as well as health conscious people who enjoy the taste of beer but do not want to experience any alcohol side effects. Our powdered beer-tasting beverage is an instantly made beverage that provides a fat free energy source that can be enjoyed anywhere, at any time of the day.

The concept of positioning applies to products in the broadest sense. Services, tourist destinations, countries, and even employee careers can benefit from a well-developed positioning strategy that focuses on a niche that is unoccupied in the mind of the customer or decision-maker.

We will start our business in the Bay Area because this area has diversified ethnic groups, lots of places to go, and relatively higher levels of median income.

Based on our analysis, we would set out target market for positioning our products
as follows:

Target Market

California — Ethnically diverse
Middle— and high—income level professionals
Outdoorsy people — Campers, family people with active lifestyles
Beer lovers who have health and safety concerns

Our unique benefits

Healthy — Fat free energy source
Safe — A beverage for enjoyment with no alcohol side effects.
Convenient — Instant drink which is easy to use and carry.
Variety of flavors

The easiest way of getting into customer's mind is to be first. It is easy to remember who is the first, and much more difficult to remember who is second.

Our product is the first product that delivers not only beer taste but also energy to customers in the chosen market. We assume we can benefit as the first mover.

We will build a range of our products based on a single brand name, because our brand's name is the most important factor affecting perception of our products. Our Sun Dust™ conveys imagery of summer heat and will hopefully make consumers thirsty. The Gun Powder™ name is meant to give consumers the image of a real blast, either in the sense of a good time or a jolt to the energy system, or whatever they are doing. Our Moon Lite™ brand alludes to imagery of moon beams, and people dancing, tripping the light, while maintaining full control of their faculties, because our beverage is non—alcoholic.

Our intent with the Jamayka Dust name is to convey an image of a valuable entity, with hints of gold dust, and also to make people thirsty, by thinking of the dust choking the back of the consumer's throat on a hot, humid summer day.

Our Logo of the product and company

Present by use of the dawn and the waves to be the symbol because the non—alcoholic powdered beer comes from the natural resources. Sunshine potentially represents feeling fresh and the ocean waves give you energy.

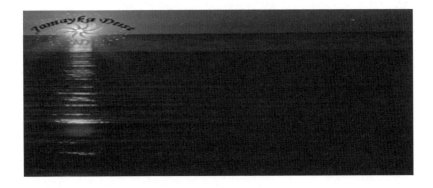

3 Marketing Strategy

Jamayka Dust's marketing strategy includes creating a health benefit image by informing potential customers of our great tasting energy beverage that tastes like beer. We will reach customers through advertisements such as fliers, television ads, radio ads, newspaper ads, and through grand opening ceremonies.

Special promotional program will also incorporate offering coupons for nearby restaurants, grocery stores, sports stores, exotic product stores, gourmet stores, and wholesalers to customers who purchase any product of Powdered Beer.

4. Pricing Strategy

The equipment and building purchase to produce our powered beer beverage exceeds 20 million dollars, so we have decided to license our technology to a large beer producer, allowing us to save on the financial burden a large capital investment required to produce the product ourselves. We have signed a five-year non-competition agreement with our manufacturer, and we expect to pay higher prices for the outsourcing of our product. Although our cost of sales will increase through outsourcing, we will not have the large depreciation costs and interest expense charges for borrowing 20 million dollars. Jamayka Dust will use the mark-up pricing method to determine our sales price, so we expect our product will cost 25% more than our competition, since we have outsourced the production phase.

Jamayka Dust's beer flavored beverages make us unique to the marketplace. We base our value proposition on our products and their healthy, safe, fat free and beer tasting qualities and on the fact that no other company offers the same product. Since the cost of our product represents a small part of the buyer's total income, the premium price over our immediate competition will not hinder our sales.

Our products' suggested retail sales price for the 1st year of operation:

	Package type	Weight	Glasses of beer	Price
Individual size	1 packet like Tea bag	1 oz.	One glass	$1.25
	6 packets in a Barrel	5	Five glasses	$5.95
Family size	30 packets in a large Barrel with a washable, plastic measuring cup	20	Twenty glasses	$28.99

5. Distribution Strategy

Our Powdered Beer beverage offers real beer tasting refreshment without any alcohol. It's a new and an innovated healthy alternative to beer as well as soft drinks and sport drinks. Therefore, Jamayka Dust will sell our products as an alternative healthy beverage in grocery stores, sports stores, exotic product stores, and gourmet food stores, so that customers can buy Powdered Beer when they go grocery shopping. We plan to place our product in the same aisles of the grocery store where beer is sold. Additionally, customers can purchase our product direct, via our inter—net website. In the future, Jamayka Dust will consider distributing our Powdered Beer beverage to restaurants, gas stations, and vending machines.

6. Promotion and Advertising Strategy

Jamayka Dust will promote Powdered Beer to customers by:
Television and radio advertisements during the first three months of business to attract potential customers.

Placing print advertisements in the sports section of local newspapers and outdoor travel magazines. We will also place weekly and monthly advertisements during the first six months of business so that the image of our Powdered Beer becomes recognized by consumers.

Flier distribution to consumers' homes in the Bay Area.

Jamayka Dust will offer discounts to customers who buy large volumes for the purpose of wholesaling and retailing.

Offer discount for any orders placed on our website that total more than $100.

Jamayka Dust will hold taste-testing campaigns at several gourmet grocery stores throughout the Bay Area, will promote our product through displays, and will offer the stores incentives for sales of our product.

Jamayka Dust will also send its catalogs and samples to the buying centers of wholesale stores, grocery stores, sports stores, exotic product stores, and gourmet stores before we make a contract to supply Powdered Beer to them.

Radio Advertisement Story Board

Intro:
[music] Tangerine Dream pulsating music from "Stratosfear" album⋯⋯. Imagery of running and movement

fade in sounds of two joggers running in the summer or early autumn⋯.

[sound effects] panting, running shoes crunching on gravel, a bird chirping⋯.

Decrease music in background to fade out during the first lines of conversation.

conversation:

first jogger: "Time out, Break, Break⋯⋯.no fair going over 3 miles at a time⋯⋯let's take five⋯."

second jogger: "Oh, come on, no pain no gain⋯⋯⋯⋯."

First jogger: "no, let's take five⋯⋯⋯I need something to drink⋯⋯⋯⋯do you have anything?"

"Yeah, I have some Gun Powder Stout with me."

[sound effect]− mild explosion⋯.

first jogger: "let's mix up some of that⋯it's quick and easy, and it tastes good too."

third person male narrator: [commanding voice] "Try Gun Powder™ Stout, which will give your running game a real blast⋯."

Second jogger: "yeah, I always carry some, it's good stuff⋯"

[Music] creep up Tangerine Dream "Stratosfear" underneath second jogger conversation⋯.

subdued attractive female voice underlying music repeat five times in

일범의 평범한 사람 이야기

synch will pulse of music: Gun Powder, Gun Powder, Gun Powder, Gun Powder, Gun Powder."

Music trails off with the sounds of jogging fading into the distance….

Project Paper 3:
ERP Application for POSCO Process Innovation

1.Introduction

POSCO, a Korean steel maker, started its Process Innovation in order to build the total optimized information management system that is clear and speedy. POSCO established the master plan of PI in September,1999. The goal of POSCO PI is to build the most efficient and speedy work process by linking the workflows which are distributed over the whole organization such as manufacturing, facility management, purchasing, R&D, business, and administrations. POSCO introduced ERP and SCP packages as tools for supporting their optimal system.

ERP that was originally developed from MRP (Material requirements Planning) is the package name for Enterprise Resource Planning. There are several kinds of ERP packages such as BaaN, BPCS, Oracle Application, SAP R/3, MFG−PRO, GLOVIA, etc. POSCO chose

Oracle Application for their PI system. Oracle ERP solution which is called Oracle Application consists of about seventy software modules for Financial & Accounting, Manufacturing, Supply Chain, Project, Human Resource, Strategic Enterprise management, and Customer Relation management, and so on.

2.Needs of introducing ERP

ERP is a tool with the optimal business practicability suitable for global standards in order to meet the rapidly changing economic situation.

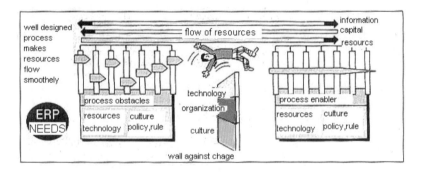

The needs of ERP can be explained by the viewpoint of enterprise environment and information technology.

In terms of enterprise environment,

1) The efficiency of enterprise management for win—win strategy of company and customer

2) The needs of process innovation

3) The integration of functions for the whole process chain

4) The total optimized process flows integrated manufacturing and sales

5) The flexibility for the speed and changes.

In terms of information technology,

1) The execution client server system by downsizing

2) The decline of existing system and Y2K problem accelerated the transformation of enterprise information system

3) The expectation for using package software by outsourcing

4) The new value creation by the ledger type database.

The followings are the characteristics of ERP.

1) Commonplace: ERP is not developed for a particular company or industry but developed for every company and every industry's application.

2) Real-time: ERP processes data by real-time and provides timely the useful information the user. So, the speed and transparency of affairs would be improved by ERP.

3) System integration: ERP is designed that all affairs with logical relations should be processed at the same time. Every data is processed by just one input so that duplication and discordance is not permitted. So, the efficiency of affairs would be improved.

4) Convenience for users: ERP supports icons and graphic symbols in Window environment so that users can easily inquire and analyze

data.

5) Open system: ERP can be used in any hardware and system technology. ERP also support the flexible and expandable IT for the rapid changing environment.

6) Globalization: ERP supports a lot of languages, currencies and accounting system of many countries.

However, ERP is not the almighty tool for every company. POSCO has performed a lot of preparations in order to apply ERP successfully, such as • Process Innovation first • Clear objectives • Users to be the subject • Clear policy of top management • Out—side consulting • System oriented process and so on.

3.Characteristics of the new system for POSCO PI

The new system of POSCO can be explained by the following four characteristics.

1) Application Architecture

POSCO new system is on the basis of Oracle ERP system and consists of Rhythm SCP package of i2 technology, VBM (Value Based Management), BSC (Balanced Score Card) and ABM(activity Based Management). POSCO has linked the new system covering execution ~ planning ~ strategy with the existing production system, and linked the internal system with the external system so that e—business system for synchronizing the internal and external processes has been established. A lot of companies usually enlarge their system to planning level or strategy level after the execution level stabilized. But POSCO started at the same time to operate the integrated system that has the whole system of execution, planning and strategy. It's a kind of big bang that maximized the synergy effect.

⟨Fig.2 ⟩ERP/SCP/Enlarged ERP sytem

	Enlarged			
strategy level	ERP	BSC/ABM	DATA WAREHOUSE	
planning level	SCP	Integrated sales/ manufacturing plan	procee plan	Standardization data dictionary
execution level	ERP	LOGISTICS	FINANCE/ ACCOUNTING	
infra level	production site system(legacy)			

2) The structure of Item/BOM/Routing and its application

It is most difficult to standardize affairs and have 100% accurate master data in many companies. But POSCO had already a remarkable infra system such as the work standards for each material unit by process and by factory. The cost per steel grade at each factory transferred to

451

them, and BOM/outing could be designed in consideration of the existing work order process and cost center.

Item/BOM/routing integrated process (order~production~shipping~accounting part)

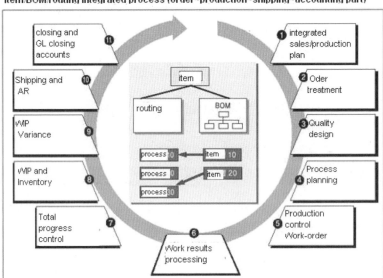

3) Application of IT new technology

POSCO applied Super Dome, the extra-large server which may be the biggest in the world and the newest version Oracle 11i, and applied the new technology EAI in order to integrate the various platform, and e-business system which is 24 hrs. non-stop and completely opened. The infra environment is perfect for preparing the future technological development by adopting Giga bit network, HA (High availability), e-Group ware, VPN (Virtual Private Network), and e0-learning.

일범의 평범한 사람 이야기

4) Hot run and End—users' participation

If any system developed by some special group transferred to the users who had not participated in the development, there would be a lot of confusions and problems. POSCO had prepared those kinds of situation. So POSCO opened the system to all end—users who would use the system for the period of System Link test, System test and Application Test. By doing this, the end—users could understand the system better and many potential issues could be solved during the test period.

4.Examples of ERP system

4—1) Human Resource Management

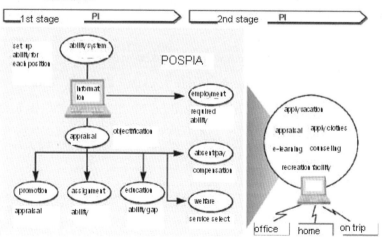

The human resources part of PI is classified two stages. During the first stage of PI, Job ability required to each position was set up and Appraisal process was improved, so that the connection between appraisal result and job–allocation, promotion, and salary was strengthened. The learning culture was built up by training Leaders for change, performing MAPPERS conference, and enlarging On–line study classes. The work system was improved by introducing non–working day on every other Saturday, enlarging vacation for refresh, and improving work shifting. And the labor/welfare supporting procedures such as payment of business trip expense has been simplified.

Based on the performance of 1st stage, salary, absenteeism, welfare, and employment system were developed during 2nd stage of PI. The main ideas of HRM system are as follows.

1) Information transaction between ERP and legacy system without any interface system.

2) The employment system would be linked with internet.

3) The welfare system like the highly developed country system.

4) HRM system would be developed on EP (Enterprise Portal) base, so that employee can use easily.

4-2) Financial Process

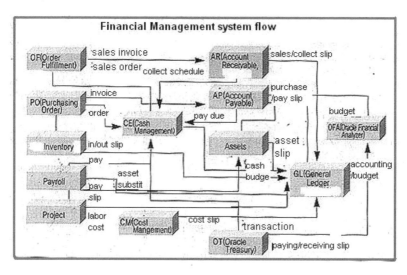

Financial Management system flow

The main objectives of financial process system are • Improve standard cost system • Introduce Activity Based Cost • Real-time closing account • Improve budget administration system • Automatic forecasting of income and expenditure • Transparent account system • Increase the accuracy of data.

1) Cost management

Standard cost per item was calculated by using of BOM*/ Routing*Base data/unit cost of raw material. CST (Cost Management module) of ERP was chosen for daily profit & loss calculation and Cost differential analysis. Activa module of ERP was a little modified for cost allocation and standard cost calculation in order to meet the law.

2) Budget management

The main target of budget management system is shortening the period for making up budgets and improving budget management. ERP toll was OFA (Oracle Financial Analyzer) which is working in coordination with the general ledger.

3) Financial administration

The target of this part is supporting top management's decision making and other key processes in company by providing accurate and efficient financial information. Financial administration system consists of Closing accounting, Credit management, Debit Management, Asset management, Connection closing, and Taxation planning.

4) Capital management

The main objectives of this part are to cope effectively with the rapidly changing situation by the automatic forecasting of capital needs and the risk management. Treasury module of ERP was chosen for this system.

4-3) Business & Manufacturing Process

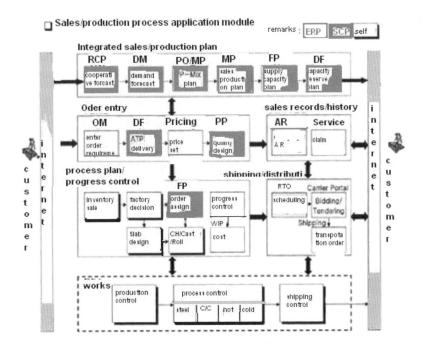

Business and manufacturing process is the most important key process of a company, which is alpha and omega in a company. This process aimed to • Customer oriented system • Improve the accuracy of demand & supply information • Maximize the efficiency totally removed the time delay • Improve the service level • Cost reduction and • Use the practical material flow information. Business and manufacturing process system consists of 6 process chains, 33 sub-process chains and 133 tasks.

ERP was applied the execution part which includes Order entry, Progress control, and Cost link. SCP system was applied for the optimization part which includes Sales/manufacturing plan, Process plan, and Transportation plan.

1) Integrated sales/manufacturing plan

The periods for making sales/manufacturing plan was shortened from 60days to 15 days, so the company's management plan can be updated quarterly. SCP package system supplied by i2 Technology was chosen for this system. RCP (Rhythm Collaboration Planner) for demand forecasting with customers, DM (Demand Management) for demand forecasting, MP(Master Planner) · PO(Profit Optimizer) for product mix · sales/manufacturing plan, FP(Factory Planner) for supply capacity plan, DF(Demand Fulfillment) for capacity reservation plan per customers modules were applied. But OFT (Oracle financial Analyzer) was applied for sales · price plan.

2) Order entry, Quality design

This system supports to response the delivery as soon as order input by performing automatic order data processing and quality design. OM (Order management) module for order entry and PP (Product Planner) module for quality design were applied.

3) Process planning, Progress control

This system shortened the delivery (for Hot coil) from 30 days to 7 days by transferring the control to business division from production works. FP (Factory planner) of SCP for order assignment planning and

ERP WIP (Work In Process) · BOM(Bill Of Material) for progress control and cost link modules were applied respectively. But the legacy systems were improved and applied for order match, factory determination within works, slab design, grouping of charge/cast/roll unit.

4) Shipping/distribution management

Introducing the bidding system for determining the transport company for every transportation event contributed cost reduction. The total transport information provided to customers by using GPS. And the export orders would be processed according to the shipping schedule, so that the Products in stock level decreased remarkably. Carrier Portal and Shipping module of ERP were applied for bidding and shipping direction, and RTO (Rhythm Transportation Optimizer) and DS (Dock schedule) of SCP were applied for transportation planning and daily planning.

5) Sales records management

Account receivable management for supporting "D+1-day financial closing", without slip system, and work cooperation system for claims would be automatically processed. ERP AR (Account Receivable), Work Flow module for work cooperation and Service module for cash payback, etc were applied.

6) New product/ New demand development

CFT (Cross functional team) which consists of development, quality, laboratory, and business group would investigate customers' needs for new product, and the duration for developing a new product were shortened from 4 years to 1.5 year.

5. Conclusion

The management environment and information technology have been changing rapidly since 1990's. A lot of time, money and works had been needed for upgrading the existing system to meet the changes. But ERP has the spearhead IT which is flexible and enlargeable for coping with the changes. POSCO had performed Process Innovation successfully with the long–term vision. And the speed, transparency, and efficiency of business could be highly improved through ERP system, because all business processes in the company such as production, purchasing, material, accounting, etc. could be integrated by IT and treated by real time. POSCO have pursued the total optimization over the company–wide through ERP, not the optimization of each sub–organization.

Over the past thirty–some years, hard work and perseverance have made POSCO the moving force in the world of steel. Today, POSCO is the most competitive steel company in the world. Like any other company, POSCO could not exist without customers. And POSCO's win–win management philosophy ensures customers stay POSCO's No. 1 priority. POSCO are now driving forward Six Sigma over the

company—wide in order to keep the reputation and to meet customers'
needs in innovative, cost—effective new ways.

References:

1. www.posco.co.kr

2. www.weekly.poco.co.kr

3. www.oracle.com

4. Smart steel, POSCO research institute, 1996

Research Paper 4: Pickle Deflector Roll Improvement

1. Introduction

USS—POSCO Industries (UPI), a joint venture company established
by U. S. Steel Corporation and POSCO of Korea, is located in
Pittsburg, California. The company employs almost 1,000 people and
converts hot rolled steel coils into three main product lines: cold rolled
sheet, galvanized sheet, and tin plate. (See Exhibit 1: The Material Flow
in USS—POSCO)

Tin Plate is typically utilized in the following applications: Food
Cans (Soup, Tuna, Fruit, Vegetable, Coffee) and Pet foods, Easy Open
End, Oil Filters, Crown Caps, Screw Caps, Motor Oil Cans, Paint and
Lacquer Cans, and Aerosol Cans. Western canners and food processors

use more than 600,000 tons of tin plate annually. UPI is the West's only tin plate producer, maintaining the leadership position held by the plant since the 1920s.

UPI has two Electrolytic tinning Lines, #1 ETL and #3 ETL, #2Line was closed in 1985. #3ETL produces Tin coated steel only, but #1ETL produces Tin products and Tin Free Steel which is Chrome coated steel. The line layout of #1 ETL is shown at Fig. 1.

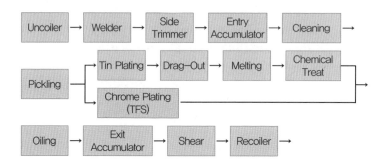

TFS was originally developed as lower cost alternative to Tinplate and is used primarily for two-piece drawn cans and as end stock on tinplated and composite can. The surface of TFS product is more sensitive than Tinplate, so TFS stains are easily revealed in case the strip is not perfectly treated in Pickling unit. In 2002, a problem-solving team for improving TFS stains had an excellent result during six months (See Exhibit 2: TFS production analysis).

The purpose of Pickling unit is to remove oxides and rust from the strip and lightly etch the strip surface so as to prevent as clean a steel surface as possible to the plating step. 5 to 10 percent sulfuric acid is used for the pickle solution which is very solvent. Rubber lined roll or steel strip is easily dissolved or etched by the pickle solution. Pickling is a very critical operation since any non—uniformity in the treatment will be revealed in the appearance of the finished product. Poor pickling can cause scratches or stains on the surfaces of finished products. Tin plate or TFS steel with such defects cannot be used for can manufacturing to the above mentioned applications.

After TFS stains project was successfully finished, there was still a problem at the pickling section. We had to change pickle deflector roll very frequently for ensuring good quality without defects. Rubber—lined pickle deflector rolls were easily damaged or worn by the pickle solution, poor strip tracking, or by the heavy burr on the strip edges. Therefore, there is an opportunity for reducing costs in pickle section while maintaining or improving quality.

2. Problem Solving Steps

2—1 Team Charter

The problem—solving team for Pickle section was organized with a team leader (Production Assistant Manager), facilitator, and six team members (Process manager and Lead operator from operation part, Mechanical supervisor, Mechanical group leader and a worker from maintenance part). The team set the team's scope and method of measurement at the first meeting.

Scope: Reduce Pickle Deflector Roll Change Frequency by 25% while Maintaining or Improving Quality
Method of Measurement: Roll Change Frequency, Delays, Costs, and Quality diversions

2-2 Identification of the problem

The most outstanding issue was the status of too frequent roll change whatever the reasons were. Frequent roll change would greatly impair the productivity, quality, and costs at all. As the first step, the team gathered the operational and maintenance data for the year and calculated the costs generated by the roll changes. The number of roll changes in pickle section was forty-nine times for eight months and the cost amount due to those roll changes was approximately $190,000 as shown in Table 1 and 2.

일범의 평범한 사람 이야기

⟨Table 1: Number of Roll Changes in the Pickle Section⟩

3/2003 thru 11/2003

	Scheduled	Emergency	Total
#1 Pickle	4	3	7
#2 Pickle	8	6	14
#3 Pickle	9	5	14
#4 Pickle	13	1	14
Totals	34	15	49

* 31 Rolls Changed During a TFS Run

* 18 Rolls Changed During a Tin Run

⟨Table 2: Cost of Rolls Changes in the Pickle Section⟩

3/2003 thru 11/2003

	Frequency	Amount
Re-grind	21	$ 7,350
Re-rubber	24	$ 55,220
Delay	30Hr	$ 49,140
Labor	147M/Hr	$ 4,704
Quality	200Tons	$ 70,000
$ Total		$ 186,414

NOTE: Quality Based On $350 a Ton in Diversions

Labor Based On 3 Man Hours per Emergency Roll Change

The team had listed total sixteen reasons of Deflector roll changes by a brainstorming. Table 3 shows the results of brainstorming with votes. The most critical reason of changing rolls is for preventing defect (in this case, stains). The damaged rolls (for examples, worn by the pickle solution, grooved by the burr of the strip edge, or scratched by the strip through bad tracking) might contain the residual sulfuric solution which cause stains on the strip surface after plating. Figure 2 is the Pareto graph of the brainstorming results.

⟨Table 3: Reasons of Changing Pickle Deflector Rolls⟩

by Brainstorming

1. Stain = 30(wear, grooving, surface finish) 2. Trial = 4
3. Creases = 3   4. Dents = 0
5. TFS run/PM =19   6. Bad Bearings = 3
7. Cuts = 7   8. Scratches/Abrasion = 8
9. Tracking = 7   10. Material Failures = 0
11. Broken Shaft = 0   12. Roll Delaminating = 0
13. Wrong Diameter = 4   14. Roll Becoming Dished = 5
15. Roll Profile = 0   16. Poor Pickling = 0

〈Figure 2: Pareto of Roll Change Causes by Vote〉

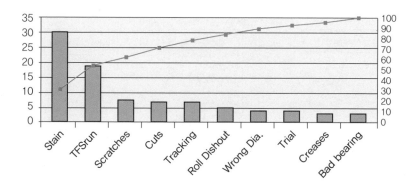

2-3 Analysis of root causes of the problem

The team had analyzed the reasons of TFS Stains, Scratches from the Pickle Deflector rolls, Cuts on the Pickle Deflector rolls, and Bad tracking by the Pickle Deflector rolls. The Fish bone diagrams are shown as Figure 3 and 4. The causes for Scratches, Cuts, and Tracking are shown at the same diagram.

The Type I, II, or III means the problem type. Type I is the controllable problem which the team members can eliminate the reasons by their own operational and maintenance efforts. Type II is semi-controllable, and type III is the uncontrollable problem that is fixed condition by environment or raw materials.

⟨Figure 3: Cause and Effect for TFS Stain⟩

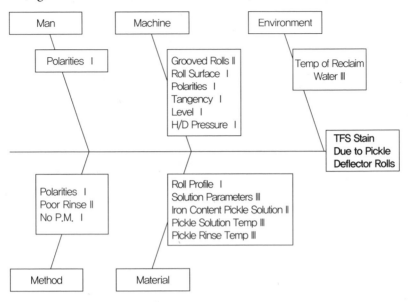

Figure 4: Cause and Effect for Scratches, Cuts, and Tracking⟩

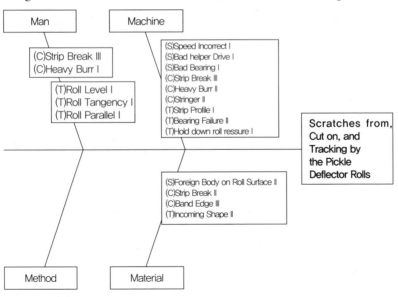

일범의 평범한 사람 이야기

2-4 Plan and implementation of action items

The team had suggested possible solutions for each problem by brain storming based on the cause effect diagrams created. The team took out ten solutions for solving TFS Stain and six solutions for the other problems. All of the suggested solutions could not perform because of the limitation of cost and resources. So the team had evaluated the solutions by Effort—Impact analysis and selected the solutions with higher priority (low effort—high impact is the best).

〈Figure 5: Probability/Impact Analysis for TFS Stain〉

1. Carbide Roll

2. Heat Exchanger for Pickle Solution

3. Control Pickle Spray Rinse Temperature

4. Polarity Switching Practices

5. Better Control of Solution Parameters

6. Different Rubber Materials

7. More Accurate Roll Inspection P.M.

8. Improved Burr Control

9. Better Scheduling of Orders

10. Better Rinsing

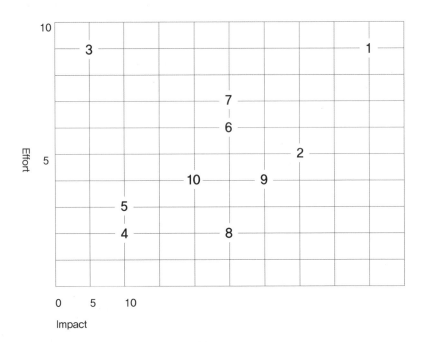

⟨Figure 6: Probability/Impact Analysis for Scratches, Cuts, Tracking⟩

1. Carbide Rolls
2. Roll Installation Practice
3. Laser Alignment P.M.
4. Speed Match More Often
5. AC Drives on Rolls
6. Digital Display on Gauges

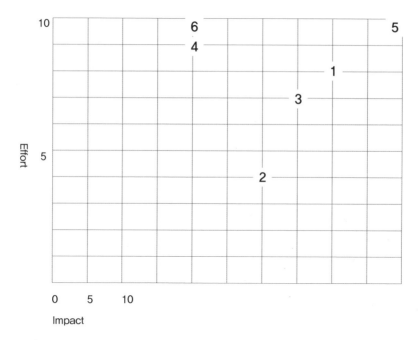

The team had built the implementing plan for action items which were selected by the Effort-Impact Analysis. The team also recommended some action items for the future which would be also helpful to improve the problems.

⟨Table 4: Action Plan⟩

1. Carbide Rolls in the Pickle Spray Section	12/11/03	Justin Eckhart
2. Maximize R.O. Water in the Up pass of #2 Pickle Spray Tank	12/31/03	Justin Eckhart
3. Scheduling Practice for Gauge & Width	12/31/03	M.D. Amin
4. Burr Control Measurement System (temp run burr masher on strip over 80 Gage)	1/2/04	Team
5. Install a Heat Exchanger / Pickle Solution	2/1/04	Justin Eckhart
6. Develop Roll Checklist for Pickle Section	1/9/04	Team

⟨Table 5: Recommendations⟩

1. Trial Materials for #1 & #2 Pickle Deflector Positions

2. Standardize Roll Installation Procedure

3. Set P.M. on Roll Inspection Data

4. Install AC Drives

5. More Frequent Speed Matches

6. Install Fiberglass Tank at Tops

7. Automated Burr Detector after the Trimmer

The Team started to take action according to the action plan. The first action was to install Carbide rolls in the pickle spray by 12/11/03, but it was delayed due to the electro coating until the first part of January. The first carbide roll was installed in #4 pickle spray by the startup of the TFS starting January 9th. And the second carbide roll was installed in the #1 pickle tank on Feb. 22nd. The #2 action was

472

to maximize R.O water in the up pass of the #2 pickle spray, and it was done as scheduled. The #3 action was a better scheduling practice for gauge & width was on schedule for 12/31/03. The #4 action item was Burr control System of when to run the burr masher. The team recommended operators to run the burr masher on all 80 gauge and up and it seemed to be working great. So the Team will inform the rest of the crews to run burr masher on 80 gauge and up. The #5 action item was to install a heat exchanger on the pickle solution by 2/1/04, but the Team concluded that the ambient temperature on canal water would be fine. The last action item was to develop a roll checklist for pickle section. The Team established the checklist after the full discussion between operation part and maintenance part.

2-5 Checking effectiveness of action taken.

As of March 10th, the carbide roll installed in #4 pickle spray tank is still using without any quality problem such as stains. If we had not replaced it to carbide roll, we would have changed it several times for regrinding and re-rubber lining. And also, no stains due to poor pickling were produced. Table 6 is the summarized savings amount for last 3 months. The total savings reach up to $47,664 and it will be approximately $190,000 per year.

〈Table 6: Savings Amount by the improvement for 3 months〉

1. Three regrinds $3 \times \$350 = \$1,050$
2. Three rubber $3 \times \$2,300 = \$6,900$
3. One emergency & 5 standard roll change labor $2,700
4. No production for three hours delays for roll change $4,914
5. 33 tons non−prime per run $\times$ 2 runs $\times \$350 = \$23,100$
6. Life of elevated carry overextended $9,000.
   Total = $47,664

2−6 Standardization of process improvement

After Team confirmed the operation results of three months which was satisfactory, Team revised the SQPs (Standards Quality Procedures) of Scheduling Practice for Gauge & Width and of Burr Control Measurement System in order to ensure the revised method would be continuously performed (See Exhibit 3). Besides SQP update, the maintenance parts developed a roll check list for pickle section which contains who check the rolls, when, and how. The accumulated data on the check sheet would be helpful for the further improvement in the future.

2−7 Future actions

Any facility without a large investment for rationalization for long period should have various issues due to wear, fatigue and un−match with newest technology and control system. For examples, AC drive motors are required a lot of maintenance jobs, the melting capacity is not enough to meet the increasing speed, and the accumulating tin trees and dust can increase the dents on the strip surface. So the process should be continuously improved for achieving the better quality, the higher productivity, and the lower cost. In #1 electro−tinning line, another team was organized for reducing Drag−out dents as one of the six−sigma project. Exhibit 4 is the outline of the drag−out dents reduction team which is still in the stage of implementation.

3. Conclusion

Quality and process improvement in the steel manufacturing company is the essential part of maintaining the competitiveness. And the continuous improvement cannot be achieved by an individual. It requires teamwork between operation, maintenance, sales and/ or purchasing department. Team leader should be well qualified for coordination, motivation, technology and skills, and leadership. Team members also should actively participate in their roles and be trained to new techniques and changes. The pickle roll improvement team had good team works during the project performing period. And all team members became more confident to challenge to solve any new issues in the future.

(Exhibit 1)

The material flow in USS−POSCO

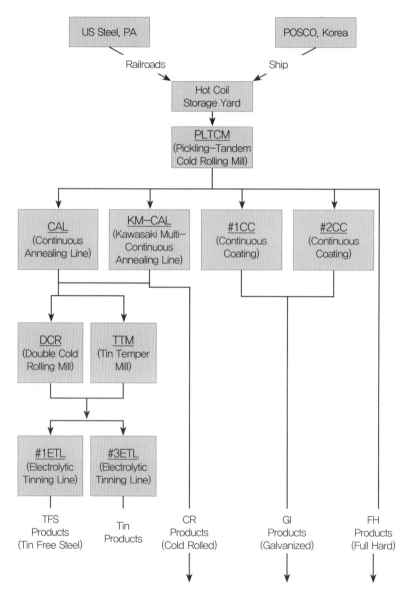

일범의 평범한 사람 이야기

(Exhibit 2)

TFS Production Analysis during First half in 2002

1. Main Corrective Actions

➤ Control Chlorides: Wash down water, Carry over water from pickle section, Cooling water leak, Quench water.

➤ Control iron

➤ Build a better understanding with crew: solution Temp' vs. Amps, Catalyst ratios.

➤ Roll alignment in the cell.

➤ Install new Deflector roll (elevated, weld detector)

➤ Install new Flow meter.

2. Production data in the first haft of 2002

(Unit: ton)	Jan. Run	Apr. Run	May Run
Prime Production	19,686	13,523	6,742
Diversion Total	1,201	384	43
Stains	617	115	13
Arc	2	110	0
Rust	133	0	0
Others	449	159	30
% Stains per prime Production	3.1	0.9	0.2
% Yields per Prime Consumed	93.0	97.3	99.4

Diversion per TFS Run

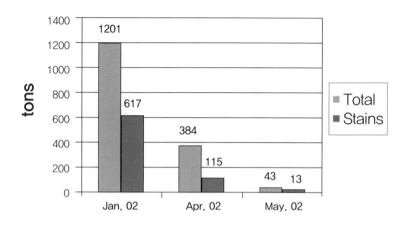

(Exhibit 3) Standardization of Process improvements

Scheduling Guideline — ETL #1 & #3

No. SQP—T 6.201 Revd.

PURPOSE

Scheduling Guidelines ETL #1 & #3

RESPONSIBILITY

Business Services, ETL stocker, Shift Manager

PROCEDURE

I. SOURCES OF STEEL:

1. Tin Temper Mill

2. DCR Mill

3. Side Trimmers #3.

4. #1 Re-coiler Unit.

5. O.K. Ferro -From Reclamation or after service work.

II. SEQUENCING PRIORITY : (See *Note at bottom of page if these guidelines cannot be met)

1. Coating Weight :

Coating weights should be increased from light to heavy when possible (e.g., 20lb to 25lb to 50/20lb to 75/25lb to 100/20lb to 75/20lb to 50/25lb to 25lb). Coating weight changes should not exceed more than two increments.

2. Marking :

Rule for Marking Changes : When possible, symbol mark orders with different type symbols should not be scheduled following one another. Either a line marked order, an order with no marking, or waste coil must be inserted between symbol marks to prevent a line stop. Line marking orders may be scheduled in any manner.

3. Oiling :

Oiling weights should increase and decrease in single increments when possible (e.g., 5/15 to10/20 to 40/60lb to 10/20 to 5/15). Increasing from a 5/15 oil weight order to a 40/60 oil weight is allowable but not preferable.

4. Width:

    Line should be scheduled wide to narrow then narrow too wide. Scheduled width changes should not exceed more than two (2) inches in either direction. **

5. Gauge:

    Scheduled gauge changes should not exceed more than 0.0030 inches on most size changes. The gauge change should not exceed 0.0055 inches for transitions into or out of 0.0184 inches and heavier material. **

6. Start—Up: After scheduled downturns.

    Never run from heavy coated (50/20 and heavier) to un—melted.

    Minimum of 4 coils 20# and or 25# coated order needed to start—up.

    Never run coffee body orders for 8 hrs. after startup.

    Never run salmon ends as first prime order after startup.

7. Trial orders should be scheduled to run Monday—Friday "B" Turn, when possible. Trail orders should not be scheduled within 8 hours after startup. **

8. Orders that can be scheduled and run on #3 ETL only are: Ross Labs, Salmon Ends, D&I, and 40/60 oils.

* Note: Trial Orders requiring ETL non–standard operating procedures must be cleared by process manager or shift coordinator before schedule.

** Note: If these scheduling guidelines cannot be met, the schedule must be approved by the Shift Manager or Process Manager.

No. SQP–T 6.202 Revd.
Scheduling Guideline – #1 ETL (TFS)

PURPOSE
Scheduling Guidelines for #1 ETL (TFS)

RESPONSIBILITY
Business Services, ETL Stocker, Shift Manager

PROCEDURE
1. All T.F.S. run on #1 ETL.
2. Block schedule T.F.S. orders using guidelines from tin schedules. (Refer to SQP–T 6.201, items 2, 3, 4)
3. Startup orders should be scheduled from wide to narrow. *

4. Block schedule any DCR T.F.S. together, when possible.

5. Van Can and Impress orders cannot be scheduled within 8 hours of startup. *

6. Trial orders should be scheduled to run Monday — Friday "B" Turn. Trial orders should not be scheduled within 8 hours of startup. *

* If these scheduling guidelines cannot be met, the schedule must be approved by the Shift Manager or Process Manager.

Scheduling Guideline — #1 ETL (Coated)

No. SQP—T 6.203 Rev.D

PURPOSE

Scheduling Guidelines for #1 ETL (coated)

RESPONSIBILITY

Business Services, ETL stocker, Shift Manager

PROCEDURE

1. Line limitations (melted)

  Width: 1) Max. width = 37"

           2) Min. width = 28"

  Gauge: 1) Max. gauge (melted) = .0123"

           2) Min. gauge (melted) = .0053"

2. Line limitations: (Un−melted − Matte finish)

Width: 1) Max. width = 37"

2) Min. width = 28"

Gauge: 1) Max. gauge (un−melted) = .0205"

2) Min. gauge (un−melted) = .0053"

3. The maximum coating weight that can be run on #1 ETL is 25#.

4. Orders that cannot be run on ET #1: Ross Labs, Salmon Ends, D&I, and 40/60 oils.

Burr Reduction

No. SQP−T 6.410 Rev.New

PURPOSE

Assuring proper Burr on In−Line trim coils

RESPONSIBILITY

ETL Finishers, Operators, Feeders, Assistant Operators

PROCEDURE

1. Check Burr on Bottom East and West edges of sample with fingernail.

2. If Burr is determined to be excessive reduce gap by .20 (two tenths) If reduced, knives don't need to be in maintenance. Refer to SQP−T 6.415 −.

Use caution as gap should not be reduced less than .50 (five tenths), if gap has been calibrated to 1.0/1.0.

3. If Burr is still present and further adjustment cannot be made the Burr Masher Rolls must be applied.

4. If Burr is still present with Burr Masher Rolls on and the gap at the minimum adjustment, the knives and gap must be checked physically, and appropriate corrective action must be taken.

NOTE: If the problem is occurring every 33" − 34" it is possible knife damage has occurred, in which case applying the Burr Masher Rolls should be tried. If problem still exists a knife change or flip should be performed.

(Exhibit 4) Six-sigma project: Drag-out Dents reduction.

Brainstorming on Drag-Out Dents

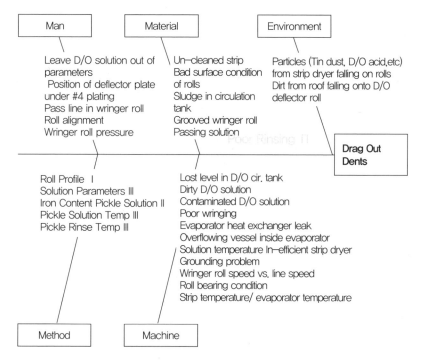

Project Description

- Reduce Drag-Out Related Dents by 70%

  - Drag-Out dents occur after the tin plating in the drag-out section. Excess tin and acid build up on roll surfaces and eventually causes dents.

  - Internally: yield reduction, additional labor cost

  - Externally: poor "promise performance", customer claim cost and customer process interruption.

－Rust occurs in tin plated products where dents are present. Lacquer-coated products will also rust due to dents. Can also cause structural failure.

Current Status of Action Items

• Replace 2 broken up pass brush rods for self-cleaning spray headers － completed 11/16/03.
• Replace 2 down pass brush rods 1/22/04.
• Replace steam sparker with steam envelope － completed 9/2/03.
• Bring filter press into operation － parts on site, 50% installation complete, fully complete 2/29/04.
• Install 3-way valve to transfer D/O directly to pickle sump － design stage for process improvement.

Drag-Out Dent Project Schedule

Week 1	-Team members selected
Weeks 2 – 5	-Developed Process Map -Brainstormed cause and effects
Weeks 6 – 12	-Developed FMEA -Discussed possible DOEs
Weeks 13 – 19	-Investigated Quality Walk data- analysis –I.P. -Bringing filter press to operation Developing measurement system -Installed ceramic deflector rolls -Investigate dirty d/o to pickle sump
Weeks 20 – 30	-Complete data analysis -Complete maintenance items -Set up measurement system -Choose variables and plan DOE.

Project Paper 5: Nucor Corporation

1. Overview

Nucor Corporation is the largest steel producer in the United States, has over $4.1 billion in sales annually, and has more than 98,000 employees who work hard to keep Nucor a leader in its industry. Nucor is the nation's largest recycler, recycling over 13 million tons of scrap steel annually.

2. Value Chain

Nucor produces steel and steel products by melting recycled ferrous scrap in electric arc furnaces. Products produced are carbon and alloy steel in bars, beams, sheet, and plate; steel joists and joist girders; steel deck; cold finished steel; steel fasteners; metal building systems; and light gauge steel framing. The main customers are the companies of construction, automotives, containers, appliances and machineries.

3. Culture

Nucor's success in large part is driven by its culture, developed over many years. It contains so many elements: Commitment to employees, Teamwork, Safety, Customer focus, High quality standards, Ethics and integrity, Continual improvement and risk-taking, Pay for performance, Environmental focus, Decentralized divisions, Entrepreneurial spirit, Profitability, etc.

4. Strategic Intent

The Strategic intent of Nucor can be summarized as "Produce high quality steel and steel products at low cost in order to satisfy customers and maintain the market leader through the process of continual technological improvement."

5. Issues and Growth Strategy

Under the depressed economic situation for steel industry, Nucor also is faced to some significant issues such as the price fluctuation of steel scrap and the challenges from the newly developing countries. In order to keep its position as a leading producer of quality steel and steel products, Nucor's business strategy should be focused on optimizing existing operations and continuous investing to new technologies with the security of safety and environmental protection.

1. A Brief Background of Nucor

Nucor's origins are with auto manufacturer Ransom E. Olds, who founded Oldsmobile and then Reo Motor Cars. Through a series of transactions, the company Olds founded eventually became the Nuclear Corporation of America. Nuclear Corporation was involved in the nuclear instrument and electronics business in the 1950's and early 1960's.

The company suffered through several money-losing years, and when facing bankruptcy in 1964, installed F. Kenneth Iverson as President and

Samuel Siegel as Vice President of Finance. This change in management led to a restructuring and a decision to rebuild the company around the major profitable operations; the steel joist businesses in Florence, South Carolina and Norfolk, Nebraska called Vulcraft.

The company moved its headquarters from Phoenix, Arizona to Charlotte, North Carolina in 1966, and expanded the joist business with new operations in Texas and Alabama. Management then decided to integrate backwards into steel making by building its first steel bar mill in Darlington, South Carolina in 1968. In 1972 the company adopted the name Nucor Corporation. Since that time, Nucor has built three more Vulcraft facilities, eight steel mills, and expanded into other steel products. In 2002, Nucor completed the purchase of substantially all the assets of Birmingham Steel Corporation, which includes four operating mills in Alabama, Illinois, Washington, and Mississippi.

2. Description of Business

Nucor Corporation has received a great deal of attention in the business media in recent years because of its success in an industry beset by a multitude of problems. Nucor has been able to remain a growing, profitable steel and steel products producer, because Nucor's work force is strongly committed to Nucor's basic philosophy — to build steel manufacturing facilities economically and to operate them productively.

Today, Nucor Corporation is the largest steel producer in the United States, has over $4.1 billion in sales annually, and has more than 98,000 employees who work hard to keep Nucor a leader in its industry. Nucor is the nation's largest recycler, recycling over 13 million tons of scrap steel annually.

3. Performance trends

Nucor, a pioneer of the world's mini—mill industry, increased its crude steel production capacity by 15.4 % per year, and improved its revenues by 16.4% per year, during the ten—year period from 1985 to 1995. The company 's net profits increased by 16.7% every year even though it was declined during last two years.

Income Statement	Dec-02	Dec-01	Dec-00	Dec-99
Net Sales	4,801.78	4,139.25	4,586.15	4,009.35
Cost of Goods Sold	4,025.18	3,531.24	3,666.11	3,223.84
Operating Inc	293.91	160.19	477.49	374.09
Pretax Income	309.53	173.86	478.31	379.19
Net Income	162.08	112.96	310.91	244.59

Balance Sheet	Dec-02	Dec-01	Dec-00	Dec-99
Assets				
Total Current Assets	1,424.14	1,373.67	1,381.45	1,538.51
Net PP&E	2,932.06	2,365.66	2,340.34	2,191.34
Total Assets	4,381.00	3,759.35	3,721.79	3,729.85
Liabilities and Shareholders' Equity				
Short-Term Debt	16.00	0.00	0.00	0.00
Total Current Liabilities	591.54	484.16	558.07	531.03
Long-Term Debt	878.55	460.45	460.45	390.45
Total Liabilities	1,841.36	1,274.00	1,278.57	1,186.73
Total Common Equity	2,322.99	2,201.46	2,130.95	2,262.25

Cash Flow Statement	Dec-02	Dec-01	Dec-00	Dec-99
Net Cash Flows from Operations	497.22	495.12	820.75	604.83
Net Cash Flows from Investing	901.41	360.40	410.28	374.28
Net Cash Flows from Financing	160.85	-162.94	-492.09	32.93

Key Ratios	
P/E	24.50
Earnings Per Share (EPS)	2.07
Dividends Per Share (DPS)	0.76
Dividend Yield	1.60
Quick Ratio	1.19
Current Ratio	2.41
Return On Equity (ROE) Per Share	7.33
Return On Assets (ROA)	4.71
Return On Invested Capital (ROIC)	6.02
	in millions of USD

4. Value proposition

The economy made the 1980s a horrible time for the steel industry. All companies reported sales declines, most lost profitability and some, in both major and mini—mill operations, closed or restructured. However, Nucor was the only one mini—mill operator who making moneys and holding on profitability.

Despite the doubts voiced by world steel experts, Nucor introduced the Thin Slab Caster in its Crawfordville Plant and successfully put it into operation in 1989, thus becoming the world's first commercial plant of the thin slab caster.

Today, Nucor has operating facilities in 14 states. Products produced are carbon and alloy steel in bars, beams, sheet, and plate; steel joists and joist girders; steel deck; cold finished steel; steel fasteners; metal building systems; and light gauge steel framing.

5. Nucor's locations and products

Divisions	Products	Facilities	Tons/Year
Sheet mill	Carbon steel in hot rolled, cold rolled, pickled, floor plate, and galvanized coils	Crawfordsville,IN Hickman, AR Berkeley, SC	8.4 million
Bar mill	Carbon steel angles, channels, flats, reinforcing bars, rounds, and squares	Utah, Texas, South Carolina, Nebraska, Utah, Alabama,Illinois, Mississippi, Washington	5.8 million
Fastener	Carbon and alloy steel standard hex head cap screws, hex flange bolts, structural bolts and nuts, and finished hex nuts	Indiana	75,000
Vulcraft	Carbon steel in joists, joist girders, composite floor joists, and floor and roof deck	South Carolina, Nebraska, Texas, Indiana, Utah, New York	400,000
Cold Finish	Rounds, hexagons, flats and squares in carbon and alloy steels	Nebraska, Utah, South Carolina	350,000
Building Systems	Pre-engineered metal buildings and metal building components	Indiana, Texas, South Carolina	145,000
Nucor-Yamato Steel Company	Carbon steel wide-flange beams, sheet and H-piling, miscellaneous and standard channels, angles, and CZ and CSC car building sections	Arkansas, South Carolina	3.2 million

일범의 평범한 사람 이야기

6. Value Chain

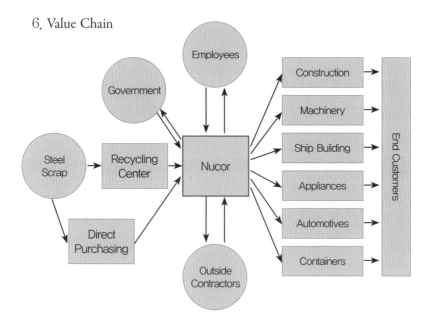

Nucor is the world largest recycler of steel scrap. Nucor buys steel scrap from the scrap-downed industrial equipment to the junk auto part. Those steel scrap are put into the electric arc furnace and melted. The melted steel is poured into a ladle to be carried by an overhead crane to the casting machine. In the casting machine, the liquid steel is extruded as the continuous red-hot solid steel and cut into lengths called slabs and billets. Slabs and/or billets are carried into the rolling mill and placed in a reheat oven to bring them up 2000 °F at which temperature they would be malleable. In the hot-rolling mill, presses and dies progressively converted the slabs into hot-rolled coils and the billets into the designed round bars, angles, channels, flats, and other products. Some of the hot-rolled coils would be directly sold to the customers such as construction companies or ship building companies.

The other hot coils are carried to the cold—rolling mill where those would be re—rolled, annealed and/or Zn—coated and then sold to the construction companies, the housing companies and the automobile companies.

7. Business Model

Nucor is committed to uncompromising quality, responsive service, and competitive pricing. Through continuous innovation, modern equipment, dedication to the customer, and concentration on productivity from a highly motivated work force, Nucor has distinguished itself as a leading producer of quality steel and steel products. Many Nucor locations are ISO 9000 Certified. Nucor employees are committed to providing customers with the highest quality levels at the most competitive prices. And, while steel and steel products are Nucor's business, the real business of Nucor is its commitment to each and every customer on each and every order.

8. Nucor's Culture

Nucor's success in large part is driven by its culture, developed over many years. It contains so many elements: Commitment to employees, Teamwork, Safety, Customer focus, High quality standards, Ethics and integrity, Continual improvement and risk—taking, Pay for performance, Environmental focus, Decentralized divisions, Entrepreneurial spirit, Profitability, etc.

Organization and Employee

Nucor has a simple, streamlined organizational structure to allow employees to innovate and make quick decisions. The company is highly decentralized, with most day—to—day operating decisions made by the division general managers and their staff. The organizational structure at a typical division is made up of only three management layers: General Manager, Department Manager, Supervisor/Professional, and Hourly Employee.

Employee relations at Nucor are based on four clear—cut principles:

1. Management is obligated to manage Nucor in such a way that employees will have the opportunity to earn according to their productivity.

2. Employees should be able to feel confident that if they do their jobs properly, they will have a job tomorrow.

3. Employees have the right to be treated fairly and must believe that they will be.

4. Employees must have an avenue of appeal when they believe they are being treated unfairly.

By implementing these four basic principles within a relatively simple organizational structure, Nucor has been able to attract and retain highly talented and productive employees.

The incentive system

All employees are covered under one of four basic compensation plans, each featuring incentives related to meeting specific goals and targets.

1. Production Incentive Plan: Operating and maintenance employees and supervisors at the facilities are paid weekly bonuses based on the productivity of their work group. The rate is calculated based on the capabilities of the equipment employed, and no bonus is paid if the equipment is not operating. In general, the Production Incentive bonus can average from 80 to 150 percent of an employee's base pay.

2. Department Manager Incentive Plan: Department Managers earn annual incentive bonuses based primarily on the percentage of net income to dollars of assets employed for their division. These bonuses can be as much as 80 percent of a department manager's base pay.

3. Professional and Clerical Bonus Plan: This bonus is paid to employees that are not on the production or department manager plan and is based on the division's net income return on assets.

4. Senior Officers Incentive Plan: Nucor's senior officers do not have employment contracts. They do not participate in any pension or retirement plans. Their base salaries are set lower than what executives receive in comparable companies. The remainder of their compensation is based on Nucor's annual overall percentage of net income to stockholder's equity and is paid out in cash and stock.

In addition to these established bonus plans, Nucor has periodically issued an extraordinary bonus to all employees, except officers, in years of particularly strong company performance. This bonus has been as high as $800 for each employee.

9. Industry Analysis

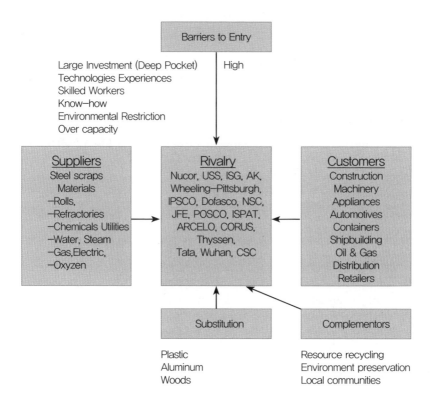

Barriers to Entry — High

Large Investment (Deep Pocket)
Technologies Experiences
Skilled Workers
Know-how
Environmental Restriction
Over capacity

Suppliers
Steel scraps
  Materials
–Rolls,
–Refractories
–Chemicals Utilities
–Water, Steam
–Gas,Electric,
–Oxyzen

Rivalry
Nucor, USS, ISG, AK,
Wheeling–Pittsburgh,
IPSCO, Dofasco, NSC,
JFE, POSCO, ISPAT,
ARCELO, CORUS,
Thyssen,
Tata, Wuhan, CSC

Customers
Construction
Machinery
Appliances
Automotives
Containers
Shipbuilding
Oil & Gas
Distribution
Retailers

Substitution
Plastic
Aluminum
Woods

Complementors
Resource recycling
Environment preservation
Local communities

10. Competition

There are over 100 operating mini mills in the U.S. Mini mills now account for about 38% of total U.S. steel industry shipments. Mini mills have both a labor and capital cost advantage compared to integrated steelmakers. Mini mills are very sensitive to scrap prices, however, and lose their cost advantage compared to integrated mills when scrap prices rise above $90/ton.

There are also many integrated steel mills which produce steel from iron ore, coal, and lime, and typically supply a full range of products, with an emphasis on flat-rolled carbon steel, strip, and plate products. The capacity of integrated steel plants ranges from two million tons to four million tons per mill per year. During the last 20 years, the U.S. steel industry has undergone a drastic and painful restructuring process that resulted in a 30% reduction in capacity and a loss of 375,000 jobs. Over half the integrated mills shut down or de-integrated their operations.

American steel manufacturers are supported by the U.S. government policy. Without the 201-tariff policy against the imported steel products, many of American steel manufactures would not be survived at this high competition market. American steel companies have not invested enough capitals to new facilities and high technologies during last two decades.

Nucor is the only one steel company with mini mills which makes profit.

11. Strategic Intent

Ken Iverson, chairman of Nucor, had explained clearly about the Nucor's future business: "We are going to stay in steel and steel products. The way we look at it. This company does only two things well, builds plants economically and runs them efficiently. That is the whole company. We don't have any financial expertise, we're not entrepreneurs, and we're not into acquisitions. Steel may not be the best business in the world, but it's what we know how to do, and we do it well."

The Strategic intent of Nucor can be summarized as "Produce high quality steel and steel products at low cost in order to satisfy customers and maintain the market leader through the process of continual technological improvement."

12. Core Competency
The Nucor's success is based on the following competencies.

■ Financial Strength
Nucor invested $182 Million cash at the close of Q1-2003 and only 26% of total capital is debt. On 10/1/02, Nucor issued $350 million of 4.875% notes due 2012. Cash provided by operations is up to $497 million In economically depressed 2002 (exceeded $800 million in 2000). Cash dividends increased every year since Nucor began paying dividends in 1973.

Nucor has kept a conservative financial & accounting practices and its financial statement has been reported in plain language format which is easy to understand.

■ Market Leadership

Nucor has been the Largest U.S. structural steel producer, Largest U.S. steel bar producer, Largest U.S. steel joist producer, and Largest U.S. steel deck producer.

■ Diversified Product Mix

	Product Mix
2002 Sales Tons	Steel Sheet: 43%, Structural Steel: 20%, Steel Bars: 22%, Steel Joists: 3%, Steel Deck: 2%, Cold Finished Steel: 2%, Steel Plate: 6%, Other: 1%
2002 Steel production	Sheet: 48%, Bars: 6%, Structural: 20%, Plate: 6%
End User Markets	Construction: 60%, Oil & Gas: 15%, Auto/Appliance: 15%, Various: 10%
Steel Production Capacity	Hot Rolled Sheet: 8.4 million, (incl. Cold rolled sheet 3.0, Galvanized 1.4) Bars: 5.8 million, Structural: 3.2 million, Plate: 1.2 million Total: 18.6 million
Steel Products Production Capacity	Steel Joists: 685,000 tons, Cold Finished bars: 350,000 tons, Steel Deck: 400,000 tons, Steel Buildings: 145,000 tons Total Steel Products:1.6 million

■ Technological Innovation

In 1986, the Crawfordsville plant was the first to launch one of Nucor's most ambitious projects -- production of hot-rolled and cold-rolled sheet steel using a new thin-slab process that would yield flat-rolled steel at low capital cost. Work on the plant began in September of 1987, and operation began in August of 1989.

Nucor began operations of its 100% owned Strip-casting facility in Crawfordsville in May 2002. This facility uses the breakthrough technology of strip casting, to which Nucor holds exclusive rights in the United States and Brazil. Strip casting involves the direct casting of molten steel into final shape and thickness without further hot or cold rolling. This process allows lower investment and operating costs, reduced energy consumption, and smaller scale plants than can be economically built with current technology. This process also reduces the overall environmental impact of producing steel by generating significantly lower emissions, particularly NOx.

Today, Nucor is also focus on new disruptive technologies called His melt which converts iron ore to liquid metal (eliminates need for sinter/pellet plants and coke ovens)

■ Low-cost Position

Minimills have both a labor and capital cost advantage compared to integrated steelmakers. The advantages of Thin Slab casting and flat rolled facility are: ①the construction cost per ton is below the half of the blast furnace mill ②the labor cost (1.3 man-hour/ton) is much lower than the integrated steel mill (4.3 man-hour/ton) ③the fixed costs can be minimized ④Mini mill is more flexible to the economic fluctuation

Nucor has a very minimum number of management levels by the decentralized, flat organization which can save the total cost.

Also "Can Do" attitude and energy level of Nucor people creates efficiencies.

13. R&D and Innovation

Nucor's strong emphasis on employee communication and commitment carries with it the commitment to provide the work force with the best technology available to get the job done right in a safe working environment. As evidence of that commitment, Nucor aggressively pursues the latest advancements in steel making around the world to determine what technology it can adapt in its facilities.

This pursuit of technical excellence led to the joint venture with Yamato Kogyo of Japan to build Nucor—Yamato Steel Company in 1988. At Nucor—Yamato, Yamato—Kogyo's technological expertise in structural beam blank casting was successfully combined with Nucor's management philosophy and talented personnel to build one of the premiere structural steel mills in the United States.

In addition, the Nucor Steel sheet mills in Indiana, Arkansas, South Carolina, and Alabama represent a revolution in the thin slab casting. Nucor was the first "mini mill" to successfully commercialize the technology developed by a company in West Germany.

14. Value Migration

The steel industry in America is facing significant labor issues including rising health care costs and under—capitalized pension plans. Nucor has a incentive—based pay system for everyone and No lay—off practice, so Nucor has to maintain the good relation with its employees instead of struggling against them like at other union companies.

There are some other issues to be overcome by Nucor in the future.
①Mini mills are very sensitive to the price fluctuation of steel scrap, therefore Nucor needs to develop any scrap-replacing material (for example, DRI or molten iron instead of steel scrap) for its rainy days.
②the increase of steel products in newly developing countries such as China and India which have lower labor cost and higher demand of steel products can threaten Nucor's competitive power.   ③ Nucor also has to prepare the challenges of new technologies such as Finex process in POSCO and Japanese mills.

15. Business Strategy
Nucor has 4-Pronged Growth Strategies
1) Optimize existing operations
■ Continued Quality Improvements and Cost Reductions
■ Improve Sheet Steel Mill Volume and Profitability (continue moving up the value chain)
■ Nucor announced Bar Mill Group Capital Projects in early 2002 and more than $200 million on capital projects to be completed by 2004.
Projects include Rolling Mill Modernization at Nebraska, New Melt Shop at Texas, and New Reheat Furnace & Finishing End at South Carolina

2) Continue greenfield growth—opportunities to capitalize on technology

- Hertford County, North Carolina steel plate mill continues successful penetration of plate market.
- Chemung, NY Nucraft plant starting production in a new geographic market
- New facility using Cantrip technology in Crawfordsville, Indiana began commercial production in Q2—2002

3) Pursue acquisitions

- Former Auburn Steel was acquired in late March 2001
- Former Trico Steel Mill acquisition completed on 7/22/02.
- Annual capacity of 1.9 million tons———increasing our sheet capacity by roughly 30%. Plant located in Decatur, Alabama
- Nucor Steel – Decatur began production start—up less than 60 days from acquisition close. Expect to produce approximately 1.5 million in 2003.
- Birmingham Steel – in December 2002 acquired substantially all the assets for $615 million in cash (included roughly $117 million of working capital)
- The four operating bar mills have combined annual capacity of roughly 2 million tons – increasing Nucor's annual bar steel annual shipment capacity by more than 50% to 5.8 million tons.

4) Grow globally through joint ventures based on new technologies

16. Performance Expectations

This is the contents of Nucor's presentation for investors. The worldwide economic situation is not so easy to overcome by Nucor itself, but the performance expectations look like persuasive based on Nucor's history.

- 10% or better annual compound earnings growth (through the economic cycle)
- Minimum average return on equity of 14%
- Return on sales of 8% or better.
- Market leadership in every product group and business in which we compete.
- Continue Nucor tradition of emerging from economic down-cycles stronger than before (use downturns to gain market share, penetrate new steel product markets, implement new disruptive & leapfrog technologies, and focus on cost / quality

References

1. www.nucor.com
2. Nucor's annual report for 2002
3. Case Study – Nucor by Harvard Business school
4. Interview – Peter Markus, President of WSD by Weekly POSCO
5. Iron and Steel Overview by Metals Advisor

6. Smart Steel by POSCO

7. News Releases — CHARLOTTE, N.C., PRNewswire

8. American Metal Market —www.amm.com

Project Paper 6:
The Operations of a Purchasing Function in USS-POSCO Industries

⟨Executive Summary⟩

1. Background

USS—POSCO, a joint venture company between US Steel and POSCO in KOREA, has a lot of inefficient procurement processes even though it has almost one hundred of operation history. That's why the people in process are too rigid and obsolete to accept the rapid changes of technology. They even worry about losing their position if processes are transformed to automatic.

2. Key Findings

— The raw materials are supplied by both parent companies by 50:50. UPI has no choice to determine the quantity and price of Hot Bands

— The purchasing organization which consists of six purchase specialists is very limited in the purchasing decision— making process.

일범의 평범한 사람 이야기

- Two computer systems, MAXIMO and WALKER, are used for processing purchase orders.
- The recent cost reduction by the reverse auction is very successful.

3. Issues and Recommendations
- Hot Bands purchasing: Ensure its own authority to buy from the 3rd sources
- Limited buyer's role in decision-making: Strengthen the buyer's responsibility and authority and perform job rotations between operation and purchasing.
- Higher cost than competitors: Introduce periodical open bidding, enlarge reverse auction, and organize supplier qualification team.
- Inefficient order processing system: Enlarge MAXIMO functions, introduce e-procurement, and Share information with suppliers.

4. Conclusion
UPI has to understand the importance of supply management which is far more strategic than purchasing. The purchasing professionals have to spend more time focusing on higher value activities like long-term contract management and supplier performance management instead of processing paper and following-up on transactions.

1. Introduction
USS-POSCO Industries (UPI), a joint venture company established by U. S. Steel Corporation and POSCO of Korea, is located in

Pittsburg, California. The company employs almost 1,000 people and converts hot rolled steel coils into three main product lines: cold rolled sheet, galvanized sheet, and tin plate.

The first Pittsburg steel facility opened in 1910 under the name Columbia Steel. The plant had expanded during the 1920s to 1940s, facilities and equipment were added to help supply major public works projects – the most notable being the San Francisco/Oakland Bay Bridge – and to meet the demand for steel products during World War II. But the plant had been faltered during the next several decades due to the increased use of alternative materials (like aluminum and plastic), and growing competition from foreign imports. In 1986 U. S. Steel entered into a 50/50 joint venture with POSCO in Korea, a partner that could supply high quality raw material for use at the plant. The new partners began a comprehensive modernization program designed to upgrade the processes and equipment of the facility. The $450 million modernization was completed in April 1989, representing one of the largest investments in manufacturing facilities in California. Because of the modernization, UPI is now among the most efficient steel finishing facilities in the world.

Today, UPI manufactures cold rolled, galvanized and tin mill products from hot rolled steel. With the support of nearly 1,000 hourly and salaried employees, UPI ships steel daily to more than 150 customers, primarily in the thirteen western states. (See Exhibit 1, 2: Financial conditions and The Material Flow of USS—POSCO)

2. Purchasing Function

UPI has two different purchasing functions. One is for the raw materials (Hot Bands) from both parent companies. Another one is for MRO (Maintenance, Repair, and Operating) supplies and other goods. Hot Bands purchasing is one of the responsibilities of Business Services organization, because the quantity and specifications of Hot Bands are determined according to the Sales Plan. All other purchasing and contracts except Hot Bands are the responsibility under purchasing division (See Exhibit 3: Organization chart of UPI).

2-1. Hot bands Purchasing

UPI is a joint venture company between US steel and POSCO, and the raw materials (Hot Bands: Hot rolled Coils) are supplied by both parent companies by 50:50. The quantity, steel grade, and specifications of Hot Bands are determined according to the sales mix. The yearly sales plan is usually established until the end of October. So, the purchasing plan for Hot Bands for next year is also determined until November. The Hot Bands Purchasing plan includes the quantity for each product line, the quantity from USS and POSCO, the quantity required for each month, and the price per ton. The Hot Bands price is determined by both parent companies based on the market price and the transportation fee from east to west, and the financial situation of UPI.

The business service people who work for purchasing Hot Bands from POSCO and USS update the order files every month according to the monthly sales plan. The transportation carriers from POSCO, Korea are private ships which equipped de—Nox facility for preventing air pollution in California. The transportation carriers from Gary, PA , Birmingham, IN, or Granite city, IL are rails.

2—2. Buying center in UPI Purchasing

The buyers in UPI's purchasing organization are consisted of one general manager who is a steering member, one department manager, four buyers, and one assistant staff. A department manager is responsible for purchasing Metals, Utilities, and Insurance. Four buyers are responsible for purchasing 1) Electrical, Outside Processes, Mill Equip., Coil Packaging 2)Services, Cars, Office Equip., Rental Equip., Production Supplies 3)Mechanical Components, Outside Mechanical Repairs 4)Chemicals, Lubricants, Mobile Equip., Mechanical Equip. The initiators who request that something be purchased and the users who will use the product or services are same people. They initiate the buying proposals and define the product requirements. In most case, the deciders and approvers are also the division manager or vice president of the organizations of the user group.

2—3. Procurement System and Purchasing Flow

UPI has two different systems for procurement process. One is MAXIMO supplied by MRO Software; the other is WALKER system.

MAXIMO, installed at UPI four years ago, is used widely for work management, preventive maintenance, inventory control, job plans, resource allocation, and purchase management for mainly operation and maintenance department. Walker system, which is originally a financial system, has been used for procurement system for purchasing department for twenty years ago. Figure 1 shows the basic relation of the two systems.

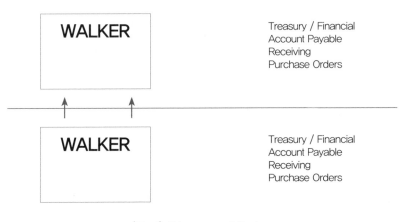

⟨Fig.1⟩ Procurement System

The purchase order processes in UPI can be classified to Regular Process Order Process, Contract Order Process, Contract Service Order process, and Blanket Order Process. These processes have somewhat different flows according to the characteristics of the contracts.

The regular order process for MRO items is as follows. 1) Purchase requisitions are uploaded in MAXIMO by the users. 2) It is approved by department manager or division manager in MAXIMO. 3) The purchase requisition approved is sent to buyers from MAXIMO to Walker. 4) A buyer requires quote to potential suppliers. 5) A buyer issues purchase order to the best proposal and makes a contract through negotiation. 6) Walker system allocates the cost to the cost center by monthly on the base of items delivered. 7) MAXIMO has the statistics and history of purchasing.

The process of selecting supplier and negotiating prices for contract order process items, such as a project, is different from the regular order items. 1) The user groups in operation or maintenance department search the potential vendors. 2) The user group people send letters for requesting proposals with requirements to the selected potential vendors and sometimes have an explanation meeting with them. 3) The user group people receive the proposals from the multiple potential vendors. 4) The user group people evaluate the proposals and select the most suitable supplier on the base of specifications, technology, manpower, experiences, and price. 5) The user group people send the purchasing order to the purchasing department by MAXIMO system, and the buyers negotiate the price with the supplier and make a contract. (See Exhibit 4: purchasing Order Processes)

2-4. Purchasing Cost Management

UPI has almost one hundred years history since its first operation in 1910. It has been operated with the strongly related suppliers for a long time. So the suppliers for almost of all MRO items have not been changed to new vendors. For examples, Bingham for Roll repairing and rubber—lining, Quaker for Alkali solution, Atotech for Chrome—plating solution, D.A. Stuart for Rolling oil and rust—inhibitor, and etc. The prices for these existing suppliers' items are determined by the market price for every shipment. And the price negotiations are performed by the UPI buyers at purchasing department by annual base for some items. UPI recently introduced the Reverse Auction technique in its purchasing in order to reduce costs. UPI has suggested its target cost or price for a lot of items that the plants need to the potential suppliers and chosen the lowest—priced suppliers since last year. The items for power transmission, office supply, electrical parts, and safety supplies were complete and many other MRO items and Contract service orders are under processing. The estimated savings by one year's reverse auctions are $6 million.

3. Assessment of the Present Processes

3—1 Raw Materials

UPI does not use MRP system for its procurement of raw materials (Hot Bands), but the functions of existing system are simple because many important parts of procurement processes are already fixed by the parent companies who are main suppliers. There are no processes for preparing specifications, selecting suppliers or bidding, negotiating prices, or making contracts. The processes for yearly planning, short term planning and monthly planning are working very well. Updating order files are automatically linked to POSCO ERP (Enterprise Resources Planning) system which is Oracle Application. There are not many issues in purchasing Hot Coils in UPI.

3-2 Buying Processes

Buyers have to have formal authority to select the supplier and arrange the purchase terms in the well-working purchasing organizations. And also buyers have to play role in selecting vendors and negotiating and may help shape material specifications. However, the buyers in UPI seem not to play their roles sufficiently. The users decide the material/equipment specifications without involvement of buyers, the users almost select the vendors who can meet the requirements before sending purchasing orders to the purchasing department. The main role of buyers is negotiating and documentation according to the processes. For the routine supply items such as office supply, spare parts, and pre-determined suppliers' items, the buyer's role is very standardized. For the new project, the most important decision making in buying process is performed by the user group people. That's because the user group have the more technical knowledge and project experience than the buyers.

3-3 Procurement System

Two computer systems are used for procurement processing in UPI; one is for MRO in production site, the other is for general stuffs in Purchasing Department. That's because people insisted their ways and did not accept the new system, MAXIMO, even though MAXIMO had a lot of functions which could be helpful to reduce manual processes. MAXIO, as the procurement software, provides the integrated modules for automating material requisitioning, procurement, and supplier relationship management processes. But in UPI, MAXIMO is mainly used for work management and job plans for maintenance department and partially used for procurement of MRO items. There are still many paper-based, manual processes for procurement in the Walker system. Figure 2 shows the SWOT analysis of UPI's Purchasing function.

Strength	Weakness
- Purchasing Experts - Long relationships with suppliers - User oriented supplier selection - Simple process for buying raw materials - Independent division leading by a steering member.	- Two computer systems for processing purchase order - Many paper based, manual processes - Buyers not involving in setting up purchase specifications - No authority to negotiate the price of raw materials - Not-satisfiable delivery performance
Opportunity	Threats
- Rapid development of Internet technology - The steel industry is rebounding due to Chinese growing demand - Cost reduction strategy - New general manager - Already installed MAXIMO	- Higher cost than competitors - Cost reduction by e-procurements in competitors - Many M&A in the steel industries - Too many MRO required due to the old facilities. - Not enough supplier qualification

⟨Fig. 2⟩ UPI's Purchasing Function

4. Suggestions to Improve the Operation

Issues	Recommendations
1) UPI has no choice to determine the quantity and price of Hot Bands	- UPI has to have its own authority to purchase Hot Bands from the 3rd source, it will help for UPI to buy the raw materials at lower cost.
2) Buyers' role is very limited in the purchasing decision-making process.	- Strengthen the functions of buyers by modifying the responsibility and authority description of the company's organization. - Job rotation between maintenance or operation and the purchasing department would be working for better understanding each other's position and share information and common goals.
3) The cost is higher than competitors.	- Introduce open bidding annually or every 2~3 years to select suppliers for regular order items. - Enlarge the reverse auction to Contract order item. - Organize a supplier qualification team including engineer, purchasing, and financial specialist in order to select the best supplier for a new project.
4) The inefficient order processing by using two separated systems.	- Enlarge the functions of MAXIMO to manage the whole processes of procurement including asset management, inventory management, and documentations between buyer and suppliers. - Install an e-procurement system for the routine items (regular purchase orders and balnket orders) - Share production and purchase& supply information with supplier through a common network.

5. Conclusion

The competitiveness of a company is determined by the sales increasing and total cost lowering. These two factors cannot be achieved by the company alone. These can be actualized through the entire supply chains from raw materials suppliers through factories and warehouses to the end of customers. UPI's purchasing functions, system, and organization are following the ways as it has been for its long history.

일범의 평범한 사람 이야기

That results in the inefficient process and cost—rise. Supply management is far more strategic than purchasing. Now it's the time to change UPI's purchasing functions to supply management which is the key to supply chain management. All supply information should be stored in computer and shared with suppliers. The purchase order should be processed automatically in a integrated system or e—procurement which can reduce cost and shorten delivery. And the purchasing professionals have to spend more time focusing on higher value activities like long—term contract management and supplier performance management instead of processing paper and following—up on transactions.

Bibliography
1. World Class Supply Management by Burt, Dobler, and Statling
2. The management of Business Logistics by Coyle, Bardi, and Langley
3. USS—POSCO Business Update
4. Presentation materials designed by Purchasing department in UPI.
5. Literature Articles provided during the classes.
6. www.ussposco.com, http://internet.ggu.edu, www.purchasing.com
7. e—procurement by Oracle and SAP

(Exhibit 1) Financial Status of USS–POSCO

	1998	1999	2000	2001	2002	2003	04 (BP)
Production(ton)	1,465	1,604	1,496	829	1,178	1,231	1,321
Sales (ton)	1,517	1,621	1,505	836	1,180	1,236	1,330
Sales ($)	765,637	749,415	758,057	411,807	580,625	655,246	742,083
Net Profit ($)	-21,215	-21,867	3,596	-12,519	36,234	-37,111	5,148
Asset ($)	565,655	491,198	459,096	469,330	475,250	426,374	379,046
Debit ($)	346,595	294,006	258,308	285,382	275,354	266,653	214,177
Capital ($)	219,060	197,192	200,788	183,948	199,896	159,721	164,869

* BP: Business Plan

* In May 2001, UPI suffered a devastating fire to one of its operating facilities – the Tandem Cold Mill (TCM). The TCM was destroyed and had to be rebuilt from the ground up. Showing remarkable resiliency, UPI was able to rebuild the TCM in less than eight months, and it now stands as one of the world's most technologically advanced mills of its kind.

일범의 평범한 사람 이야기

2. CT (Contract) Order process

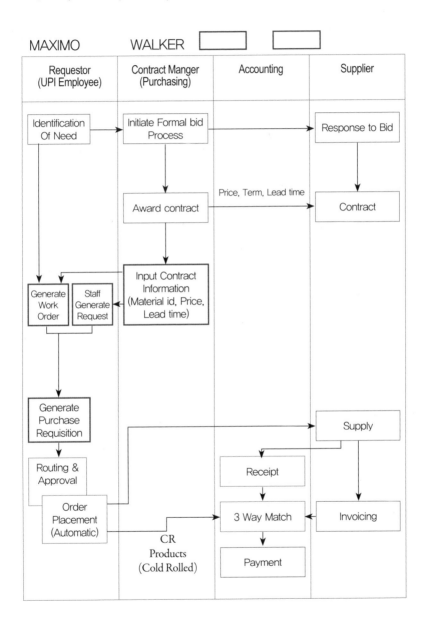

MAXIMO   WALKER

Requestor (UPI Employee)	Contract Manger (Purchasing)	Accounting	Supplier
Identification Of Need	Initiate Formal bid Process		Response to Bid
	Award contract	Price, Term, Lead time	Contract
Generate Work Order / Staff Generate Request	Input Contract Information (Material id, Price, Lead time)		
Generate Purchase Requisition			Supply
Routing & Approval		Receipt	
Order Placement (Automatic)	CR Products (Cold Rolled)	3 Way Match	Invoicing
		Payment	

(Exhibit 3) Organization Chart of USS-POSCO

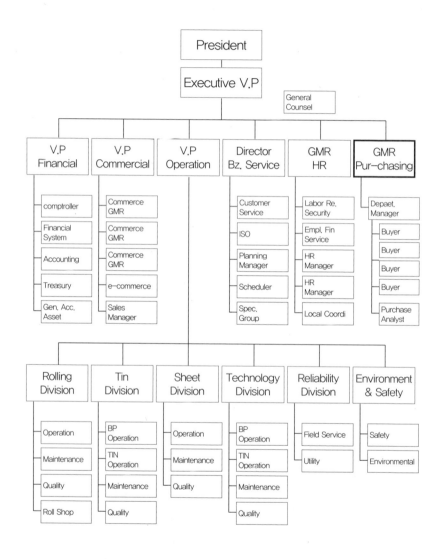

일범의 평범한 사람 이야기

(Exhibit 4) Purchase Order processes

1. Regular Purchase Order Process

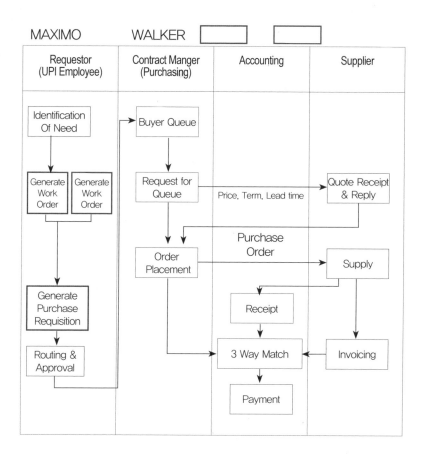

• 3 Way Match

-PO Exist in WALKER

-Invoice Price matches PO Price

-Receipts in WALKER

• Staff Generate Request

-Staff: Non-MRO

    (Maintenance, Repair, Operating)

2. CT (Contract) Order process

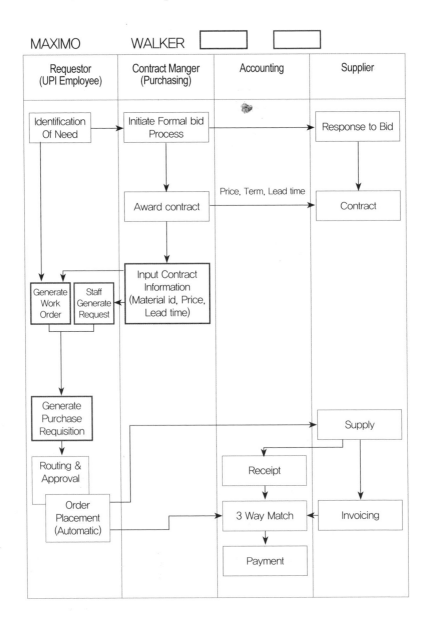

3. CS (Contract Service) Order process

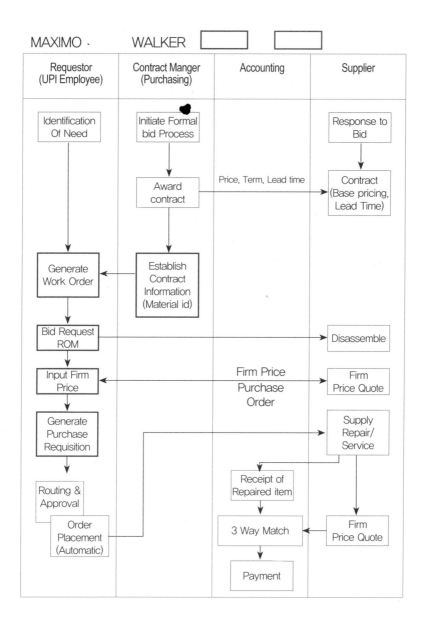

4. Blanket Order process

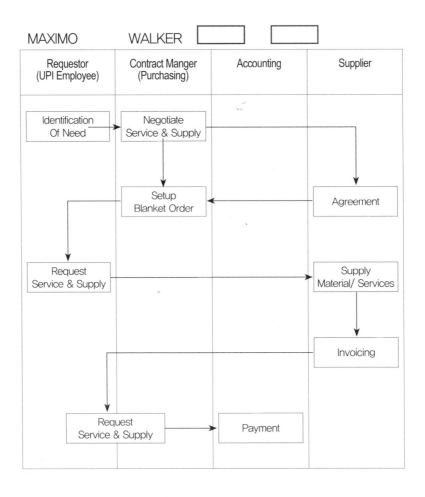

* Invoice Approval: done by Dept. Mgr./Div. Mgr./Contract mgr. according to $ amount

Project Paper 7: Carnival Glass, Inc.

1. What is the Problem?

How can Carnival Glass upgrade its logistics system to increase customer service level and to ensure efficient order processing?

2. The Critical Factors and Issues

1) Packaging and distribution of consumer products take place primarily at a single facility in York, PA.

2) York facility has expanded several times, but the approximately 60,000 square feet of outside warehousing is still utilized

3) Items are put away at random in the warehouse.

4) Market planners at headquarters in Ohio forecast the demand.

5) When the ware has been packaged and palletized, it once again is taken into the warehouse for staging or storage and ultimate distribution.

6) 83 percent of all orders are shipped in volume-type shipment, with the remaining 17 percent of orders are shipped in less-than-volume shipment, UPS, or parcel post shipments.

7) The company allows customers to pick up their own orders at the warehouse.

8) The current manual order processing system has a lot of inefficiencies.

   - Customer service representatives (CSRs) take down the order on a standard ordering form and collect all the data needed to process the form.

- Twice a day, orders that had been keypunched are sent to the mainframe computer in a batch mode.
- Various types of errors occur frequently in processing orders, which results that 34 percent of the orders are not validated the same day as received.
- The system for checking order accuracy is costly and time—consuming.

9) Customer service level is low.

- It is very difficult to provide the best customer services because Carnival Glass has too many numerous types of customers such as wholesale distributors, major retailers, retail outlets, catalog or mail business, grocery stores, export, tableware business, and special market business.
- Lead times are not satisfactory to customers (Actual 86 % in 4 weeks for 95 % order fill of customer's requirement)
- The percentage of order shipped complete is 69 percent.
- A shortage in supply new products takes place because of the difficulty in forecasting demand.
- There are quality problems with the new products.

3. My Recommendations to Solve the Problem

1) Simplify the types of customers

- Carnival Glass has too numerous types of customers to meet customer requirements, to perform accurate demand forecasting, and to meet volume—type shipment.

— In order to solve above mentioned problems, I recommend Carnival Glass to reorganize the marketing and distribution networks to have wholesale distributors, major retailers that have their own distribution centers, an export only. Do not sell directly from plant to retail outlets and grocery stores and stop the catalog or mail business, tableware business, and special markets.

— This can increase the volume—type shipment from 83 percent to almost one hundred percent because the inventory control would be performed by the distributors. For the retail outlets or private customers, UPS or parcel post shipments will be utilized at the lower cost die to the shorter transportation distance.

— This distribution systems shows as figure1.

⟨Figure 1⟩

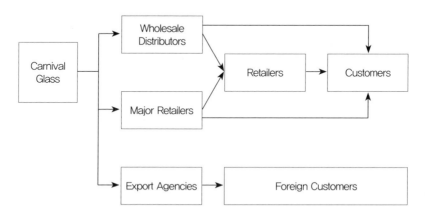

2) Install a computer network between Carnival Glass and customer (wholesale distributors, major retailers, and export agencies) for improving order management and sharing information.

— Demand forecasting is performed by each customer. Carnival Glass collects the demand data from each customer and consolidates them for scheduling packaging and transportation.

— Carnival Glass and the customers communicate information relating to demand and orders. For example, each customer can see the inventory data Carnival's facility and track the order progress through the network computer terminal.

— Introduce the CPFR (collaborative planning, forecasting, and refreshment) for achieving the true supply chain integration.

— This system would shorten the lead time as the customer requirement to 95 percent within 4 weeks.

— This would increase the accuracy of demand forecasting and reduce stock—out due to the difficulty in forecasting demand.

3) Develop and install a new computerized order management system.

— Set up a data base in the mainframe computer which contains all of the necessary information related to each product code such as price, design, available production plant, packaging type, transportation route, and etc.

— The function of order management system should include from receiving orders and entering them in the system to delivering orders and measuring the service levels.

- It will contribute to reduce errors and shorten the order and replenishment cycles.

4) Redesign the warehouse layout
- Divide the warehouse space into the separate areas for receiving packaging materials, packaging, storage, and shipping. So, do not put items away at random in the warehouse.
- Avoid the reverse material flows in the warehouse. The warehousing configuration shown as figure 2 can be one of the choices.

⟨ Figure 2.⟩

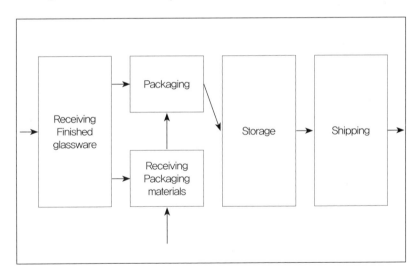

- This can eliminate the twice movement in the warehouse. The existing

- The existing warehouse layout causes a twice material handling, i.e., when the ware has been packaged and palletized, it once again is taken into the warehouse for staging or storage and ultimate distribution.
- This modified layout does not allow customers to pick up their own orders at the warehouse which increase the efficiency of material handlings in the warehouse

5) Build a new packaging and distribution facility in Western area such as in California.
- York facility is already saturated (outside warehousing is utilized) and not enough for covering the potential demand from over the states and exports.
- A western plant would save a big amount of outbound freight costs to customers in the western area and to export to foreign counties.

6) Develop a website to provide information about products, prices, collections, orders, advertisement, and linkage to its distributors.
- The website should focus on contemporary carnival glass and on the further education about glasses for customers.
- Customers can also use this website for ordering, so the detail direction of how to order and should be provided.
- Carnival Glass' distributors would receive orders from customers and directly link to the order management system.

4. The Alternative Solutions

1) Keep the existing numerous types of customers and add e—sales.

— This alternative is not selected because the company would meet a lot of inefficiencies in its business.

— The percentage of "in volume—type shipment" would be decreased due to the consolidation difficulty of frequent small orders.

— The average inventory level would be increased and therefore inventory carrying costs would be increased.

— Stock out would be occurred more frequently.

— Demand forecasting would be more inaccurate.

2) Increase the work force for order entry and checking order accuracy.

— This alternative is not selected because it raises the cost without a significant improvement.

3) Increase private carrier and customers' pick up instead of contract carrier

— This alternative is not selected because it is not helpful to increase 'in—volume shipment' and causes more complicated logistics.

4) Increase the space of York facility in order to reduce over—handling and stock out.

— This alternative is not selected because it increases the transportation costs to western areas and inventory levels.

Bibliography:

The Management of Business Logistics— 7th edition by Coyle, Bardi, and Langley

World Class Supply Management—7th edition by Burt, Dobler, Starling

Case Literature: Carnival Glass, Inc.

The contemporary carnival glass website

제4부 미국생활

일범의 평범한 사람 이야기

초 판 1쇄 2023년 03월 31일

지은이 손영징
펴낸이 류종렬

펴낸곳 미다스북스
총괄실장 명상완
책임편집 이다경
책임진행 김가영, 신은서, 임종익, 박유진

등록 2001년 3월 21일 제2001-000040호
주소 서울시 마포구 양화로 133 서교타워 711호
전화 02) 322-7802~3
팩스 02) 6007-1845
블로그 http://blog.naver.com/midasbooks
전자주소 midasbooks@hanmail.net
페이스북 https://www.facebook.com/midasbooks425
인스타그램 https://www.instagram.com/midasbooks

ISBN 979-11-6910-198-1 03810

값 50,000원

미다스북스는 다음세대에게 필요한 지혜와 교양을 생각합니다.